AF758506

P

T... ...an the last date
...extended on request
...ook. **Books may not be**

...eader it will be recalled and
the... ...e, or fines will

The Heterodox Economics of GARDINER C. MEANS

STUDIES IN INSTITUTIONAL ECONOMICS

GARDINER C. MEANS
INSTITUTIONALIST AND POST KEYNESIAN
Warren J. Samuels and Steven G. Medema

THE HETERODOX ECONOMICS OF GARDINER C. MEANS
A COLLECTION
Frederic S. Lee and Warren J. Samuels, editors

UNDERGROUND ECONOMICS
A DECADE OF INSTITUTIONALIST DISSENT
William M. Dugger

The Heterodox Economics of GARDINER C. MEANS

A Collection

Edited by
Frederic S. Lee
and
Warren J. Samuels

with the assistance of
Caroline F. Ware and Steven G. Medema

M. E. Sharpe, Inc.
Armonk, New York ■ London, England

UNIVERSITY OF BATH
LIBRARY
11 17 FEB 1993
330.18
5064564

UNIVERSITY OF BATH
LIBRARY
26 JUN 2023
Withdrawn

Copyright © 1992 by M. E. Sharpe, Inc.

All rights reserved. No part of this book may be reproduced in any form without written permission from the publisher, M. E. Sharpe, Inc., 80 Business Park Drive, Armonk, New York 10504.

Available in the United Kingdom and Europe from M. E. Sharpe, Publishers, 3 Henrietta Street, London WC2E 8LU.

Library of Congress Cataloging-in-Publication Data

Means, Gardiner Coit, 1896–
The heterodox economics of Gardiner C. Means : a collection /
edited by Frederic S. Lee and Warren J. Samuels.
p. cm.
Includes bibliographical references (p.) and index.
ISBN 0-87332-717-9
1. Means, Gardiner Coit, 1896– .
2. Economics.
I. Lee, Frederic S., 1949– .
II. Samuels, Warren J., 1933– .
III. Title.
HB119.M43A3 1990
330.1—dc20
90-8836
CIP

Printed in the United States of America

The paper used in this publication meets the minimum requirements of American National Standard for Information Sciences—Permanence of Paper for Printed Library Materials, ANSI Z39.48-1984.

♾

TS 10 9 8 7 6 5 4 3 2 1

To
Caroline F. Ware
in memoriam

Contents

Figures and Tables

Figures

Tables

Preface

Gardiner C. Means was not principally an academic economist but an activist in government and the world of ideas and policy. He was, with Adolf A. Berle, the coauthor of *The Modern Corporation and Private Property*, one of the three or four greatest and most widely cited books in the social sciences in the twentieth century. Means was a major investigator not only of the institutions of the corporation and private property but also of industrial structure and concentration, price formation and inflexibility, and stagflation—and their interrelationships. His ideas have had enormous, though controversial, impact on scholarly thought in several disciplines and in the major fields of economics.

This collection brings together some of Means's principal writings, several of which were hitherto unpublished, including the provocative chapters from his proposed dissertation which his Harvard committee found objectionable. The collection includes material from each important area in which Means wrote: the corporate revolution and its implications, the nature and consequences of inflexible administered industrial prices, industrial concentration, and the macroeconomics of such a world. Most of these writings are not otherwise readily available. Caroline Ware's essay, "Academic Resistance to Administered Prices," which critically interprets some of the resistance of some economists to her late husband's work, is also included. Finally, we include what we hope is a complete bibliography of Means's writings.

Frederic S. Lee
and
Warren J. Samuels

Acknowledgments

The authors and publishers are grateful for permission to reproduce the material in this volume. We wish to thank Macmillan Publishing Company for permission to reprint Chapters 1 and 13 from *The Corporate Revolution in America* (1962, pp. 15–19 and 47–73); The University of Chicago for permission to reprint from the Charles E. Merriam Papers (Box 185, Folder 1), Chapter 5; Yale University Library for permission to reprint from the Jerome Frank Papers (Box 33, Folder 472), Chapter 6; Burt Franklin Publishers for permission to reprint Chapter 17 from *The Roots of Inflation: The International Crisis* (1975, pp. 1–31); The University of Chicago Press for permission to reprint Chapter 19 from the *Journal of Law and Economics* (vol. 26, June 1983, pp. 467–485); the American Statistical Association for permission to reprint Chapter 14 from the *Proceedings of the American Statistical Association: The Business and Economics Statistics Section* (1962, pp. 118–126); the *University of Miami Law Review* for permission to reprint Chapter 15 which appeared in the journal (vol. 25, Fall 1970, pp. 1–40); *Wage-Price Law & Economics Review* for permission to reprint Chapter 16, which appeared in the journal (vol. 1, 1975, pp. 47–74); M.E. Sharpe, Inc. for permission to reprint Chapter 18 which appeared in *Challenge* (July–August 1976, pp. 61–63); and Caroline F. Ware for permission to reprint Chapter 11, which is located in the John M. Blair Papers at the National Archives, Washington, D.C. Chapter 3 was originally published as *Industrial Prices and Their Relative Inflexibility* (Senate Document No. 13, 74th Cong., 1st sess., 1935). Finally, from the Gardiner C. Means Papers at the Franklin D. Roosevelt Library we have reprinted the papers that appear as Chapter 2 (Series I, "The Corporate Revolution"), Chapter 4 (Series I, "The Major Causes of the Depression"), Chapter 7 (Series III, "Antitrust Policy"), Chapter 8 (Series II, "Prices—Administered"), Chapter 9 (Series IV, "International Trade—1"), Chapter 10 (Series IV, "Economics—Macro—2"), and Chapter 12 (Series V, "Prices").

We were assisted in the preparation of this collection by Caroline F. Ware and Steven G. Medema and by a grant from the Franklin D. Roosevelt Foundation.

Introduction: Gardiner C. Means, 1896–1988

by Frederic S. Lee and Warren J. Samuels

Early Life, 1896–1927

Gardiner Coit Means was born on June 8, 1896, in Windham, Connecticut, and spent his precollege days growing up in Massachusetts and Maine. He entered Harvard at the age of eighteen and majored in chemistry. With the outbreak of war in 1917, Means left Harvard to enlist in the army and was sent to an officer's training camp in Plattsburgh, New York.[1] After receiving his commission, he transferred to the Aviation Section of the Signal Corps in January 1918 and was sent to aeronautics school at Hazelhurst Field on Long Island, New York. Although he crashed a plane at Hazelhurst, he qualified as a reserve military aviator and was sent to Texas to hone his skills. Means was stationed at Ellington Field near Houston, Texas, when the war ended. With time on his hands, Means and a friend obtained a small brownie camera and roamed over the airfield taking pictures of flights, crashed planes, and other items of interest. They developed the film by renting a room at a Houston hotel, filling the tub with water, putting a sheet across the middle, and using one end of the tub to develop and the other to rinse the prints. The resulting packets of small pictures sold so well that others with better cameras started to compete. Means and his friend withdrew with their profits (Means, 1975, 1986; Eichner, 1980; Ware, 1988; *New York Times*, 1918).

In 1919, Means was discharged from the army and joined the Near East Relief. The Near East Relief was a charitable fund organized in August 1915 in response to the systematic murder and dispersion of the Armenians by the Turks. Over twenty-six million dollars was raised in 1915–16 in the United States and was turned over to the U.S. embassy in Istanbul, which, in turn, ensured the distribution of the money via consuls and missionaries to the surviving Armenians and other refugees throughout the Ottoman Empire. However, with the entry of the United States into the war, this flow of funds was halted and did not resume until after the hostilities had ended. Resuming its operations after the war, the Near East Relief sent to Turkey on January 2, 1919, three ocean liners packed with food, medical supplies, and relief workers. It was during these early days of renewed operations that Means joined the Near East Relief and went off to Turkey (Sachar, 1969, pp. 340–346).

Because of his ability to fly planes, the Near East Relief initially assigned Means to act as an air-chauffeur for the relief executives. But this turned out to be impractical so he was sent to Harput (now Elizaer), Turkey, where he provided technical training and industrial expertise to the industrial activities set up by the Near East Relief for the Armenian (and Greek) orphans under its care. To understand the conditions under which Means lived and worked, it is necessary to consider how one actually got to Harput in 1919. If a relief worker came from Istanbul, as Means did, he would take a train over the Baghdad railroad to Ulukisla, Turkey, the last stop before reaching the tunnels of the Taurus mountains. The relief worker would then set out by truck to cover the five hundred miles of rocky, mountainous roads to Harput. If the relief worker came from Halab (Aleppo), Syria, or Baghdad, it was usually by some sort of motor transportation and/or camel caravan over rocky, desert landscape. Upon reaching the rather isolated Harput, the relief worker's impression was probably not unlike this:

> Just before sunrise we at last reached the foot of the hill on which Harpoot is situated. . . . Up the winding heights we went on a strip of road barely as wide as our wheels. At last a mud wall, a sleepy dog, and a rocky vacant square. We crossed it diagonally, and went through a narrow passage between tall houses. Then we passed along a rocky, sloping ledge with a high wall on one side, and a drop to unknown depths on the other. At last we turned down a silent street and came to a gate. At the entrance to the gate an Armenian beggar child waited, a thin, little wraith of tragedy. Her starved figure proclaimed her a child, but her sad little face seemed to bear the marks of years of pain. Evidently, she had slept out of doors all night, and had no idea of where to go for her breakfast. Eventually, the Near East Relief authorities would find her and take her to the Harpoot orphanages, but now she was without family, or help, or home. [Miller, 1920]

Harput itself was one of the principal cities into which the Near East Relief brought orphan children for their care. When Means arrived, there were nearly two thousand children housed in orphanages in and around Harput, and when he left there were over five thousand, with nearly 2,400 being cared for in the thirty American orphanages in the area. Of these children, about seventy-five percent were younger than fifteen years of age. Because of the disruption of the local economy caused by the killing and dispersion of the Armenians and by the war and its aftermath, it was not possible for the Near East Relief to obtain the clothing necessary to clad the children, especially through the harsh winters. Consequently, it set up "shops" to make the needed clothing. The shops also performed another important function of providing vocational training for the older children. The Near East Relief was acutely aware that with the destruction of the Armenian community and the absence of mothers and fathers, the children would not have the opportunity to learn the skills and trades needed to maintain them for the rest of their lives. Thus, the Near East Relief undertook the responsibility of providing such training for the children.

It was in this context of providing vocational training and supplying the orphanages that Means applied his energy while in Turkey. He developed a putting-out system of children knitting wool stockings, sweaters, and caps on machines sent from the States; he also supervised shoe shops, hand-weaving and hand-spinning shops, a dye shop, a tailor shop, a blacksmith shop, a tin shop, and a carpentry shop; and finally he developed a putting-out system for cotton and wool spinning. Although the industrial levels of operations were primitive, nearly pre–Industrial Revolution, the children apparently enjoyed the activities and turned out over five thousand dollars worth of goods monthly, all of which was absorbed into the operations of the orphanages.[2] Besides developing and supervising these activities, Means had to work with the local merchants who imported the raw materials for the shops, and with the merchants in Halab and Damascus. In all cases, the merchants had a fixed amount of stock on hand, of which Means required only part, and the prices that Means paid for the raw materials were determined in the transaction itself. The Near East merchants with whom Means dealt operated within the context of an "oriental" bazaar (or *souk*) in which each merchant had a given amount of stock on hand and there were no established prices prior to the actual transaction. Consequently, Means had to bargain with the individual merchants as to both price and quantity, and the particular figures arrived at were specific only to that transaction. Thus, a buyer following on the heels of Means (or if Means returned the following day to the same seller) would have to engage in the bargaining process anew and arrive at his own price and quantity relationship. For the tourist who bargains only over a few goods, this process of establishing a selling price can be enjoyable; but for Means who had to purchase a vast array of raw materials, the process was long and exhausting, especially when he had to bargain with more than one seller of a particular item in order to get it at a reasonable price (Means, 1933, 1975; Barton, 1930; *The New Near East*, 1920; Ware, 1988).

Returning to the United States in 1920, Means entered Lowell Textile School in September, a decision prompted by his exposure to hand-weaving in Turkey. After two years of studying wool manufacturing, he left in March 1922 to set up Means Weave Shop to make a high-quality (and high-priced) hand-woven blanket of his own design that was very different from any made by other blanket manufacturers. Means marketed his blanket through many small shops instead of seeking a large one that could leave him high and dry if a large shop's order were not renewed and would tax his small staff of workers for whom he preferred steady and unpressured work. Through the running of his firm, Means became well acquainted with the Boston wool market and the textile machinery market, and quickly came to the conclusion that American industrial life was far different from what he had experienced in the oriental bazaar in Harput. In particular, Means found himself setting his price prior to any transaction in the market and then engaging in many sequential transactions at this price. For one five-year period in the 1920s, he maintained the same price, even though his costs and sales varied, and sold many thousands of blankets. When Means did change his price in 1929, he did so more in response to a fall in the price of wool than to a decline in sales and the subsequent price was also administered to the market. In any event, Means felt that he was acting rationally in adopting such a price policy. He continued this business until 1933 when he sold it and moved to Washington to take part in the New Deal (Means, 1975, 1983, 1986; University of Lowell; Carter, 1934; Ware, 1988).

While still maintaining his textile firm, Means became interested in learning more about business methods and about the operation of the economy, such as the causes of business depressions and unemployment. Therefore, he thought of enrolling in the Harvard Business School, but then changed his mind. Instead, in February 1924, he became a graduate student in Harvard's famed Department of Economics. The course he took from W.Z. Ripley on the corporation and industry undoubtedly met his goal of learning how the American economy operated. Between 1924 and 1927 Ripley's course dealt with railroads, trusts, and corporations. Ripley argued, both in his classes and, subsequently, in his best-seller, *Main Street and Wall Street* (1927), that this dispersion of stock ownership was permitting the senior-level management and directors of the corporation to enrich themselves at the expense of the stockholders. In addition to Ripley's course, Means took a course titled ''Valuation'' and thus spent the 1926 spring semester listening to James Bonbright, who commuted from Columbia University to lecture on public utility regulation. As for courses in economic theory, Means took F.W. Taussig's well-known course and A. Young's course, ''Money and Banking.'' In these courses, he was introduced to the writings of Smith, Ricardo, Mill, the Austrians, Marshall, and Edgeworth. In addition, he was also probably introduced to Walrasian general equilibrium theory at this time, as presented by G. Cassel in his book *The Theory of Social Economy*, which first appeared in English in 1923. In spite of his excellent introduction to neoclassical economic theory, Means found it hard to take it seriously as a theory that could explain the operations of the American economy of the twentieth century[3] (Blitch, 1983; Weintraub, 1983; Mason, 1982; Carlson, 1968; Means, 1960, 1975; Green, 1986; Hon, 1987; Law, 1986; Ware, 1988).

Means thought that the neoclassical economic theory he was taught at Harvard was clearly relevant to explaining the economic activities of Great Britain at the time of Adam Smith and David Ricardo, the American economy prior to the

1840s, and the kind of economy he experienced in the oriental bazaars while in Turkey. In all cases the great bulk of production and distribution activities was carried on by quite numerous and very small owner-controlled and owner-operated enterprises. Moreover, in all cases the act of exchange was essentially an act of trading, in the sense that the buyers and sellers were trying to get the best price for the goods that existed in the market that day. Consequently, prices were determined in the trading (or bargaining) activity itself, rather than being established beforehand, and hence were extremely flexible, especially with respect to variations in demand since supply was largely given. Thus, Means concluded that in these economies the equating of supply and demand at the market price can be posited without too great a distortion of the facts and the whole economic process can be summed up as an intricate system of trades (Means, 1933, pp. 130–131, 135).

With the advent of the Industrial Revolution, symbolized by the emergence of the factory system, Means thought that the economic system underwent significant and irreversible change. In particular, the scale of production of the individual enterprise increased greatly and with it the number of workers employed on its premises. As a result, the owners of the enterprise developed a managerial structure to supervise the workers and the production processes. In addition, the owners also began to administer their market activities, such as the wage rate and the market price. Thus, the market ceased to be the sole regulator of economic activity and the determiner of the market price. Finding these changes in economic reality significant, Means observed, with great dismay, that neoclassical theory did not in a significant way take these changes into account:

> In F.W. Taussig's course on Economic Theory, I was made to read Adam Smith and was seized with the fact that Smith, despite his pin factory example, was really talking about a factoryless economy like my part of Turkey, not an industrial economy like that of the United States. When we studied Ricardo, Mill, and Marshall, I watched to see what changes in basic theory were made to take account of this notable difference. I could find none. [Means, 1975, p. 150]

So by the time he received his M.A. in 1927, Means had become quite disappointed with orthodox theory.

The Modern Corporation and the Corporate Revolution, 1928–1933

Between 1923 and 1927, A.A. Berle turned out a series of provocative and highly speculative articles dealing with the fate of the stockholders who as owners of the large corporations were losing control of them to corporate management. In all his articles, Berle sought protection for the stockholders in the courts of equity. Claiming that common law could be utilized to work out a set of rules of fair play, he argued that the powers of management were subject to the tacit limitation that they be used only for the equal advancement of the interest of all shareholders and that any use not adopted in this sense may be stopped by injunction or remedied by a judgment for damages. In advancing the argument, Berle was formulating for the first time what later became known as the fiduciary theory of corporations (Burrowes, 1966; Schwarz, 1987; Berle, 1928, 1973).

Wanting to continue his research on corporate finance, and to develop his fiduciary theory of corporations, Berle, in 1927, presented a research proposal titled "A Study of the Trends of Recent Corporate Development" to the Social Science Research Council. The Council reviewed the proposal and accepted it in late August of the same year because "the procedure recommended in this study [the combined use of law and economics to study the modern corporation] well illustrates the type of joint attack fostered by the Social Science Research Council" [Social Science Research Council, 1927, p. 25]. However, to carry out the project, Berle had to be connected with a recognized university, so he approached Young B. Smith, Acting Dean of the Columbia Law School, who was quite happy to appoint Berle as a lecturer in law on November 1, 1927, and let him carry on his research under the auspices of the University's Council for Research in the Social Sciences. Safely ensconced in Kent Hall at Columbia, Berle began to put his research project together, using the $25,000 allotted to him for the first year of the supposedly two-year project. Needing an associate as a statistical and economic research assistant, Berle asked Means, whom he had known at Plattsburgh and had renewed acquaintance with after the war through the friendship between their wives, to join him on his research project on the modern corporation. Thus, with the hiring of Means and a stenographer-assistant, the research project commenced, with Means collecting the statistical evidence and providing the economic analysis, and Berle providing the legal analysis (Berle, 1973; Goebel, 1955; Eichner, 1980; Kirkendall, 1961).

Berle viewed the research project as a vehicle through which he could show the changes in property rights brought about by the existence of the corporate enterprise. Consequently, he restricted the project, and hence *The Modern Corporation and Private Property*, to the relations between the corporation as managed by the group in control, and those who hold participation in it. Thus, while he carried out the legal analysis, Berle directed Means to determine the relative importance of large corporations in the American economy and the dispersion of stock ownership, since the former would determine the extent of the system of corporation finance in the economy while the latter would indicate the extent "that a small, dominant management group [could] control the business operations of any corporation of reasonable size" (Berle, 1928, p. 190).[4]

Believing that Berle's distinction between management and ownership lacked economic significance, Means was worried that his statistical work on the corporation would not be effectively utilized. Thus, he convinced Berle that instead of thinking in terms of ownership and management, it would be more useful to employ three distinct concepts—ownership, control, and management. This threefold distinction did not affect Berle's legal investigations because he was only concerned with the activities of the directors and the senior officers of the corporation with regard to the stockholders. However, it did permit Means to analyze the implications the separation of ownership and control had for neoclassical price theory (Berle and Means, 1932; Eichner, 1980).

Means's statistical research clearly showed, for the first time, how large the modern nonfinancial corporations were, the extent to which they controlled aggregate nonfinancial assets and net income and dominated the economic landscape, and the extent of the separation of ownership from control among them. In addition, he contributed all of the economic arguments found in *The Modern Corporation and Private Property*. This is particularly evident in Book IV where Means drew out the implications that the separation of ownership from control had for traditional theoretical roles of private property, wealth, and the profit motive in directing economic activity and increasing social welfare.[5] Secondary to these implications, Means's statistical research relating to the size and economic dominance of the modern corporation led him to question the adequacy and relevance of many theoretical concepts found in neoclassical economics, such as Marshall's concept of the representative firm, the doctrine that the size of the firm was limited by the wealth of the individual owners or by technological inefficiency, the determinacy of costs of the modern corporation, and the coordination of economic activities by the forces of supply and demand in the marketplace. However, because the main theoretical focus of *The Modern Corporation and Private Property* was on the implications of the separation of ownership from control, Means did not follow up on these secondary implications until he turned to writing his dissertation.

As of June 1930, Means's statistical research for Berle's project on the modern corporation was virtually completed, leaving him with free time on his hands. At this same time, W.M.W. Splawn, the special counsel of the House Committee on Interstate and Foreign Commerce, commissioned J.C. Bonbright to prepare an economic study on the problem of railway holding companies. However, because of his special interest in the regulation of public utilities combined with the recent creations of large public utility holding companies, Bonbright extended the study to holding companies in general. To help him with the study, which eventually was published as *The Holding Company* (1932), he turned to his old student for assistance. Recalling the course Bonbright gave at Harvard on public utility regulation and the fact that the course provided him the initial foundation for his thinking about the modern corporation, Means quickly agreed to Bonbright's request. His duties apparently consisted of searching for early examples of pure holding companies; however, he also seemed to have assisted Bonbright in other ways, especially with respect to analyzing the economic consequences of holding companies. Aside from becoming better acquainted with a specific legal device for securing the concentration of control and management, Means also became more thoroughly convinced that business enterprise could be efficiently organized and managed on a large scale, especially if the holding company form of corporate organization were used (Bonbright and Means, 1932; Means, 1930, 1960; Bonbright, 1930; Hon, 1987; Columbia University, 1931).

After finishing his work for Berle and Bonbright and the subsequent publication of his articles in the *American Economic Review*, and the *Quarterly Journal of Economics* (see Berle and Means, 1930; Means, 1931A, 1931B, 1931C), the Harvard Department of Economics invited Means to combine these articles with an additional section interpreting their significance, and submit the manuscript as his doctoral dissertation. Means did this and in January 1933 submitted as his dissertation, "The Corporate Revolution: The Modern Corporation and Its Effect on Certain Fundamental Economic Postulates." His dissertation committee, which consisted of E.S. Mason, E.H. Chamberlin, and A.E. Monroe, however, did not accept the dissertation as is because they felt that the theoretical section was not "well developed." Perhaps the truth was that they rejected it because they did not like the theoretical interpretations that Means drew from the factual evidence since they boldly attacked neoclassical theory. Nevertheless, possibly with some prodding from Berle, the committee did accept the first part of the dissertation which contained the factual material, and so in 1933, Means was awarded his Ph.D. However, inadvertently, the summary of the entire dissertation, including the theoretical implications, was published in the summaries of Harvard theses for the year 1933 (and reprinted here as Chapter 1). Means never attempted to rework the rejected theoretical section to put it into publishable form and although many of its theoretical ideas, especially administered prices, found their way into his later works, it dropped entirely from sight, buried under the mounds of papers, letters, and manuscripts accumulated over a lifetime of research and writing. Lost from sight, Means eventually assumed that it was lost for good; but the archivists at the Franklin D. Roosevelt Library found the theoretical section among his papers when cataloging them and it is reprinted here as Chapter 2 (Eichner, 1980; Means, 1933, 1962B, 1975, 1986; Green, 1986; Berle, 1973).

In the theoretical section of his dissertation, which was titled "Certain Theoretical Implications of the Modern Corporation," Means presented a more detailed explanation than he had previously done in his articles and in *The Modern Corporation* of how the existence of the large corporation and the separation of ownership from control called into question the "scientific" validity of neoclassical economic theory. Restricting himself to what he considered the most fundamental postulates of the theory—the principle of supply and demand in determining prices, the determinacy of costs, the saving and investment process, and the role of the profit motive in directing economic activity—Means argued that they could not be sustained in their traditional form once the large corporation and the separation of ownership from control became the dominant features of the economy. In particular, he argued that the demise of the principle of supply and demand in determining prices rested primarily upon the mere size of the corporate enterprise, as opposed to the separation of ownership from control. Consequently, Means devoted a chapter of the theoretical section, which he titled "The Modern Corporation and Basic Economic Thought," to the concept of administered prices and its destructive implications for supply and demand determination of prices.

The Roosevelt Years: Administered Prices and National Economic Planning, 1933–1940

Part of Franklin D. Roosevelt's attack on the farm crisis was the establishment of the Agricultural Adjustment Administration (AAA) in the Department of Agriculture.[6] After this Administration had been in existence for two months, it became obvious to Henry Wallace and Rexford Guy Tugwell, the Secretary and Assistant Secretary of Agriculture respectively, that the success of the AAA depended to a large degree on the recovery of the industrial sector, and hence on the recovery policies of the National Recovery Administration (NRA). Thus, to obtain the kind of specialized information they needed, Wallace established, at the prodding of Tugwell, an advisory position to be filled with an individual who would busy himself in seeing the staff aides of the other federal agencies in order to learn what recovery policies were brewing that would have an impact on the recovery of the farm sector. The individual would then draw up reports of his findings and submit them to Wallace. So in late May or early June 1933, Tugwell called Means, who was teaching a summer school course at Columbia Law School, and asked him whether he would consider joining Roosevelt's war on the farm crisis. Means went to Washington to talk with Tugwell and Wallace; the outcome of their meeting was that Wallace immediately appointed Means to the advisory position and gave him the informal title of Economic Advisor on Finance. Working out of an office that was adjoined to Tugwell's, Means took Wallace's orders to heart and quickly became a member of committees in the NRA, including the Consumer Advisory Board, and a participant in the growing controversy over the NRA's price policy.

In taking the job with Wallace, Means took it for granted that he would be trying to develop policies and instruments that would make the economy work more effectively. Upon arriving in Washington, he began articulating an explanation (see Chapter 4) for the Great Depression that was based on the belief that the American economy was not flexible enough to adjust to recent economic developments, such as the disappearance of the frontier, technological improvement in industry resulting in greater output per worker, and the farm debt, without causing significant unemployment and a decline in economic activity. The principal culprit, according to Means, was the increasing concentration of economic activity resulting in inflexible administered prices. Other factors that also reduced the flexibility of the economy included the building up of internal debt and the incapability of governmental institutions to deal with the economic problems growing out of the new conditions established by the rise of economic concentration. Means found that his explanation was well received, but not by the policymakers. Believing that the policymakers would take his arguments more seriously if they were accompanied by dramatic empirical evidence, he undertook, in the late spring of 1934, a statistical analysis of wholesale prices to bring out the basic difference in behavior between farm commodity prices and the administered prices of industry. Upon the completion of the investigation, he found the results much more startling and in conflict with neoclassical price theory than he had expected. Consequently, drawing upon his previous analysis of administered prices, Means used the statistical evidence as a lead to writing a paper delineating the reasons for the failure of the NRA and the AAA with regard to the making of industrial policy and the possible techniques that both the NRA and AAA could use for making better industrial policies. Although the paper was entirely analytical, Means expected it to be used by the makers of industrial policy.[7]

Thinking the paper important, Means gave it the title ''NRA and AAA and the Reorganization of Industrial Policy Making,'' and had it typed up (by August 29) and widely distributed. The paper did in fact generate a great deal of response with regard to his statistical and economic analysis and his discussion of industrial policy-making. Although largely tied up with his work for Wallace and, beginning in November, for the National Resources Board, he was able to respond to his critics and, in October, to revise the paper.

Erroneously suspecting that Means's paper was being suppressed, the longtime foe of monopoly and bitter enemy of the NRA, Senator William Borah of Idaho, had the Senate pass a resolution on January 3, 1935, titled ''Monopolistic Influence upon Industrial Prices,'' demanding that Wallace submit the paper to the Senate. Wallace did so on January 15 under the (nearly) original title ''N.R.A., A.A.A., and the Making of Industrial Policy''; however, when published two days later as Senate Document No. 13, it bore the title of *Industrial Prices and Their Relative Inflexibility*, with the original title appearing on the first page (see Chapter 3). The publication of *Industrial Prices* occurred with much fanfare and caught the attention of economists and politicians alike. The *New York Times*, *Washington Post*, and *Washington Herald* all noted Borah's resolution and gave a quick summary or flavor of the pamphlet. Consequently, *Industrial Prices* received much play in the popular press and journals. More importantly, Means received many requests for the pamphlet from economists and institutions. By the end of February 1935, over seven thousand copies of *Industrial Prices* had been distributed.

When writing *Industrial Prices*, Means confined the analysis solely to the intraindustry problems of prices and production that emerge when firms can make their own business policy. Hence, he argued that the problem of making industrial policy, in so far as it concerned the NRA and AAA, lay in finding the key decisions for each industry, which, if made right, would so condition the other elements of industrial policy that the latter could be left to the actions of individuals and the operation of the market. However, in spite of the narrow focus of *Industrial Prices* on intraindustry problems of prices and production, it was clear to Means that many of the most important key decisions would concern interindustry relationships and could be made right only in terms of interindustry balance and within the context of the national economy. Thus, he soon realized that the NRA, AAA, and other specific recovery programs could not repair the poorly functioning economy and that partial planning in general, whether done by business enterprises or public institutions, would more likely make matters worse than better. So, given this emerging interest in national economic planning, Means accepted Tugwell's suggestion (made in October or November 1934) that he go to work, at least on a part-time basis, for the National Resources Board.

Appointed as Acting Director of the Industrial Section of the Industrial Committee of the National Resources Board (later to be called the National Resources Committee) in November 1934, Means made his first act the drawing-up of a research proposal suggesting that the industrial capacity of the blast furnace industry be investigated, primarily for the purpose of developing techniques for making further industrial capacity studies. Later, in February 1935 after reading H. Loeb's book, *The Chart of Plenty*, he revived an old idea of his of modeling the American economy in terms of both production and consumption. With such a model, he argued before the Industrial Committee, it would be possible to construct production-consumption patterns that would reflect the economical use of resources to serve human requirements under a variety of possible conditions. The Committee accepted his argument, so in May 1935, Means initiated research projects on industrial capacity and consumption and thus was on his way to developing a series of production-consumption patterns or a model of the American economy that could then be used for national economic planning.

In November 1936, Means wrote a memorandum on national economic planning (see Chapter 5) in which he argued that one of the concerns of a federal planning organization would be to bring about and maintain effective overall balance of the use of the nation's resources. This, in turn, implied that his production-consumption projects had to be expanded to include an investigation into the forces that affect the coordination and organization of economic activity and hence the overall balance of the economy. Thus, Means suggested that the National Resources Committee initiate a study of the structure of industry that would (1) be concerned primarily with the administrative or controlling units through which industry is now carried on; (2) consider the present and possible roles of competition and administration of economic activity; (3) be concerned particularly with corporations, trade associations, labor unions, farms, and consumer organizations; (4) be concerned with possible techniques for coordinating economic activity with the minimum concentration of power; and (5) result in recommendations as to the structure of planning and acting for overall balance toward which this country should work. The Industrial Committee accepted Means's suggestion in July 1937, permitting Means to develop a comprehensive multi-industry model of the American economy that could be used for national economic planning.

The research undertaken by Means and his colleagues in the Industrial Section was published between 1938 and 1940. In particular, Means used the model in *Patterns of Resource Use* (1938) to determine the pattern of consumption, resource use, and labor employment at three different levels of consumer income, including the full-employment level. His model was also used (see Paradiso, 1940) to determine the amount of capital equipment required by the iron and steel industry, over the existing equipment, at various levels of consumer income, including the full-employment level. Finally, in 1939 Means's work on the structure of industry was published under the title of *The Structure of the American Economy Part I: Basic Characteristics.* Although these publications combined with those on consumption develop various features of Means's multi-industry model of the American economy, no single publication emerged that presented the model in its entirety. This was due to the rise of American Keynesianism and its approach to national economic planning. That is, beginning in late 1937, the Industrial Committee began to have second thoughts about Means's approach to national economic planning, and by June 1938 the Committee had virtually come to accept Keynesianism and its aggregate approach to national economic planning. Consequently, it ceased to support Means's research projects and stipulated that the active ones be completed as soon as possible. Denied the research he wished to do, Means did not fit in with the Keynesian NRC or its successor, the National Resources Planning Board. He resigned from the Planning Board in June 1940.

Aside from his work with Wallace and the NRC, Means also found time to write a short note (see Chapter 6) in which he argued that corporate enterprise expenditure was a function of the current and the preceding year's level of production. This is quite possibly the first description of the sales-accelerator investment function popularized by Robert Eisner in the 1960s. Means also maintained his interest in economic concentration and its impact on the operation of the American economy. However he did not think that the neo-Brandeisians' insistence on enforcing the antitrust statutes was the answer to getting the economy moving again (see Chapter 7). He therefore passed up the opportunity to serve as economic coordinator of the Temporary National Economic Committee, although later in life he regretted this decision. Finally, Means was a lecturer at American University between 1936 and 1939 where he taught a seminar titled "The Problem of Economic Coordination in a Modern Democracy." One of his students was John M. Blair, who took his seminar in 1937. Means was also an instructor at the Graduate School of the United States Department of Agriculture where he taught a course on the economics of administered prices (see Chapter 8).[8]

War and Postwar Years, 1940–1988

Means left the National Resources Planning Board for the new Fiscal Division of the Bureau of the Budget. The Fiscal Division had been created after the Bureau of the Budget was reorganized, expanded, and placed in the new Executive Office of the President created by the Administrative Reorganization of 1939. The Division included an economics group and an accounting/reporting group. The economics group had responsibility for analysis of a wide range of matters related to the budget, and it drafted the President's budget message. It was also involved in the Bureau's function of clearing legislative proposals and reports on legislation prepared by other government agencies. In 1940–41 defense expenditures were rapidly increasing and the threat of shortages and inflation was a growing concern. Relying on his previous research on administered prices in which commodities were grouped on the basis of their frequency of price changes, Means argued that with expanding output, prices in the more flexible groups could be expected to rise and return to their pre-Depression relationship with the administered prices. This kind of price movement Means called a price rotation and he did not consider it a cause of concern; on the other hand, if the index for administered prices began to rise, thus transforming all the price relationships, this would indicate that inflation is taking place and hence it was something to be concerned about. Means believed that the price rises in 1940–41 were of the price rotation type and thus not a cause of concern. However, Gerhard Colm, the head of the Fiscal Division, thought otherwise and this difference of opinion about the inflation threat, combined with Means's failure to shape the Director of the Bureau of the Budget's advice to the President, led him to leave the Bureau by the end of 1941 (Eichner, 1980; Goode, 1987).

In 1943 Means became associate director of research for the Committee for Economic Development (CED), a business-sponsored, private research group originally concerned with government policies to assure a full-employment transition to a peacetime economy. While at the CED he instigated the collection of the statistical series on money flows now regularly published by the Federal Reserve Board in its flow of funds accounts. While on the CED staff, Means also played the role of the gadfly—often he was in a minority of one, and hard to persuade. He was valued, however, because he enlivened the discussion and made the young theorists who populated the CED look hard at points they were tempted to brush aside. Means also served as Economic Consultant for the Committee and on its Research Advisory Board. He retired from the Committee in 1958 and spent his remaining years writing, lecturing, appearing before Congressional Committees, and working as an economic consultant for several companies involved in antitrust suits (Eichner, 1980; Hart, 1987).

The two decades following his service in the federal government found Means hard at work on developing the concept of administered prices into a doctrine of administered prices. In 1943 he extended the concept to international trade (see Chapter 9). Next, in 1947 Means produced a manuscript (that was never published) in which he developed a non-Keynesian monetary theory of employment (see Chapter 13). His theory was based on his concept of administered prices and on his monetary theory of aggregate demand. The former explained why changes in aggregate demand would work themselves out through changes in both prices and employment, while the latter explained the level of aggregate demand in terms of the relation between the demand for money and the stock of money outstanding. Thus, when the price level increased, the real stock of money declined and so, as a consequence, did the propensities to consume and invest that determined the level of aggregate demand. Therefore, in order to restore the real level of aggregate demand, Means argued that the stock of money had to be increased. Finally, in the 1950s, Means devoted much effort to developing a macroeconomic equilibrium model that included both flexible and administered prices (see Chapter 10). The *American Economic Review* rejected his papers on the topic and George Stigler ridiculed his attempts, but the great interest economists of all persuasions showed in the Hicksian and other fix-flex price models of the 1960s and 1970s shows that Means was ahead of his time.

The 1940s and 1950s also saw Means lay the firm, pricing, and price foundation for his doctrine of administered prices. Stung by comments from economists that he failed to utilize Chamberlin's description and analysis of monopolistic competition, Means attempted in a series of papers to fashion an explanation of administered prices based on traditional monopoly analysis but without utilizing the marginalist apparatus associated with the Chamberlin-Robinson theories. This project, however, which took place over a ten-year period between 1943 and 1953, was undertaken against Means's better judgment since his own experience as a monopolistic competitor led him to reject the relevance of Chamberlin's theory as early as 1934, and moreover, since he completely rejected marginalism. Consequently, when the Brookings report on pricing in big business appeared in 1958, Means quickly refashioned his explanation of administered prices, now basing it on target rate of return pricing procedures. Second, in the 1940s Means had begun dismissing the notion that management tried to maximize current profits. He subsequently reached the more revolutionary position that management seeks neither short- nor long-period maximum profits, nor frames its business strategies in terms of long or short periods. Rather, Means argued, management seeks profits over time which would not induce entry or otherwise inhibit the growth of corporate profits or the corporation itself. Third, Means integrated the concept of pricing period and the flow principle of production into his definition of administered prices. Fourth, he reviewed the trend of economic concentration in light of his previous findings (see Chapter 14). And finally, Means began to take seriously the importance of perverse prices which John M. Blair had brought to his attention.

The 1950s also saw Means introduce the concept of administrative inflation.

In 1957 Senator Estes Kefauver became chairman of the Senate Subcommittee on Antitrust and Monopoly. He selected John Blair as his chief economist and Blair in turn convinced Kefauver to embark on a tedious investigation of administered prices. The Subcommittee hearings began in 1957 and at the first hearing Means, whom Blair had invited to testify, introduced the concept of administrative inflation to help explain the general rise in the price level for the last two years. He continued to work on the concept and to appear before government committee hearings for the next five years (Eichner, 1980; Nossiter, 1962).

These developments during the 1940s and 1950s permitted Means to develop his doctrine of administered prices which delineated the forces that affected the coordination of economic activity and determined the actual manner in which the modern corporate economy operated (see Chapter 11). With the doctrine in hand, Means could not only account for the persistent inflation that characterized the American economy since World War II, but also propose economic policies to deal with it (see *Pricing Power and the Public Interest* [1962A]; *The Corporate Revolution in America* [1962B]; and Chapters 15, 16, 17 and 19). He also saw his doctrine of administered prices as a direct challenge to neoclassical economics (see Chapters 13 and 19). As could be expected, the neoclassical economists responded in a variety of ways (see Chapter 20). The most direct attack leveled at his doctrine of administered prices came from Stigler in his book with James Kindahl called *The Behavior of Industrial Prices* (1970). Means analyzed the price data in the book and came to an opposite conclusion that it did in fact support his doctrine of administered prices. His findings were published in the *American Economic Review* in 1972 and Stigler responded with a piece in the same journal in 1973. Means in turn submitted a rejoinder alleging no less than seventeen errors of fact or in the interpretation of his position made by Stigler (see Chapters 12 and 20). The editor of the *AER* refused to publish the paper. However, subsequent research by D. Carlton (1986) on the Stigler-Kindahl price data clearly showed that Means was correct in his allegations and that Stigler came very close to perpetrating a fraud when he claimed otherwise. Needless to say, there is an enormous literature, with quite diverse conceptual and quantitative specifications and conclusions, on all aspects of administered prices. A critical evaluative basis seems to be one of consonance or dissonance with Means's accepted paradigm: The facts do not speak solely by themselves to the hypothesis of administered prices; they are interpreted on the basis of selectively chosen supplementary hypotheses.

Means died on February 15, 1988, and his obituary shortly appeared in such papers as the *New York Times*, the *Washington Post*, the *Chicago Tribune*, and the *Independent* (a U.K. newspaper). Economists generally ignored his death. As strange as this seems, such treatment is altogether fitting for an economist who served his country and fellow citizens so well while at the same time incurring the displeasure of neoclassical economists by trying to forge new non-neoclassical concepts and pictures of economic relationships appropriate for a corporate economy.

Notwithstanding the alienated relationship between Means and orthodox economics and the consequent quite mixed reception of much of his work, Gardiner Means, while very much a solitary figure, was a major contributor to institutional economics and a founder of post-Keynesian macroeconomics. *The Modern Corporation and Private Property* is undoubtedly one of the major social science works of the twentieth century. For post–World War II Institutionalists, Means's ideas on the corporation—specifically, concentration and size, the dispersion of stock ownership, the separation of ownership from control—the corporate system, the changing meaning of private property, the economy as a system of power, and the corporation as private government were very important and useful. His analysis of administered prices comprised a new microeconomics, including theories of the price adjustment process and of the firm in relation to the market, and a macroeconomics somewhat congruent with, but also somewhat in conflict with, that of Keynes and the orthodox Keynesians, especially with regard to the role of inflexible, administered prices in macroeconomic coordination failures, which was readily absorbed in post-Keynesian economics. Central to all of Means's institutional, microeconomic, and macroeconomic work was the role of power which was enough to distance him from his more orthodox brethren (see Samuels and Medema, 1990).

Notes

1. When Means entered the army, he had not yet completed the course work required for a B.A. degree in chemistry. However, in keeping with the patriotic fervor of the time, Harvard awarded B.A. degrees to members of the Class of 1918 who were in the armed forces and had not completed the necessary course work.

2. Caroline Ware has described Means's activities in Harput in the following manner:

> Both as a method of training and of production, Gardiner introduced two basic industrial features: division of labor and mechanization. In his shoe shop, for example, he seated the boys in a circle. A master shoemaker cut out the parts. The first boy sewed two parts together over and over again until he got expert at doing it just right. He passed each shoe on to the next boy who learned to do the second process in the same manner until he became expert at it. When all the boys were expert at doing their particular bit they all moved one seat to the right and learned the next process. After every boy had had a turn at each step he went to another room where he was given all the pieces for a single shoe and had to put them together from scratch. Finally they learned to cut the pieces from the hides. With respect to mechanization, the women who spun yarn used only a spindle which they rubbed along their thigh to set it twirling and then they wound the resulting yarn up on the shank of the spindle. Gardiner found a picture of a spinning wheel in a dictionary. He got his carpenter shop to make the parts from the picture, got the spinning wheel working and taught the younger women and children to use it. [Ware, 1988, p. 6]

3. Other courses taken by Means between 1924 and 1927 included "Economic History since 1750" given by E.F. Gay, and "International Trade" given by J.H. Williams (Green, 1986; and Mason, 1982).

4. From the evidence that is available, it appears that Berle was the sole author of Books II and III, while Means was the sole author of Chapters II through VI of Book I. The other chapters of Book I and all of Book IV were coauthored. When preparing *The*

Modern Corporation, both Berle and Means had difficulty understanding each other's technical jargon. As Caroline Ware has noted:

> This became so serious from time to time that they would talk about the possibility of having to write two separate books, one from the legal viewpoint and one from the economic. So I intervened as a listener and translator. I got the lawyer to explain what his technical statements meant in lay terms. Then I got the economist to put his technical ideas into lay terms. Then I gave the lay versions to the opposite person and helped them to reach a common understanding from which they could go on. The result gave the final book its uniqueness and importance. [Ware, 1988, pp. 2–3]

5. Absent from *The Modern Corporation and Private Property* and Means's dissertation is any discussion of profit maximization and its applicability to the modern corporation. In spite of the claims made by many economists (e.g., see Stigler and Friedland, 1983), Means never considered this question to be one of the book's arguments for two reasons. First, he accepted Berle's fiduciary theory of corporations which was designed to repair the theoretical breach between the owners and the controllers. Second, up until 1947, Means believed that the managers and controllers strove to maximize the profits of the corporation.

6. Material in this section is drawn from Lee (1988, 1990).

7. Although aware of Chamberlin's book, *The Theory of Monopolistic Competition*, when writing the paper, Means used neither its terminology nor its theoretical approach largely because he did not find business enterprises behaving in the manner it suggested. This has led neoclassical economists to question the soundness of Means's analysis of prices and the usefulness of his terminology.

8. In 1936 Means and Caroline Ware jointly published *The Modern Economy in Action*. Ware wrote the book while Means furnished the ideas (Ware, 1988).

References

Barton, James L. 1930. *Story of Near East Relief*. New York: Macmillan.

Berle, Adolf A. 1928. *Studies in the Law of Corporation Finance*. Chicago: Callaghan and Co.

———. 1973. *Navigating the Rapids 1918–1971*, ed. Beatrice B. Berle and Travis B. Jacobs. New York: Harcourt Brace Jovanovich.

Berle, Adolf A., and Means, Gardiner C. 1930. "Corporations and the Public Investor." *American Economic Review* 20 (March): 54–71.

———. 1932. *The Modern Corporation and Private Property*. New York: The Macmillan Company. Rev. ed. New York: Harcourt, Brace and World, 1967.

Blitch, Charles, P. 1983. "Allyn A. Young: A Curious Case of Professional Neglect." *History of Political Economy* 15 (March): 1–24.

Bonbright, James C., 1930. Letter to Felix Frankfurter. August 6. James C. Bonbright Papers, Box 1. Columbia University.

Bonbright, James C., and Means, Gardiner C. 1932. *The Holding Company*. New York: McGraw-Hill.

Burrowes, Robert D. 1966. "Adolf Augustus Berle, Jr.: Brandeis of the Future." Ph.D. dissertation. Princeton University.

Carlson, Valdemar. 1968. "The Education of an Economist before the Great Depression." *The American Journal of Economics and Sociology* 27 (January): 101–112.

Carlton, D.W. 1986. "The Rigidity of Prices." *American Economic Review* 76 (September): 637–658.

Carter, John Franklin [Unofficial Observer]. 1934. *The New Dealers*. New York: Simon and Schuster.

Cassel, Gustav. 1924. *The Theory of Social Economy*. New York: Harcourt, Brace.

Chamberlin, Edward H. 1933. *The Theory of Monopolistic Competition*. Cambridge: Harvard University Press.

Columbia University. 1931. *Report of the Dean of the School of Law for the Period Ending June 30, 1930*. New York: Columbia University.

Eichner, Alfred S. 1980. "Gardiner C. Means." *Challenge* 22 (January-February): 56–59.

Goebel, Julius. 1955. *A History of the School of Law Columbia University*. New York: Columbia University Press.

Goode, Richard. 1987. Personal communication. September 8.

Green, Jerry. 1986. Personal communication. November 13.

Hart, Albert G. 1987. Personal communication. September 9.

Hon, Ralph C. 1987. Personal communication. September 8.

Kirkendall, Richard S. 1961. "A.A. Berle, Jr. Student of the Corporation, 1917–1932." *Business History Review* 35 (Spring): 43–58.

Law, Margaret E. 1986. Personal communication. October 8.

Lee, Frederic S. 1988. "A New Dealer in Agriculture: G.C. Means and the Writing of *Industrial Prices*." *Review of Social Economy* 46 (October): 180–202.

———. 1990. "From Multi-Industry Planning to Keynesian Planning: Gardiner Means, the American Keynesians, and National Economic Planning at the National Resources Committee." *Journal of Policy History*, 2:186–212.

Loeb, Harold. 1935. *The Chart of Plenty*. New York: Viking Press.

Mason, Edward S. 1982. "The Harvard Department of Economics from the Beginning to World War II." *The Quarterly Journal of Economics* 97 (August): 383–433.

Means, Gardiner C. 1930. Letter to Edwin F. Gay. August 6. G. C. Means Papers, Series I, Holding Companies. Franklin D. Roosevelt Library, Hyde Park, New York.

———. 1931A. "Growth in the Relative Importance of the Large Corporation in American Economic Life." *American Economic Review* 21 (March): 10–42.

———. 1931B. "Stock Dividends, Large Scale Business and Corporate Savings—A Criticism." *Quarterly Journal of Economics* 45 (May): 536–540.

———. 1931C. "Separation of Ownership and Control in American Industry." *Quarterly Journal of Economics* 46 (November): 68–100.

———. 1933. "The Corporate Revolution." G. C. Means Papers, Series I, "The Corporate Revolution." Franklin D. Roosevelt Library, Hyde Park, New York.

———. 1938. *Patterns of Resource Use*. Washington, D.C.: Government Printing Office.

———. 1939. *The Structure of the American Economy. Part I: Basic Characteristics*. Washington, D.C.: Government Printing Office.

———. 1960. Letter to James C. Bonbright. August 14. James C. Bonbright Papers, Box 3, Folder Me. Columbia University.

———. 1962A. *Pricing Power and the Public Interest*. New York: Harper and Brothers.

———. 1962B. *The Corporate Revolution in America*. New York: Crowell-Collier.

———. 1975. "Remarks upon Receipt of the Veblen-Commons Award." *Journal of Economic Issues* 9 (June): 149–157.

———. 1983. "Corporate Power in the Marketplace." *The Journal of Law and Economics* 26 (June): 467–485.

———. 1986. Interview. December 31.

Miller, Hugh S. 1920. "On the Road to Harpoot." *New York Times* (January 11): section III, p. 5.

New Near East. 1920. "In Isolated Harpoot." 6 (December): 14.

New York Times. 1918. "Airman's Life Saved in 2,000-Foot Fall." (May 30): 20.

Nossiter, Bernard. 1962. "The World of Gardiner Means." *The New Republic* 146 (May 7): 17–20.

Paradiso, Louis J. 1940. *Capital Requirements: A Study in Methods as Applied to the Iron and Steel Industry*. Washington, D.C.: Government Printing Office.

Ripley, William Z. 1927. *Main Street and Wall Street*. Boston: Little, Brown.

Sachar, Howard M. 1969. *The Emergence of the Middle East: 1914–1924*. New York: Alfred A. Knopf.

Samuels, Warren J., and Medema, Steven G. 1990. *Gardiner C. Means's Institutional and Post Keynesian Economics: An Interpretion and Assessment*. Armonk, NY: M.E. Sharpe.

Schwarz, Jordan A. 1987. *Liberal: Adolf A. Berle and the Vision of an American Era*. New York: The Free Press.

Social Science Research Council. 1927. *Third Annual Report, 1926–27*. New York.

Stigler, George J., and Friedland, Claire. 1983. "The Literature of Economics: The Case of Berle and Means." *The Journal of Law and Economics* 26 (June): 237–268.

Stigler, George J., and Kindahl, J.K. 1970. *The Behavior of Industrial Prices*. New York: National Bureau of Economic Research.

University of Lowell. Registrar. Permanent Record Card of Gardiner Coit Means.

Ware, Caroline F. 1988. "Some Notes on Gardiner C. Means, Economist." Unpublished.

Ware, Caroline F., and Means, Gardiner C. 1936. *The Modern Economy in Action*. New York: Harcourt, Brace.

Weintraub, E. Roy. 1983. "On the Existence of a Competitive Equilibrium: 1930–1954." *Journal of Economic Literature* 21 (March): 1–39.

Part I

Selected Writings of Gardiner C. Means

1

The Corporate Revolution

This thesis presents statistical evidence of a change in the fundamental character of economic organization which has been brought about through the growth of corporate activity, and attempts to indicate certain of the more important changes in the assumptions of economic analysis which this development requires. It is suggested that this development, culminating in the separation of ownership and control, has brought a change in the character of industry as revolutionary as that produced by the industrial revolution with its corresponding division of function, the separation of labor and control.

The statistical part of the thesis shows (1) the increasing extent to which economic activity is conducted under the corporate form of organization, (2) the increasing role which corporations of tremendous size have come to play, (3) the increasing dispersion of stock ownership, and finally (4) the increasing separation of ownership and control which is involved in the modern corporation.

The theoretical section takes four major postulates of received economic theory—the trading character of the market, the determinacy of cost, the unity of the process of real saving, and the efficacy of the profit motive—and suggests that modern corporate enterprise makes it necessary to replace these, in so far as corporate enterprise is concerned, with (1) the administrative character of the market, (2) the indeterminacy of cost, (3) the duality of the process of saving, and finally (4) the possible ineffectiveness of "profits" as a motivating force.

Following an introduction, the thesis sketches the development of corporate economic activity in the United States from the 335 corporations of 1800 to the half million corporations of the present day. It is shown that the corporation has come to dominate field after field of business enterprise, coming earliest in those fields invested with a public interest (banks, insurance companies, and common carriers), or in those requiring large aggregate fixed capital (railroads or mines);

Reprinted with permission of Collier Books, an imprint of Macmillan Publishing Company, from *The Corporate Revolution in America: Economic Reality vs. Economic Theory* by Gardiner C. Means. Copyright © 1962 by The Crowell Collier Publishing Company.

latest in those involving little public interest (public services, agriculture, etc.), and in those requiring little fixed capital (wholesale and retail trade). The trend of the last century indicates that in the very near future virtually all economic enterprise will be conducted by corporations with the possible important exception of farming.

The thesis then indicates that in the growth of corporate enterprise very large corporations have come to be the dominant form. In 1927, two hundred non-financial corporations controlled 45 percent of non-financial corporate wealth, received over 40 percent of corporate income, controlled 35 percent of business wealth, and between 15 and 20 percent of national wealth. The rate of growth of large corporations between 1909 and 1927 has been such that if it were to continue 80 percent of corporate wealth would be in the hands of two hundred corporations by 1950.[1]

The thesis also shows the growth in the number of book stockholders in recent years for three of the largest corporations in the country, for thirty-one representative big companies, and for all corporations (estimated). The latter increased from 4.4 million in 1900 to 12 million in 1920 and 18 million in 1928. Customer and employee stock ownership is considered and a shift of ownership from the rich to the less well-to-do is shown from income tax statistics.

The statistical section of the thesis examines the separation of ownership and control in the large corporations in the United States. Five types of control are considered: complete ownership; majority control; control through a legal device; minority control; and management control. Examination of the ultimate control of the two hundred largest American corporations indicates these striking facts: 65 percent of them by number and 80 percent by assets are controlled by management or by a legal device under which ownership and control are separated; 23 percent by number and 14 percent by assets represent control by minority ownership. This leaves 12 percent by number and 6 percent by assets which are actually controlled by majority of the ownership. It is suggested that this corporate development calls for a re-analysis of the economic process in which the individualism of Adam Smith's private enterprise has given way to the collective activity of the modern corporation.

The theoretical section examines the central core of received theory as it was developed by Adam Smith and given greater precision by later writers. The received theory can be summarized as the application of the principle of substitution to both the factors of production and the means of consumption, under the assumption of markets for both in which supply is equated to demand through a perfectly flexible price. It assumes what might properly be called a trading market. Earlier writers have recognized that economic activity is only in part trading and that the element of administration enters in, but they have tended to minimize this administrative aspect. The modern corporation has not only increased this aspect by bringing a greater part of economic activity within the administrative limits of single units, but has altered the character of the market by making *price* not an outgrowth of trading but of administration. Prices fixed over periods of time have replaced flexible prices, and supply as defined by classical economists is seldom equated to demand. Rather, *production* tends to be equated to demand at the fixed prices and a disequilibrium between *supply* and demand results not in a fall in price, but in the failure fully to employ the factors of production, or in their overemployment.

The next section suggests that as all enterprise activity involves "overhead costs" and as these are essentially "joint costs," it would be more precise to assume that every product of enterprise activity is a product of joint cost and, correspondingly, that every product involves joint utility. The importance of the organized relationship of items of wealth in the modern corporation makes this assumption essential. Under this assumption both cost and utility become indeterminate.

It is then suggested that the process of saving has come to be a dual process conducted by two independent groups of individuals, whose actions do not necessarily mesh, with the result that two separate and independent markets exist, one for capital goods and one for interests in capital goods. It is indicated that prices in these markets may move in opposite directions or in the same direction.

Finally the thesis indicates that where ownership and control are completely separated and profits are destined only for the " owners" they cannot perform their customary role of inducing the efficient management of enterprise, though they can perform the role of inducing the taking of risk. It is suggested that if the logic of traditional profit theory were to be followed, any profits over and above enough given to the "owners" to induce the continued supply of new capital should be received by control as a prize to induce the efficient management of enterprise. Because such great profits to control would presumably involve diminishing returns, the question is raised whether profits are a socially effective method of inducing enterprise activity [where the modern corporation in concerned].

Note

1. It should be noted that this statement was not a prediction but an indication of the magnitude of the rate at which growth was proceeding in the twenty-year period. Concentration did continue after 1929 but at a much slower rate. Government action under the Roosevelt and subsequent administrations has operated to slow the rate of concentration, breaking up utility holding companies, impeding railroad consolidation, preventing industrial mergers, and, in the case of aluminum, eliminating monopoly by facilitating the creation of effective competitors.

2

Theoretical Chapters from Proposed Dissertation

Chapter VI. The Modern Corporation and Basic Economic Thought

Thus far we have examined four major aspects of corporate development: the increasing proportion of economic activity that is conducted under the corporate form, the increasing proportion carried on by tremendous corporate giants, the dispersion in the ownership of these giants, and the separation which has developed between their ownership and their control.

The effect of this fourfold development on the character of our economic system has been little understood. Though the changes themselves, with perhaps the exception of the separation of ownership and control, have been common knowledge and apparent to most observers, their implications with respect to the economic process and our understanding of that process have not been developed. Throughout the nineteenth and the early part of the twentieth century, the analysis of the economic process has continued to be in terms of private enterprise and that beautiful logical structure, the organon of received theory, has been primarily a logical refinement of the economic symphony first publicized by Adam Smith.

In order to bring out the revolutionary effect of the modern corporation on the economic process as described in received theory, we will first outline the core of nineteenth century theory and then compare the economy out of which this analysis sprang and which the analysis presupposes with the present day economy of corporate enterprise.

The central core of received theory is to be found clearly developed in *The Wealth of Nations*. In summary statement, it is the application of the principle of substitution to both the factors of production and the means of consumption

January 1, 1933. From the Gardiner C. Means Papers at the Franklin D. Roosevelt Library.

under the assumption of markets for both in which supply is equated to demand through a perfectly flexible price.

The assumption as to markets need not detain us. It is the stock in trade of every textbook writer and is typified with a false clearness in the customary crossed lines of [the] supply and demand curve. In such a market an increase in supply relative to demand will cause a drop in price sufficient to equate supply and demand under the new conditions while a relative decrease in supply will cause a rise in price of a corresponding nature.

The application of the principle of substitution is not so easily covered. The principle itself as applied to the business man has been clearly expressed by Alfred Marshall:

> At the beginning of his undertaking, and at every successive stage, the alert business man strives so to modify his arrangements as to obtain better results with a given expenditure, or equal results with a less expenditure. In other words, he ceaselessly applies the principle of substitution, with the purpose of increasing his profits.[1]

Adam Smith employed the same principle in respect to two factors of production when he said:

> *The whole of the advantages and disadvantages of the different employments of labour and stock must, in the same neighbourhood, be either perfectly equal or continually tending to equality.* If in the same neighbourhood, there was any employment evidently either more or less advantageous than the rest, so many people would crowd into it in the one case, and so many would desert it in the other, that its advantages would soon return to the level of other employments. This at least would be the case in a society where things were left to follow their natural course, where there was perfect liberty, and where every man was perfectly free both to choose what occupation he thought proper, and to change it as often as he thought proper. Every man's interest would prompt him to seek the advantageous, and to shun the disadvantageous employment.[2] [Emphasis added.]

The same principle, he applies to land when he indicates that it will be shifted from corn to pasture or the reverse[3] or from corn into grass[4] depending on the relative prices which these products bring. We would generalize his position with relation to the factors of production by saying that anyone in control of a factor of production—land, labor, or stock—would be constantly striving to shift its use so "as to obtain better results with a given expenditure or equal results with a less expenditure"[5] of the particular factor concerned. On the consumption side it goes without saying that Adam Smith assumed that each individual strives to spend his available income so as to obtain the optimum results, substituting for any prospective purchase, any other which promised greater advantage.

In applying the principle of substitution to give a unified picture of the economic process, Adam Smith pictured a system of "natural" prices for the factors of production—worker, stock, or land—such that no shift to some other employment would at the prevailing prices[6] bring a greater return to the possessor of that factor and no substitution of the purchase of one commodity for that of another at the existing prices would (or could be expected to) bring greater satisfaction to any consumer. He assumed that if all factors and commodities were to exchange at their "natural prices," a condition of optimum satisfaction from the available factors of production would be reached.[7]

With this picture of natural prices in mind, Adam Smith maintained that in practice in the economy of his time actual prices tended to approximate the natural prices, except to the extent that competition was impeded by unnatural restraints erected by men through government or otherwise. The reasons for this he gives as follows:

> The quantity of every commodity brought to market naturally suits itself to the effectual demand. (i.e., to the demand which would exist at the natural price. This is equivalent to saying "demand which would cause the actual price to be the same as the natural price.") *It is the interest of all those who employ their land, labour, or stock, in bringing any commodity to market, that the quantity never should exceed the effectual demand; and it is the interest of all other people that it never should fall short of that demand.*
>
> If at any time it exceeds the effectual demand, some of the component parts of its price must be paid below their natural rate. If it is rent, the interest of the landlords will immediately prompt them to withdraw a part of their land; and if it is wages or profit, the interest of the labourers in the one case, and of their employers in the other, will prompt them to withdraw a part of their labour or stock from this employment. The quantity brought to market will soon be no more than sufficient to supply the effectual demand. All the different parts of its price will rise to their natural rate, and the whole price to its natural price.
>
> If, on the contrary, the quantity brought to market should at any time fall short of the effectual demand, some of the component parts of its price must rise above their natural rate. If it is rent, the interest of all other landlords will naturally prompt them to prepare more land for the raising of this commodity; if it is wages or profit, the interest of all other labourers and dealers will soon prompt them to employ more labour and stock in preparing and bringing it to market. The quantity brought thither will soon be sufficient to supply the effectual demand. All the different parts of its price will soon sink to their natural rate, and the whole price to its natural price.
>
> The natural price, therefore, is, as it were, the central price, to which the prices of all commodities are continually gravitating. Different accidents may sometimes keep them suspended a good deal above it, and sometimes force them down even somewhat below it. But whatever may be the obstacles which hinder them from settling in this centre of repose and continuance, they are constantly tending towards it.[8] [Emphasis added.]

This picture of an economic system in which for the factors of production and for the means of consumption the interplay of supply and demand operate through price to yield the optimum or, in Marshall's phrase, the maximum satisfaction, has been given greater precision since it was elaborated by Adam Smith, but in its essentials it has remained unchanged and at the heart of economic theory to this day. It was given mathematical precision as a complete structure in the system of simultaneous equations presented by the mathematical economists; it was given mathematical precision on a "one-thing-at-a-time" basis by Alfred Marshall; it was given physically perceivable precision by the hydrolic tour-de-force of Irving Fisher; and has been reaffirmed in the most competent recent work on "Modern Economic Society" by Sumner H. Slichter of the Harvard Business School. Because this book is so recent (1931) and because it has been so widely received as an up to date description of our present day economic system, it is worth quoting to show the close tie which binds the economic thought of today with that of 1776.

In sketching the fundamentals in "The Operation of the Existing Economic Order," Slichter starts with prices[9]:

> Any explanation of how prices are determined must consist *very largely* of an explanation of how they are interrelated. For every price, it must be remembered, is related to every other price. The relationship between prices may be compared to the relationship between bodies in a gravitational field. Just as a change in the position of any body in the field affects every other body, so a change in the price of any good starts a multitude of changes running throughout the whole system of prices. For this, there are two principal reasons. In the first place, the amounts which buyers are willing to spend upon different goods depend upon the relative prices of the goods. A change in the price of any one commodity, therefore, alters the amounts which buyers are willing to spend for a myriad of other goods. In the second place, the distribution of income among different persons in the community depends upon prices. Any change in price is almost certain to increase or to decrease the incomes of the sellers of the good and likewise to decrease or increase the incomes of the sellers of other goods. But no two persons have precisely the same desires. Consequently, every shift in the distribution of income produces changes in the demand for goods. *Thus each change in the price of a good causes other prices to change and these in turn cause still other prices to change.*

Here we have the same conception of a system of highly flexible prices shifting to adjust supply to demand. Using the market for berries as an example, he explains that "(1) when a seller finds that he can obtain more for his supply than he is asking, he tends to raise his price; (2) when he finds that he has a greater supply than he can sell at the prevailing price, he is likely to ask less rather than not sell all of his product. Consequently, when more product is *demanded than is offered*, price tends to rise; when more is offered than is demanded, price tends to fall."[10] His link with Adam Smith's "natural price" is still further emphasized when he says:

> It is desirable to observe that in one important respect any other price would be less advantageous than the one established by competitive buying and selling. At any other price, a smaller volume of goods would be sold. If the price were higher, the sales would be less because a smaller quantity would be taken; if it were lower, the sales would be less because a smaller quantity would be offered. At any other price, therefore, fewer persons would be able to satisfy their desire to buy and fewer persons would be able to satisfy their desire to sell. In this respect and to this extent, the prices established by competition are ideal prices.[11]

When we turn to the economy of the eighteenth century out of which this economic harmony was first developed we find that the great bulk of production and distribution was carried on either by independent individuals and extremely small independent enterprises or by individuals and small enterprises operating under the restrictions of guild and binding custom. The harmony itself was supposed to apply only to that part of the economy which operated in unrestricted fashion and it is therefore this part alone which need hold our attention. In such an economy, transactions between economic units, whether individuals or small enterprises, are conducted by individuals who have a direct interest at stake in the price arrived at. Prices grow out of the higgling and bargaining of the market place in such an economy much as they do today in an oriental bazaar[12] and the assumption of the flexibility of price appears to be a justified one.

If one were to designate such an economy by a single word, unquestionably the most satisfactory term would be a *trading economy*. Not only is such an economy primarily a process of buying and selling, but the buying and selling is essentially a matter of trading in the sense of getting the best price. Price does not *precede* a trade, but is determined *in* a trade and therefore flexibility of price can be assumed to exist. An equating of supply and demand at the market price can be posited without too great a distortion of the facts and the whole economic process can be summed up as an intricate system of trades.

It must be recognized, however, that even in such an individualistic economy, trading is not the sole economic activity. The proper combining of the factors of production is a part of the economic process just as much as the buying and selling at the best price. The business of the proper combining of the various factors of production within any enterprise can be variously described as business management or as engineering, though the latter term seems the more suitable. This dual character of business is clearly expressed by Marshall when he says of business men, "They 'adventure' or 'undertake' business risks; they bring together the capital and the labour required for the work; they arrange or 'engineer' its general plan, and superintend its minor details. Looking at business men from one point of view [the engineering aspect] we may regard them as a highly skilled industrial grade, from another [the trading aspect] as middlemen intervening between the manual worker and the consumer.''[13] He indicates that in some types of enterprise, the trading aspect dominates as in the case of "the dealer on the stock exchange or the produce markets, whose daily purchases and sales are of vast dimensions, and who yet has neither factory or warehouse, but at most an office with a few clerks in it.'' In other enterprises "administration counts for most.''[14]

It is apparent, however, that the earlier economists minimized the element of administration in their analysis. This is clearly brought out in Adam Smith's repudiation of the joint stock company—the prototype of the Modern Corporation—as an effective method for organizing economic activity. He pointed out that the directors of such companies,

> being the managers rather of other people's money than their own, it cannot well be expected that they should watch over it with the same anxious vigilance with which the partners in a private copartnery frequently watch over their own. Like the stewards of a rich man, they are apt to consider attention to small matters as not for their master's honour, and very easily give themselves a dispensation from having it. Negligence and profusion, therefore, must always prevail, more or less, in the management of the affairs of such a company. It is upon this account that joint stock companies for foreign trade [at the time he was writing the only important manifestation of the corporation outside of banks, insurance companies, and water or canal companies] have seldom been able to maintain the competition against private adventurers. They have, accordingly, very seldom succeeded with one. Without an exclusive privilege they have commonly mismanaged the trade. With an exclusive privilege they have both mismanaged and confined it.[15]

When we attempt to analyze the changes which the Modern Corporation has brought about in the character of the economic system, perhaps the most important single change is the shift in emphasis between these two aspects of economic activity. In the modern huge corporation, business enterprise has come to be primarily a problem of administration, of engineering, while the aspect of trading has been reduced to a minimum. This shift has carried so far that in contradistinction to the Trading Economy of Adam Smith's day in which production was organized through trading in the market place, we have an Engineering Economy in which within large areas, production is organized on an administrative or engineering basis and *in which the markets on the periphery of these areas take on an engineering character as price becomes a matter of administration rather than a matter of trading.*

If the development of large scale enterprise *had not affected the character of the market*, one might continue the description of the central economic process in the terms of Adam Smith, treating each great enterprise as if it were simply one of the buyers or sellers in the market place, while adding a section to the analysis to cover the economics of production within the single enterprise. This is precisely what economists have done, Marshall with great refinement, Slichter with the most recent additions. True, greater emphasis has been placed on monopoly problems than in earlier works. Yet, this has involved not a change in the assumed fundamental character of the market, but only a change in the point at which price is arrived at.

How then does a market in an engineering economy differ from a market in a trading economy—or at least from the type of market assumed by traditional economists to have existed in such an economy? *In an engineering economy prices are fixed by administrative action for periods of time.* Price is determined before a transaction occurs. In a trading economy prices are developed in the process of trading and price is not determined until the transaction occurs. *In an engineering economy supply and demand never equate except by coincidence.* In a trading economy supply and demand necessarily equate.[16]

In examining a market in which the price is administratively determined, it will be convenient to take the typical department store market since we can here see this phenomenon in a simple form. Here all prices are determined by administrative action. In fact, it is almost inconceivable that each transaction in a department store should be a matter of higgling and bargaining between the shop girl and the customer. Before the store is opened in the morning virtually all the articles for sale have been priced. To plot supply curves for that somewhat restricted market, one must construct a most unusual set of curves. If one takes a single article, let us say a standard type of women's black suede shoes, size 5C priced at $5.00, the supply of this article in this particular market is zero at $4.99, or any price below that, while if in the salesroom there were just twelve pairs of this size and style of shoe, the supply would be twelve units and no price greater than $5.00 would be asked. Anyone could walk in and get one pair or all twelve pairs at $5.00 each, but none at less than this price. At the moment of opening the store, and as of that moment, the supply curve indicates twelve pairs at $5.00. But if no customers have yet come into the store, the demand curve at that moment and as of that moment would be zero at any price. Here of course supply and demand would not equate. By extending the time represented by the supply and demand curves to say one hour each, then the supply curve would still indicate no supply at $4.99 or less, but the supply at $5.00 would perhaps be augmented by a half dozen pairs which lie in crates in the basement and which could be opened in a few minutes if the demand for such shoes at $5.00 was depleting the supply in the show room. On the other hand, demand for shoes at $5.00 might still remain zero if no customer turned up, so that by extending the curves to cover one hour we have supply at $5.00, 18 pairs; demand at $5.00, zero. Still no equating.

Let us suppose that the first customer is going to turn up at noon, three hours after opening the store. Then by extending the curves to cover three hours we would have curves at the moment of opening, but covering a period of three hours, showing supply at $5.00—18 pairs; demand at $5.00—1 pair. No equating of supply and demand.

Suppose further that two sales will be made in the afternoon and three sales will be made each business day thereafter. Then, if we make the supply and demand curves cover a full day, the supply at $5.00 will be 18 pair and the demand 3 pair.

When we extend the time period of the curves to cover a full week, it would at first appear that an equating of supply and demand would be reached. At the rate of three purchases a day the demand at $5.00 will be 18 pair (for a six day week). But the supply at $5.00 may be even greater, since the head of the shoe department can place an order (perhaps already has placed an order) for immediate delivery from say the manufacturer nearest the warehouse. Since this delivery can be assumed to take less than a week, the supply at $5.00 available to customers of the store during the week is very much more than the supply on the premises. Perhaps it is this supply plus the total supply on hand at the local warehouse of say 500 pairs. Therefore, the curves at the time of opening of the store in the morning and covering a week's period would show, supply—518[17]; demand 18. Again, there is no equating of supply and demand.

If we extend the period covered still further—a month, a year—we will get much the same result. With a period of a month, the supply will have to include perhaps the finished and part of the unfinished shoes in the hands of the manufacturer, since, if demand increases to such an extent that at $5.00 both the stock in the store and in the local warehouse is depleted, the stock in the factory could be rushed to fill the gap. Furthermore, we must add to the total supply, the number of shoes that the manufacturer would make and ship to the store or local warehouse during the month if no change in demand over that expected by the manufacturer in making up his production schedule were to take place.

So far we have chosen situations in which supply was ahead of demand at the existing price though without any result in lowering price. But, suppose demand were ahead of supply, what would occur? Let us say that during the first day customers came in demanding shoes at the rate of six pair an hour. At the moment of opening and as of the moment of opening only, supply would be ahead of demand since there would be 12 pair of shoes and no customers. Likewise, the curves covering one hour and presumably that covering two hours would show supply ahead of demand—supply 18 pair—demand 6 pair, and 12 pair respectively. (Presumably as the supply on the floor was depleted, say when it reached 3 pair at the end of one and a half hours, it would be replenished by the 6 pair in the basement.) The curves covering three hours would show an equating of supply and demand, each being 18 pair. But the curves covering four hours would show a greater demand than supply. Any purchaser coming after the third hour would be politely told that the current supply was exhausted. He could be supplied tomorrow (when shoes had been delivered by the local warehouse), but not today. Clearly, in such a situation demand exceeded supply and it must have been clear to the salesmen in the shoe department that this was so at least by the end of the second hour. Yet, the price would seldom be raised on the last six pairs. Thus, we have *price constant*, and supply usually either greater or less than demand.

It should be noted that no extension of the time period covered by the supply and demand curves will result in any but an accidental equating of supply and demand. We are dealing with a phenomenon which conforms neither with the economist's short run nor with his long run supply and demand curves. Whereas there may be a tendency for the proportionate discrepancy between supply and demand to decrease in the long run, there is *no* tendency for the absolute amount of the discrepancy to decrease. One must, therefore, say that the supply and demand curves which so neatly cross in the economist's traditional description of the market cannot be employed to describe this market.

We can generalize this market by saying that the price is fixed over a period of time and that the possessors of the supply act as a reservoir or a series of reservoirs out of which goods flow to the consumers and into which goods flow from the producers. The flow of goods into any one of these reservoirs may not bear [sic: be?] closely articulated with the flow of goods out of the reservoir, with the result that at particular prices the reservoirs may to a certain extent be filled up or depleted without any effect on price. In such a situation, the effect of fluctuations in demand is to speed up or slow down flow through these reservoirs, working finally back to the factors of production themselves, where, because the rates of wages and interest are also administratively determined, the immediate effect is to throw out of use the factors of production rather than to reduce their price. . . .

So far we have not considered what, under these circumstances, will bring about a price change. In a closely articulated industry,[18] pressure upon price results from changing or abnormal rates of production. In a loosely integrated industry, pressure on price results both from the above and from variations in the volume on hand in various intermediate reservoirs. Any increase over the normal seasonal amount in the reservoirs will place pressure on the price in the direction of a downward revision. Whether any such revision takes place will depend on the sensitiveness of the administered price to such pressure. The corresponding [price change] would be true in the case of the upward pressure exerted by depletion beyond the normal amount or by an acceleration of the whole productive process. Even after these price changes have been made, there is no more justification for the assumption that supply and demand has been equated than was the original case. What we are justified in saying is that prices have been revised more in accordance with demand.

It should be noted that these price changes are of a discontinuous character so that the actual price of any particular commodity, if plotted through time, would give not a smooth, undulating curve but rather straight lines with perpendicular breaks.

If a wide variety of markets are examined, it will be discovered that some administratively determined prices are highly sensitive to fluctuations in production and in the reservoirs, while others are the reverse. Thus, the price of automobiles appears to be relatively insensitive, while that of standard cotton yarn is relatively sensitive, the latter remaining constant for days at a time, but sometimes having as many as fifty discontinuous price changes throughout the year. At one extreme we have such prices as the five cents for the *Saturday Evening Post* or the New York City subway fare, and at the other extreme we have the markets for perishables and the speculative markets in which the discontinuous price changes occur so frequently as to make those markets take on the character of the traditional trading market.

If prices were perfectly rigid, the effect of a change in consumer demand would result entirely in changes in the extent to which the factors of production were employed or in the volume of products in the intermediate reservoirs. This is in direct contrast to the result which would develop if prices were perfectly flexible, as they have been assumed to be in a trading economy. In the latter case, a change in the consumer demand would result in a change in the organization of the factors of production but no factors would be thrown out of use, except to the extent that the difficulty of shifting factors from one use to another might cause delay in their adjustment. To the extent, then, that administratively determined prices are resistant to pressure for price change, change in demand involves change in the extent to which the factors of production are used. When this involves the throwing of the factors of production out of employment, demand for the final product is itself presumably further affected by the curtailed spending power of the possessors of these factors.

That this analysis has some validity is suggested by the quite different effects which the present depression has had in the farming area and in the industrial area. In the farming area, prices have dropped tremendously, but there is little to indicate that farmers who own their farms are *unemployed*. If anything, they are likely to be working harder than ever since the product of their labor brings them such small returns. Industrial prices, by contrast, while many of them have fallen, have not declined to anything like the same extent as farm prices. Instead, industrial labor and industrial capital have, to an appalling extent, become idle. This is precisely the result which one would predict on the basis of the above analysis if the agricultural part of our economy were still primarily a trading economy, while the industrial elements had become an engineering economy.

This analysis would suggest that a market in which price is administratively determined, fixed over periods of time, and subject to discontinuous price changes must be a fundamental postulate with respect to a major part of our economy if the economist would understand the operations of that economy.

Chapter VII. The Modern Corporation and the Indeterminacy of Cost

All enterprise, because it is organized activity, necessarily involves joint cost. The very costs of organization are as much a cost of any one product as of any other. In fact, every product of an enterprise is to some extent a product of costs which have yielded other products.

Though the presence of joint cost has been recognized by economists, the analysis of enterprise activity has customarily been on the assumption that cost was determinate except in the cases in which joint cost was so dominant a factor that it could not be ignored. Under conditions of small scale enterprise, it has been possible to overlook or to minimize this factor. As the size of the industrial unit has increased and the process has become to a greater extent vertically integrated, joint cost has not only come to have major importance but it has reached such a point that it would seem necessary for the economist to shift his assumption. What formerly was the special case appears now to have become the general case, while what formerly was regarded as the general case does not exist.

The economist, in his treatment of joint cost as a special case, has been aided and abetted by the accountant who has followed in his footsteps. By the accountant, costs are assumed to be determinate and problems of joint cost are thrown into the catch-all of overhead cost, treated cavalierly with an arbitrary allocation, misunderstood and analyzed obscurely under the heading of depreciation or ignored entirely.

The all-pervasive character of joint cost even in areas thought to be determinate must be apparent when a close analysis is made. Take, for instance, the case of a shoe store in which a pair of shoes which was purchased for five dollars has been sold for ten dollars. What are the costs of the "thing" sold?—i.e., what costs have gone into bringing to the enterprise the ten dollars which is received in the final transaction? If we follow up only a single line of cost, it must be apparent that the single pair could not have been sold for ten dollars if there had not been a wide variety from which the prospective customer could select. It is common experience that some day, when the enterprise is closed out, some of the pairs of shoes which have been assisting past sales will have to be sold at a serious loss. This loss, or cost of operation, is just as much attributable to prior sales, including the pair of shoes mentioned above, as is the cash paid out in the acquisition of this specific pair. It is, therefore, theoretically impossible to discover the "cost" of this pair until the enterprise has rounded out its existence. The accountant may be justified in disregarding this fact. The economist does so at his peril.

Again, consider the production of cotton cloth on a single loom. In a single day, let us say that the loom produces fifty yards of cotton cloth at what we will accept as a total known cost of five dollars. It is customary for the business man and the accountant to impute a pro-rata share of the total cost to each unit of the production, i.e., to say that each yard "cost" ten cents. If the economist considers the case with precision, he must say not that the cost of each unit was ten cents but that, if all the units are of uniform character from the point of view of prospective selling price, the units have the same *value*. The cost of each unit alone is necessarily indeterminate. The fact that this "cost" is an imputed figure is clearly brought out when we consider the possibility that part of the yardage had been damaged so as to have a value of zero. In such a case, the accountant and business man would not hesitate to impute the total cost simply to the part of the production which consisted of marketable product. Thus, if ten of the fifty yards were valueless, their cost would be regarded as zero and the cost of each of the marketable yards would be placed at twelve and one-half cents.

In the same situation, an element of indeterminacy enters from a second source. We assumed that the cost for the total production of the period was given. Actually, since the loom is employed over a long period and finally wears out, each yard of cloth produced from it is a joint product with every other yard produced, since all of them have derived in part from the single cost of the loom. In treating the machine cost as a problem of depreciation and throwing it into the area of overhead cost, this fact of joint cost is minimized by the accountant.

Thus, even in such simple situations as are common in small scale enterprise, cost is necessarily indeterminate and its apparent determinacy has been in large measure an imputation of value.

When we turn to the corporation, the problem of joint cost becomes greatly magnified. In addition to the complexities of mass production involved in large scale enterprise, the giant corporation has intensified the fact that production is the result of a functioning, interrelated organization. In the large corporation, direct, easily attributable costs are at a minimum. It is this which has made it so difficult for accountants to apply to the accounts of large corporations the technique of accounting which was developed to meet the conditions of smaller enterprises in which most of the problems arising out of joint cost could be dodged by throwing those which could not be imputed with ease into the catch-all of overhead. The arbitrariness of the allocation of the costs lumped into overhead increases as these assume a larger proportion in relation to total costs. The long-winded arguments over the problem of depreciation suggest that clarity in corporate accounting will not be developed until the whole process represented by corporate enterprise is treated as a continuous process of joint costs with the cost of any product, or even of large categories of products, thoroughly indeterminate. Nor can the economist hope to aid this clarification unless he in turn accepts joint cost as a fundamental postulate.

In attempting to bring some sort of order out of the chaos into which this aggravated problem of joint cost throws accounting, it seems apparent that recourse will have to be taken in part to an accounting analysis in terms of utility. That this recourse is already being extensively employed has been clearly indicated by the most penetrating analysis of accounting which has yet been made.[19] It has been admitted in some of the areas in which cost itself has come to be recognized as thoroughly indeterminate, as, for instance, in the cost of production of copper where no basis is given for the amount to be attributed to depletion, or in the meat packing industry where a single unit of raw material—e.g., a cow—involving a single cost is broken up into so many products. Canning even goes so far as to suggest that all accounting should be conducted on a basis of something which approaches what we might call utility accounting.[20] It must be apparent, however, that any form of pure utility accounting (or value accounting on a basis of utility) will suffer much the same fate as cost accounting when it reaches the reciprocal problem of joint utility.[21]

As careful analysis indicated that all production is conducted under a condition of joint cost, so it must be apparent that all production is also accomplished under conditions of joint utility. Even in the simple shoe store described above, the final utility—the ten dollars derived from the sale—was a product of many costs.

The large corporation, characterized by an important measure of vertical integration, has made joint utility as dominant as joint cost. In some industries, such as meat packing, the feature of joint cost is most conspicuous. In others, such as the automobile industry, it is joint utility which stands out. Accounting and economic analyses based on the assumed determinacy of either cost or utility are thus doomed to confusion. It would seem, therefore, that the analysis of an economy dominated by the corporation must proceed on the basic assumption that all production is under conditions of joint cost and of joint utility.

Chapter VIII. The Modern Corporation and the Process of Saving

One aspect of the effect of the corporation upon the process of saving has already become well recognized, namely, the increasing extent to which saving in the community is done out of corporate income rather than out of the income of individuals. This differs from saving as the economist has been familiar with it in that the individual having an interest in corporate income is not in a position to determine whether or not he will save out of that income. Such decision is made by corporate control. While this necessitates an elaboration of economic theory, it does not involve any far reaching change in the operation of the economic system, since the postulate of received theory—that the decision to save and the decision to acquire new capital equipment lie in the same hands—still holds good. In so far as saving out of corporate income is concerned, corporate control has simply supplanted the private entrepreneur.

With respect to the savings of individuals, this postulate no longer holds. The separation of ownership and control has separated the customary process of saving into two independent stages under the control of separate groups of individuals. On the one hand, the decision to save lies in the hands of individuals in the community who "save" through buying corporate securities. On the other hand, the decision to add to the capital goods of corporations, and, correspondingly, to issue new securities with which to supply the funds for this expansion, lies in the hands of control. This means that we have two independent processes going on which by no means necessarily mesh—the process of saving by individuals and the process of acquiring new capital goods through the issue of securities by corporations. It likewise means that we have two separate and only indirectly related markets, that for securities and that for capital goods, which may operate in quite dissimilar fashions.

This separation of the process of saving into separate and quasi-independent processes is of particular importance to monetary theory. It is the failure to recognize the independence of these two processes, perhaps more than any other factor which tends to weaken Keynes' most able analysis of monetary phenomena. As Robertson has pointed out,[22] Keynes definitely confuses "real capital" (factories, machinery, etc.) with "investment" (securities, etc., exclusive of those involving "loan capital") and regards the value of "real capital" even in the hands of corporations as identical with the value of the interests in that real capital represented by securities.[23] Actually these values not only may be quite different, but may move in opposite directions.

In order to indicate clearly this possibility, let us consider a highly abstract situation. Let us assume that in a closed system all production is carried on by corporations of the modern type, and that all capital goods are owned by corporations whose securities are in turn held by individuals lacking full control over the corporations. Let us further assume for simplicity that all corporate earnings are paid out in dividends, thereby abstracting from corporate saving. In such a system, individuals would, on the one hand, supply labor (in the widest sense) and the use of savings to the corporations, and, on the other hand, buy goods and services for consumption from the corporations. One market, that for capital goods, would exist between corporations, some producing the capital goods, others making use of them in production. A second market, that for securities, would exist between the corporations and individuals and among individuals themselves.[24] Finally, let us assume that, before we introduce a disturbing factor, a condition of approximate equilibrium has been reached such that: the corporations are producing both consumption goods and capital goods, selling the former to individuals and the latter to other corporations; individuals are receiving income both from their labor and from their investments, part of which they are spending on consumption goods, and the remainder of which they are saving and investing in securities newly issued by the corporations; and, finally that the funds acquired by the corporations as a result of the issue of new securities are being invested in newly created capital equipment bought from other corporations or created by each corporation itself. Necessarily, such a balance would exist only if the individuals are saving and the corporations are issuing new securities at a parallel rate. With such an economic process in smooth operation, let us assume that, perhaps because of fear engendered by a European pestilence or by suddenly rising tariff barriers, the corporations decide to cease capital expansion and completely stop the issuance of new securities and the purchase or creation of new capital goods, while no other changes in the intention of individuals takes place except as a direct outgrowth of this change on the part of the corporations.

What would be the effect of this change on the market for capital goods and on the market for securities? Presumably, with no new capital construction being undertaken, the producers of capital equipment would be under pressure to drop their prices and such price changes as resulted would be downward. At the same time, if the individuals in the community *tried* to continue to save at the old rate, the new funds coming into the security market without any corresponding inflow of new securities would tend to lift the price of securities, and since their prices are highly flexible, security prices would rise. Furthermore, *as long as new net savings*[25] *sought investment with no addition to the securities outstanding in the community, security prices would continue to soar to infinity.* Presumably, at some point below infinity, the desire to save would be decreased, the corporations would be induced to issue new securities, or both actions would occur and the security price rise would be stopped. The decrease in savings would presumably result partly from the reduced return on a given value of an investment, partly from the increase in the *apparent* income of individuals as a result of the rising prices of securities, partly as a result of the greatly augmented money value of the wealth of individuals, and partly from the reduced income of the individuals connected with the production of capital goods. The issuance of new securities would result partly from the ease of selling new securities and the lowered return which they need to promise and partly from the lowered prices of capital goods, which would induce the corporations to expand their capital equipment. It is not necessary here to go into the less direct results of the initial change as they multiply through the system. What it is important to notice here is that the unbalance brought about by the stoppage of the flow of new securities is ultimately brought into adjustment (if at all) by the movement of prices in the capital goods and the securities markets in opposite directions.

It is not here suggested that in such a simplified economy the prices of capital goods and of securities *necessarily* move in opposite directions, but only that they *may* do so, a development not contemplated in Keynes' analysis. Of course, in the case given above, the event which induced the corporation to stop the expansion of capital equipment and the issuance of securities might have been such as, at the same time and in the same degree, to stop the new net saving by the community. In this case, there would be pressure downward on the capital goods market, while securities remained constant (except those of capital goods producing corporations whose prospect of income is reduced). Or, again, the combination of men thrown out of work in capital goods production, combined with the effect of the originating event, might cause the community to *attempt* to consume part of its past savings, such an attempt which would have [yielded] results not at all consistent with received theory, and deserving of further consideration.

Because of the separation of ownership and control posited in this simplified case, the attempt of the community as a whole to consume part of its past savings, i.e., for individuals who save to save less than is spent out of savings by those who trench on their accumulated wealth, will be directly frustrated; while the wealth of individuals, i.e., the value of their securities, will be destroyed, unless the attempt to trench on savings is given up, or the corporations are made by control to retire part of their outstanding securities. This result can be more clearly followed if we assume as the initial equilibrium condition one identical with the previous one except, first, that corporations, on balance, are neither issuing new securities and adding to capital equipment, nor retiring outstanding securities with a corresponding reduction in capital goods; and second, that individuals on balance are neither saving nor trenching on past saving. In such a situation, the producers of capital goods would be supplying only replacement equipment, etc. If we then introduce into this smooth running economy, a disturbing element such as a burst of extravagant living, or a scientific prognostication (believed because scientific) that the world was about to come to an end, or the increasing pressure of a high degree of unemployment which induced the community as a whole to attempt to trench on its past savings, the direct result will be a fall in the value of securities—Peter trying to sell Paul—without *any* increase in the amount of goods which individuals could consume.[26] At the same time the value of capital goods would remain constant. If the effort to consume past savings were continued, and if the corporations did not, on balance, retire part of their outstanding securities, the value of securities would decline to zero. Here, as in the earlier case, such a wide change in value might be stopped by a decrease in extravagance as securities fell in value, by a retirement of corporate securities, or by a combination of the two.[27] Whatever the final result, what is important here is that the attempt to consume past savings would result primarily in the destruction of the money value of the wealth of individuals, that is, in the destruction of the money *value* of their *interest* in the product of their past savings. It would not result in allowing them to consume the product of past saving. That this should be so is not surprising since the individuals having an interest in the product of past saving have no control over their product and so cannot of their own volition consume it. Only by the intermediary action of corporate control, would this be possible. If no such action by control occurs, the value of securities will melt away while the goods in which the securities represent an interest, though badly wanted by the community, will remain on the shelves of the corporation.[28]

From this discussion it must be apparent that any analysis of an economic process which is largely dominated by corporations in which ownership and control are separated, must assume that, to the extent of this domination, the process of saving is a dual process; that two separate and independent markets exist, one for capital goods and a second for securities; and that the failure of these two to be brought into consonance may cause serious disequilibrium in that economy.

Chapter IX. The Modern Corporation and the Profit Motive

In the era of private enterprise which this thesis indicates we are leaving, society has relied in the main on two forces to give order and effectiveness to economic activity—profit seeking and competition. Both by custom and by law the individual has been encouraged to undertake enterprise for private gain. At the same time, the forces of custom and law have been exercised to maintain competition between separate business enterprises.

The economic justification for the reliance on these two forces has been found in the stimulating effect of profits and in the regulating effect of competition. Profits are regarded as a prize offered to induce the individual to assume the risks and responsibilities of enterprise and to spur him to conduct enterprise with his utmost ability. In his search for profits it has been supposed that the business man would seek to produce those things for which the community had the most pressing demand and that in supplying this demand he would strive to combine the various factors of production in the most economic fashion, at least within the limits of his own enterprise. At the same time, the competition of different enterprises, both for the use of the factors of production and in the sale of their product, has been supposed to insure the economical distribution of the factors among enterprises and in particular to maintain the profits of enterprises as a group within reasonable bounds. Thus, in an atomistic society in which each individual and especially each business man sought solely his own private gain, the twin forces of profit seeking and competition were supposed to make for the most effective ordering of economic life.

We need not here consider how successfully these forces have, in the past, accomplished the great role which has been assigned to them. It is our business rather to examine the role of profits in the light of the Modern Corporation.

As the various functions which must be performed in the conduct of enterprise have become more clearly differentiated, economists have further analyzed the profits received by the business man. They have distinguished between that part which may be thought of as interest on capital invested, that part which may be thought of as the wages of management, and the remainder or "pure profits."

With such a division it is clear that the interest component is a return on capital—presumably the rate of return which the owner could have obtained if he had invested his capital in a riskless bond. Likewise the wages component is a return for the labor of management—presumably the wage or salary which the entrepreneur's degree of skill would command if he were to be employed as a manager. The remainder, "pure profits," is not so easily tagged.

While most writers agree that "pure profits," if made, are received by the entrepreneur and that they alone out of profits constitute the prize which induces him to undertake the risks and responsibilities of enterprise, two divergent views have developed with regard to their source. One group of writers regards them as primarily a return for risk taking, while the other treats them as essentially the return for acting as the initiating force in enterprise, for taking on the authority and responsibility of the man who gives orders in contrast to a hired manager or employee who received them. S.H. Nulove, in discussing recent writings on profits, reports that "Practically all of the economic students who have attempted to explain profit as a distinct distributive share have related it in one way or another to risk.'' Yet ''some of the early economists . . . subordinated the risk element and emphasized the 'managerial-services' of the entrepreneur as the significant origin of profits.''[29] These two differing emphases are to be found even more clearly marked in contemporary writing, particularly in that of F.H. Knight and that of Maurice Dobb.[30] The first of these writers indicates that the ''pure profits'' which the entrepreneur receives are ''associated with the performance of his peculiar twofold function of (a) exercising responsible control and (b) securing the owners of productive services against uncertainty and fluctuation in their incomes.''[31] But while he thus recognizes both control and risk-bearing, he finds the source of profits primarily in the latter, the necessity that owners should assume the inevitable risks of enterprise. He states categorically that ''profit arises out of the inherent, absolute unpredictability of things.''[32] It is the owner of a business who takes the risks due to this uncertainty, and ''in the typical modern business organization the responsible owner furnishes no labor services to the business, but property services only''[33] and receives the profits. He concludes that without risks to be borne there would be no profits, that the entrepreneur receives his profits primarily as a result of taking this risk, and that in the modern corporation it is the stockholders ''who take the risk and receive profits.''[34]

In contrast to this view, Dobb holds that ''though the Entrepreneur Function is connected with the bearing of uncertainty, it is connected incidentally rather than essentially.''[35] He finds that ''the growth of this economic differentiation creates the need for some integrating force, without which differentiation would collapse into chaos,''[36] and that in our present society this integrating force is the entrepreneur whose activity gives rise to profits. He points out that a business does not run itself, ''it needs the leadership and strategy of a general.''[37] This leadership is supplied by the group in control, those two or three ''having a guiding hand on the firm's destinies.''[38] It is they who perform the entrepreneur function and ''the problem of profits will arise as a distinct form of payment owing to the special power which one class of capitalists—those who combine capital with the work of undertaking—has of securing capital increment.''[39]

The conflict between these two views is based primarily on a difference in emphasis. Those who hold that ''pure profits'' are primarily a return for risk recognize the position of the entrepreneur in control of his enterprise but tend to minimize its importance, while the opposing camp, as we have seen, recognize but tend to minimize the importance of risk-taking. In view of this agreement as to the two elements involved, but disagreement in emphasis, the suggestion seems warranted that ''pure profits'' are a return for the performance of two distinct *and separable* functions, risk-taking and the exercise of control.

If we had to deal only with private enterprise, this suggestion would have little more than academic interest. In such enterprise the entrepreneur combines both functions in a single individual and receives the ''pure profits'' which his risk-taking and initiating vigor may make possible. A distinction between that part of his profits which may be thought of as a return for risk-taking and that part which may be thought of as a return for exercising control would have little importance.[40]

But in the Modern Corporation we have seen that these two functions have become separated. On one side we have the body of owners exercising only a few minor and residual elements of control while on the other side the group in control have only a very minor proportion of the total ownership. The stockholders supply the capital and take the ultimate risks. Control exercises ultimate authority over the enterprise and takes the responsibility of operation. The two functions of risk-taking and control which we suggested were performed by the entrepreneur of private enterprise are thus performed by two separate groups in corporate enterprise.[41] What then becomes of "pure profits"?

Both in popular thought and legal tradition the corporation "belongs" to the stockholders and likewise to them "belong" any profits remaining after its contractual obligations have been met.[42] According to this view, the very reason for the existence of the corporation is to make profits for its stockholders.

In practice, however, it is well recognized that part of the profits of corporate enterprise are frequently obtained by those in control at the expense of the stockholders. Frequently this diversion of profits is accomplished by illegal means though in ways to avoid the scrutiny of the stockholders. Perhaps more often it is accomplished by means which are regarded as legal by those employing them. Some methods have long been recognized, such as the creating of "service companies" to supply the controlled enterprise at "highly profitable" rates or trading in the securities of the controlled company on the basis of advance and often manipulated information. Other methods are of more recent origin. The new corporation laws of Delaware and Maryland have greatly enlarged the opportunities for "plundering" a corporation or its stockholders in a legal fashion. Some writers regard the new clauses introduced into corporate charters on the basis of these laws as "thieves licenses."[43] It is therefore apparent that some of the "pure profits" can be diverted into the pockets of control quite apart from the small proportion of profits which they may receive as stockholders.

Without going into detail as to the methods or extent of such diversion of profits, we can raise the question of whether there are any limits to the extent to which profits can be thus diverted. The activities of the early railroad wreckers and the most recent case of Kreuger and Toll suggest that there is no limit. In the case of the modern corporation this conclusion does not necessarily apply. If we assume, as appears to be generally the case, that the control wishes to maintain its position, this at once limits the extent of the possible diversion. Except in cases in which control is maintained by a legal device, the stockholders must be kept in a reasonably contented frame of mind or the existing control is in danger of losing its advantageous position. If a fair amount of profits is not earned and earmarked for the benefit of the stockholders, their discontent may encourage some other group to organize a proxy fight and seek control. In case the dissatisfaction of the stockholders is sufficiently deep seated—stockholders are reputed to be a particularly phlegmatic body—the existing control will lose its position to the new group. Thus a return sufficient to prevent serious discontent among the stockholders would be the first limitation on the profits which the controlling group could divert if it wished to maintain a secure position.

A second limit arises from the usual desire of control to enlarge its economic power through the expansion of the enterprise which it dominates. Expansion presumably involves the raising of new capital. But additional funds are unlikely to be supplied regularly unless the preexisting supplies of capital have been reasonably well treated—have obtained an acceptable return on their investment.

Both of these limits are of a somewhat indefinite character but at the same time they are probably sufficiently definite to be recognized by control in specific cases. A body of stockholders is unlikely to be dangerous except when it is vociferous, thereby bringing the discontent to the attention of control. Likewise, difficulty in marketing new issues of securities is a fact of which control must be all too clearly aware.[44] Thus, where the group in control seeks to maintain its position and to obtain new capital for expansion, it will have to ensure to the corporation profits in an amount sufficient to satisfy both existing and prospective stockholders. This limiting amount would appear to be something in the nature of a supply price for risk-bearing capital. It would involve a return which would not only be equivalent to interest on riskless capital, but which would also, in the eyes of the investor, compensate for the risks involved. Thus, part of "pure profit" would have to go to the stockholder as a return for risk-bearing.

In so far as this analysis correctly mirrors the current situation, it follows that a diversion of profits would, in general, take place in appreciable amount only if the profits of an enterprise were more than sufficient to yield a satisfactory return on the risk-bearing capital.[45] The real problem of what becomes of "pure profits" when risk-taking and control are separated must center around any surplus in profits remaining after a return has been made on the risk-bearing capital.[46] It is this surplus, this remainder out of "pure profits" which control has the power to divert to its own pocket, to distribute to the stockholders, to divide between the two groups, or to dispose of otherwise. For convenience we shall refer to it as the ex-risk profit. It makes its appearance in the short run at least, as a residual profit after the costs of all capital and hired management have been met. Who should receive the ex-risk profits?

Though "pure profits" have never, so far as the writer is aware, been subdivided in the foregoing manner, two conflicting sets of opinion can be found among economists with regard to the diversion of profits into the pockets of control, presumably a taking of part or all of the ex-risk profits. Nulove, after summarizing some of the ways in which the diversion can be accomplished, concludes, "It is apparent, therefore, that the 'insiders' can, within very wide limits under present social and legal institutions, increase their income-streams *without rendering any service to society.*"[47] In contrast to this, Field, after showing how the service companies can be employed in the public utility industry to divert profit into the hands of control, says: "Group service organizations are separately incorporated . . . partly *to provide legal channels for compensating the motivating geniuses* of these systems more nearly in accordance with the contributions which they have made."[48] One writer would presumably have the ex-risk profit go entirely to the stockholders, while the other would have them go, in part at least, to the "motivating geniuses"—control. How to choose between these views?

The problem is in its first incidence one of law. It is within the power of the courts to make illegal every diversion of profits. At present the law is in a state of flux. The courts are faced, not with the simple question of who should receive the ex-risk profits, but with an extremely complex one involving the fundamental nature of the corporation. Is the corporate charter essentially a contract to which the stockholder is a party by his very purchase of stock? Then any specific powers granted to the directors are contractual powers which can be freely exercised within the limits of the charter. If these include the power to profit at the expense of the corporation or its stockholders, let the stockholders beware in buying into such a contract. By taking this point of view, the courts can legalize the diversion of profits.[49]

In opposition to this view is that which holds the charter to be essentially an agreement between a group of individuals associating for a common purpose. In such a case the courts could properly find that these powers granted to the directors are actually "powers in trust"[50] which can be employed legally only in the interests of the whole body of associates. This would place those in control of a corporation in a position of trusteeship both toward the corporation and toward the stockholders. Any diversion of profits into their own pockets, while undoubtedly still possible, would at least be illegal under such an interpretation.

Both of these interpretations of the corporate charter appear to have equally valid legal support. The courts are, therefore, in a position to choose between them, either encouraging the diversion of profits to corporate control, or making such diversion entirely illegal, as there seems to be no compelling legal tradition which would determine their choice. The law can be of little help in answering our question—who should receive the ex-risk profits. The answer must be sought in economic and social considerations.

In seeking to analyze this problem, the economist should first recall to mind the functions which profits are traditionally supposed to perform. We saw that profits have been regarded as a prize which induced individuals to assume the risks and responsibilities of enterprise, acting as an incentive both to the taking of risks and to the vigorous operation of enterprise. Since in corporate enterprise one group, the stockholders, takes the risks of enterprise[51] while another group, the control, exercises power over the enterprise and has its destiny in its hands, the full function of profits can no longer be performed if they are given to a single group. The first function, that of inducing risk-bearing, will be performed when profits have been allowed to the stockholders, as we saw they generally would be, sufficient to induce the supplying of risk-bearing capital—sufficient in the eyes of investors to constitute a satisfactory return for the taking of risk. But at the same time the stockholders have surrendered control and responsibility. Beyond the risk-taking, they contribute nothing to the success of the enterprise. Ex-risk profit distributed to them would seem to perform no useful function. Such an extra return would of course be kindly received by the stockholders, but they have by hypothesis already received sufficient to induce their continued supplying of capital and, since they are not in control, the hope of additional profits cannot result in their operating the enterprise more efficiently. Thus, the distribution of ex-risk profits to them would appear to be economically wasteful.[52]

The second function of profits, that of inducing the vigorous conduct of enterprise, can be performed only to the extent that the controlling group have a hope of receiving profits. According to the traditional logic of profits it should therefore follow that the ex-risk profits should be distributed to this controlling group so that, in the effort to increase their own income, they will operate the enterprise in the most profitable manner. It is control and not the owners who have become the driving power behind modern enterprise. It is they who should be stimulated to the maximum effort. If profit seeking is to be the basic motive force of enterprise, it is they who should receive the residual profits.

This is a radical conclusion, for the assumption that all profits belong to the stockholders is a deep seated one. The logic is, however, inescapable so long as we hold the view that enterprise should be conducted with the aim of making the maximum profit and apply that view to the great quasi-public corporation in which ownership and control have become almost completely separated.

Yet, the proposal to hand the residual profits over to control may well give pause—the power of this group in our larger corporations is already immense. Practically self-perpetuating in their dictatorships, invested with tremendous legal powers, becoming increasingly dominant in their economic might as a larger proportion of industry comes yearly under their sway, the few men in control of the largest corporations threaten to become the uncrowned kings and economic masters of the land. Shall we then give them still more power by giving to them any residual profits which corporate enterprise may yield?

This question forces us back to the basic assumption of profit theory—that profits are an effective incentive and that competition will so limit profits that the social cost in profits taken will be more than outweighed by the social advantages of efficiently conducted enterprise. It gives rise to two interrelated questions which must challenge the attention of the economic and business world:

First—Are profits the most effective incentive for the conduct of modern corporate enterprise?

Second—Is competition an effective regulation of profits where the great modern corporations are concerned?

It is not our purpose here to do more than pose these questions. We cannot enter into a discussion of the weaknesses inherent in profits as an incentive or into the alternative incentives to which the masters of modern industry might, and perhaps do, respond. We can only suggest a few of the points which would have to be considered in such a discussion. In the first place, profits as an inducement are presumably subject to diminishing returns when, as in the great modern corporations, they amount to huge sums, far beyond the uses to which an individual can put them in his private life. At the same time the social cost of handing over so large a fragment of the national income to a few individuals, however great their services, would become increasingly severe. It is evident, moreover, that a monetary inducement to efficient operation may be offered in other ways, such as the bonus system or the tantieme of Germany, without relying on the prize of the whole of ex-risk profits.

Possible alternative motives are even more difficult to appraise than the weaknesses of the existing one. It is a matter of mere conjecture whether the motivations of industrial leaders might become that of the professional man, of the public servant, of the statesman or the empire builder rather than that of the profit seeker. Such considerations, however, are certainly within the realm of possibility. To the question raised in the body of this chapter—"To whom should ex-risk profits be distributed?" we counter with the question, "Should such profits be made at all?"

This question becomes all the more pertinent when we consider the second problem, is competition the effective regulator that traditional profit theory assumed it to be? Again we can only suggest a few of the considerations pertinent to the discussion of this question. First it must be recalled to mind that when competition was assumed to be an effective regulator, industry involved a multitude of small concerns without large amounts of fixed capital and without elaborate organizations. Such firms could be easily brought into being to challenge those who exacted unnecessarily large toll in the form of extortionate profits. With the domination of industry by the great modern corporation, these conditions no longer obtain. As their power grows it becomes increasingly difficult for new concerns to enter into competition[53] with those already in the field if the latter's profits become excessive, while existing large units find it more to their advantage to divide the field and rule supreme than to cut each other's throats in competition. In such circumstances, competition as the faithful watchdog standing guard over the national income to prevent its diversion into the hands of the powerful becomes, perhaps, an economic myth.

The profits dilemma, followed to its logical conclusion, thus resolves itself into a challenge: can the basis of the old economic order of private enterprise in which risk-taking and motivating activity were combined and in which enterprises were many and weak be carried over into the highly integrated, engineering economy in which control is in such a large measure independent of ownership? An analysis of our economy in terms of the postulates suggested in the preceding three chapters may assist us in arriving at an answer to this question.

Notes

1. Alfred Marshall, *Principles of Economics*, 8th edition (London, 1930), p. 355.
2. Adam Smith, *The Wealth of Nations*, Everyman's edition (New York, [1912]), p. 88.
3. Ibid., p. 135.
4. Ibid., p. 136.
5. Marshall, op. cit., p. 355.
6. More prescisely—"at the prices which would prevail after the shift."
7. While this idea of optimum satisfaction is not clearly stated in Smith, it is implied in his use of the term "natural price." In the philosophy of his time a law of nature as applied to human conduct was understood to indicate not something which must be, but rather as setting forth an ideal course which man would follow if he were to benefit himself to the utmost. In the same sense the "natural price" is a price which would bring ideal or optimum results.
8. Smith, op. cit., pp. 50–51.
9. Sumner H. Slichter, *Modern Economic Society* (New York, 1931), p. 268. Italics by the present writer.
10. Ibid., p. 271.
11. Ibid., p. 272.
12. The bazaars of Kharput, Alleppo, and Damascus in which the present writer has had extensive business experience, are typical.
13. Marshall, op. cit., p. 293.
14. Ibid., p. 293. The reader familiar with Marshall will note that in the passages cited, Marshall is contrasting speculation and administration. It is clear, however, that as he uses the word, speculation is primarily trading.
15. Adam Smith, *The Wealth of Nations*, Everyman's Library edition, Vol. II, p. 229.
16. It should be noted that the conception of the market in a trading economy is derived from the economists' generalized description and is a necessary postulate to their picture of a competitive equilibrium. The present writer is most doubtful if any actual market ever corresponded to this picture, though the picture is useful as a tool of exposition in describing the operation of a trading economy.
17. Subject of course to depletion by other shoe stores, etc., to the extent of 500.
18. For simplicity, we are assuming here that this industry is so perfectly articulated that the use of the factors of production is made a perfect function of demand for the final product at the *fixed price*,—i.e., that no abnormal accumulation or depletion of stocks on hand takes place.
19. John B. Canning, *The Economics of Accountancy* (New York, 1929).
20. Ibid., passim.
21. Joint utility, as here used, bears the same relation to Marshall's joint demand that joint cost bears to his joint supply (cf. Marshall, op. cit., pp. 381–393). A joint utility situation exists when a single utility (product) derives from two or more costs.
22. D.H. Robertson, "Mr. Keynes' Theory of Money," *Economic Journal*, Vol. XLI (1931), pp. 395–411.
23. See John Maynard Keynes, *Treatise on Money*, in two vols., (New York, 1930), Vol. 1, pp. 128–131, particularly p. 130.
24. Banks would also have access to this market.
25. By net savings we mean that the total of new savings by individuals in the community more than counterbalances the spendings out of savings by other individuals.
26. It is here assumed that the volume of money (including deposits) remains constant and that the proportionate distribution of this money between individuals and corporations remains constant. Its velocity of circulation may fluctuate or remain constant as conditions determine.

27. Or by other changes too involved to be worth presenting here.

28. It is worth suggesting that this hypothetical case may have some bearing on the present economic situation. Whether detailed examination will prove it to have any significance remains to be seen.

29. S.H. Nulove, "Recent Writings on Profits," *The Journal of Business of the University of Chicago*, Vol. II (1929), p. 363.

30. F.H. Knight, *Risk, Uncertainty and Profit* (Boston and New York, 1921); Maurice Dobb, *Capitalist Enterprise and Social Progress* (London, 1925).

31. Knight, op. cit., p. 278. The "owners" of productive services apparently refers only to those who supply a service on a contractual basis.

32. Ibid., p. 311.

33. Ibid., p. 309.

34. Ibid., p. 293.

35. Dobb, op. cit., p. 38.

36. Ibid., p. 10.

37. Ibid., p. 53.

38. Ibid., p. 54.

39. Ibid., p. 96.

40. The separation of profits into interest, wages of management and "pure profits" can be justified on the ground that they are in fact frequently separated to a greater or lesser degree, and can therefore be estimated. Most of the labor of management is frequently performed by hired managers and capital may be supplied which carries a minimum of risk. A basis is thus given for estimating a hypothetical interest return on the owner's capital and hypothetical wages for the labor of management he actually performs.

41. The most important distinguishing feature between private enterprise and corporate enterprise, as the term is here used, is this separation of ownership and control.

42. Most economists recognize that element of income received by the bondholder or other creditor over and above the amount he would receive on a "riskless" investment as "pure profits," a return for risk-taking and for the exercise of judgment in the selection of risks. For the purpose of this discussion the bondholder's share in profit can be disregarded.

43. Cf. Henry R. Seager and Charles A. Gulick, Jr., *Trust and Corporation Problems* (New York, 1929), p. 634.

44. It is not so clear, however, that these manifestations will appear in time to allow control to change its policy unless the latter is on guard.

45. Such a conclusion does not apply, of course, to a controlling group which is willing to rifle a corporation and retire from the position of control nor does it apply to a group in legal control (through a legal device) which is willing to allow a corporation to fall into a decline.

46. Assuming that the prior claims of creditors, etc., have been met.

47. S.H. Nulove, "Insiders and Corporate Income Streams," *The Accounting Review*, Vol. V (June 1930), p. 156. Italics by the present writer.

48. Kenneth Field, "A Study of the Intercorporate Structure of Service Corporations in the Electric Light and Power Industry," *Journal of Land and Public Utility Economics*, Vol. V (Aug. 1929), p. 302. Italics by the present writer.

49. Lawyers who support the view that the charter is a contract which grants absolute powers do not do so as a rule on the ground that control should be enabled to divert profits, but rather on technical grounds to protect some particular act of management which frequently has no direct bearing on the division of profits.

50. See Berle and Means, *The Modern Corporation and Private Property* (Chicago, 1932), pp. 247–276.

51. It must be recognized, of course, that the workers, the controlling group, the creditors and others in the community also share to a greater or less extent in the risks involved in any enterprise.

52. To the extent that the controlling group own a small proportion of the total stock, the hope of additional profits may be an incentive to efficient operation of enterprise. Where, however, they own but 2 or 3% of the total, the remaining 97 or 98% of the extra profits would be wasted from the point of view of obtaining efficient operation.

53. The competition of many small concerns, each making a single line of products, against a large integrated concern would not appear to be adequate protection against undue profit by the latter. It would only be protection where the production costs throughout the small concern were as low as or lower than in the large competitor.

3

Industrial Prices and Their Relative Inflexibility

Introduction

The attached charts point to the wide-spread presence in our economy of inflexible administered prices which have produced highly disrupting effects in the functioning of the economy and which are largely responsible for the failure of a policy of laissez faire. The charts indicate that there are two essentially different types of markets in operation—the traditional market in which supply and demand are equated by a flexible price and the administered market in which production and demand are equated at an inflexible administered price. In the first type of market economic adjustments are brought about primarily by fluctuations in price. In the second type of market economic adjustments are brought about primarily by changes in volume of production, while price changes are of secondary significance in producing adjustment.

The difference between market prices and administered prices is clear. A market price is one which is made in the market as the result of the interaction of buyers and sellers. The prices of wheat and cotton are market prices as are many other agricultural products. This is the type of price around which traditional economic theory has been built.

An administered price is essentially different. It is a price which is set by administrative action and held constant for a period of time. We have an administered price when a company maintains a posted price at which it will make sales or simply has its own prices at which buyers may purchase or not as they wish. Thus, when the General Motors management sets its wholesale price for a particular model and holds that price for 6 months or a year the price is an administered price. Many wholesale and most retail prices are administered

From U.S. Congress. Senate. *Industrial Prices and Their Relative Inflexibility,* Letter from the Secretary of Agriculture. 74th Cong., 1st sess., S. Doc. 13.

rather than market prices. For administered prices the price is rigid, at least for a period of time, and sales (and usually production) fluctuate with the demand at the rigid price.

Administered prices should not be confused with monopoly. The presence of administered prices does not indicate the presence of monopoly nor do market prices indicate the absence of monopoly. In many highly competitive industries, such as the automobile industry, prices are made administratively and held for fairly long periods of time. On the other hand, it is conceivable that, in a monopolized industry the product might be turned out according to some fixed production schedule and sold for what it would bring in the market regardless of price. Thus, in the first case, we would have administered prices in a competitive industry and in the second market prices in a monopolized industry. In general, monopolized industries have administered prices, but so also do a great many vigorously competitive industries in which the number of competitors is small. The bulk of the administered prices shown below are in competitive industries.

Chart I [Figure 3.1] indicates the very great importance of administered prices in the American economy. It shows all the commodities making up the Bureau of Labor Statistics' wholesale price index (except railroad and utility rates and a few composite items) distributed according to frequency of price change. The chart covers the number of changes from month to month for each item during the 8-year period from 1926 to 1933. In the right-hand column of the chart are 125 items which changed practically every month in the 8 years. In the left-hand column are 95 items which changed price less than five times in 8 years. The remaining 527 items fall between these extremes. The U-shaped character of the distribution curve carries the usual suggestion that there are two quite different types of price. It is clear that the highly flexible prices of the right-hand group of items are for the most part made in the market, and are the type of prices around which traditional economic analysis has been built. The inflexible prices of the group of items at the left of the chart are established administratively and held for appreciable periods of time. More than half the items covered in the chart averaged less than three changes a year. These items represent a type of price essentially different in its effects from the flexible market price on which the policy of laissez faire has been founded.

Chart 2 [Figure 3.2] shows clearly that frequency of price change and magnitude of price change in the depression have gone together. In this chart the same items as in chart 1 are distributed along the horizontal axis according to the same scale of frequency of price change used in the first chart while the vertical scale represents the ratio of prices in 1932 to prices in 1929 taken as 100. Each dot represents one item and its distance from the base line of 100 reflects its price change between 1929 and 1932. If it is below the base line it has fallen during the depression; if above, it has risen. At the right are the flexible priced items

Figure 3.1. **Rigid and Flexible Prices**

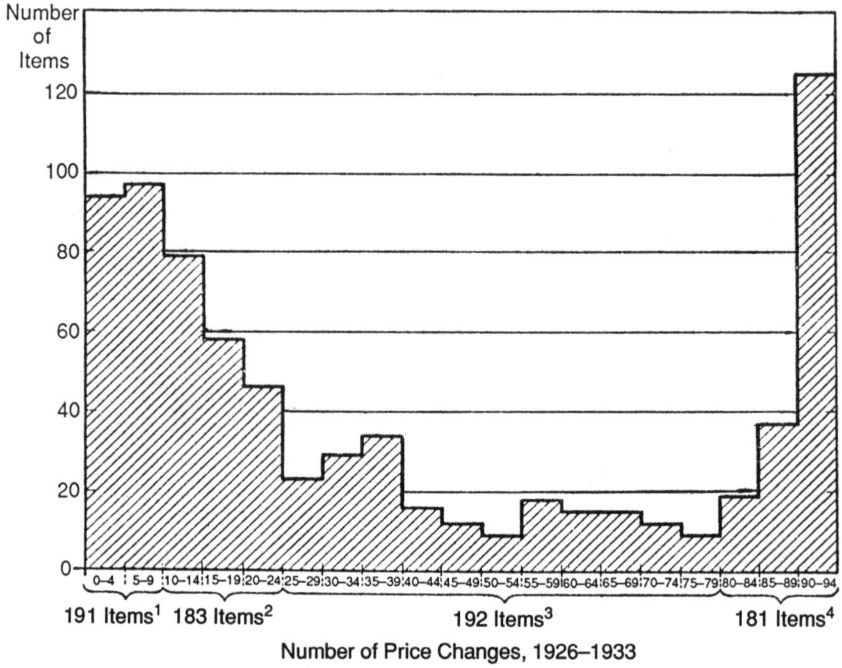

Note: 747 Items from B.L.S. Wholesale Price Index Distributed According to Frequency of Price Change

[1]Changed at the rate of less than once every 10 months.
[2]Changed at the rate of less than once every 4 months but more than once every 10 months.
[3]Changed at the rate of more than once every 4 months and less than 3 times every 4 months.
[4]Changed at the rate of at least 3 times every 4 months.

whose prices in 1932 centered around a price level half that of 1929, while the bulk of the administered prices at the left are centered around 90 percent of the predepression levels though with a considerable dispersion. The items which changed frequently in price show a large drop during the depression while those having a low frequency of change tended to drop only a little in price.

Chart 3 [Figure 3.3] indicates even more clearly this tendency of frequency of price change and magnitude of price drop in the depression to go together. It shows 10 unweighted price indexes computed by grouping into one index the prices of items which did not change at all in the 8-year period; grouping in another index those which changed in price every month; and dividing the remaining items into 8 groups approximately equal in number, selected and arranged according to increasing frequency of price change. Again, the big drop in

Figure 3.2. **Relation Between Frequency of Price Change and Magnitude of Price Change during Depression.**

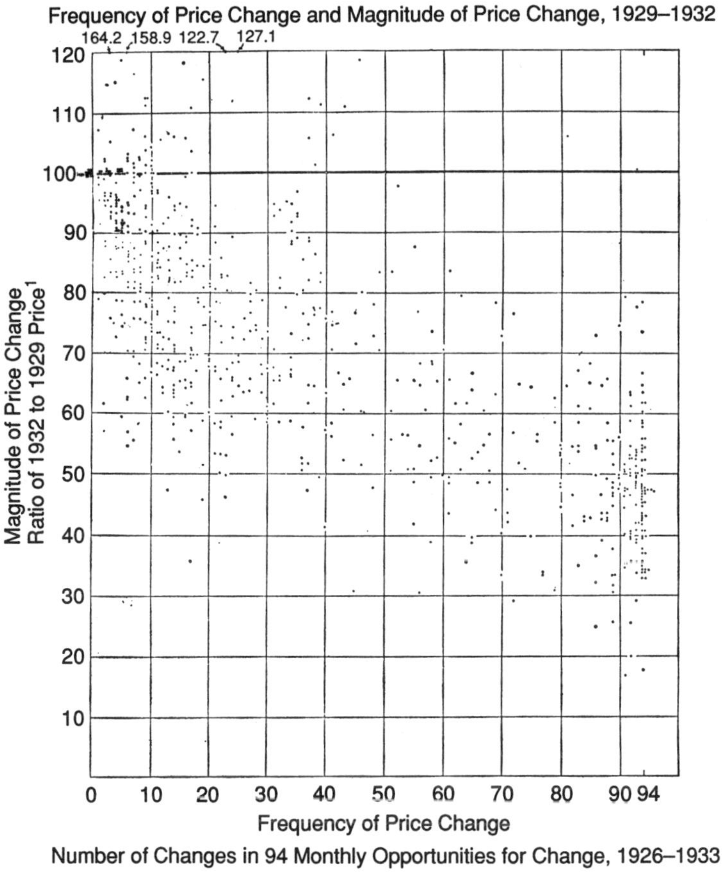

Note: Distribution of 750 Price Series Included in B.L.S. Wholesale Price Index

[1]Average of monthly prices

price is in the items which were clearly not administered while the administered prices tended to show less price drop.

Charts 4 [Figure 3.4] and 5 [Figure 3.5] indicate the wholly different economic effect of flexible market prices and inflexible administered prices. Chart 4 shows the character of the adjustment which takes place in a market of the traditional type in which prices are flexible. It reflects the change in prices and production for agriculture as a whole during the depression. Not until the control program in 1933 was there any significant drop in agricultural production. Practically the whole impact of falling demand worked itself out in falling prices.

Figure 3.3. **Relation between Frequency of Price Change and Magnitude of Price Change during Depression**

Index	No. of Items	Frequency of Price Change[Δ]
I	14	0
II	77	1–4
III	76	5–8
IV	82	9–13
V	96	14–21
VI	88	22–35
VII	86	36–60
VIII	85	61–87
IX	83	88–93
X	63	94
	750	

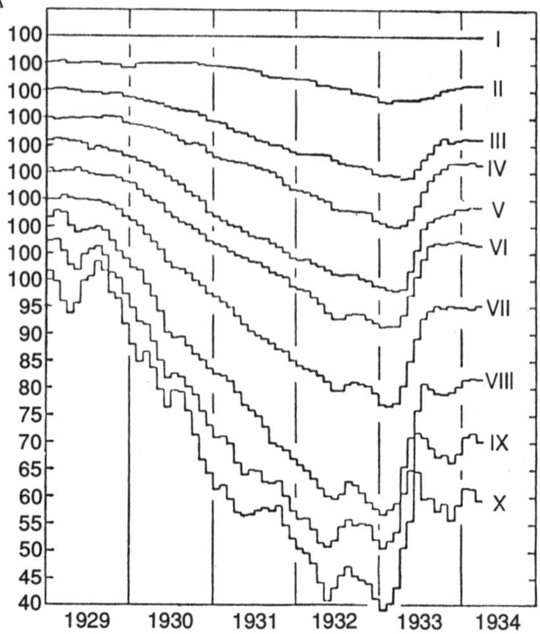

Note: Price Indexes for 750 Items Included in B.L.S. Wholesale Price Index Grouped According to Frequency of Price Change (1926–1933)[1]

[1]Arithmetic Average of Monthly Price Relatives Based on Average of Monthly Prices in 1926 as 100.
[Δ]Number of Changes in 94 Opportunities for Change.

Chart 5 shows in somewhat exaggerated form the opposite development which takes place in a market of the second type in which prices are held essentially rigid by administrative action. It reflects the changes of prices and production of agricultural implements. Practically the whole of the impact of falling demand worked itself out in falling production and only to a secondary extent by falling prices. The exaggeration comes partly from the fact that such partially counterbalancing items as improvements in quality and reduction in the direct costs of production are nowhere indicated and partly because certain minor concessions in the time payments on certain items were made, based on fluctuations in the price of certain agricultural products. Neither of these affect the essential picture told by the chart, the rigid prices and fluctuating production, which is in so much contrast to the flexible prices and stable production assumed by traditional economists and typical of the field of agriculture.

Figure 3.4. **Prices and Production for Agriculture, 1926–1933**

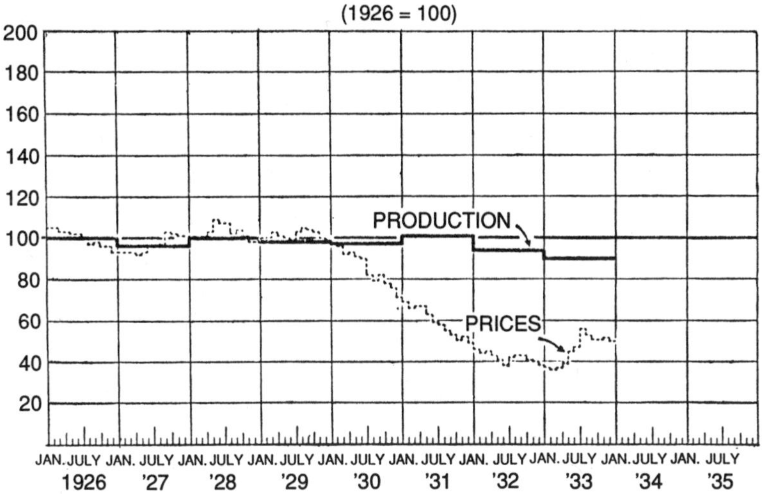

Source: U.S. Department of Agriculture, Bureau of Agricultural Economics.

Figure 3.5. **Prices and Production for the Agricultural Implements Industry, 1926–1933**

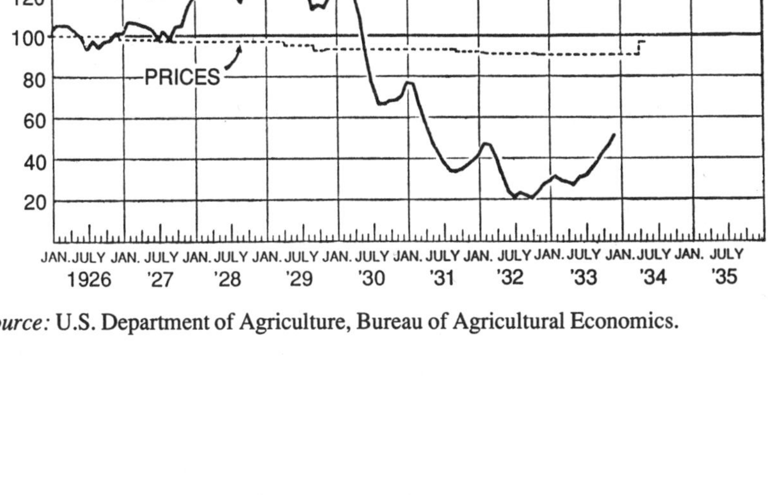

Source: U.S. Department of Agriculture, Bureau of Agricultural Economics.

Figure 3.6. **Relative Decline in Prices and Production, 1929–1932**

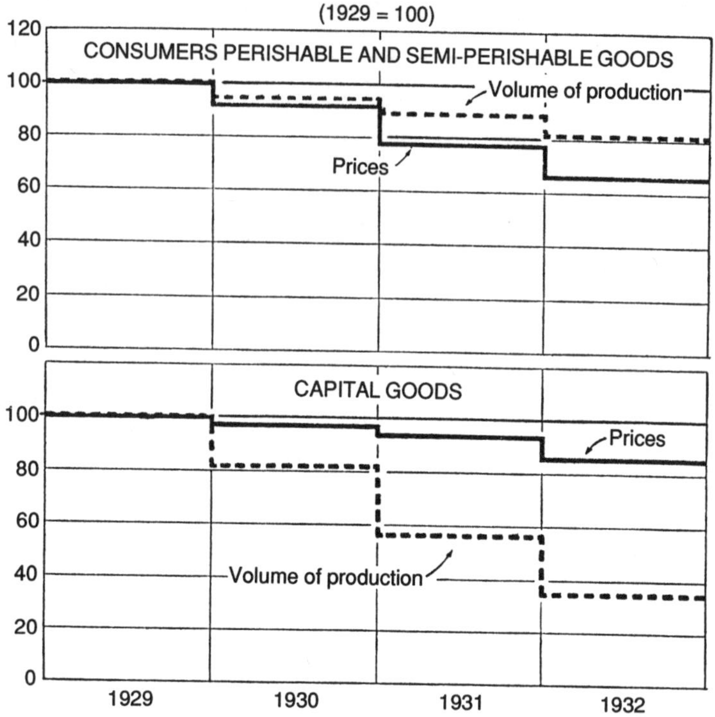

Source: U.S. Department of Agriculture, Bureau of Agricultural Economics

Chart 6 [Figure 3.6] indicates the difference in economic effect of administered and market prices. It shows the relative changes in prices and production for the consumers' perishable- and semiperishable-goods industries and the capital-goods industries. For consumers' goods, prices dropped appreciably while production dropped to a lesser extent. For the capital-goods industries, the prices dropped little while production dropped out from under the relatively inflexible prices. An important part of the difficulties in the capital-goods industries must be attributed to this fact that prices did not adjust.

Chart 7 [Figure 3.7] indicates the disrupting effect of administered prices on the price structure. It shows the downswing of prices during the depression and their subsequent upswing since March 1933. The indexes for the same 10 commodity groups covered in chart 3 are arranged in a new fashion with time represented by the successive lines on the chart and the price relatives for different commodity groups arranged along the horizontal axis according to increasing frequency of price change. Thus, at the left are the commodity groups made up of items that changed infrequently in price. At the right are the commodity

Figure 3.7. **Relative Price Changes for Ten Commodity Groups Arranged According to Increasing Frequency of Price Change**

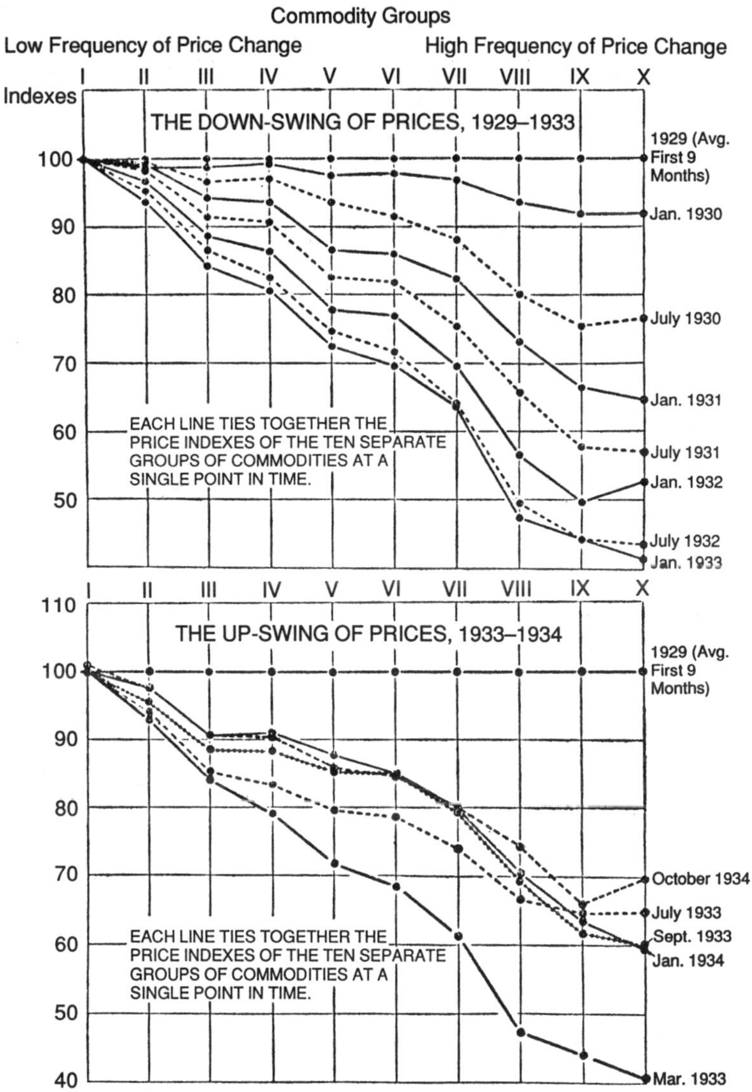

groups made up of items which changed price frequently. Each group is represented by a series of dots indicating the level of prices at successive dates with the 1929 prices as 100. Thus, the prices of group X dropped as follows: 1929, 100; January 1930, 91; January 1931, 64; January 1932, 52; January 1933, 41. For the inflexible group I, prices remained constant. For intermediate groups, the successive prices fell to intermediate degrees. Each line on the chart ties together the price relatives of the 10 different commodity groups at one particular date. Thus, for January 1930, the price relatives for the 10 groups lie along the second line while their price relatives for January 1933 lie along the bottom line. The progress of the depression is shown by the general swing down of the successive lines. The whole price structure pivoted around the rigid prices. The relative uniformity of the swing down should be noted for it seems to reflect a very real set of basic price relationships. The corresponding upswing of prices since March 1933, is shown in the lower part of the chart.

If the corresponding indexes of production for each group of items were available, they would show that the downswing of production had pivoted around the group of flexible priced commodities. Production at the right of the chart would have stayed up while production at the rigid price end of the chart would have dropped most. While exactly corresponding production figures are not available, the relation of price drop and production drop for 10 major industries from 1929 to the spring of 1933 are shown below:

	Percent drop in prices	Percent drop in production
Agricultural implements	6	80
Motor vehicles	16	80
Cement	18	65
Iron and steel	20	83
Auto tires	33	70
Textile products	45	30
Food products	49	14
Leather	50	20
Petroleum	56	20
Agricultural commodities	63	6

One can make the broad generalization, having of course many exceptions, that for industries in which prices dropped most during the depression production tended to drop least, while for those in which prices were maintained the drop in production was usually greatest. Indeed, the whole depression might be described as a general dropping of prices at the flexible end of the price scale and a dropping of production at the rigid end with intermediate effects between.

* * *

The shift from market to administered prices reflected in the foregoing charts is the development which has destroyed the effective functioning of the American economy and produced the pressures which culminated in the new economic agencies of government.

The following memorandum attempts to examine the implications of this shift as they relate to national policy and particularly to the structure and functions of A.A.A. and N.R.A.

Part I. The Basic Cause for the Failure of a Laissez Faire Policy

1. The National Recovery Administration and Agricultural Adjustment Administration were created in response to an overwhelming demand from many quarters that certain elements in the making of industrial policy (including agriculture as an industry) should no longer be left to the market place and the price mechanism but should be placed in the hands of administrative bodies—code authorities, crop control committees, etc. This demand is not only a product of emergency conditions, but is also a reflection of more basic dissatisfactions with the results of laissez faire, such as are reflected in the demands for weakening the antitrust laws, strengthening labor organization, intervening to aid the farmers, and for such economic reorganization as will bring the higher standard of living made possible by modern technology.

2. The whole trend of social development both in this country and abroad has been to recognize the failure of a complete laissez faire policy.

3. The basic cause for the failure of a laissez faire policy is to be found in the very same forces which have made possible a high standard of living for all, namely, the gradual, century-long shift from market to administrative coordination of economic activity which has resulted in modern industrial organization and modern technology. This shift to administration has brought a new type of competition and inflexible administered prices which disrupt the workings of the market.

4. A century ago the great bulk of economic activity in the United States was conducted on an atomistic basis by individuals or families—as is most of agriculture today—while the actions of the separate individuals were coordinated by the market. The individual produced for sale and his activity was geared to and in part controlled by flexible market prices. Balance between the actions of individuals was maintained—insofar as it was maintained—by the impersonal forces of the market and the law of supply and demand. Through the market, the apparently unrelated activities of individuals were thus made to mesh into a single coordinated whole and industrial policy was made by the market as a result. The policy of laissez faire has rested on the assumption that the market would continue to make industrial policy and would remain a satisfactory coordinating mechanism.

5. But gradually more and more of economic coordination has been accomplished administratively. Great numbers of individuals have been drawn into large factories or business organizations and their activities have come to be coordinated within the separate enterprises by administrative action. In a single factory the separate activities of thousands of workers are coordinated by the factory management so as to mesh into a single producing organization. Within single corporate enterprises, tens and even hundreds of thousands of individuals have their economic activity coordinated by administrative direction. In 1929 the activity of over 400,000 workers was meshed into a great communication system

by the management of the American Telephone & Telegraph Co. Contrast the coordination and balance among this group of workers with that among 400,000 separate farmers whose action in producing more or less of each product is controlled and balanced only by the market. In the first, we have the extreme of administrative coordination; in the second, the extreme of market coordination.

6. The shift from market to administrative coordination has gone so far that a major part of American economic activity is now carried on by great administrative units—our great corporations. More than half of all manufacturing activity is carried on by 200 big corporations while big corporations dominate the railroad and public-utility fields and play an important role in the fields of construction and distribution.

7. This development of administrative coordination has made possible tremendous increases in the efficiency of industrial production within single enterprises. The large number of workers brought into a single organization has allowed a high degree of subdivision of labor and the use of complicated series of machines so that the volume of production has been expanded way beyond the capacity of the same number of workers operating independently. Organization has made for rapid and extensive development of technology and the improving technology in turn has increased the advantages of administrative coordination. The telephone, the automobile, modern plumbing, are the joint product of technology and administration. The possibility of a high standard of living for all rests on these two interrelated factors.

8. But the very concentration of economic activity which brought increased productivity has by its nature destroyed the free market and disrupted the operations of the law of supply and demand in a great many industries and for the economy as a whole. (See appendixes A and B.)

9. Evidence of this disruption is to be found in the administrative character and relative inflexibility of price in a great many industries and the fact that on the whole prices during the depression have tended to go down least where the drop in demand has been greatest.

10. The failure of prices to adjust is perfectly familiar to business men in nearly every industry. But the implications of this familiar fact for the economy as a whole have not been recognized.

11. In a large part of industry, the market is not equating supply and demand through a flexible price mechanism, but is bringing an adjustment of production to demand at administratively determined prices. Thus, General Motors may set the f.o.b. price of a 1934 Chevrolet at $500 and produce the half million cars demanded at that price, yet be willing and eager to produce and sell a million cars at that price if only there were buyers. (See appendix C.)

12. The presence of administered prices, while it does not indicate monopoly, does mean that the number of concerns competing in the market has been reduced to the point that the individual concern has a significant power to choose within limits between changing its prices and changing its volume of production

or sales. (See appendix D.) When any small drop in demand occurs, it is in a position to hold its price and reduce its production without losing all its business. As a result it tends to hold up price and reduce volume of production for the industry as a whole.

13. But this means that individuals have a direct power over industrial policy which they exercise in making business policy for their own enterprise.

14. The distinction drawn here between industrial policy and business policy is of the greatest importance.

15. According to laissez faire principles, industrial policy was supposed to result from the interaction in the market of the business policies of a large number of independent units, no one of which had any significant power. In the truly atomistic economy to which the principles of laissez faire applied, no individual buyer or seller alone had any significant power over either price or total volume of production for the industry. Prior to A.A.A., agricultural products, such as wheat and cotton, were produced and marketed under these conditions.

16. Where the number of competing units in a particular industry have been reduced to a relatively small handful, industrial policy is no longer made wholly by the market but in part by individuals. Industrial policy becomes subject to administrative control even though there is no monopoly or collusion between the separate enterprises.

17. But when the business man has the power to affect industrial policy, he almost necessarily makes wrong industrial decisions. The very position, experience and training of the business man which lead him to make the correct decisions on business policy tend to force him to make the wrong decisions on industrial policy in spite of the utmost public spirit which he, as an individual, may seek to exercise. The fact that his decisions are wrong from the point of view of the public interest is no necessary reflection on either his character or his intelligence, but arises from the nature of the situation within which he operates and the functions which he performs.

18. The business man is expected to make business policy in a way to maximize the profits of his own enterprise. When he has the power to choose between lowering price and lowering production, good business policy frequently requires him in the presence of falling demand to hold price and curtail his production even though this means idle men and idle machines. The amount by which he can count on increasing his sales by lowering price is usually so small that the whole balance of his interest as a business man points toward a restriction of production. The fact that he can lay off his workers enables him to cut production without having to carry the burden of idle workers as he does that of idle machines. His interest dictates lowering price only when he is able to squeeze his costs, particularly his labor costs. At best, it is an even choice whether he will choose to maintain profits or minimize losses by seeking a relatively large profit margin on a reduced volume or a small margin on a maintained volume of sales,

and in such a situation the easier device, and the one involving the lesser risk, is the device of holding price and accepting curtailed volume. It is only because this holding of prices has become widespread and customary that the term "price chiseler" could be a term of opprobrium in an economy supposed to be coordinated through flexible prices.

19. The net effect of business control over industrial policy is, therefore, to aggravate any fluctuations in economic activity and prevent any necessary readjustments. An initial drop in demand would result, not in price readjustment, but in maintained prices and curtailment of production, thus throwing workers and machines out of employment, reducing money income and spending power, and further reducing demand. The inflexible administered prices resulting from the shift from market to administration thus act as a disrupting factor in the economy and could cause an initial small drop in demand to become a national disaster.

20. Only as the business man was willing to go directly counter to the interests of his enterprise as a profit-making concern and against business tradition would he make the kind of decisions which, if made throughout industry, would keep the economy functioning and would serve the fundamental interests of business itself. If during the depression individual business men throughout the economy had been persuaded to lower their prices, thus making decisions which appeared by all the standards available to them to be adverse to their interests, the result would actually have been in their interest since it would have reduced the severity of the breakdown.

21. So long, therefore, as concentration exists and important powers over industrial policy are exercised in the guise of business policy and result in inflexible administered prices, the market cannot be expected to coordinate and balance economic activity under a policy of laissez faire.

22. Thus, administrative coordination—the very thing that has made modern technology and a high standard of living possible—has destroyed the effectiveness of the market as an overall coordinator by the inflexible administered prices which are inherent in the reduction of competing units it has produced.

23. It is the effects of this failure of the market mechanism which have brought the overwhelming demand from many quarters for governmental intervention in economic matters. This inflexibility has impeded the balancing of trade between nations, disrupted the workings of monetary policy, brought the banking system to its knees, obstructed the full use of human and material resources, disorganized the flow of savings into useful equipment, brought an unbalanced national budget and greatly increased economic insecurity.

Part II. The Basic Choice in Social Policy

1. Since the administrative coordination which promises a high standard of living carries with it inflexible administered prices which destroy the effectiveness of the market as an over-all coordinator, it is necessary to choose between

two alternatives if an effectively functioning economy is to be established—either (1) atomize the administrative units to the point where inflexible administered prices disappear and the free market can become an effective coordinator, or (2) supplement the market mechanism with institutional arrangements (N.R.A., A.A.A., money system, etc.) sufficient to allow the economy to function effectively in the presence of and in spite of inflexible prices.

2. The first road would require the breaking up of large corporate units into a very great number of separate and wholly independent competing enterprises with the loss in efficiency which it would entail. Few realize the extent to which it would be necessary to pulverize industry. Each of the big automobile companies would probably have to be made into a hundred or more independent concerns; the big chemical companies would have to be broken into very much smaller units; and even after the break-up of the unregulated part of industry, the inflexible prices in the railroad and utility fields would impede economic adjustment, unless they also were broken up and made competitive. In order to make a laissez faire policy truly effective, productive efficiency would have to be greatly impaired and a lower standard of living accepted than is made possible by modern industrial organization and modern technology.

3. The second road, while employing the market as a major instrument, would seek to supplement the market at the points where it tends to fail. Many have held that this would require Government ownership or dictatorship since they can see no other alternative to a laissez faire policy.

4. Actually, the choice does not lie between private ownership and Government ownership because the problem is primarily the distribution of controls, not the locus of ownership. (See appendix E.)

5. Nor does the choice lie between the atomization of industry and an economic dictatorship, since it is only necessary to set up an institutional framework through which certain key industrial decisions are made and within which private or corporate enterprise and initiative can function effectively.

6. If inflexible administered prices are to be accepted as an inevitable product of modern technology and modern industrial organization, the following lines of action would be called for to prevent them from being a disrupting influence and to allow the optimum use of human and material resources.

(*a*) First, all pressure making for a general revision of prices either upward or downward would have to be eliminated from the economy, since any development requiring a general change in the inflexible prices would result in a change in production and economic unbalance. This would mean that a monetary policy would have to be adopted which aimed to keep the flexible prices as a group approximately in line with inflexible prices as a group (see appendix K) and that a mechanism for the adjustment of international trade balances through general changes in prices would have to be replaced.

(*b*) Second, new techniques of control would have to be worked out for establishing the necessary elements of industrial policy so that the self-interest of individuals working through the market but limited by the framework of policy established would tend to produce the optimum use of human and material resources.

(*c*) Finally, violent dislocations in the flow of savings into capital goods would have to be minimized.

The remainder of this report will be devoted to the problems of making industrial policy.

Part III. The Problem of Making Industrial Policy

1. The National Recovery Administration and the Agricultural Adjustment Administration are in part a product of the economic break-down resulting from inflexible administered prices. The major task ahead of them, if they are to facilitate the functioning of the economy, is to participate in the making of industrial policy where the market cannot produce satisfactory results.

2. The basic problem of both N.R.A. and A.A.A. is, therefore, to devise techniques of control for establishing the necessary elements of industrial policy.

3. Until this is recognized as the basic function of N.R.A. and A.A.A. the economic policies of these two agencies tend to be contradictory and confused; once the true function of these bodies has been recognized, the organization and policy implicit in this function will clarify much of their economic activity.

4. In establishing certain elements of industrial policy, the purpose of N.R.A. and A.A.A. should be to set up a framework within which the actions of individuals or groups, operating on their own initiative and in their own interest, will result in a fully functioning economy. The objective should be to accomplish what the market is supposed to accomplish, namely, a balance of the interests of the various interest groups which constitute industry so as to produce the most effective use of human and material resources.

5. To do this it is only necessary to find key decisions for each industry which, if made right, would so condition the other elements of industrial policy that the latter could be left to the actions of individuals and the operation of the market. Thus, in the peach canning industry, the single act of setting the number of cases of peaches to be packed is said to be a sufficient supplement to the market to establish all the other elements of policy in the industry. Because of market forces, the fixing of the size of the pack is said to determine within fairly narrow limits—

(*a*) The price to and the money receipts of peach growers.

(*b*) The profits of the peach canners.

(*c*) The amount of employment given to labor in picking, packing, and transporting peaches, making tin cans, etc. (wage rates are mostly determined by other factors).

(*d*) The amount of peaches received (at wholesale) for a consumer's dollar.

6. The setting of key elements of industrial policy by administrative bodies to facilitate economic functioning is a new technique.

(*a*) Earlier interventions of government in industry have been essentially different.

(1) Antitrust legislation tried to maintain competition and the market as the maker of industrial policy and failed because it confused the absence of monopoly with the existence of a free market. The market break-down is not a matter of monopoly (as the courts have interpreted the term), but of the making of industrial policy by private individuals.

(2) Public-utility regulation establishes a major element of industrial policy—namely rates—but, because it is focused on the interests of property and not on balancing the interests of investors, workers, and consumers, it tends to aggravate the faults inherent in business decisions—witness the efforts to increase railroad rates during the depression. It has neither tackled the problem of getting service to the public under optimum conditions nor has it taken account of the problem of price rigidity introduced by the process of rate making.

(3) Government ownership and operation has involved taking on the whole job of industrial and business operation instead of simply the key industrial decisions. Government has here had to determine not only industrial policy but also business policy as well, with all the centralization which this involves.

(*b*) Collective bargaining has been a technique for establishing certain elements of industrial policy, but it tends to place the whole emphasis on the division of the spoils and loses sight of the other major aspects of industrial policy having to do with increasing the spoils to be divided.

7. In determining industrial policy by the making of key decisions, the essential problems are, first, to discover, industry by industry, what, if any, elements of industrial policy need to be established administratively and, second, to set up a mechanism which will get those key decisions made "right."

(*a*) Finding key decisions is a highly technical matter of applied economics and should become increasingly effective with experience.

(*b*) Getting the right decisions made is primarily a matter of: (1) adequate research and planning; and (2) appropriate organization to obtain the adoption of policies worked out as a joint product of the research staff and the various interests in the industry.

(*c*) "Right" decisions are those which will achieve the results that the market has been supposed to produce, i.e., if the "right" decisions are made throughout all industries, the net effect will be the smooth functioning of the economic machine, the full use of human and material resources, and a balance of interest among individuals and groups. The "right" decisions are thus "ipso facto" in the public interest (see appendix F). In a depression, the decisions in each industry could only tend in the direction of fuller utilization of human and material resources, but as each industry utilized its resources to a fuller extent its expansion would allow other industries to expand further so that the making of the "right" decisions throughout all industries would gradually lead to full utilization. (When the decisions are made to maximize profit, they tend in the reverse direction, or in a manner to minimize the impetus toward recovery coming from other directions.)

Part IV. Possible Techniques for Making Industrial Policy

1. If the N.R.A. and A.A.A. are to develop a partnership technique wherein government and industry are in some way combined to establish the necessary elements of industrial policy, the location and division of power and responsibility in making decisions will importantly affect the likelihood that key decisions will be made "right." Four different methods of distributing responsibility appear to be within the realm of immediate possibility.

(*a*) Decisions could be made by a body (code authority or control committee) made up of business men (or farmers) with the Government acting as a rubber stamp, reserving its veto power for extreme cases. This is the method which the N.R.A. and, to a lesser extent, the A.A.A. employed for the most part during their first year.

(*b*) The Government might undertake to make these decisions and impose them on industry, using Research and Planning Division to determine what would be "right," perhaps using the code authorities and control committees as channels for carrying out the decisions, supplemented by some method of enforcement.

(*c*) The code authorities and control committees might constitute a balanced partnership between government and business in which government represented not only the public interest but also the specific interests of other groups in industry, i.e., labor and consumers.

(*d*) The several interests might jointly be represented in making the key decisions with the Government, in possession of all the necessary factual data, exercising a veto power and responsible for seeing that the interactions of the several interests produced a balance in the public interest.

2. A body of business men constituting a code authority will almost necessarily make the wrong decisions on industrial policy for their industry for the same reasons that in an individual enterprise power over industrial policy leads to harmful industrial decisions. As has been indicated, this is due not primarily to lack of business foresight and intelligence but to the fact situation with which each industrial authority has to deal. Partly because of the particular interest which the business men have in the industrial policy established, and partly because the experience and training of business men have been primarily in the exercise of business judgment, the decisions on industrial policy inevitably tend to be made in terms of business policy. The result for each industry is comparable to the result when individual business men make elements of industrial policy through their own, strongly situated enterprises. The pressure to create

values by establishing higher prices and lower production will persist. In each industry, the only sound business answer to falling demand is to restrict production so as to hold prices. The fact situation does not allow of any other business decision, even though the business interests of each industry would ultimately be better served if all industries lowered prices in the presence of falling demand.[1] (See appendix G.)

It is thus apparent that sound industrial policy cannot be expected if left to business groups alone, whether because in making industrial policy they act in their own business interest or simply because they exercise sound business judgment. When the lumber code authority raised prices, thus impeding recovery, it was acting according to sound business policy in the interests of the business men in the industry. To blame the lumber code authority for not establishing an effective industrial policy is to place the blame where it does not belong. It should rest on those who would place such a responsibility upon business men alone on the assumption that business policy, which aims to create values, and industrial policy, which aims to get things to people, are the same, and that those who are familiar with and interested in the one can be expected to accomplish the other. Only as business men failed to act as business men and failed to follow their business judgment would their decisions on industrial policy result in a properly functioning economy.

3. If the Government took on the whole job of making industrial decisions, it would be better equipped with the information necessary to the making of sound decisions than would anyone else; it is committed to the public interest as the basis for those decisions; and it commands the powers of enforcement.

On the other hand, it is doubtful whether the Government could effectively exercise the whole function of making industrial policy without using almost dictatorial methods. It would inevitably become the focus of group pressures vastly more vigorous and disruptive than those now existing; it would expose itself to political attack as dictatorial, and errors in detail would be used against it as political ammunition; industrial policy making by Government itself would call for a very high degree of centralization.

4. The third possibility—joint action of Government and business, with the Government representing not only the public interest, but also the specific interests of labor and consumer groups—would probably provide the most effective available method for getting the interests of the nondominant economic groups represented in the immediate future.

On the other hand, the Government would thereby be placed in the position of playing a dual role. In behalf of the public interest it should act as arbiter between conflicting interests; as representative of labor and consumer interests it should play a partisan role. It would be most difficult for the Government to perform this partisan role, for it would be constantly under pressure from business, the strongest of the economic interest groups, to act at least equally in its behalf; democratic government rests upon the philosophy that it is an impartial rather than a partisan body; and even if this present administration, or any other particular administration, succeeded in acting on behalf of the nondominant groups, there is neither guaranty nor likelihood that the political commitments of future administrations would permit them so to act.

5. In the fourth possibility, that of having the several interests impinge upon each other under Government supervision, the Government would be placed in a favorable position to influence the decisions in the direction of the public interest as it would not have to play a partisan role and it would not have to thrust industrial policy upon those who had not shared directly in the making of that policy. Most of the conflict between economic interests would take place between representatives of these interests rather than focusing upon a representative of Government.[2]

The introduction of the other interests besides those of business would tend to push the decisions in the direction of the balance of interests which the market is supposed to achieve and whereby it is supposed to produce the optimum functioning of the economy. (See appendixes H, I, and J.) The pressure from labor representatives to maintain or increase employment and from consumer representatives to lower price and maintain the fullest use of labor and machines would be set against the business man's normal tendency to establish higher prices and lower production than the public interest demands.

Thus, in the case of canned peaches, the size of the peach pack was actually decided by a control committee composed of growers and canners, with the Secretary of Agriculture exercising a veto power over the decision. The figure finally fixed was probably not as large as the public interest demanded. The growers wanted a somewhat larger pack, the canners a smaller pack. Both consumers and picking and canning labor would have been better served by a larger pack. If consumer and labor representatives had also participated in making the decision, it is probable that the size finally set would have been somewhat larger. At the same time, if the consumers and workers had attempted to increase the size of pack too far, the growers would have shifted sides and joined the canners in resisting further increase since too large a pack would have been just as much against their interests as too small a pack.

It would be essential for the consumer interest to be represented as well as those of business and labor, for labor cannot always be relied upon to counteract the inclination of business to create value by restricting production. Too often labor representatives, by focusing their attention on the division of the spoils, would be persuaded to join business in using the scarcity technique in return for higher money wages. This is indicated by the experience of some of the German cartels in which business and labor combined to exploit the consumers—i.e., the owners and workers in other industries—and of some American cities where organized labor and organized business in the building industry have combined for similar exploitation. The inclusion of consumer representatives along with those of business and labor would insure a direct pressure for the full use of resources.[3]

The chief disadvantages of such a set-up would be (1) that the diverse interests are not equally strong as pressure groups, so that the greater and more effective organization of business would make business interests still dominant; and (2) that the veto power in the hands of the government and the necessity of getting agreement on the part of conflicting groups may lead to stalemates in particular situations—a disadvantage which might also present itself if the government represented the nondominant groups in a partnership with business.

6. Whichever method of determining the key elements of industrial policy is adopted, problems distinctive to each solution must be met.

(1) If the Government is to do the whole job, an effective enforcement machinery must be developed; it would be essential to secure public acceptance of the idea that government should exercise such power over industry; the problems inherent in centralization would have to be solved. The direct impact of conflicting groups upon the Government could be minimized by the creation of an advisory body for each industry within which the conflicting interests were represented.

(2) If the Government is to represent the nondominant economic groups, the problem becomes that of pitting the political power of these groups against the economic power of the business group. This would call for a definitive realinement of political parties on the basis of economic interests.

(3) If the interests are to impinge on each other, labor and consumer interests must be strengthened as pressure groups, presumably through the building up of their organizations. Such organizations would gain a status which they do not now have by being given a constructive role to play in the making of industrial policy, and the Government might properly take positive steps to encourage their growth, just as it did in the case of business organizations in the first year of N.R.A. and in the case of farmers through the encouragement of farm cooperatives and the farm-extension service. As the interest groups became more nearly equal in power, their decisions would tend increasingly to be in the public interest.

The danger of stalemate is inherent in any solution which contains the element of democracy and which avoids both a positive dictatorship and the complete atomization of industry necessary to make laissez faire operate effectively. By shifting the major emphasis in industrial relations from the division of the spoils to making the economic machine work—a shift which is basic to the whole technique here described—a chief reason for stalemate would automatically be removed.

7. The choice among these possible ways of determining key elements of industrial policy should be made with reference to the basic requirements for a satisfactory American program. It should be geared to the conditions established by modern technology; it should leave existing economic and governmental organization intact as far as possible; it should provide the minimum centralization compatible with necessary coordination, and avoid as far as possible bureau-

cracy and political influence; it should secure industrial decisions in the direction of the optimum use of human and material resources and a balance of economic interest among various groups; it should meet the traditional American demands for liberty, opportunity, and democracy as far as the need to provide security will permit, and it must be compatible with the Constitution. (See appendix K.)

Appendixes

Appendix A. The Break-down of the Market Mechanism

Underlying the many-sided demand for the abandonment of laissez faire is the disruption of the law of supply and demand which has resulted when the power to determine certain elements of industrial policy has become lodged in the hands of individuals instead of lying with the impersonal market mechanism. This development, arising largely out of the concentration of economic activity into great enterprises, has not been recognized by traditional economists, yet it is of the greatest significance. To understand its full implications it is necessary to see clearly how it affects the basic elements in the traditional theory.

The whole structure of traditional economic theory is built on the "law of supply and demand"; i.e., the assumption that supply, demand, and price will so adjust themselves in the market that supply and demand will be equal at the price which is arrived at. On the basis of this law was built the picture of how our whole economy was supposed to work. Under the pressure of individual self-interest, the supply, the demand, and the price for each article and service was supposed to adjust itself, so that the right amount of each thing would tend to be produced at the right price. Thus the operations of the free market world tend to produce the optimum use of human and material resources.[4]

According to this theory, the mechanism of the market was impersonal and the whole of industrial policy was determined by the market—both the amount of a thing produced and sold, and the price at which it was sold. Industrial policy was the result of the individual decisions of a large number of buyers and sellers. The business policy of individuals interacted so as to produce industrial policy, but no one individual or enterprise had significant control over any element of industrial policy. This operation of the free market is clearly shown in the case of most agricultural products (before A.A.A.). The individual farmer produced wheat or not, depending on what he expected the price of wheat to be, and offered his produce for what it would bring in the market. He had no significant control over either the total amount of wheat produced or the market price of wheat. His contribution to the total supply was too insignificant to give him any control over industrial policy.

But this theory was set forth by Adam Smith to explain the workings of an economy quite different from that now existing. He was dealing with an atomistic economy in which the great bulk of economic activity was carried on by independent artisans, by one-man businesses, or by business units so small that they could be treated for most purposes as though they were one-man affairs. Most of agriculture still corresponds to this Adam Smith picture, but today a large part of industrial activity has been concentrated into units so large that certain important elements of industrial policy are now made by individuals and no longer by the impersonal market mechanism. In 1931, 200 corporations controlled approximately 54 percent of all nonfinancial corporate wealth. If we leave out the highly concentrated fields of railroads and public utilities and the relatively unconcentrated construction and distribution industries and confine our attention to manufacturing alone, we still find a very high degree of concentration.

In 1931 the 200 largest manufacturing corporations controlled over 55 percent of all manufacturing corporate assets, and over half of all manufacturing assets, whether incorporated or not. At least half of the gainfully employed population of the country were engaged in industries in which control over certain major elements of industrial policy were in the hands of individuals.

In some of these industries, the business policy of one or a few big enterprises actually determines essential elements of industrial policy. Thus, the management of the Aluminum Co. of America can control, within limits, either the volume of pig aluminum sold in the whole industry or the price at which it is sold. It cannot control both of these elements of industrial policy, but the control of either element by a small group of individuals is contrary to the assumptions underlying the laissez faire philosophy of automatic market adjustments. In the regulated monopolies, an element of industrial policy—railroad and utility rates—is under the combined control of a group of business executives, a governmental commission, and the courts. In industries such as automobiles or agricultural implements, a few big companies so dominate the field that, within limits, they can control either prices or production. There is ample evidence that this partial control over industrial policy is very widespread throughout industry and does not require monopoly conditions or collusion to bring it about. Competition of a sort may be very active as in the case of the four big tobacco companies or the big automobile companies, yet it may be of such a character that the big companies can choose as individuals to establish either price or volume of production and, because their operating conditions are similar and they sell in the same market they tend to establish and hold the same price and make their production conform to the sales at that price. It should be noted that this partial control over industrial policy does not necessarily mean that the big enterprises make too much profits. The matter is vastly more fundamental than that.

The danger of industrial policy making by individuals is that policies will be adopted which interfere with the working of the economic machine and thus defeat the effectiveness of a laissez faire policy on the part of government. It is clear that during the depression the effect of falling demand has been quite different in the atomistic and in the concentrated industries. In the atomistic and highly competitive industries like agriculture, the volume of production and sales have been maintained while prices have dropped. Each producer has continued to use his productive facilities to the full, selling the product for what it would bring. Such industries have thus acted according to traditional theory. In more concentrated industries, however, the depression drop in demand has been met primarily by holding prices and reducing production. In the case of agricultural implements, the prices reported to the Bureau of Labor Statistics for 20 agricultural implements declined on the average only 6 percent, yet production and employment in the industry declined 80 percent.[5] Case after case could be cited in which the prime reaction to depressed demand was to curtail production and not to lower prices. Here we have evidence, not only of the power to choose between lowering production and lowering price but also evidence that the power tends to get exercised in the direction of lowered production and not lowered price.

This reduction in production is of the utmost importance because it is, in itself, destructive of the workings of the economy. A reduction of production throws workers out of employment, reduces their money income, and further reduces the demand for goods without in any way increasing the income or buying power of anyone else either by increasing their money incomes or reducing prices. If all industry operated in this way, the result of an initial drop in demand would be an overpowering depression, unless some other factor, monetary, or otherwise, intervened to prevent the initial drop in demand from destroying demand entirely. Only if the power to choose between lowering price and lowering production was consistently used to lower prices to the point where full use of machine and labor resources was reached (regardless of how many bankruptcies were produced) could we expect the results predicted for a policy of laissez faire to be reached. Yet it can be shown both in theory and in practice that the power to choose between reducing production and reducing price to meet lowered demand will on the whole tend to be used to hold price and reduce production where it is exercised to maximize profits or minimize losses. Thus, industrial policy making by individuals is not only contrary to the assumptions of laissez faire but it tends to produce results quite opposite to those necessary for a harmoniously functioning economy.

Appendix B. The Disruption of the Law of Supply and Demand

The failure of traditional economists to recognize the extent and harmful effects of industrial policy making of individuals is easily understood when the law of supply and demand is examined in reference to the power of individuals partially to control industrial policy. According to the law, the supply and the demand for an article are supposed to be equated at a price. Unfortunately, the meaning of "supply" is today most ambiguous. Is "supply" "the amount of an article sold at the price," or is it "the amount which would be forthcoming at the price if

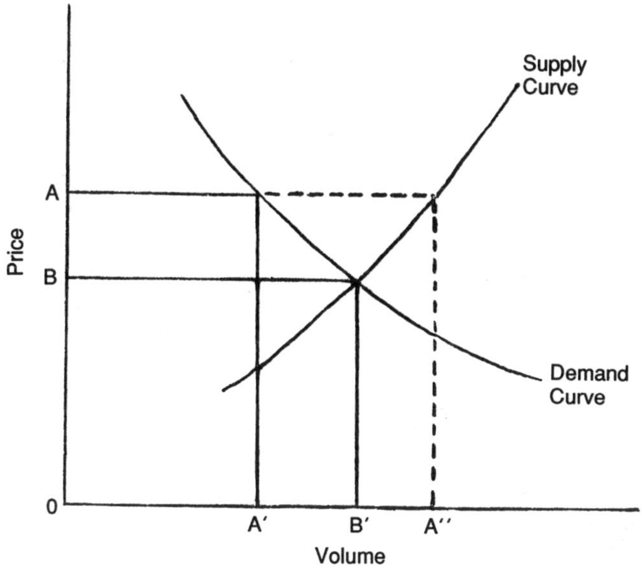

someone would buy it at that price''? In a truly atomistic economy, such as Adam Smith was discussing, these two amounts would be the same so that to him there was no ambiguity. But where concentration or other factors have entered in so that individuals can, within limits, control either price or volume of production, there can be a wide difference between these two amounts. Thus, General Motors might set the price for 1934 Chevrolets at $500 f.o.b. Detroit and sell only 500,000 cars. Yet the company might be willing (and eager) to produce and sell 1 million cars at the price of $500 if buyers were available to take the extra cars off their hands at that price. The amount sold at $500 would thus be 500,000 cars. The amount forthcoming at $500, if only buyers would come forward and buy, would be 1 million cars. Which of these figures constitute supply?

The traditional economist calls ''the amount sold'' the supply when he is dealing with actual markets. If he called ''the amount forthcoming if there were takers at the market price'' the supply, then it would become at once obvious that in a large number of industries today supply and demand are not equated by price. But when the traditional economist comes to defend the general policy of laissez faire, he unconsciously shifts his ground and means by supply ''the amount forthcoming at a price'' rather than the amount actually sold. Only as price is adjusted so as to equate ''the amount forthcoming at the price'' and the demand at the price will the economy work as the traditional economists assumed.

The gradual widening of the difference between ''the amount sold'' and ''the amount forthcoming'' has bit by bit disrupted the working of the old law of supply and demand. Today, instead of having ''the amount forthcoming'' and demand equated by price, we have "amount sold" and demand equated at a price.

If we translate the law of supply and demand into terms of production (assuming all produced is sold), the two meanings of supply would be "the amount produced" and "the amount that would be produced if there were takers at the price set" or what we can refer to as "willing capacity."[6] Today, in a very large number of industries, individuals have sufficient control over industrial policy so that prices tend to be held in a depression and actual production is allowed to drop way below "willing capacity" for considerable periods. Production is equated to demand at the price set rather than having supply and demand equated by price.

The essential difference can be indicated in the symbolism usually employed by economists.

In the above diagram the customary supply and demand curves are indicated. If price was such as to equate supply and demand the price would be *OB* and the amount sold *OB′*. If the particular producers were in a position to restrict production so as to hold up prices, the price might be *OA* and the volume sold *OA′* while the "willing capacity" at the price *OA* would be *OA″*. Thus where the amount sold (*OA′*) and the "willing capacity" (*OA″*) are different amounts, the price is not established according to the law of supply and demand on which a laissez faire policy has been based.

Appendix C. Inflexible Administered Prices versus Flexible Market Prices

The fact that the prices of a great many commodities tend to be extremely rigid has only come into prominence in very recent years. The full significance of this rigidity is only beginning to be understood.

A study of the behavior of prices reveals that there are two quite different techniques of price making, each dominating a section of the market. The first involves prices made in the market and highly flexible. The second involves prices made administratively which tend to be inflexible and by their nature to be changed infrequently.

Most economic studies have dealt only with the magnitude of price change and not with the frequency of price change.[7] The varying degrees of price change during a depression have been recognized, but these differences have been attributed to differences in the characteristics of either supply or of demand (differences in the slopes of the supply or demand curves). While the difference in prices might be explained by this factor, they might equally be explained by the existence of administered prices as is suggested by the infrequency of price changes. Undoubtedly both factors have been at work, though the first two charts at the beginning of this report suggest that the factor of administration has dominated during the depression. Otherwise, one would not have found the striking correlation between frequency of price change and magnitude of price drop from 1929 to 1932. It is well known that the demand for food is relatively inelastic while that for automobiles is much more elastic yet production has been curtailed most in the latter industry.

The difference between the two methods of price making can be clearly seen in the case of concrete examples. The farmer sends his hogs to market or carts his carrots to town in the early morning. The price that he gets for those hogs or carrots depends upon market conditions—how many other farmers have sent in hogs or brought in carrots that day, and how many people are there to buy. The prices are the result of a bargain struck under these conditions. When the farmer sends his hogs or brings his carrots, he does not know just how much he is going to get for them. He is sure that they will all be sold, because he is not going to pay the freight to have the hogs shipped back to him, or drive home with a load of carrots to rot on his hands; but he cannot tell what the price is to be.

Contrast the fate of a Chevrolet with the fate of a hog. In the offices of General Motors, the managers decide on the 1935 price. They print their price lists and mail them out to their salesmen. They may arrange ahead of time to buy the materials which go into the Chevrolet at prices for materials which promise to give them a profit on each car at the price which they decide upon for the car. They do not know how many Chevrolets they are going to sell; but they do know at what price they will be sold. The contrast between the price of the farmer's hogs or carrots and the price of a [1935] Chevrolet is the contrast between the two kinds of price determination.

The essential difference between the two types of prices is that one represents an equating of supply and demand by price while the other represents the equating of production and demand at a price. (See appendix B.) The first type of price facilitates economic adjustment, the second tends to interfere with adjustment by bringing a drop in production and purchasing power when demand drops.

It will be said by many that this drop in production occurs primarily in the capital-goods industries and not in consumer-goods industries. It is undoubtedly true that a greater drop in production has occurred in the capital-goods industries. But it is also clear that prices in those industries have been very much more rigid. The usual expectation of the economist would be that in general where demand had dropped most prices also would have dropped most. The exact opposite appears to have been the case, for consumption goods, particularly agricultural products, fell markedly in price during the depression while capital goods did not fall in anything like the same proportion. Also, where the prices of consumption goods were held rigid, the drop in production was more nearly like that of the capital goods industries.

It may also be said that the failure to reduce prices has been due to the increased unit cost of production resulting from the burden of overhead. Once the business man has made the initial decision to hold his price which prevents a maintenance of production, increased unit costs exert a progressively strong pressure to maintain and accept a progressively lower level of production. This factor would not enter into price determination if industrial policy were really determined in the market. Though practically the whole of the farmer's cost is overhead, the market does not consider such costs in the price which it gives him.

The importance of these two types of pricing processes lies not only in the control over industrial policy which is reflected in rigid prices, but in the fact that all adjustment to changing economic conditions which are made through price are made in the area of flexible prices, thereby destroying the price relationships between the flexible-price and the rigid-price industries. The adjustment of production instead of price in the inflexible areas aggravates the initial price adjustment in the flexible industries by reducing purchasing power and throws the burden of further price adjustment on the flexibly priced commodities. This situation can be clearly seen in the effect of the depression upon agricultural prices and the destruction of the price relationship between agricultural and industrial goods. It is also seen in the fact that during the depression the total income of all farmers and the total income of all industrial workers dropped in approximately the same proportion, but the drop in farm income reflected a drop in prices while the drop of workers' income reflected primarily loss of employment.

The net result of administered prices under a laissez faire policy is thus to impair or destroy the adjustability of the economy.

Appendix D. The Requirements of a Free Market

In order that a free market should exist so that prices will be made competitively in the market the most important single requirement is a sufficient number of buyers and sellers in the market so that no one buyer or seller is in a position to affect prices sufficiently by changing his own volume of purchases or production to make this a factor in making his own calculation. No individual farmer producing cotton will affect the price of cotton sufficiently by increasing his production to make it worth while even to consider the effect of his action on price. On the other hand the management of General Motors know that if they increased their production appreciably, an appreciably lower price would be required to dispose of their output and since the lower price would affect their receipts on each item sold, they would have to balance carefully the lower price on the cars they would otherwise sell at the higher price and the possible profits on the added cars they would sell at the lower price.

This can be shown clearly with the customary marginal cost and demand curves.

Under freely competitive conditions it is assumed that each producer will produce up to the point where his marginal cost will be equal to or just short of the price, since each producer is supposed to be unmindful of the effect of his action on prices. This would mean that in the situation represented by the above diagram, the single producer will produce OA′ units and sell them at a price OA. (Such a result would require a demand curve for the particular producer's product with a much more gentle slope than is indicated above.) However, where the

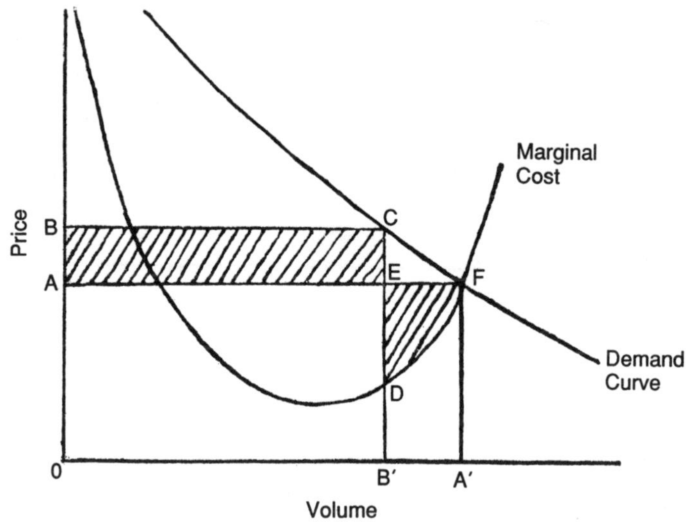

particular producer was a major factor in the market, perhaps one of three or four big competing enterprises, the producer would have to consider the effect of his own action on the price prevailing. Thus, if he curtailed his production from A′ to B′ and would as a result lift the prevailing price from OA to OB then he would have to consider whether the profit indicated by ABCE was greater than the profit indicated by DEF. If the first were greater, then it would pay him to reduce production. His most profitable action would, of course, be conditional by the action of his competitors, but the presence of three or four independent and active competitors would not eliminate the possibility of gaining advantage by reducing production though the action of competitors might reduce the range of profitable curtailment. In such a market the producer would certainly have to consider the effects of his own production policy on price.

If administered prices were present in an industry this would be prima facie evidence that the free market, in the sense posited in the laissez faire philosophy, did not exist. If administered prices are present in a major part of our economy and since they exist in a great many areas which are not monopolized but in which there is active competition between a few units, it is clear that they do not necessarily reflect monopoly conditions but something more wide-spread—namely, the reduction in the number of competing units in many industries.

Appendix E. Not a Problem of Government Ownership Versus Private Ownership, but of the Distribution of Controls

In the modern corporation, "private property" in the traditional sense, i.e., in the sense that an "owner" has power over, responsibility for, and interest in his property, does not exist, for the interests and controls which have been combined to constitute traditional ownership have become lodged in different hands. In the modern corporation, most of the ownership interests are in the hands of stockholders, but where stock is widely dispersed, power does not lie with the stockholders but with the directors and officers of the corporation. The ordinary stockholder can do as he pleases with his share of stock—sell it, hold it, or burn it up—but over the corporate enterprise as such, and over its physical property, he has practically no control. The control exercised by corporate management, on the other hand, does not rest on ownership, for in most of the great corporations the controlling group holds a negligible proportion of the stock.

This situation makes it possible to shift threads of control from one place to another without changing either the character or the locus of ownership interest. This means that the threads of control relating to business policy and those relating to industrial policy could be sorted out and the latter relocated, leaving ownership interests untouched.

The separation of control from interest in respect to ownership is only one of the ways in which modern economic organization has made this separation between interest and control. Under the factory system, the worker surrenders much of the control over his own activity during working hours. So long as the factory enterprise was small and one of a large number competing for the services of workers, the worker still retained an important measure of control, for he could always transfer to some other enterprise. But as the administrative units have become ever larger, the direct control of the worker over the conditions under which he works has become less and less. To some extent this loss in direct control has been counterbalanced by a measure of control through labor organization, but, for the most part, workers have ceased to be in a position to exercise an important element of control.

The consumer, likewise, has lost much of the control which he had through bargaining as the business units with which he deals have become less numerous and more powerful.

Thus, the shift of large segments of economic activity from coordination through the market to coordination through administered activity has gradually sucked controls over industrial activity away from the three parties mainly at interest, the security holders, the workers, and the consumers. It has placed this control in the hands of administrators, nominally responsible to the one group, the security holders, but factually responsible in all too many cases to no one. Such a concentration of controls leaves the investors, the workers, and the consumers with great and basic interests in industrial activity but with a minimum of control over it.

In that major part of industry which is dominated by modern corporations, the crucial problem is not the transfer of ownership or of any other interest, but rather the locus of control over industrial policy.

Appendix F. The Public Interest

It is a part of the American tradition that it is the function of the Government to protect and foster the public interest. In any concrete situation it may be and usually is most difficult to determine what action is in the public interest. Yet no one would claim that the Government should be the tool of any special group. Even when special interests seek action favoring them, they word their arguments in terms of the public interest. All guides to action on the part of Government should therefore start with the public interest.

The discussions of the public interest during the eighteenth and nineteenth centuries centered around the assumption that the political and the economic spheres should be and could be kept wholly separate and that the free market would supply all the coordination and control of individual economic activity necessary to bring the optimum use of human and material resources. It was therefore held that the public interest called for a policy of laissez faire and all matters of immediate policy have been discussed with this basic element of policy already determined. As a result, there has been almost no discussion of what would constitute the public interest as to questions of immediate policy if a change in the character of economic activity necessitated a change in basic policy away from complete laissez faire.

In considering what would constitute action in the public interest in cases where the market mechanism was being supplemented by administrative action, light can be thrown by examining the reasons why a policy of laissez faire was formerly considered in the public interest. It was assumed that under a policy of laissez faire each individual would be fully employed—to the extent of his desire—in producing for the market and that as a result of the price mechanism, the individual would receive for his activity a corresponding volume of the product of some other worker. Likewise, so long as capital was scarce relative to its effective uses, investors would receive a return on their investment related to the degree of scarcity of capital.[8] As a result of the operations of the free market under a policy of laissez faire, a balance between the conflicting interests of buyer and seller—of worker, investor, and consumer—was supposed to be established. If perfect balance throughout were established, it would mean that no new worker would find an appreciable advantage in going into one industry or employment rather than another (except as he had peculiar qualifications), no new savings seeking investment would find an appreciably higher return commensurate with the risks in one industry than another, and no new consumer coming into the market would find appreciable advantage in buying from one group of producers rather than from another except as special qualities of commodity or service were required. Finally, the average return on capital would correspond to the actual scarcity of capital in relation to the possible uses. If a policy of laissez faire actually produced the above results, we should have, not idle men and idle machines, but the optimum use of human and material resources. Presumably a laissez faire policy was regarded as in the public interest because of these promised results and though a general laissez faire policy has failed to produce the expected results, we may accept the basic objectives sought by that policy as in the public interest.

This means that the basic objective in making industrial policy in the public interest would be to bring a coordination and balance of the conflicting interests of the same character which a laissez-faire policy was supposed to bring. Thus, if the size of the cotton crop has to be established administratively, the basic aim of public policy should be to make a decision which would represent an appropriate balance between the conflicting interests of cotton raisers, cotton manufacturers, cotton-mill labor, and cotton-cloth consumers.[9] Here public interest calls for the finding of the common interests and the balancing of the conflicting interests in order that the results of economic activity will more nearly conform to the balance which the policy of laissez faire was formerly expected to produce.

To the extent that industrial policy is to be made administratively, the major interests involved in the system of interchanges will resolve themselves into three major categories: The business interest primarily seeking more money income for less use of capital, the labor interest primarily seeking more money wages for less work, and the consumer interest primarily concerned with obtaining more or better goods and services for less money. The farmer interest will sometimes be a producer's interest, either as worker or owner or both together; at other times it will be a consumer interest. The public interest, therefore, calls primarily for a balancing of the business, labor, and consumer interests which together constitute industry. This conflict of interests is clearly recognized in the three advisory boards attached to the N.R.A.—the Industrial Advisory Board,[10] the Labor Advisory Board, and the Consumers Advisory Board—and in their equal representation on the Advisory Council. The conflict is only partially recognized in the great departments of the Federal Government, the Commerce (business) Department and the Department of Labor. The Department of Agriculture combines the three interests for a large part of our economy which still operates on an atomistic basis.

The lack of any department of the consumer undoubtedly grows out of the recurrent confusion between the public interest and the consumer interest. It is said that since everyone is a consumer and everyone is the public, therefore the two are the same. This is true with regard to the most general problems. But when any specific problem comes up, it is at once clear that for all the population the interest affected in making policy is not their consumer interest. The workers in, let us say, the shoe industry are interested in higher wages, yet the consumer interest, that is, the interest of all buyers of shoes except those making shoes, is in lower prices and presumably lower money wage rates. The policy involved is really one of the ratio of exchange in part between the workers in the shoe industry and the workers in other industries. To say that the public interest and the consumer interest were the same, i.e., that the public interest excluded the shoe workers would be just as partial and unproductive of an effective operating balance in the economy as it would be to say that workers in the shoe industry alone constituted the public and that wages for the particular industry should be set wholly without regard to the interests of the buyers of shoes. The public with respect to any particular industry includes both producers and consumers, and the public interest requires the balance of these conflicting interests.

Appendix G. The Business Interest

Although much has been said here of the bad effect on the economy of industrial policy made by business men and of the necessity of counteracting this tendency to make bad industrial decisions, yet industrial policy determined in the public interest would actually be more to the ultimate interest of business men than the policy which they themselves would set.

To question the quality of industrial decisions made in the interest of maximizing profits or minimizing losses is to condemn neither profits as such nor the men who make such decisions. It is probable that if decisions had been so made as to properly balance the interests of investors, workers, and consumers during the last 5 years, business profits would have been very much greater and business losses would have been less, or would have been turned into profits. This would have been accomplished, not by taking from the money income of workers or from the money outgo of consumers but rather by greatly increasing the national income available for distribution.

The men who made these decisions were not violating the rules of the business game. On the contrary, the very gravity of the situation arose out of the fact that they did, for the most part, play according to the rules of the game. Unfortunately, the play according to the rules of the business community—rules laid down for an atomistic economy—brought economic death to innocent bystanders.

The increased power placed in the hands of single enterprises has made the rules of the business game almost as inappropriate as the Marquis of Queensberry rules would be to a fight in the pit of Madison Square Garden between two armored tanks mounting machine guns. In both cases the power of the contestants to do damage by their actions has extended far beyond their immediate sphere. The remodeling of the Ford product brought economic depression to the whole region of Detroit just as effectively as the machine guns of one of the contestant tanks could mow down a large section of the audience. Even where some outstanding men sought to break the rules of the business game by making industrial policy, not solely in the interests of the immediate profits of their enterprise, but in the public interest, their actions were nullified by the actions of the mass of other business men.

In changing the rules of the game, the problem is not unlike that of the crowded excursion boat which capsized when a large body of excursionists rushed to one rail to see what was happening. In both industry and excursion boat rugged individualism works well so long as a multitude of different individuals decide individually to do different things. Each passenger can walk where he chooses so long as the passengers choose to scatter over the ship. But when most of the passengers rush to one rail great damage is done. Of course, we might say that God is just and drowns those foolish enough to rush to the rail. This is exactly what the traditional economist says of business. Yet the boat takes down with it all its passengers, whether they rushed to the rail or not, and so does business.

In the case of the excursion boat, a line of obstructions down the center of the boat and a few deck stewards trained to break up any undue rush would be sufficient to prevent a recurrence of the upset without the necessity of interfering with the passengers' normal individual liberty to walk around the deck as they pleased. The individual business man has everything to gain from having his actions impeded or deflected at the points where they are likely to produce destruction or economic collapse.

Appendix H. Labor Interest

The effect of pressure from labor upon industrial policy will vary with the particular aspect of labor interest which its representatives are pressing at any time. In each industry, labor has two interests: (1) An interest in full and steady employment which calls for the full and continuous operation of that industry; and (2) an interest in higher money wages which calls for a division of the money spoils more nearly in its favor. It has usually no consumer interest in its own industry, although the individual workers have an important consumer interest in other industries.

American labor organization (except for the revolutionary unions) has been built upon the principle of securing a favorable division of the money spoils through collective bargaining. It has not been primarily concerned with maintaining employment or protecting real wages through price. In the face of rising prices, its pressure has been to raise wages to cover those prices rather than to keep prices down. Moreover, where labor has been represented by the spokesmen for exclusive groups of workers, as in the building trades, its interest in high money wages for its own group of workers has led it to disregard the interests of the rest of labor and to agree to or to force industrial policy which often curtails employment and raises prices.

In only a few cases—e.g., the Amalgamated Clothing Workers or the role played by organized labor in Josephine Roche's Rocky Mountain Fuel Co.—has labor shared in industrial policy making beyond seeking its share of the spoils. The N.R.A. has given labor a new role. The spokesmen for labor, whose experience has frequently been that of representing an exclusive labor group rather than the whole body of labor in the industry, have not infrequently carried to their new policy-making responsibilities the attitudes which have gone with collective bargaining. Labor representatives are always in danger of being persuaded by the offer of a slightly larger share in the spoils (witness the agreement of labor to restriction of production in the cotton-textile industry) to accept a policy which is neither in the interest of labor nor the public.

The problem of building labor into the structure of industry as a participant in the making of industrial policy thus involves a shift on the part of labor representatives from almost exclusive preoccupation with the sharing of the money spoils by any exclusive group of workers to the increase in the total spoils to be distributed, not only in money but, through low prices, in goods. It means a primary regard for the interest of the whole body of workers in employment and real income for all. It involves the reorienting of labor organization to a new kind of job, the technical training of its representatives which will enable them to recognize labor's interest in a complex industrial situation, and the recognition of the importance of the interests of workers as consumers. This does not mean that collective bargaining over a division of the spoils does not remain a function of labor organization, but only that a new responsibility of sharing in the making of industrial policy needs to be assumed.

Appendix I. The Consumer Interest

The consumer interest as an organized interest administratively represented is new to both economic and political organization in America. The Consumers Advisory Board of N.R.A., the Consumers' Counsel of A.A.A., and the Consumers' Division of the National Emergency Council are the first specifically consumer agencies to be set up in Washington. Except for the relatively weak consumer cooperative movement, and the small membership organization, Consumers' Research, organized consumers have played no significant industrial role.

Under traditional laissez faire conditions, the consumer had a large share in determining the course of economic activity through his purchasing here or there, buying or refraining from buying. Indeed, the primary justification for a system of laissez faire has been the assertion that if each individual were allowed to produce and sell freely in the market in the interest of his own profit, the net result would be a system which approached the ideal from the point of the consumer. The great advantage of the traditional thesis was the perfect and reasonable service which it promised the consumer. In many cases the consumer has been deified as the arbiter of industrial policy, since the loss of his patronage was supposed to be so immediately effective in causing price readjustments.

Undoubtedly, in the days of small enterprises, there was much validity in this picture. The consumer was in a position to shift his trade from one competitor to another offering the same article, to come face to face with the seller and bargain with him on relatively equal terms, to know perhaps as much as the seller about the qualities of the article offered for sale. The consumer could exercise a very real control over production and over the prices at which sales were actually made. So long as the organization of economic activity was brought about primarily through the free market, the consumer was in a position to carry his share in controlling the economic process.

The development of administrative power in place of market coordination has greatly weakened the position of the consumer. The concentration into great units has steadily reduced the control which the consumer can exercise over enterprise activity through the market place. The consumer is faced with administered prices, a "take it or leave it" policy, and only a few sellers of each particular product. No longer can he come face to face with the owner of the enterprise with which he is doing business. Nor has he a multitude of sellers whom he can pit one against the other for his business. To an increasing extent he is in an unfavorable bargaining position and is forced to take what is offered at the price at which it is offered or go without.

His position is further weakened by the barrage of advertising to which he is subjected. In a great number of cases, moreover, he has to buy commodities of whose characteristics he can know little, yet whose qualities are well known to the seller or manufacturer. Unlike like consumers in a simpler economy, the modern consumer meets the bulk of his wants through purchases and tends to be unfamiliar with the actual making of the commodities which he buys. Yet these commodities are to an increasing extent made of highly fabricated materials about which science has given the manufacturer a wealth of knowledge. Thus, not only is the consumer no longer in a position to bargain face to face with the seller and share directly in the determination of price, but he is bludgeoned into buying something about which he knows vastly less than the seller or manufacturer. Though the consumer is frequently hailed as the objective of all attention, the effect of the shift from coordination of activity by the free market to administrative action has steadily reduced the direct influence of the consumer on price-and-production policy.

Weak though the consumer is, his point of view would seem to be an essential ingredient in the making of industrial policy, for his interest is in the very things which constitute industrial policy, namely, the production and distribution of goods and services, while business interest remains preoccupied with creating value.[11]

It has been traditional among both economists and business men to view the economic process as a process of production, looking down the stream of goods and regarding consumption as the last step where the goods go over the Niagara Falls into the maw of the consumer. Actually, there is just as great logical justification for describing the whole economic process as one of consumption. We consume raw materials, we consume labor, and each step in the process is a step in the consumption of available resources. Here the point of view adopted is at the lower end of the stream of goods looking upstream. Goods move toward the observer not away from him.

These two opposing points of view do not change the character of the economic process, but they do cast into the foreground different aspects in that process and make for a quite different emphasis. To the producer-minded, the first thought in an industrial program is: "How can the existing productive instruments be made to return value?'' To the consumer-minded, the first thought is: ''What goods are needed for ultimate consumption?'' To the producer-minded, the curtailment of production, limitation of hours, and lifting of prices can appear to be a satisfactory solution to a specific problem. The person habitually adopting the consumer point of view will never be misled into producing scarcity of goods.

In meeting any specific situation, it is essential to recognize that the public interest and the consumer interest are not identical. The consumer interest is only one of the many economic interests involved in our economy—it is the interest of buyers rather than that of investors, workers, producers, sellers. To confuse the public interest with the much more specific consumer interest is to lose sight of the even-handed balance which is implicit in the term ''the public interest,'' even though all persons are consumers and all persons are also the public.The lack of identity between consumer and public interests is apparent in any specific situation where the difference in interest between the various groups involved is clear, and the general identity of those who constitute the body of consumers and the public does not obscure this difference. Thus, if the size of the cotton crop is under consideration, the consumer interest and the cotton farmer's interest may be in conflict. Yet both groups together constitute the public. To place any Government official in the position of having to represent both the public interest and the consumer interest is to make him both judge of all parties and counsel for one of the parties at interest. The confusion between consumer and public interests has made the N.R.A. fail in the past year to give such weight to the consumer interest in arriving at its decisions as would best serve the public interest to which the N.R.A. is devoted.

The organization and effective representation of the consumer point of view could take two quite distinct forms—the organization of individuals as consumers and the organization of the consumer interest. The difficulty of organizing consumers as individuals has often been pointed out. Nobody is a consumer, because everybody is a consumer; everybody is also a producer and people are more likely to act in their interest as producers than as consumers. The weakness of the consumers' cooperative movement in the United States is frequently cited as evidence of the failure to get organized consumer activity.

Much more feasible is the organization and representation of the consumer interest, for existing organizations which are not specifically producer organizations —e.g., professional groups, engineers, chemists, etc., or women's organizations—can function in the interest of their members as consumers, and even definitely producer organizations, such as farm or labor organizations, can act for their members in the many specific situations in which the interest of their members is primarily a consumer interest. Most importantly, the technicians are the logical representatives of the consumer interest, since their interest and skill are devoted to producing goods and services, not values.

Appendix J. The Farmer's Interest

The farmer is the prototype of the enterprise unit to which laissez faire applied and for which the market tends to operate most nearly according to the pattern indicated by that philosophy. If it were not for the concentration in other fields, it is quite probable that industrial policy in the field of agriculture could be left entirely to the market. As it is, the farmer has been forced to deal with large organized units, both in buying agricultural implements, fertilizer, etc., and in selling to packers, milk distributors, tobacco manufacturers, sugar refiners, etc., so that he is no longer connected to the ultimate consumer by a free market. The flexibility of his prices has made him bear the brunt of price adjustments, while as a purchaser of industrial goods he has been confronted with a policy of high price maintenance. The market for his products has at the same time been curtailed by the destruction of the purchasing power of the unemployed resulting from the industrialist's policy of curtaining production. It is, to a large extent, his relations with the rest of the economy rather than the problems of his own industry which place the farmer in a difficult position.

It is quite probable that, once recovery has been brought, and if a suitable industrial policy can be established in the processing and marketing industries, most agricultural problems with respect to policy can be left to the market, except as techniques are developed for insuring against crop failures, facilitating the removal of submarginal land from cultivation, etc.

The farmer has a vital interest in the industrial policies of the processing and marketing industries and in the industries making the things which he buys and would need to be represented either as farmer or as consumer on any bodies making policy with respect to those industries.

Appendix K. An American Basis for Economic Reorganization

1. Any satisfactory technique for the making of industrial policy must be relevant both to the factual situation and to American traditions.

2. The facts to be met are:

(*a*) Laissez faire has failed; i.e., the market mechanism has broken down.

(*b*) The banking and money system has failed to meet the needs of modern technology and modern industrial organization.

(*c*) Modern technology makes possible a high standard of living for all.

(*d*) Modern technology requires great administrative organizations.

(*e*) These industrial organizations must be coordinated and their operation in the public interest insured.

3. The American tradition demands that a solution be sought which preserves the maximum of liberty, democracy, and opportunity and at the same time provides plenty and security and lies wholly within the framework of the Constitution.

4. Neither the evidence of the facts nor the conviction of the American people has established or accepted the principle that democracy itself has failed, or that the social management made necessary by modern technology and the break-down of the market requires dictatorship, regimentation, the loss of civil liberties, or the elimination of profit making and a reduction in the exercise of individual initiative.

5. The positive principles for economic reorganization which fit the fact situation and which are consonant with the American tradition are:

(*a*) Responsibility should be linked to power, wherever such power lies, whether in the hands of business, labor, farmer, or consumer groups.

(*b*) Any group should have the free right to organize and act for the furtherance of its own interest, provided that such action is responsible and that it does not impair the operation of the economic machine.

(*c*) A balance of economic interest should be maintained among the groups which make up industry.

(*d*) A balance should be achieved between centralization and decentralization, with the maximum decentralization compatible with adequate coordination.

(*e*) Human and material resources should be used to the full.

(*f*) To government should be entrusted those things which government can do best, leaving to the separate elements in industry those things which each can do best and assigning to groups combining both government and the elements of industry those things which neither government nor the several groups in industry can do well alone.

6. The essential structure of a reorganized economy should—

(*a*) Maintain existing institutions, both economic and governmental, intact as far as possible.

(*b*) Use the market mechanism wherever it can continue to function.

(*c*) Supplement or supplant the market mechanism by devices for the determination of industrial policy—code authorities, crop-control committees, etc., which adequately represent the several economic interests involved and which are neither wholly private nor wholly governmental but constitute a "partnership" between government and industry.

(*d*) Make further provision for the smooth and equitable functioning of the economic machine through a banking system designed to meet the monetary needs of the economy, such adjustment of the flow of investment as will insure a balance between saving and spending, and adequate provision through social insurance or otherwise for the victims of the accidents and adjustments from which no economic system can be free.

Appendix L. The Necessity for Supplying the Right Amount of Monetary Medium

1. The present banking system is organized to fit an atomistic economy—i.e., an economy in which practically all industrial policy is made in the imper-

sonal market and in which no individuals or organized groups have any significant power over industrial policy. It assumes that prices are highly flexible and that adjustment to changing conditions takes place rapidly through changing prices.

2. In our actual economy, such extensive powers over industrial policy are exercised by individuals in many industries that prices in those industries become relatively inflexible and adjustment to declining demand is made through reduction in volume of production rather than in price, with the resulting curtailment of employment and dearth of spending power.

3. It is this introduction of wide-spread price rigidities into the economic system which necessitates a rebuilding of the banking system to fit this changed condition.

4. Where prices are highly flexible, a moderate change in the volume of the monetary medium (including commercial bank deposits as part of the monetary medium) produces very little economic disruption. If the volume of the monetary medium is reduced, there will be a slight contraction in the demand for all sorts of different commodities, prices will drop slightly in almost every industry, and a new price level will be established which is in balance with the reduced supply of money. The same thing would happen whenever conditions developed such that a larger volume of money was needed to support the existing level of prices and the actual volume of money remained constant. Prices would readjust at a lower level without serious economic dislocation. The presence of rigid debt would, of course, mean that a drop in price level would make the debt burden heavier on particular individuals, but, if there were no depression and no serious drop in prices, the shifting burden of debt would be of secondary importance. This means that changes in the volume of money could then be looked upon as unimportant. In such an economy, there would be no problem of supplying the right amount of money.

5. The present Federal Reserve System was drafted with the express aim of taking advantage of this assumed unimportance of changes in the volume of money and of price level so as to insure the utmost safety of the money medium by having it based, at least so far as deposits are concerned, on prime commercial paper. This meant that the volume of money was expected to fluctuate with the volume of business activity so that a drop in business activity would bring a drop in the volume of money outstanding.

6. Where, in an important number of industries, individual business men are in a position to hold prices and reduce production—i.e., where prices are inflexible and changes in demand affect not price but volume of production and volume of employment—a change in the price level due to a moderate change in the volume of money (or in the need for money) becomes a matter of major consequence. If the volume of money is reduced, it tends to produce a slight drop in demand for all sorts of commodities. In those industries in which prices are flexible, prices drop as a result of the drop in demand for all sorts of commodi-

ties. In those industries in which control over industrial policy is sufficient to hold prices, the drop in general demand tends to result in a drop in production, increased unemployment, reduction in the incomes of both workers and investors, and a further drop in general demand. This in itself could set up a serious recession in business which could amplify itself into a serious depression. Likewise, if the volume of money were to remain constant when conditions developed such that a larger volume of money was required to support the existing price level, a general drop in demand would result with the same effect as if the volume of money had been reduced. (Perhaps something like this happened in the latter part of 1929, thus aggravating the recession in business activity in the capital goods industries, which was already under way.) It is thus apparent that where prices are inflexible a serious decline in business activity could result from purely monetary causes and that in such cases the remedy would be an expansion in the volume of the monetary medium at the time when business activity was declining.

7. This means that the banking system has been organized on the assumption of flexible prices, with the aim of reducing the volume of money when business activity declined, yet, due to the rigidity of prices it is expansion of the volume of money which may be, and probably is, required to prevent further decline in business activity. This means that the present banking system, insofar as it works as its creators intended, tends to reduce the volume of money at the very time when its increase is required for a proper functioning of the economic machine.

8. It is thus clear that where extensive price inflexibility exists in the economy, the banking system must not only perform its well-recognized function of supplying safe money, but it must also supply the right amount of money.

9. The right amount of money would be the amount which would put the least pressure for a general revision, upward or downward of the relatively inflexible prices. When an economy was functioning properly, this would mean keeping the relatively flexible prices in line with the less flexible prices. This would also tend to keep debt, and particularly money, at a more constant purchasing power. In a depressed economy, this would mean a gradual increase in money volume (or a decrease in the need for money) to bring the prices of the more flexibly priced commodities into line with the rigidly priced commodities; i.e., those in which important elements of industrial policy tend to be made by individuals rather than by the market. Such a lift in the more flexible prices could not be brought about effectively by monetary action unless the making of industrial policy were in appropriate hands, since the phobia with respect to inflation would lead to arbitrary lifting of the prices in the industries in which prices are subject to the control of individuals (witness the price history of some industries in 1933), thus defeating the objective of monetary policy.

10. The establishment of appropriate monetary policy (assuming industrial policy is taken care of) requires (1) that a technique should be established for

keeping close track of prices of varying degrees of flexibility and particularly their relation to each other as an indication of appropriate policy and (2) that control over the volume of money should be in some central body, presumably the Federal Government.

Notes

1. Even if in a particular case all other industries had lowered prices, it would not be sound business policy for a particular industry to lower its prices but rather to reap the benefits at the old prices of the increased volume of activity resulting from the actions of the other industries. Only if the lowering of prices on the part of all other industries were dependent on the action of the particular industry would sound business policy call for a lowering of price and even then sound business policy would mean attempting to force other industries to lower prices as much as possible while the particular industry lowered its prices as little as possible.

2. This principle was made use of in the N.R.A. when the advisory council was set up composed of representatives from the three advisory boards (business, labor, and consumer), thereby removing from the administrators the impact of conflict among the advisory boards.

3. Determination of industrial policy by either labor or consumer groups alone, or by a combination of the two, is not a realistic possibility in America at present, short of a violent revolution.

4. This statement, though greatly oversimplified, gives the essentials of the laissez faire philosophy. There is no need at this point to go into just what constitutes the ''right'' amount or ''right'' price for things.

5. Some further reduction over quoted prices was made in certain cases through giving credit for abnormally low prices for certain agricultural products, but this does not affect the principle that the primary effect of the depressed demand was on production, not prices.

6. For any manufacturer who was willing to produce and sell at the current price more than he was actually producing, ''willing capacity'' would exceed amount produced.

7. Frederick C. Mills, in *The Behavior of Prices*, has distributed certain price series according to frequency of price change but presented the statistical results without drawing conclusions. His figures showed the same U-shaped distribution.

8. Differential returns to particular investors would reflect the differences in risk. The average return was expected to reflect only the scarcity of capital.

9. Other interest groups could be included as the transporters of cotton, whether railroad or truck, etc., but the major interests are covered above and the minor interests would usually only supplement one or another of the major interests.

10. It should be more properly called the ''Business Advisory Board.''

11. When labor organizations act in the interest of wages rather than of employment, they are exerting pressure toward value rather than toward production.

4

The Major Causes of the Depression

The causes of the present depression are not simple. Neither are they easily disentangled from all the varying influences which have been at work in our society during the last decade or more. The present memorandum is an effort to set forth what appear to be the major influences that resulted in the present depressed economic conditions.

The main problem is to discover why, in the short three year period from 1929 to 1932, the National Income produced dropped from 83 billion dollars to 39 billion dollars[1]; why the total farm cash income dropped from $12 billion to $5 billion[2]; why the total number of unemployed increased by over ten million and the total wages and salaries of workers dropped from $52.8 billion to $31.5 billion[3] and why interest and dividends declined from $12.2 billion to $8.4 billion.[4] No drought or war, earthquake or pestilence came to scourge the American people and force this contraction of income on practically every group in the community. Both men and machines were available to produce greater income. Yet tremendous unused capacity to produce existed side by side with dire want and distress from the lack of the very things which could be produced. Men and machines were increasingly idle while the standard of living of the American people declined. Why did this "poverty in the midst of plenty" develop and why did it continue?

No certain answer can be given to this question yet there are many developments in the period leading up to the depression which stand out as more significant and which in combination must be regarded as largely responsible for the decline in economic activity.

These developments take the form of slow or more rapid changes in the technical or institutional conditions under which our economy is operating. They produce their effect, not directly by instituting a depression, but indirectly by

June 19, 1935. From the Gardiner C. Means Papers at the Franklin D. Roosevelt Library, Series I: National Recovery Administration, "Depression."

making the economy particularly susceptible to violent fluctuation in activity. They are developments which in combination prevent the maintenance of the balance which is essential to a healthy economy.

The more important developments of this kind in the years before the depression can be grouped under three heads:

1. those which necessitated great and rapid economic readjustments if the economy was to be kept in balance;
2. those which decreased the flexibility of the economic structure and tended to impede automatic readjustment;
3. and those which transformed the usual economic drives from forces working toward economic readjustment into forces tending to produce further maladjustment and greater unbalance in the economy.

In the first group belong such developments as the rapid increase in automobile transportation, the shift of this country from a debtor to a creditor nation, and the expansion in the use of electricity. Each of these brought the necessity for great and rapid change in ways of living or in the character of industrial activity.

In the second group belong such developments as the increasing height of tariff barriers, the increased inflexibility of prices, and the increasing concentration of industrial control. Each of these helped to reduce economic flexibility and to impede the economic readjustments called for by the first group of developments.

The developments in the third group are more complex in their action and will be considered in more detail below. They involve the forces which determine the money supply, the rate of industrial production, etc. which have traditionally been depended upon to work in the direction of maintaining or reestablishing economic balance but which, under certain conditions, work in the opposite direction.

The developments of the predepression years will be considered under the three headings above, even though it is not possible to determine the exact extent to which each development or each type of development contributed in producing the depression. Almost certainly the decline of industrial activity was the result of the *interaction* of many different developments, one set requiring economic readjustment, another set impeding adjustment, and a third set aggravating the unbalance already created. It is believed that the more important developments of each type are covered below and their interaction indicated.

I. Developments Requiring Economic Readjustment

Developments calling for important economic readjustments within the American economy in recent years can be roughly grouped into:

a. those in evidence before the World War;
b. those appearing in the postwar years.

For the United States, probably the five most important long-time developments have been:

1. The disappearance of the frontier;
2. The increase in the production and use of the automobile, bus, motor truck and tractor;
3. The development of electricity;
4. Technological improvement in industry resulting in greater output per worker;
5. The shift from a debtor to a creditor nation.

In the war and postwar years added factors developed calling for extensive and rapid economic readjustment and greatly accelerated the factors already mentioned. The more important of such developments are listed below:

1. Acceleration in the rate of technological improvement producing displacement of men by machines.
2. Wartime expansion of agricultural production to meet a temporary demand.
3. Rapid and temporary expansion in construction activity to fill in the wartime deficit in housing.
4. Rapid and temporary acceleration in automobile production.
5. Increased importance of automobile transportation.
6. A heavy increase in the burden of urban mortgage debt—frequently based on real estate values out of line with real estate requirements.
7. The decrease in the stability of monetary units—devaluation of currencies, etc.
8. A capitalization in the security markets of the increased and impermanent profits arising from the displacement of labor by machines.
9. The development of an increasingly large and complex superstructure of financial and holding companies based largely on the capitalization of the temporary profits of labor displacement or of financial manipulation.
10. Rapidly and arbitrarily changing tariffs, import quotas, etc.
11. The changing character of the relations between nations as to the payment of interest and principal on war debts.
12. Rapid and irresponsible or unskilled expansion of loans to foreign governments, companies, or individuals.

All of these developments called for significant economic readjustments. In some cases a change in the character or rate of expansion of a particular economic activity was called for. In other cases a positive contraction or a complete relocation of productive effort was required if economic balance was to be maintained. The World War speeded up the developments calling for change, increased their impact, or introduced new developments. The complexity of forces at work and the magnitude of the changes and adjustments required to maintain economic balance are clearly indicated in the following section which takes up separately each of the more important changes calling for economic readjustment.

1. The Disappearance of the Frontier

The disappearance of the frontier has been so frequently discussed that it needs no intensive discussion here. It is clearly reflected in the cessation of the century-long expansion of the acreage under cultivation. The rapid growth in cultivated acreage and the break in that growth after 1918 is clearly indicated in Chart I.* If the war expansion in acreage had not occurred, it is probable that the end of the expansion in acreage would have come more gradually. But the war only brought the expansion period to a close more suddenly and in a manner to place an unusually heavy burden of adjustment on the individual farmer.

This ending of acreage expansion called for a reversal of the long-time momentum of agricultural development. No longer could agriculture absorb large numbers of new workers. No longer could the farmer's son or the unemployed worker find new cheap land to develop. Further economic expansion had to take the form of industrial expansion or the slow development of more intensive cultivation in agriculture. The whole status of agriculture was altered by this disappearance of the frontier, and extensive adjustments to the new status were made necessary. The whole thrust of economic expansion was shifted away from agriculture and into the field of industry.

2. The Development of the Automobile, Bus, Tractor, and Truck

Coincident with the passing of the frontier, has been the development of an automobile civilization. Probably no single development has forced more rapid change on the American economy than the widespread use of automotive equipment, particularly automobiles, tractors, and trucks. Change has come through the tremendous increase in the production of such equipment and through its actual use. The rapid growth in automobile production since 1900 is shown in Chart II, while Chart III shows the great increase in the number of automobiles (including trucks) in use. Horses were displaced by metal; hay and grain by gasoline. This eliminated a significant market for agricultural products, both horses and feed, and at the same time shifted much of the tractive power used on the farm from horse power raised on the farm to horse power produced in the factory and chemical plant. The automobile and truck shifted passengers and freight from the railroads, and their widespread use called for significant changes both in the character of railroad terminal facilities and in railroad operation. The automobile brought great development of highways and radically altered the interrelation between urban and rural centers, developing intermediate urban areas which drew population out of the cities with consequent effect on real estate and other values.

---

*The charts referred to in this chapter were not prepared.

The above are only a few of the many effects produced by the production and widespread use of the automobile (and tractor and truck) on economic and social organization. Yet these important effects have been condensed into a few short years—mostly since the World War. The rapidity with which they have come has placed a tremendous burden of adjustment on the economic system.

3. The Development of Electricity

A third development of major significance is the great development of electric power and the shift from steam driven to electrically driven machinery. In the short period from [dates not specified] the installed electric capacity has mounted from [dates not specified]. The flexibility of electricity has called for greater decentralization of industry and for shifts of industry away from the older centers of production. The rapid expansion in its use has facilitated another development, the improvement of industrial techniques.

4. Technological Improvement in Industry

The fourth great sphere of change is to be found in the great and continuous process of technological improvement in industry. As technology improves, the number of workers necessary to do a given job decreases. If technological improvement takes place slowly enough the men displaced by the machine tend to be reabsorbed elsewhere with sufficient rapidity to present no serious social problem. When technical improvement takes place at a rapid rate, however, technological unemployment becomes serious as the men thrown out of work fail to be reabsorbed quickly in other directions. The social gain from rapidly increased productivity thus places a heavy burden of unemployment on individual workers. Technological improvement in recent years is reflected in Chart IV which shows estimates of the productivity per man-hour over the last thirty-five years. The estimates are admittedly crude yet their general import is clear. The continued progress in technology which they show has necessitated continuous adjustment while the extremely rapid increase in productivity in the postwar years has aggravated the problem and even before the depression appears to have produced extensive technological unemployment.

5. The Shift from a Debtor to a Creditor Nation

A fourth significant development, likewise aggravated by the war, has been the shift of the United States from a debtor to a creditor nation. Before the war this country was a debtor country. Great sums of money had been borrowed from foreigners to construct many of our railroad systems, etc. The country regularly had a so-called "favorable balance" of trade as it was exporting goods to pay interest on this debt and to repay principal. However, the country was approaching the point at which it would be exporting more capital than it imported. A continuation of this process even without the war would have brought the country to the point where, on balance, it was a creditor rather than a debtor nation. The war greatly speeded up the repayment of American debt to foreigners particularly as European holdings of American securities were sold to Americans. At the same time the great war loans to foreign nations tipped the balance way over to the point where this country was, on balance, a major creditor nation. The country thus became a creditor nation long before it would have at the earlier rate of change. This development is clearly shown in Chart V. The huge size of the credits existing after the war called for a heavy "adverse" balance of trade—that is, if the interest and principal of foreign debts both private and public were to be paid, the United States had to receive goods and services greatly in excess of those sold to foreigners.[5] This meant either a great restriction of exports, a great increase in imports, or a combination of the two, if international economic relations were to be maintained on a stable basis.

In addition to these major long-time developments the war period introduced new factors which made necessary extensive and rapid readjustment if economic stability was to be maintained.

6. *The Postwar Construction Boom*

Of these perhaps the most important was the rapid expansion in construction after the war which filled up the wartime deficiency in housing. This boom in construction is clearly indicated in Chart VI. The lack of construction during the war necessitated a temporary acceleration in construction activity which drew men and material resources into the construction field to an extent much greater than could be maintained once the deficit in construction had been made good. As the supply of housing, etc., was brought more nearly into balance with the population, a decline in the rate of construction was to be predicted, necessitating a shift of resources out of the field of construction and into other fields. This decline in construction activity was clearly in evidence by the end of 1928, as the chart indicates. Such a decline called for a shifting of resources of men and materials into other avenues of use.

7. *Instability of International Monetary Relationships*

The war also brought great instability in the relationships of the monetary units of different countries. Nearly every war country inflated its monetary medium to such an extent that by the end of the war the values of the units of different countries were seriously out of equilibrium. The direct impact of disequilibrium was postponed during the war by stringent exchange regulation but after the war one country after another lost control of its monetary medium until the monetary stability which had been developed in the prewar years was largely destroyed.

This instability in money units necessitated more frequent and more violent adjustments in the trade relations between different countries.

8. The Development of Great International Balances

Partly as a result of the monetary instability and partly as a result of other factors, great pools of inter-country short-term debt-credit were developed after the war. One country would build up credits in a foreign country as part of its own bank reserves while individual lenders placed large sums of short-term credit in foreign countries, shifting them from country to country as opportunity for more profitable use made its appearance. These huge mobile pools of credit developed to the point where shifts in their location from one country to another tended to become more important than shifts in the normal trade balances between countries and tended to submerge the adjustments which the changes in internal price levels have been relied upon to produce. The repeated and unpredictable shifts or potential shifts in short-term credit balances made necessary great and repeated shifts or potential shifts and readjustments in the currents of international trade.

9. The Changing Status of War Debts and Reparations

A further factor calling for change in adjustment was the uncertainty which surrounded the international war debts and reparations. So long as it was uncertain what part of the war debts and reparations would ultimately be paid, the complex international relationships were in a constant state of flux. Successive changes in the status of war debts and reparations made necessary important and often unpredictable readjustments in the economic relationships between countries.

10. Postwar Expansion in American Loans

Coupled with the war debt problem was an extensive expansion in loans by American bankers to foreign governments and companies. These loans were made easy by the peculiar strains established by the war debts, etc., and were made largely in an unskilled or irresponsible fashion. They amounted to significant sums (see Chart V) and largely postponed the economic readjustment made necessary by the shift of this country to the position of a creditor nation. It was inevitable that when the insubstantial character of many of these loans was realized, the whole flow of American loans to foreigners would come to a swift halt—a reversal in the flow of credit that would in turn necessitate rapid adjustment in the flow of international trade.

11. Development of Economic Nationalism

Combined with the breakdown of monetary stability and the building up of material foreign balances and of the shift in debtor-creditor relationships, a vigorous trend toward economic nationalism developed. The effect of this development of nationalism in impeding economic adjustment will be considered below. For the present its importance lies in the unpredictable and arbitrary character of the changes which this growing nationalism introduced—changes which in turn forced adjustment on different parts of the world economy. This economic nationalism took the form of tariffs, import quotas, and other restrictive measures which introduced sudden and artificial changes in the trade relationships between countries, thereby necessitating quick changes in the flow of trade itself.

12. Farm Debt

One more factor calling for adjustment growing out of the war deserves mention—the great increase in farm mortgages. As Chart VII indicates, the total debt on farms nearly tripled in the few short years of the war period. This heavy burden of debt was built on the temporary wartime values of land and was out of line with more normal farm values. This abnormally heavy debt called for positive readjustment.

Many other developments took place in the predepression years which made rapid economic readjustment a necessity. Certain of these appear to have grown out of postwar maladjustments and will be considered later as the interaction of the increased need for adjustment and increased barriers to adjustment are taken up. These developments include the great expansion in urban mortgages, the pyramiding of the complex structure of financial and holding companies, etc.

The effect of all the foregoing developments and the many lesser developments which are not considered here combined to place on the economic system a tremendous burden for making extensive and rapid economic adjustments if economic stability was to be maintained. While in some cases these developments may have, in a measure, offset each other, in the main they combined to necessitate greater adjustment—adjustments of a magnitude little realized at the time—adjustments which could only take place with the necessary rapidity in an economy in which all or most of the elements were highly flexible.

II. Developments Reducing Economic Flexibility

At the same time that the foregoing developments were calling for important economic readjustments and requiring a highly flexible system, other developments were taking place which greatly reduced the flexibility of the economic system and impeded the making of the necessary economic readjustment. The more important of these developments are listed below.

1. The increasing concentration of economic activity into great administrative organizations which resulted in relatively inflexible administered prices.
2. The development of economic nationalism which undertook to prevent or impede economic adjustment.

3. The development of international cartels or price agreements in many commodities.

4. The building up of debts which inhibited economic adjustment.

1. The Increasing Concentration of Economic Activity Resulting in Inflexible Administered Prices

Probably the most important single factor increasing the inflexibility in the American economy has been the greatly increased concentration of economic activity. The growing concentration of economic activity into large units is indicated in Chart VIII which shows the proportion of all non-financial corporate wealth controlled by the 200 corporations largest in each successive year. According to the best available figures, over 55 percent of corporate wealth (exclusive of banks, etc.) is controlled by 200 companies. These figures do not indicate the full degree of concentration since interlocking directorates, banking control, etc., are not covered. Yet standing alone they show clearly the extent to which the economy has developed away from the simple one-man enterprise such as exists in farming and in much of retailing and upon which so many of our institutions have been built.

Part of this concentration has involved a shift of economic activity from the unregulated to the regulated sphere—railroads at an earlier period and more recently electric power. Such concentration almost necessarily carries with it relatively inflexible rates or prices for service and though these are subject to some measure of governmental control the inflexibility of the rates established may be just as significant in impeding economic readjustment as inflexibility of prices in unregulated fields. At the same time, the protection of wealth afforded to the utilities by the courts in the guise of protecting property makes adjustment still more difficult.

A major part of the economic concentration has taken place in the areas supposed to be adequately governed by the market and price mechanism. Here the concentration has frequently developed to the point where a few large units, though perhaps competing among themselves, dominate the industry. This has resulted in inflexible administered prices which have in themselves also impeded economic adjustment, as will be seen below. The actual extent to which the inflexible prices have come to dominate the unregulated part of the economy is indicated in Chart IX.[6] The chart covers the bulk of the items in the Bureau of Labor Statistics Wholesale Prices index and distributes them according to frequency of price change. The inflexible administered prices—prices which change infrequently and which impede adjustment—are represented at the left of the chart and the traditional flexible prices which facilitate adjustment are indicated at the right. More than half the items belong to the inflexible group.

In addition to the economic concentration in the corporate form, concentration has developed to a lesser extent in other forms, presumably in large part as a protective reaction to corporate concentration, and reduced the flexibility of the market. This concentration has mostly taken the form of farm cooperatives, business associations, labor organization, and consumers cooperatives. In most fields this concentration into bargaining organizations has not carried to a significant extent. In a few industries one or another of these types of organization had become sufficiently strong by 1929 to markedly reduce the flexibility to adjustment through the market mechanism. The whole development toward economic concentration has tremendously reduced the flexibility of the price mechanism through which economic adjustment is supposed to be brought about.

2. The Development of Economic Nationalism

A second major influence making economic readjustment more difficult has been the development of a positive economic nationalism which attempted to prevent readjustments in the trade relations between countries from taking place. This economic nationalism has taken the form of building prohibitive tariff walls, etc., in a manner to prevent readjustments which otherwise would have taken place. Thus, the American tariff of 1922 and again that of 1930 tended to thwart the readjustments called for by the shift of this country from a debtor to a creditor nation.

3. International Valorization Schemes or Cartels

A third development of great significance in impeding economic adjustment has been the creation of national or international valorization schemes which sought to control prices. A list of a few important schemes is given in Table I [Table 4.1]. While these efforts were seldom successful in maintaining prices over a long period of time, they would act often, during the period of several years, to maintain prices and prevent basic readjustment.

4. The Building Up of Internal Debt

The fourth development of importance impeding adjustment has been the extensive building up of internal debt in the United States. Debt in and of itself tends to prevent normal economic readjustment or even to distort it. Thus, the increase in farm debt, already mentioned, tended to maintain farm land in cultivation even when in absence of debt the land would be retired from use. The heavy increase in urban mortgage debt has tended to inhibit readjustments in real estate rentals in a similar manner. In other fields debt has mounted in the war and postwar periods to the point of acting at least to some extent as a resistance to adjustment.

5. The Lag in Governmental Institutions

Finally, as American economic institutions have developed and the economy has become more closely interrelated and more closely integrated, the American

Table 4.1

Postwar Valorization Schemes*

Commodity	Period of valorization project	Participants in project
Crude rubber	1922–28	Great Britain, colonial governments (Stevenson plan)
Coffee	1922-	Sao Paulo Coffee Institute, backed by State of Sao Paulo (and Brazilian government to 1924)
Wheat	1923-	Canadian cooperative pools
	1929-	United States Federal Farm Board
Silk	1914–22	Japan, producers, with government cooperation
	1926–28	
	1929-	
Sugar	1925–28	Cuban government
	1929	Cuban government
Cotton		
Long staple	1921–30	Egyptian government
Short staple	1929-	United States Federal Farm Board
Copper	1926–30	Copper Exporters, Inc. backed by 90% of world production
	1929-	Copper producers
Nitrates	1919–27	Chilean Nitrate Producers' Assn.
	1928-	Chilean Nitrate Producers' Assn.
	1929-	Internatl. agreement of Chilean, British, & German producers
Potash	1924–25	Agreement of Germans and Alsatian cartels
	1926-	Internatl. cartel of German & Alsatian producers
Mercury	1928-	Internatl. cartel sanctioned by Spanish and Italian govts.
Sulphur	1923-	Agreement of Italian and American producers
Sisal	1920-	Mexican & Yucatan govts. with producers' assn.
Quinine	1918-	Assn. of most producers & all manufacturers outside of U.S.; dominated by Dutch
Camphor	1899-	Japanese & Formosan govts.
Major international cartels, not directly affecting prices in the U.S.		
Steel	1926–	Producers of Belgium, France, Germany, Luxemburg & Saar Basin & from 1927 Czechoslovakia, Austria & Hungary
Aluminum	1926-	French, British, Swiss & German producers
Margarine	1927-	English and Dutch trusts
Rayon	1927–29	English, German, Italian, Dutch & Belgian producers
Zinc	1928-	Belgian, Dutch, French, German, Polish, British, & Spanish producers

*From *Economic Tendencies in the United States,* by Frederick C. Mills, National Bureau of Economic Research (New York, 1932), pp. 327–329.

political institutions have lagged far behind. They have been incapable of dealing with the intricate problems growing out of the new conditions established by economic concentration. While the lag in the development of political institutions has occurred both in the legislative and the administrative arms of government, the primary force impeding development has been the judicial arm. By a long line of decisions the Supreme Court has impeded the development of powers on the part of the Federal Government coordinate with the responsibilities which the Federal Government has been forced to assume as economic concentration has progressed far beyond the confines of state lines and presented problems the solution of which is beyond the scope of the individual state. A slight indication of the way in which economic concentration has overpassed state lines and presented problems of regional or national scope is indicated in the attached charts. The Supreme Court has marked the dividing line between State and Federal powers at such a point that the Federal Government, in a position to deal with problems as a whole, has been allocated insufficient powers to do so while the individual states to which the powers have been allocated are in a position to deal only with isolated parts. Thus, the lack of adjustment of the governmental machinery to modern industrial conditions added one more element of inflexibility to predepression conditions.

These developments impeding adjustment have so greatly reduced the flexibility of the economic system as to raise serious doubts of the capacity of the American economy to make the rapid and heavy adjustments called for in the postwar period without social disorder, particularly in the presence of the disrupting forces which these developments have themselves engendered.

III. Positively Disrupting Factors

In addition to the developments calling for economic adjustment and those inhibiting adjustment, a third set of developments have occurred which have converted certain forces ordinarily relied upon to produce adjustment into forces which tend to aggravate any important maladjustment once it develops. The more significant of these developments are:

1. The increase in the power of special groups, particularly business groups, over industrial policy.
2. The increasing shift of production from direct to indirect labor through mechanization.
3. The increasing importance of consumer capital goods such as automobiles, electric refrigerators, etc.
4. The increasing inadequacy of the banking system in the presence of inflexible administered prices.

1. The Power of Special Groups

Probably the most important single economic development of the last fifty years has been the increasing concentration of economic activity already referred to. It has involved a great increase in productive efficiency by shifting important areas of economic coordination from the market to the hands of administrators. At the same time, it has changed the conditions under which the drive for profits operates to such an extent so that this drive may and often does become a seriously disrupting influence.

The gains from this concentration have arisen to an important extent from the closer coordination and articulation of the activity of separate individuals which it makes possible. When all enterprises were small, the action of the separate individuals was made to fit into the action of other individuals through the market and price mechanism just as was the case with the farmers before the creation of the Agricultural Adjustment Administration. Within the big corporate enterprises on the other hand, the actions of hundreds or thousands of separate individuals are combined by the management into a coordinated whole. It is the planning activity of the management rather than the market activity which makes the work of the separate individuals within the enterprise mesh into a single great producing organization. Such is the case with the great corporate enterprises like General Motors or General Electric. As a result of this administered coordination the productive capacity of the individuals in many industries is greatly expanded, thus making possible a high standard of living if the activities of the huge separate enterprises can be adequately coordinated among themselves and with the rest of the economy.

At the same time, this concentration, by greatly reducing the number of competing units in the market place, tends to increase the power of individual managements over those elements of industrial policy for which the market has traditionally been responsible. This means that *industrial* policy, instead of being made by the impersonal forces of the market place, is to an important extent made by individuals for individual gain or profit. In the case of a product like wheat the size of the wheat crop and the price which it brings is a matter which has been, until the Agricultural Adjustment Act, something quite outside the control of any individual or small group. These elements of industrial policy—the total amount of wheat produced and its price—have been made by the market. No farmer by producing more or less or by selling or not selling can appreciably affect the price of wheat or the total volume produced. His contribution to the whole wheat production is too small to be significant. In the case of the concentrated industries quite a different situation has developed. In an industry such as that of automobiles the three or four largest producers have become so important in relation to the whole market that individually and independently each can appreciably affect either price or the total volume of cars produced. When there is a drop in demand for cars each has the power, within limits, to maintain its price by lowering production. Thus, each major company has a significant control over industrial policy and acts accordingly.

But when *industrial* policy is made in the interest of profit in the guise of *business* policy it may be made in a manner to be disrupting in its influence.

Thus, when a depression sets in and the big enterprises are faced with the necessity of either lowering prices or lowering production, it is likely to be to their interest to exercise their control over industrial policy by choosing to hold prices and to curtail production. In doing this they throw workers out of employment and reduce the buying power of the community thereby aggravating the initial depressing influence. This places the major initial burden of economic adjustment upon the workers instead of on prices where it is traditionally supposed to lie. As a result, industrial policy made in the interests of special groups tends, not to further economic adjustment, but to aggravate any incipient depression which might arise. Undoubtedly this has been a major factor in making the present depression so serious and so prolonged.

2. The Unstabilizing Effect of Mechanization

A second factor tending to aggravate economic fluctuations is the increasing proportion of labor which is employed indirectly in industry to produce machines rather than directly to operate machines. This increasing mechanization has meant that a decreasing part of the labor used in production is employed at approximately the time that the goods are actually wanted while an increasing part of the labor is employed long before in producing the capital equipment. It also means that since the capital equipment is built far in advance of the actual production of the goods to be consumed, the exact time when the capital equipment is produced can be shifted. Thus, if business prospects look poor, business men can postpone erecting new factories. When business looks good they can build new factories to last many years. As a result, that part of productive labor which operates indirectly through creating capital goods tends to work in a most uneven fashion—at one time overrushed; at another time with little employment. Yet economic balance requires a fairly continuous and steady production of capital equipment if resources are not to be shifted in and out of the construction and equipment industries in a bungling and socially wasteful fashion. This increasing shift from direct to indirect labor has greatly aggravated the unstabilizing influence of the machine process.

3. The Increasing Importance of Consumer Capital Goods

Similar in effect to the increased mechanization of industry is the increased importance of consumer capital goods such as automobiles, electric refrigerators, etc. As an increasing proportion of consumer income goes into the purchase of goods which wear out slowly over a period of years, the shifts in consumer income tend to be reflected in exaggerated form in the purchase or the postponement of purchase of such capital goods. Unlike most food which has to be consumed almost at once, the consumer's capital goods wear out slowly and the actual time at which they are replaced is not established physically as in the case of food but can be advanced or postponed with variations in the consumer's income. If the consumer's income has gone up he can trade in the old car after a shorter period of use. If his income goes down, he can drive the old car another year. This means that for an important group of commodities there are significant swings in the rate of new purchases such as would not exist if all consumption were on a strictly hand-to-mouth basis. This variability in the purchase of consumer capital goods combines with the variability in the production of new industrial capital equipment to aggravate any initial fluctuations in economic activity as individuals in seeking their own self-interest are induced by favorable or unfavorable economic developments to hasten or postpone new outlays in a degree greater than any changes in income which may have occurred.

4. The Failure of the Banking System

A further contribution to economic instability is the inadequacy of the banking system to deal with the problems growing out of modern industrial organization. In this country, while industry was going through a process of concentration, the banking system was maintained as a highly disjointed system which was expected to operate effectively through the interaction of controls of a character only appropriate to an economy in which no industrial concentration had developed.

The breakdown of the banking system under modern industrial conditions needs no description here. The most important factor in this breakdown has been the inapplicability of the principles upon which the system has been built to modern conditions. The two basic principles underlying the original Federal Reserve Act (not the way it has actually operated) might be stated in oversimplified form as follows: (1) monetary medium (bank deposits) created by banks in making loans should be based entirely on *commercial* loans and (2) the volume of such monetary medium should fluctuate according to the demands for commercial credit.

Such underlying principles encounter two difficulties under modern industrial conditions. First, the *supply* of high grade commercial paper is insufficient to provide an adequate supply of the monetary medium. And second, the presence of inflexible prices as a dominant factor in the economy would make control of the volume of the monetary medium by the demand for commercial credit a highly disrupting influence.

The deficiency of high grade commercial paper is due to the fact that the large corporate enterprises have to a large extent ceased to be a significant demand for commercial credit. With their integrated operations, they are able to even out the fluctuations in working capital requirements and to obtain both their fixed and working capital from the sale of securities so that they cease to be borrowers from the banks except under the most abnormal conditions. With the increasing size of corporate units, the enterprises which had formerly been the source of the highest grade credit risks ceased to obtain funds from the bank at all while the weaker enterprises alone continued to be bank borrowers. This means that if the banking system were to rely solely on commercial credit as a basis for creating monetary medium (bank deposits), it would have to create a great body of monetary medium backed by a dangerously large proportion of second or third grade risks, as was in part the case of the banking system in 1929 so far as much of its commercial paper was concerned. A monetary medium based on such assets is essentially unstable, and would itself contribute in part to aggravating any incipient depression.

The second difficulty with operating a banking system on the principle of commercial credit is that a reduction in business activity tends to produce a drop in the demand for credit which in turn reduces the volume of the monetary medium (bank deposits) at the very time that economic stability under the conditions of modern industry with its inflexible prices and flexible production requires a stable volume or an increase in the monetary medium. Where prices tend to be inflexible, a contraction of monetary medium (bank deposits) tends not to reduce prices but to reduce volume of production. This means that when a contraction of money medium occurs the economy does not readjust itself to the new volume through a fairly general overall drop in price but rather maladjusts itself by curtailing production, increasing unemployment and reducing income until production and consumption have been reduced to the volume which can be supported by the decreased volume of money medium. Where, as in this country, the situation is mixed, part of the economy being composed of a large number of small separate productive units such as farmers who individually exercise no significant control over industrial policy and another part being composed of great corporate units with relatively inflexible prices, a contraction of money medium could be expected to push down prices in the flexible price area and production in the inflexible-price area. Thus, the effect of monetary contraction is to produce serious maladjustment as production goes down in the area of concentrated corporate initiative and production controls while prices go down in the field of individual initiative and lack of any production controls. Because significant monetary contraction in a depression would, under modern conditions, produce increasing maladjustment instead of readjustment, either a constant volume or an increasing volume of monetary medium would be called for at the beginning of a depression *if maladjustment from monetary causes* was to be avoided. Since the demand for commercial credit falls off in a depression, a monetary system based on commercial credit and controlled in volume by the demand for commercial credit would be a serious influence toward the creating and maintaining of economic maladjustments.

In practice, the basic principles on which the Federal Reserve System was organized have been largely disregarded, and banks have gone outside of the field of commercial loans in creating monetary medium. They have either loaned against the securities of these larger corporations or have actually bought the securities of the latter. This is a procedure more in keeping with the actual industrial conditions but it means that the banking system is organized on one principle—that of basing the monetary medium on commercial paper—and operates on an entirely different principle or principles not clearly established.

So long as modern industrial organization is to persist a large degree of inflexibility in prices is inevitable. Railroad and utility rates will be inflexible insofar as short periods of time are concerned. Prices of a great many industrial products will tend to be relatively inflexible over short periods. Because of this inflexibility it becomes essential to stability that the supply of the monetary medium be controlled not in proportion to the demand for commercial credit but in relation to the maintenance of a stable economy. This does not mean the maintenance of a stable price level as such but rather the maintenance of stability in production and employment. The present-day banking system was not organized with the aim of meeting this new function nor can it in its present organization be effectively employed to meet this need. It actually operates to aggravate depressed conditions rather than to remove the monetary factor as a maladjusting influence.

IV. The Interaction of Developments Producing the Depression

It is reasonably clear that the foregoing developments—some requiring flexibility in the economic system, some impeding adjustment, and some magnifying existing maladjustments—combined to produce the depression. While it is impossible to indicate the precise importance of each of these developments, certain of their interactions can be easily traced.

1. The Widening Gap between Wages and the Prices Charged for Industrial Fabrication

The most striking interaction was that between (1) decreasing production costs as a result of improving technology, and (2) increasing flexibility of prices. As a result of these two trends an increasing discrepancy developed between wage payments and prices. Labor cost per unit of manufactured product declined while prices did not decline in proportion. This is shown in Chart XI. From 1921 to 1929 the prices of manufactured products declined somewhat but this was largely a reflection of the decline in the cost of materials used. The charges made by industry for actual fabrication (i.e., the difference between cost of materials and prices charged for product) remained on the average approximately the same. Of this fabrication charge, however, a declining proportion went to labor while an increased proportion went to overhead cost and profits. This change in the proportion of the fabricating charges going to workers and the proportion going to overhead cost plus profit appears to have been partly accounted for by some increase in overhead costs but appears to be largely accounted for by increased profits and lower wage payments for a given volume of production. The relative inflexibility of prices and the decreasing labor costs from technological improvement thus established a widening gap between the money distributed to workers for the production of commodities and the charges made for fabricating these same commodities. This resulted in an unstable situation, particularly as the purchasing power likely to be spent on current consumption was curtailed.

The increased profits resulting from this widening discrepancy between prices and fabrication charges must be regarded as responsible to a large extent for the rapid increase in the prices of industrial securities and in the superstructure of holding and financial companies which were organized to capitalize these increased and unstable profits. Both the price of securities and the highly capitalized holding and financial companies appear to have rested on the assumption that the trend of increasing profits would continue and tended not only to discount the increased rate of profits actually being obtained but also the very much greater profits which were expected in the future as the result of the continuance of the trend. This discount of future increased rates of profit is clearly indicated in Chart XII which shows the very low rate of return which was actually being received on the market price of corporate securities by 1929. . . .

While the decline in the proportion of the money charged for industrial products paid out to workers established an unstable situation, it did not establish a major dearth in *total* purchasing power so long as the additional profits were spent for consumption, invested in new capital goods, or loaned abroad in a manner to increase the purchases of foreigners in the United States. Actually an expansion in new capital goods and in foreign loans occurred. As has already been pointed out, there was an increase in construction activity in the postwar period particularly in the building of new homes. There was an extension of loans to foreign countries which may have to some extent facilitated foreign purchases in this country (a development independent of the likelihood of repayment of the loans). There was a rapid increase in the investment in installment paper. In such ways the added profits could find employment and maintain total purchasing power. However, the investment of new funds in these forms could not continue indefinitely in the presence of a declining ratio of money paid out to workers per unit of product and the charge made for its fabrication. When the postwar deficiency in construction was made up and when the safety of loans to foreigners came to be seriously questioned, the outlets for investment declined and a deficiency in purchasing power appears to have developed. This is reflected in a decline in automobile purchases, in new home construction, etc. Thus, while the full adjustment of prices to the new technological improvements could be postponed for a period, a final readjustment was inevitable as the pressure for readjustment increased and the opportunities for profitable new investment diminished.

2. *Maladjustment in Foreign Trade Relations*

A second set of interactions of major importance occurred between (1) the shifting of the United States from a debtor to a creditor country, (2) increasing nationalism, and (3) the attrition of war debts and reparations. The War greatly accelerated the basic debtor-creditor development of this country so that instead of gradually shifting from a debtor to a creditor country over a long period of years, the shift was made in one sudden spurt. The great loans by this country were made in concrete form largely as exports of war materials which were almost at once destroyed by the warring countries. In themselves these exports did not involve any basic readjustment of international trade channels nor did they involve a basic shift in the direction of use of human and material resources.

Yet, the shift of this country to a heavy creditor position and in particular the magnitude of the war debts called for a very basic shift in the channels of trade and in the direction of use of resources if the payment of the debt and interest on it was to be made. To be a heavy creditor nation and receive a corresponding return on its loans, a country must, over a period of years, import more goods and services than it exports, i.e., it must have an "adverse" balance of trade such as England experienced for so many years. For the United States the shift to a creditor country called for a great reduction in exports—particularly agricultural commodities—and an increase in imports—particularly manufactured goods.

Actually, the adjustments to facilitate the payment of interest and principal on foreign debt were not made. The country sought to obtain payment on its loans and at the same time sought through higher tariffs to prevent increased imports while the difficulties of taking land out of cultivation impeded a reduction in agricultural exports. The resulting distortions in international trade relationships were further aggravated by corresponding tariff action by import quotas and by efforts to control international prices (see Table I) on the part of other countries. In part the pressure of the maladjustments was temporarily relieved through the large volume of loans made by persons in this country to foreign countries and enterprises. But the volume of such loans was insufficient to prevent the pressure for readjustment from asserting itself. This it did partly by forcing certain countries to revalue their currencies and partly by forcing a revision of debts downward. As it became increasingly apparent that this country would not allow the trade readjustments necessary for debt payment to be made, the insecurity of all loans abroad became clearer and the one method by which adjustment could be postponed thus became no longer feasible.

The net effect of this interaction of developments was thus to establish an unstable condition in which economic balance was maintained only by a temporary and abortive export of capital. The wide discrepancy which existed between the creditor position of this country and the debtor character of the basic institutions which conditioned its foreign trade was a significant factor in intensifying the depression.

A third significant set of interacting developments centered around the monetary medium. This consisted of: a decline in the relative volume of prime commercial paper to act as a backing for the monetary medium; a shift of banking away from commercial banking and toward corporate industrial banking which involved a shift from the creating of monetary medium on the basis of commercial credit to the creating of monetary medium on the basis of loans on corporate securities or their outright purchase; a decreasing flexibility of prices; and a monetary and banking system *organized* on the assumption of commercial credit and flexible prices but trying to operate in the presence of corporate industrial banking and inflexible prices. The net result of these interacting developments was likewise to aggravate the effect of other factors making for depression.

Other interacting influences of a similar but less striking character also participated in producing or aggravating the depression, though the interactions discussed above were undoubtedly the major factors. The depression can thus be attributed to many conflicting forces but can in its basic elements be attributed to the interacting effects of (1) developments calling for greater economic flexibility if economic stability was to be maintained; (2) developments increasing the inflexibility of the economy; and (3) developments converting the economic drives which have been relied upon to act as readjusting and stabilizing influences into maladjusting and unstabilizing influences.

Notes

1. National Income, 1929–1932, Senate Document No. 124, 73rd Congress, 2nd Session, Washington, 1934, p. 14.
2. Economic Trends Affecting Agriculture, Louis H. Bean and Arthur P. Chew, U.S. Dept. of Agriculture, 1933, pp. 33, 35.
3. National Income, 1929–1932, Senate Document No. 124, 73rd Congress, 2nd Session, Washington, 1934, p. 14.
4. Ibid.
5. It is well recognized that for a short period of time such an ''adverse'' balance can be postponed by the extension of further loans. Such a development is cumulative and can therefore be only temporary.
6. For a more extensive analysis of this chart and of the implications of inflexible administered prices, see Senate Document 13, p. 2.

5

Proposals for Bringing the Technical Phases of National Planning to a National Focus

The General Structure for Planning

Administrative coordination in this country has developed in the main along two quite different planes, the geographical and the functional, and has resulted in two main sets of administrative units—the political and the economic. This means that individuals tend to be aggregated, or the whole politico-economic community tends to be divided up, on two quite different principles of aggregation or cleavage. By the geographical principle we have the political units—individuals, towns or cities, countries, states, regions, the nation. On the functional basis we have the economic units—individuals, plants, businesses,[1] industries, aggregates of industries, the nation. Each of these systems of aggregation-division is well established, enters into our daily life, and has involved planning for more effective use of resources at each level indicated and at many intermediate levels not indicated.[2] This means that the structure of economic planning is already well advanced along each of these lines.

It would be practically impossible to eliminate administrative coordination and its coordinate planning on either of these planes. Even if industry were to take over most of the functions of existing political subdivisions and allow the political units to atrophy, it would have to recreate geographical divisions and work out *interindustry* coordinating agencies on a geographical basis. Likewise, if the various governmental units were to take over the whole of industry, they in turn would require *interregional* coordinating agencies organized on an industrial basis. Because of the impossibility of eliminating either the geographical or

---

November 28, 1936. Reproduced with permission from the Charles E. Merriam Papers. University Archives, University of Chicago Library, Box 185, Folder 1.

the functional plane of cleavage this memorandum will operate on the assumption that planning has to be worked out, as it has in the past, along both lines.

In general outline, this duplex system of planning agencies takes the form of a federated system involving simultaneous centralization and decentralization of function. Some planning functions are performed at the center, for the community as a whole, other planning functions are performed by the individual for himself, and other planning functions are performed at a series of points intermediate in scope, whether geographical, functional, or both. The system is federated, since the lines of authority do not run exclusively either from the agencies of broader scope to those of narrower scope or from those of narrower scope to those of broader scope.

Within this planning structure, certain functions properly fall to the federal government, and are being performed by the federal government at the present time to a greater or less extent. Each department and agency of government carries on planning in a more or less self-conscious fashion, sometimes only in broad outline but often in refined detail. As a result there already exists a federal organization of planning, part of it developed along the functional and part on the geographical basis.

It is the purpose of this memorandum to examine the federal planning functions in broad outline, to consider the distribution of planning activity within the federal government, and to outline a possible further development in the federal organization for planning which would improve the articulation of planning functions and bring planning to a central, national focus.

In discussing these federal functions the federal government will at first be treated as a single unit without attempting to indicate the particular distribution of function within government. For this purpose all the different bodies concerned with planning in the federal government will be referred to as constituting a "federal planning organization." The discussion will not be restricted to any single agency or small group of agencies within this organization which might be developed to bring national planning to a focus. The distribution of functions within the federal planning organization will then be discussed after the federal functions themselves have been clarified.

In discussing this federal planning organization a very sharp distinction will be maintained between the technical function of developing and proposing plans and the political function of deciding on policy. The latter is concerned with where you want to go and the former with how you can get there. Legally, these two functions can be sharply divided. Thus a planning agency could be set up to develop and propose plans without having legal power to decide on policy, while a second agency would have the legal power of decision. In practice, however, the line of division is not so sharp. Where the two functions are separated, policy is likely to be *determined* by the interacting of the technical and the political bodies on each other, not by either alone. Where the two functions are combined in a single individual or body, they become mingled. However, for analytical purposes, and often in practical organization, the technical advisory function and the political policy function can be separated.

Finally in discussing federal planning functions it should be recognized that planning can take two quite different forms which might be called respectively, facilitative planning and operative planning. Operative planning would be planning in which the technical agency developing and proposing plans was combined in the same administrative organization with an agency having responsibility for executing policy. Thus, in the T.V.A., one agency might be directed to draw plans for a dam, the proposed plans might be accepted as policy by the T.V.A. management, and the latter would then proceed to have the dam built in execution of the policy. This would be operative planning, i.e., planning tied to operations.

In contrast, the T.V.A. might develop plans indicating more effective use of land in the Tennessee Valley, indicating lands which were submarginal, etc., but without power to put such plans into effect. Such planning would be facilitative rather than operative. Individuals or agencies outside the control of the T.V.A. would have to be persuaded to act in order to get execution of the plans. The Regional Plan of New York is an outstanding case of facilitative planning. In practice, a great deal of effective planning is of a facilitative character rather than operative. Effective use of national resources unquestionably requires the use of both types of planning.

Technical Functions to be Focused in Federal Planning Organization

The technical functions of the federal planning organization appear to fall into the following five categories, the first concerned with the scientific materials for planning, the next three with planning itself and the last with the adoption of proposed plans.

The Technical Materials for Planning

1. Conducting and coordinating research to provide an improved scientific base for planning.

Technical Phase of Planning

2. Facilitating the planning work of planning agencies of narrower than federal scope.
3. Partial planning of national scope or federal responsibility.
4. Overall planning of national scope.

Getting Technical Planning Used

5. Facilitating the adoption, as a policy, of plans proposed.

1. Conducting and Coordinating Research

The federal planning organization is in a strategic position to coordinate the research necessary to provide a scientific basis for planning and, in part, to carry on such research. This requires the coordination of research relating to planning within the federal planning organization and the federal government. Also it requires some measure of coordination of the research activity relating to planning, but carried on outside the federal government. The extent to which the federal planning organization could go in this latter direction would have to be worked out in practice. Its leadership might facilitate the division of research fields, the adoption of standard tools, and, in many other ways, bring about better coordination without infringing upon the autonomy of planning or research agencies outside the federal government. The problem of more effective use of resources is one which ramifies into all fields, and research relating to it should be carried on with both the national picture and the local problems in mind.

2. Aiding Other Planning Agencies

The federal planning organization is likewise in a strategic position to aid planning organizations of narrower scope without having to be in any position of authority over them. This it can do, in fact is now doing to a significant extent, in five different directions. First, it can bring about an improved structure of planning outside of the federal government by clarifying the planning functions; by facilitating the reorganization of existing, or the creating of new planning bodies where better organization of planning requires; and by facilitating the relocation or adoption of new planning functions where appropriate. Second, it can facilitate the operating coordination (in contradistinction to the research) between other planning agencies. Third, it can conduct studies to develop techniques or material of use to two or more nonfederal planning agencies. Fourth, it can act as a clearing house for other planning agencies, passing on the successful work or experience of other planning agencies to each other. Finally through the performance of its other functions, a federal planning organization can provide a background against which other planning agencies can operate.

3. Partial Planning

The third group of national planning functions have to do with partial planning, i.e., planning for some part or segment of the national economy. Partial planning tends to be of a more or less intensive character. It is exemplified by the work of the homemaker in planning a meal, that of the business man in planning plant production, that of a town planning schools, that of the trade association planning for the elimination of unfair trade practices, and that of a federal agency in planning a system of arterial highways. Each of these cases has to do with the more or less detailed planning of a part of the social economy, not with the whole.

In carrying on partial planning the federal planning organization should confine its planning to those partial planning fields which are of national scope and cannot be dealt with by lesser planning agencies, and the partial planning fields in which the federal government has administrative responsibility. Examples of such partial planning fields of national scope are arterial highway planning, public works program planning, land use planning (in its most comprehensive aspects). Also federal planning has to be carried on where the federal government has administrative responsibilities, as in the case of the Army, the Navy, federally owned parks, the Panama Canal, the T.V.A. and similar activities, including the administrative activities of the separate departments and independent federal agencies.

Even where federal funds are employed on a particular piece of partial planning—say land use—it might frequently be feasible to delegate to agencies with more limited scope, parts of the planning work as it touches their particular localities, reserving to the federal organization the function of coordinating the work of local bodies and supplementing them where the problems rise to national significance.

4. Overall Planning

By the nature of the case the full function of overall planning should be carried by the federal planning organization. This overall planning is concerned with bringing about and maintaining effective overall balance in the use of resources. It necessarily deals with the social economy of the nation as a whole. At the same time it deals only with the main structural balance—the balance between the separate branches of industry (including agriculture as an industry), the balance between saving and capital creation, the balance in international trade, the balance between money supply and money requirements. It is concerned with providing a structural framework—with delineating and coordinating the main traffic arteries of economic activity. This aspect of national social-economic planning is appropriately a federal planning function.

5. Facilitating the Adoption of Plans Proposed

Finally it is a function of any advisory planning body to interrelate its activity with the activity of the administrative bodies to which it is attached in order to make its work effective. This means that the federal planning organization must be so tied into the administrative parts of the federal government that the plans proposed or recommended by it will grow out of current administrative problems and provide feasible solutions. Likewise, it must be so tied into the administrative agencies that even though the administrative agencies legally decide upon policy in fact, the planning organization combines with the administrative agencies in developing policy.

Distribution of Technical Planning Activity within the Federal Government

The distribution of technical planning activity within the federal organization involves two pairs of conflicting considerations which seem to me to present the most difficult problem in organizing the structure of federal planning. First, geographical or functional localization of planning is desirable because the planning is then closer to the field of operations. At the same time centralization of planning is desirable, because then all the ramifications of the actions contemplated can be given weight. Also combining the technical planning and the political policy deciding in a single individual or agency is desirable to insure the carrying out of plans. Yet dividing these functions is desirable in order to allow greater technical competence in developing plans at the same time that the political problem of deciding upon goals can be dealt with by those whose function it is to be sensitive to the popular will.

In certain planning cases, these conflicting considerations are not significant. Thus, where the planning problem has only local implications, the planning can be local. If it is primarily technical, say the food to be ordered for a local army encampment, both the technical planning and the political decision can be placed in the hands of a single technician. Likewise, if the decision is primarily political with no complex technical problems, say the functionally local problem of whether a Fourth of July coming on Sunday shall be celebrated on Saturday or Monday, both technical and political functions can be adequately handled by a minor politician.

At the opposite extreme, there are some questions having nationwide influence, high technical complexity, and great political importance. In this category would fall such questions as going off the gold standard or the adoption of the A.A.A. program. Here a high degree of centralization in planning is called for, and the final policy adopted should be the product of the interaction of the technicians and the politicians.

Intermediate between these extremes lie the bulk of planning tasks. They combine varying breadths of influence with varying degrees of political significance and technical complexity. Likewise they call for varying degrees of centralization in planning and varying degrees of separation between the technical and political functions.

In addition to the wide variety of planning situations calling for different treatment, the planning functions involved in any particular development can usually be broken up and treated on different bases. The planning function can usually be broken up so as to allow some to be dealt with locally, others at intermediate points and still others centrally. Thus in the running of a local post office, the planning for extra Christmas carriers can be handled locally, whereas the planning of the layout of money order blanks can be handled at the Washington headquarters of the Department. Likewise, planning functions can usually be broken up so as to allow some to be performed by the person or body in a position to decide on policy and others to be performed by technicians separate from the decider of political policy. Such a case would be that of a Cabinet officer who worked out part of a program of action, but turned over to technicians the working out of the more technical points subject to his final decision. This possibility of breaking up the different planning functions means that a highly complex organization of federal planning is possible.

In practice, the actual planning organization shows the very great complexity which could be predicted from the above analysis. It is not the purpose here to examine this organization in detail but rather to present the well known need for bringing this planning structure to a focus, and lay a basis for the better articulation of the technical planning organization.

It is an observable fact that as problems of policy become more politically significant and technically complex, there is a greater tendency to divide the technical and political aspects. At the present time the political aspects of planning, the decisions on policy, are more or less effectively[3] brought to a focus in the Cabinet and President, the Congress, and the Supreme Court. The technical aspects of planning are not brought to a focus and yet the need for bringing the technical aspects of planning to a focus is clear. The remainder of this memorandum is devoted to outlining possible steps to be taken and functions to be performed in bringing the existing structure of planning to a central focus in order that it may better and more completely serve the requirements of our political government.

Proposed Focusing of the Technical Planning Organization

In order to bring the existing technical planning organization of the federal government to a more effective head, I suggest five independent agencies concerned with planning at the top but interlocking in a National Resources Board (or National Technical Board or National Planning Board). These agencies would be as follows:

National Resources Board
Central Statistical Board
Social-Economic Council to Congress (Legislative Bureaus)
Economic Advisors (3) to the President
Economic Advisor (1) to the Supreme Court

Each of these agencies should be independent, but the National Resources Board membership should include ex officio, the Chairman of the Central Statistical Board, the Chairman of the Economic Council, one of the Economic Advisors to the President, and the Economic Advisor to the Supreme Court.

In creating or continuing the existence of these agencies it should be made amply clear that it is not their function to determine national policy. That is a political function to be performed by persons or bodies elected or appointed for that purpose. The sole function of these technical planning agencies would be to bring to a focus the technical resources of the government as an aid to the making of more effective national policy. National policy would continue to be made by Congress, the President and Cabinet or other Presidential body, and the Supreme Court.

The functions appropriate to each of the five agencies are outlined below, the National Resources Board being taken up last and most completely.

The Central Statistical Board

This agency has already fairly clearly defined its functions and they need not be covered here. It is in many respects an interdepartmental statistical committee with a permanent secretariat. Most of the federal statistical agencies are represented upon it. It has been particularly concerned with uniformity of statistical material, statistical techniques, reducing of interbureau political friction, development of new statistical series and other activities of a similar nature. As it develops further, there are many areas of statistical reporting and analysis which it might appropriately enter. The exact division of function between the National Resources Board and the Central Statistical Board would have to be worked out to insure complete coverage and avoid duplication. The Chairman of the Central Statistical Board should be ex officio a member of the National Resources Board, while a member of the latter might properly be made a member of the C.S.B. On many matters joint committees would probably be desirable with the National Resources Board members emphasizing the research content (what you want to know) and the C.S.B. members emphasizing the statistical aspects (how you know it).

Economic Council to Congress

I have not a clear idea of the appropriate organization for such a body but I believe such a body would be most desirable and could contribute a great deal to the relations between the hill and the executive and to the quality of congressional action on economic matters. It would presumably consist of several members and would have to satisfy both majority and minority parties. (The Chairman might be selected by the majority and the vice-chairman by the minority party, the individuals occupying these positions swapping places when party power shifted.) It would have a small secretariat which would supply congressional committees with economic material and technical opinions and keep in touch with the statistical sources in the executive branches. Through the membership of its Chairman on the National Resources Board, it would be in a position to interpret congressional needs to the Board and the recommendations of the Board to Congress. A member of the Council might also be made a member of the C.S.B.

Economic Advisors to the President

It would seem highly desirable that the President should have a battery of economic advisors on hand at all times—their office being within buzz call. The functions to be performed have been performed to some extent in the last four years by Dr. Tugwell, Dr. Reifler, and more recently Dr. Lubin. The highly successful use which Secretary Wallace has made of his economic advisors, Dr. Ezekiel, Dr. Bean, and in small part myself, is indicative of the technical aid which could be given to the chief executive by a small corps of economic advisors. There would be a definite advantage in having three such advisors (with small staff). One could properly concentrate on current statistical material as Dr. Bean does for Secretary Wallace and as Dr. Reifler and Dr. Lubin have done for the President. This advisor could properly be made a member of the C.S.B., and would have to be familiar with all the government statistical collection agencies. A second member might properly concentrate on international trade problems—a particularly important factor in the light of the influence of economic factors on our foreign relations. This advisor would have to keep in touch with the economic advisor's office in the State Department, that in the Tariff Commission in War and Navy Departments and in several other agencies. The third advisor would have to concentrate on internal economic matters of a longer run character not covered by the first advisor. He should be made a member of the National Resources Board and would help to interpret the President's requirements to [blank space in original manuscript] and would keep the President in mind of the findings of the Board. He would also have to be familiar with the longer run developments in the field of labor organization, farm organizations, consumer organizations, and business organizations.

Economic Advisor to the Supreme Court

It is well recognized that the Supreme Court has interpreted the Constitution so flexibly as to have become a policy deciding arm of government. So long as the court exercises this power, it has need for an economic advisor—of a philosophical cast—quite as much as other policy deciding agencies. An economic advisor with almost no staff, but sitting in on the case discussions could undoubtedly clarify the economic and social implications of constitutional and other cases. He should be ex officio a member of the National Resources Board.

National Resources Board

The National Resources Board should be the central focus of the technical aspects of planning. Its functions will be considered at length below. In composition, it should contain a nucleus executive committee composed of at least three full time members. One of these members should be ex officio a member of whatever political body the President develops as his economic policy deciding body (Cabinet, Emergency Council, or whatever).

The full membership of the Resources Board might consist of the three full time members, the four ex officio members from the agencies already mentioned, and two or three part time members drawn from outside the Federal government.

While the Board should be made up solely of technicians (broadly interpreted), it should to some extent reflect shifting political conditions. At the same time a greater measure of continuity should exist than exists in the case of political office. Each incoming President should be in a position to select his own Chairman of the Board and his own ex officio member from among his Economic Advisors.

The Chairman of the Economic Council of Congress should also shift with shifting party fortunes. The Chairman of the C.S.B. and the Economic Advisor to the Supreme Court should be above party fortunes. The length of appointments for the remaining members could be worked out to give a balance between stability and change.[4]

The National Resources Board should have a nucleus staff of technicians and should have a panel of perhaps advisory members (non-voting) or advisors to be called on for special purposes. These problems will be discussed after the Resources Board functions have been classified.

Functions of the National Resources Board

The National Resources Board should be at the central focus of the technical planning function of the federal government and, to the extent possible, of the nation. This means that it should be at the central focus in the performance of each of the five functions already listed as functions of the federal technical planning organization. These federal functions are listed again below:

The Technical Materials for Planning

1. Conducting and coordinating research to provide an improved scientific basis for planning.

Technical Planning

2. Facilitating the planning work of planning agencies of narrower than federal scope.
3. Partial planning of national scope or federal responsibility.
4. Overall planning of national scope.

Getting Technical Planning Used

5. Facilitating the adoption, as policy, of plans proposed.

Each of these functions should come to a focus in the National Resources Board but at the same time the responsibilities of the Resources Board should be kept to the minimum. Only those functions in each of the five categories which cannot be effectively performed elsewhere should be carried through to the Resources Board. As fast as the Resources Board can clarify and disentangle functions carried through to it, those which can be as effectively or more effectively performed by planning agencies of narrower scope, should be placed in the hands of such agencies. Furthermore, the technical planning agencies of the federal government constitute a system of federated agencies, each agency retaining its own autonomy except as its autonomy is limited by the political structure of the federal government. The National Resources Board should not be in a position of authority over other governmental planning or statistical agencies. Lines of authority connecting the technical planning agencies should continue to flow through the existing executive channels.

Providing the Technical Materials for Planning

The National Resources Board has three functions to perform as the central focus in the task of providing the technical material for planning. First, it can carry on explorations or pilot studies to develop techniques and approaches of significance to more than one department of government, the use of the techniques and approaches then being adopted (if desired) by the respective departments. Second, it should facilitate the coordination of research within the federal government. This it can do, preferably jointly with the C.S.B., by keeping track of research going on in the technical aspects of planning, by developing facilitative plans for a program of research, by encouraging the adoption of any or all parts of the program of research,[5] by clarifying the research functions, and by attempting to increase the articulation between researches being conducted. Third, it should facilitate the coordination of research activity in the planning field outside the federal government, in so far as this proves feasible. This means improving the coordination of research carried on by the geographical units—regional, state, etc., by the functional units, industry, enterprise, etc., by the interest groups, farms, labor, commerce, business, etc., and by other agencies such as universities and foundations. It is obvious that this task of coordinating the non-federal research in planning is a more delicate task than that of coordinating federal research. It should be of a facilitative character only and should encourage agencies outside of the federal government to carry on much of the coordinating functions.

Facilitating Technical Planning by Agencies of Narrower than Federal Scope

As the center of technical planning forms, the National Resources Board should facilitate the planning of planning agencies having a scope narrower than federal. This can be done by helping to delineate the planning functions appropriate to different levels of scope, by acting as a clearing house for planning activity, and by aiding in setting up planning agencies at the different levels of scope. The present Resources Committee (and predecessors) have already done much to facilitate the setting up of planning agencies at the different levels along the geographical line. It might properly adopt a similar program along the functional line, encouraging the establishment of planning agencies for groups of industries and for industries. In doing this a survey corresponding to the regionalism study would have to be conducted to determine suitable lines of industrial division or foci of planning comparable to the centers for regional planning. The development of such planning bodies would, of course, be a slow undertaking, being instituted first where the field seemed most fertile. They should head the technical research and planning activity of the labor, consumer, and business groups in the particular industry. The men's garment industry or the hosiery industry might be an appropriate starting point. A solid technical basis could be established in this way for dealing with wage, price, and production problems. This work of establishing functional planning bodies might be initiated by the Resources Board and be gradually taken over by other government agencies. The focus of the task of facilitating the coordination of such agencies whether geographical or functional would still remain with the Resources Board.

Partial Planning of National Scope

With much of the partial planning appropriately carried on by the Federal Government, the National Resources Board should have no more concern than with planning of comparable significance carried on, say, by states. In such cases the partial planning is carried on by the agencies or departments having operative responsibility. The Resources Board should properly have a responsibility to facilitate such partial planning in its more significant phases but on the whole the great mass of partial planning activity of the Federal Government is primarily a departmental matter.

At certain points, however, the Resources Board should have a positive responsibility in connection with partial planning. Wherever a phase of partial planning is not covered by existing federal agencies, or where, more frequently, it is covered partially by several agencies, the Resources Board could properly take the lead in covering the field as it has done with respect to Land Use, Water Use, Regionalism, etc. In such cases the Resources Board should be initiating and facilitating but not operating. Where several agencies are concerned with the subject matter, it could properly supply a secretariat to a temporary or permanent interdepartmental committee created for the purpose of planning in this partial area. However, where the partial planning area could be concentrated in a single department—as perhaps land use—the Resources Board should no longer be concerned with this area except as it is involved in overall planning. The partial planning activity of the Resources Board would thus be confined to new partial planning areas not easily covered by any single existing agency and old partial planning areas where it is not possible to concentrate the planning in a single agency. The planning committees for carrying on this partial planning activity would operate on a plane intermediate between existing government agencies and the Resources Board itself. These agencies would prepare proposed plans which might be approved or adoption of which might be recommended by the Resources Board but for which the committee would be primarily responsible. They would not be advisory to the Resources Board but would stand on their own feet proposing plans to the relevant agencies including the President.

Overall Technical Planning

Overall planning on the technical side should be a permanent function of the National Resources Board. Overall planning can only be done effectively where the whole national social economy can be brought into view. While particular functions in developing overall plans could properly be delegated to other agencies, the tying together of the final plans can only be done at the central focus of technical planning.

The overall planning activity would fall into three main categories as follows:

1. Proposing overall national goals—production-consumption patterns.

2. Proposing overall organizational structure through which these goals might be achieved.

3. Proposing current operating policies on the part of the Federal Government which would facilitate the achieving of these goals.

Proposing Overall National Goals

The first line of activity in overall planning would be the creation of production-consumption patterns from among which the political arms of government (President or Congress) would select as a current objective that which seemed at the same time most feasible and to come closest to fulfilling the national aspirations.[6] I do not need here to go into the characteristics of production-consumption patterns. It is enough to say that they would delineate for the main economic traffic arteries the activities which would constitute the outlining of a feasible and effective use of resources. The present pilot study of the Industrial Section in this field is attempting to indicate both the feasibility of drafting such patterns, the methods whereby this can be done, and the materials needed to do it. The drafting of such patterns would be a recurring function of the Resources Board though as experience developed it is probable that more and more of the concrete work could be done by other agencies leaving only the final combination and interrelation of material from other sources to the staff of the Resources Board.

Proposing Improvements in the Economic Structure

The second field of overall planning activity is concerned with the organizational structure of the economy. How can the organizing influences available to the community be more effectively adapted to provide more effective use of resources? At what points can better organization in the use of resources be brought about by increased competition, at what points by substituting administration for competition, at what points by improving the plane of competition through the social process of regulation, at what points by encouraging the acceptance of a common goal through subsidy or otherwise? And where administrative coordination promises to give better organization of resources than competition, what are the appropriate arrangements, what focus of controls and responsibility will be most likely to insure that the administrative directors will be responsible to the persons whose interests are affected by their administrative activity? What is the appropriate role of code authority, corporate ownership, government ownership, private ownership, cooperative ownership, and regulatory commissions? There is need for a pilot study in this field and following this, the development of plans for improving the structural organizations through which we act in using our national resources. An improved structure would increase the possibility of attaining an accepted national goal.

Proposing Current Operating Plans

The federal government in its role of national focus of both political and industrial activity is constantly having to make operating policy with respect to activity for which it is directly responsible. Thus the federal government has to develop a federal tax policy, a federal credit policy, a federal monetary policy, a federal tariff policy, etc. Whatever policies it develops in these areas can seriously affect the functioning of the national social-economy. It would, therefore, be appropriate that the operating policies adopted should work in the direction of and facilitate the reaching of whatever national goal is adopted by the political arms of the federal government. To this end, the Resources Board should be in a position in conjunction with the particular operating agencies directly concerned to indicate the general characteristics of operating policy which would facilitate the attainment of whatever national goal has been adopted. The Resources Board should have no control over the operating policy adopted except in so far as its chairman might be a member of the President's Cabinet, or other presidential body deciding upon economic policy.

The appropriate way to handle this third overall planning function of the Resources Board should become clearer as the work of developing production-consumption patterns and of indicating improvements in economic structure progresses. A pilot study to discover the more important form of operating policy now decided by the federal government, the process by which it is now decided, and the ways in which each policy could be coordinated with other operative policies should be fruitful.

To aid the Resources Board in developing plans for proposal in each of these three phases of overall planning, there should be interdepartmental committees *advisory* to the Resources Board, and to the staffs working on each phase. These committees should be made up of individuals from the various departments concerned and should be chaired either by the person on the Resources Board staff directing the particular phase of the work or else by someone outside of any governmental department concerned. This would be done to reduce interdepartmental conflict.

The interdepartmental committee should be made advisory to the Board and staff rather than responsible as is proposed in the case of the partial planning committees because the Resources Board itself must be responsible for the overall planning. It can delegate its responsibility for partial planning activity which it assumes only because of the absence of a single appropriate agency for doing the work. However, the Board should not delegate its work in the field of overall planning.

Probably it is better to have a separate committee advisory to the Board and staff on each of the three phases of overall planning, since different groups are particularly concerned with each phase. Thus, the drafting of production-consumption patterns would more particularly concern the statistical agencies; the planning for improved economic structure would particularly concern the technicians in the regulatory agencies and in those agencies concerned with organization; finally the planning in respect to federal operating policy would involve a third group of technicians, those particularly concerned with the technical problem of current federal operations. There could appropriately be some interlocking membership between these three committees but they deserve to be independent committees with separate orientation.

Tying Technical Planning with Political Policy Deciding in the Development of Policy

Since the National Resources Board should have no power to decide on policy, there is a problem of making its technical planning activity have its appropriate influence in the development of policy. This is a problem which a Board itself must work out but it can be simplified by the structure of the Board, the relations of its members with other agencies, and the division of functions within the Board. A composition of the Board has already been suggested which should facilitate the tying of technical planning into policy making. This is done by making ex officio members of the Board, the Chairman of the Central Statistical Board, the Chairman of the Economic Council to Congress, the Economic Advisor to the Supreme Court, and one of the Economic Advisors to the President.

A further tie-in can be accomplished by the functions and positions given to the three full time members of the Board who constitute the executive committee and the heart of the Resources Board. As already indicated, the Chairman of the Board should be a member of the Presidential body deciding on economic policy. He should hobnob with Cabinet officers and Commissioners of the independent commissions. In addition to keeping track of the work being done within the Board, he should be familiar with the technical economic problems facing the Department and independent agency heads. He would operate on this Cabinet level of planning.

A second full time member might be particularly concerned with the research aspects of federal planning. He would operate on the "heads of research and statistical agencies" level and might properly be a member of the C.S.B.

A third full time member might be particularly concerned with the planning function itself, being a member of each of the interdepartmental committees concerned with partial or overall planning and keeping in close touch with the members of the Resources Board Staff actively working on proposed plans.

The part time members might be particularly concerned with the nonfederal planning activity, one along geographical (political) and the other along functional (industrial) lines.

These divisions of function are, of course, only suggestive. The Board as a whole and each member would have to be concerned with all the aspects involved in bringing technical planning to a national focus. This would be the sole job of the three full time members and a significant part of the work of the other members.

Advisory Members to the National Resources Board

There have been suggestions that the Resources Board should have advisory members reflecting different backgrounds or representing different interests.

On the question of individuals advisory to the Board to represent special interest groups—labor, farmers, consumers, business—or at least interpret their group interests, I am convinced that such an arrangement would be most undesirable. The technical planning agency should be removed as far as possible from special pressure groups and should not be making political decisions. Individuals representing these special interest groups might quite properly be made advisory to the Presidential body deciding on economic policy but should not be attached to the Resources Board.

Likewise individuals having particular and useful backgrounds should not formally be made advisory to the Board. Such persons might quite possibly be made advisory to the interdepartmental committees dealing with problems of partial planning and perhaps to the interdepartmental committees having to do with the different phases of overall planning.

Notes

1. The legal concept, business, is not entirely satisfactory here. The concept industrial requirement, i.e., all the plants performing a common industrial function, would be better, though this also has its weakness as function could be differently defined.

2. Very often the planning has been carried on in a more or less inarticulate fashion and it has been carried on in a variety of different interests. But by its nature, administrative coordination necessarily involves planning.

3. The existence of the various commissions, F.T.C., I.C.C., etc., impedes the more effective heading up of the political aspect of planning.

4. Perhaps the three full time and two or three part time members could be appointed for six year terms rotated so as to give a new full time appointment every two years.

5. The adoption of those parts of a research program of particular significance to the Resources Board could be insured by planning appreciable funds under the control of the Board (or jointly the Board and the C.S.B.) to be allocated to other government agencies to carry on the necessary research. This would maintain the autonomy of the separate agencies, yet give the Resources Board greater influence in coordinating the federal research activity in the field of planning.

6. Since these two desiderata would often be in conflict, a balance between the two would usually have to be worked out by the politicos.

6

Incentives to Capital Creation

There is general agreement that new capital creation is essential to economic recovery. Many people seem to think that the main approach should be through (1) keeping costs low, and (2) improving the psychological milieu of the business man. They seem to think that undue emphasis has been given to the providing of increased buying power in the hands of consumers by higher wages and relief payments.

There seems to be grave danger that the major importance of increased buying by consumers as a factor in stimulating capital creation might be lost sight of.

So far as capital creation by manufacturing and mining enterprises is concerned, it seems likely that the volume of orders is a more important incentive to capital expenditure than any other single factor. When an enterprise is only operating part of its capacity and no great increase in orders is expected in the immediate future (next 6 to 8 months), there is little inducement to build new facilities no matter how satisfactory the relations between government and industry and no matter how low the level of construction costs may be. (The two significant exceptions to this statement arise where new techniques have been developed which promise very considerable reductions in operating costs, or where construction costs are likely to rise in the near future.) On the other hand, when orders are flowing in and production is at a higher level, there is a real inducement to build new capital even though the relations between government and business are unsatisfactory and even though construction costs are as high as they have been from 1932 to 1937.

This thesis is supported by the estimates of capital outlays by manufacturing and mining enterprises from 1923 to 1937, made by Dr. Terborgh of the Federal Reserve and plotted in the attached chart [Figure 6.1]. Capital outlays by manu-

June 27, 1938. Reproduced with permission from the Jerome Frank Papers, Manuscripts and Archives, Yale University Library, Box 33, Folder 472.

Figure 6.1. **Actual and Calculated Capital Outlays by Mining and Manufacturing Enterprises**

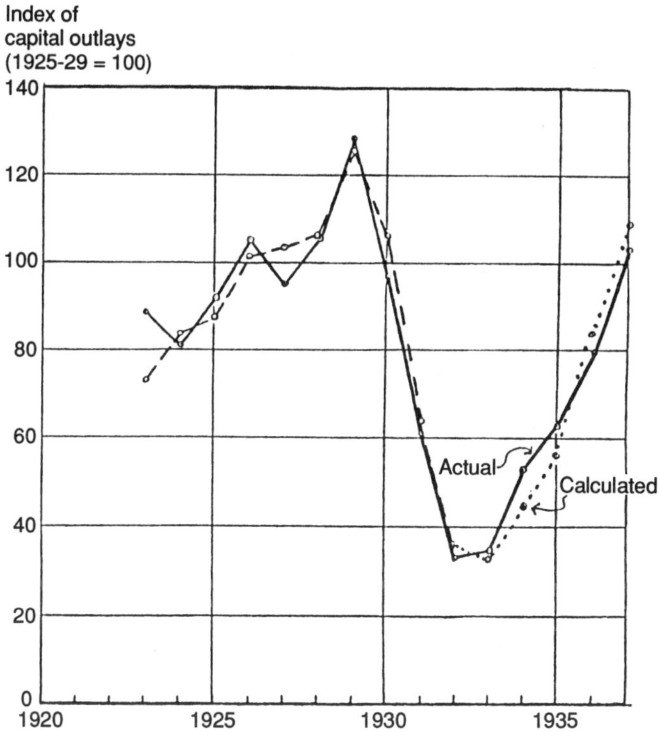

facturing and mining enterprises have increased greatly since 1932–35 and by 1937 appear to have reached a level as high as the average from 1926 to 1928, though not as high as 1929.

Correlation analysis indicates that manufacturing and mining capital outlays fluctuate fairly closely with the fluctuation of production in the current and the preceding year taken together. The magnitude of fluctuation is, of course, greater for capital outlays, the indications being that capital outlays would cease altogether if the index of industrial production based on 1923–25 = 100 were to average much below 50 for two successive years. There is not a close correlation between capital outlays and industrial production for the current year. This is to be expected since capital outlays are as a rule *decided upon* many months before the actual outlays. An index of capital outlays *authorized* would probably show a close relation to current production.

In making the correlation analysis only the data from 1923 to 1932 were used. The formula obtained was used to calculate what the capital outlays in each year from 1935 to 1937 would have been if the relation between capital outlays and the production in the current and preceding years continued to hold good after

1932. The calculated figures correspond fairly closely to the capital outlay actually made, as can be seen in the chart.

This closeness of fit between actual and calculated would appear to support the thesis that capital outlays in manufacturing and mining are closely related to the volume of production in the current and preceding years. This conclusion certainly lends color to the thesis stated above that capital creation for manufacturing and mining is largely dominated by orders (closely related to production) and is little impeded by unsatisfactory relations between government and business or recent costs of construction. Certainly there is no direct evidence of a capital strike on the part of mining and manufacturing enterprises.

It is possible that on *a priori* grounds one would expect capital outlays to be greater in relation to production in the current recovery period than in earlier years because of the low level of equipment replacement during the depression. To the extent that capital outlays *should* have been greater and were not, a case could be made either for the impeding influence of costs and the poor relations between government and business or for the claim of a capital strike. Actually I doubt if a significantly greater capital outlay could have been expected.

It seems likely that capital outlays by wholesale and retail enterprises and in the service industries would show a similar relation to output. Railroad and utility capital outlays may follow quite a different pattern. Certainly new housing and government construction follow patterns different from that of manufacturing and mining capital outlay.

The conclusion from my analysis is that so far as mining and manufacturing are concerned, and probably trade and services, the problem of inducing new capital creation must be met by inducing increased purchase of the products of industry. Of course, lower construction costs and better relations between government and business would be beneficial if they are not taken at the expense of consumer buying power.

7

Possibilities and Limitations of Antitrust Policy

The dominant economic problem in this country today is that of getting the American economy *as a whole* to work at full capacity. Part-timing and unstable production reflect basic flaws either in the organization of economic activity or in the economic policies adopted. To an increasing extent the belief has developed that these flaws are related to the high degree of industrial concentration which exists today and which is associated with inflexible administered prices.

In the last 50 years three quite different lines of approach have been extensively developed in dealing with more extreme cases of industrial concentration. The antitrust approach, typified by the Sherman and Clayton Acts, seeks to minimize industrial concentration and to maintain "competition." The public utility approach, typified in the I.C.C. and the State utility commissions, accepts concentration in certain industries and seeks to regulate the industry so as to insure "fair prices." The government ownership approach typified in the post office and the T.V.A. has been adopted in certain cases as a more direct route to "fair prices." It is the purpose of this memorandum (1) to suggest that none of these three approaches as developed in the past appears likely to contribute significantly to the maintenance of full use of resources, and (2) to indicate the functions which antitrust activity, utility regulations, and government ownership of special industries might be expected to perform successfully in bringing about more effective use of national resources. The problem of insuring full use will be discussed in a later memorandum.

In the past, major reliance has been placed on the market mechanism (operating within a framework of controls established through government) to ensure full and effective use of resources. Though, in fact, depressions have occurred frequently and wasteful use of resources has often been made, reliance on the

---

May 1939. From the Gardiner C. Means Papers at the Franklin D. Roosevelt Library, Series III, "Antitrust Policy."

market mechanism has been justified on the basis of the way an economy could be expected to operate under conditions in which *all* prices were free and flexible. Though this theoretical free-price economy is essentially different from the actual American economy of today, assumptions with respect to it are so basic to discussions of economic problems, that it seems essential to review certain of its outstanding characteristics.

The Theoretical Free-Price Economy

In a free-price economy, the market mechanism is supposed to bring about two desirable economic ends.[1] First, it is supposed to operate in such a way that economic activity is always pushed to practically full capacity;[2] and second, it is supposed to operate in such a way that an approximate balance in the use of resources results, i.e., a use of resources is developed such that no resource can be shifted from one use to another without significantly lessening the product of the whole economy. Hereafter we will refer to these desirable end results as (1) full use of resources, and (2) balanced use of resources.

In the discussion of a free-price economy, full use and balanced use of resources are usually confused or treated as one, yet their practical significances are quite different. As will be shown below, it would be quite possible to have full use of resources, i.e., no unemployed men or machines, and yet have unbalanced use of resources. Likewise, it would be possible to have balanced use of resources even in a depression when available resources were being only partially used.[3]

The practical significance of this difference between full use and balanced use revolves around the factors, price and time. Because of the time required in practice to build new plants and to shift resources from one activity to another, a system of prices which would induce a reasonably effective balance in the use of resources can be expected to develop only slowly over a period of time, perhaps a matter of years, and then only approximately. On the other hand, the essence of "full use of resources" lies in the short run. If there is significant unemployment even for short periods of time, full use of resources is not being obtained. Full use is thus a matter of months.

This important distinction can be seen more clearly by considering the way adjustment is expected to take place in the two cases. In a free-price economy, it is expected that, over a period of years, prices (including wage and interest rates) in a typical industry will fluctuate around levels such that business men are induced to construct new capital equipment in the industry as old equipment wears out or becomes obsolete and as the demand for the product increases.[4] The argument is that, if business men are to be induced to build new plants, they must expect that prices and volume in the future are going to be sufficient to cover (1) their future operating costs, (2) taxes, (3) depreciation representing the recovery of their new capital outlay, and (4) adequate profits. This means that unless there is to be a cessation of new plant construction and a gradual using up of existing plant, prices in a free-price economy must center around a level which promises to cover operating costs, taxes, depreciation, and profits on the most economical new plant that could be built. Only for rapidly declining industries would the long run prices be expected to center around an appreciable lower figure.

Two things are worth noting as to the price and cost expectations supposed to induce the construction of new plants in a free-price economy. First, the calculation of costs, depreciation and profits is based on the *most economical plant that could be built,* not on existing plants, and calculation of costs, depreciation, and profits is based on an assumption of *practically full and continuous operation* of each particular plant until it is worn out or obsolete. The basis for these presumptions will be indicated after the forces making for full use of resources have been covered.

In contrast to these long-run tendencies, the forces making for *full use* of resources in a free-price economy are expected to operate almost instantaneously. In such an economy, depressions, unemployment of men and machines, and deficiencies of buying power are supposed to be impossible. This is because any development which moved in the direction of less than full use of resources *at the initial level of prices* is presumed to set in motion forces which would bring about a lower level of prices (including wage and interest rates), thereby increasing buying power and pushing employment of resources to the full. Because prices (including wage and interest rates) would be expected to readjust quickly and all along the line, a relatively minor fluctuation of the price level is supposed to be all that would usually be necessary to maintain buying power and insure full employment of resources when any incipient decline in buying power or unemployment of men and machines made its appearance.

The quick readjustment of prices (including wage and interest rates) is presumed to maintain buying power and full employment of resources through three main influences: (1) by increasing the buying and hiring power of the money currently held by individuals and enterprises[5]; (2) by lowering interest rates which makes it feasible to expand the production of capital goods, thereby increasing current buying power without increasing the supply of consumption goods currently reaching the market; and (3) by decreasing the gross profits of business more rapidly than wage disbursements so that a larger proportion of money income would be received by individuals likely to spend it on current consumption.[6]

The last point is so important that it deserves to be considered further. It is assumed that in a free-price economy no business man is in a position to establish the prices for his products or the wage and interest rates he will pay. Prices (including wage and interest rates) are presumed to be set in the market and every producer is expected *to run at the full capacity of his existing plant whenever the prices in the market are above his direct operating costs.*[7] In the hypothetical free-price economy, each producer is thought of as though he operated like an electric pump with a price switch. At any time that the market price of his product rose above his direct operating costs at capacity operation, he would begin operating at full capacity, drawing in labor and materials and pouring his product into the market.[8] He is assumed to have no more of a selling problem than a cotton or wheat farmer today. Whenever the market price fell below the crucial operating-cost figure, he would cut off production entirely.[9] Under such conditions price could be expected to reach a point such that all the product called for at the particular price could be supplied by producers whose direct operating costs when operating at full capacity were less than the prevailing market price. The least efficient producer contributing to the supply would presumably have direct operating costs only slightly under the market price while a producer with direct operating costs equal to or above the prevailing market price would not produce.

It is important to notice that in this short-run process whereby a free-price economy is supposed to ensure full use of resources, depreciation and profit play no part. Short-run prices in such an economy are not supposed to be influenced by either depreciation or profits. Any producer whose operating costs were sufficiently lower than the least efficient producer induced to operate would be able to recover depreciation and make a profit. Other producers would suffer the losses of previously invested capital inherent in a profit and loss economy.

The significance of the above analysis lies in the wholly different factors which are supposed to be at work where prices and the market mechanism apportion resources between different uses and where prices and the market mechanism act to induce full use of resources. In the case of balanced use, prices are supposed to be dominated by the costs of constructing and operating new plants to supply a demand greater than can be filled with existing plants. In the case of full use, prices are supposed to be dominated by the costs of operating existing plants. At full use of resources, prices corresponding to balanced use would reflect operating costs, depreciation, taxes and profits on new plant. Prices at any level of activity less than full use of resources would reflect only the operating costs of existing plant, thus pressing activity toward full capacity by increasing buying power. This supposed role of direct operating costs as the dominant factor in establishing prices in the short run is of vital importance to the major economic problem of the day. *It is only because prices were expected to be controlled by direct operating costs whenever production was at less than capacity that a free-price economy was supposed to be a depression-proof economy.*[10]

The Modern American Economy

To anyone familiar with modern business the above analysis must sound quite unrelated to the conditions of actual business today. In only a few fields do conditions approximate a free-price economy sufficiently to insure full operation by each producer whenever he expects prices to be significantly above direct operating costs. In most of agriculture before crop control was instituted, farmers maintained production so long as the prices they expected were above the direct operating costs they expected to incur—and taxes, depreciation, and interest were not included in operating costs. In some sections of the textile industry and in much of the clothing industry free-market prices have persisted. Individual oil wells in Pennsylvania pump oil whenever the price of crude oil is significantly above direct operating costs and close down when it falls below this level. Junk dealers exert their energies to collect scrap iron when the price of scrap is high and lay off when the current price falls below their direct cost of collecting it.

But in the great bulk of the American economy the conditions of the free-price economy do not exist and are not even approximated. Transportation, communication, power and light, water supply, and other services are carried on by regulated industries or by government, and prices are set by administrative action. Only a relatively small part of manufacturing conforms to the conditions of a free-price economy. Most manufacturers adopt schedules of prices and control their production to meet the demand at these administered prices. Even the bulk of retail distribution is carried on through administered prices and fails to meet the conditions for free and flexible prices, while such services to the consumer as education and medical service have never met the condition of a free-price economy.

This does not mean, however, that competition is dead or that the market mechanism does not continue to perform useful and significant functions. First, there is competition between industries for the consumers' dollar. Second, there is active competition of some sort within most unregulated industries and, even, to some extent, in most regulated industries.

In order to analyze more exactly the present role of competition, it will be convenient to distinguish between two degrees of intensity in competition, defining them respectively in terms of balanced use and in terms of full use of resources.

In a specific industry competition might exist which was sufficient to produce a system of prices corresponding with balanced use of resources but not sufficient to produce that short-run flexibility of price which is supposed to ensure full use of resources. Thus, there might be enough competition in an industry to make prices corresponding roughly to the sum of operating costs, depreciation, taxes, and adequate profits on new plant, but not enough competition to force prices down to direct operating costs when depression arose.[11] If the whole economy were operating at approximate capacity, the prices in such semi-competitive industries would then correspond roughly with *balanced use* of resources. On the other hand, if these prices were to remain relatively constant while prices in more competitive parts of the economy declined under the influence of depression, the particular prices would cease to correspond with balanced use of resources at the actual depression level. They might, however, continue to be prices which approximated operating costs, depreciation, taxes, and unit profits on new plant. If full recovery were attained these prices would again correspond with balanced use of resources. This would be a case of the prices being approximately in balance in the long-run sense but insufficiently flexible to ensure the short-run adjustments supposed to ensure the full use of resources. Competition sufficient to ensure a long-run price flexibility which keeps prices in line with the sum of operating costs, taxes, depreciation, and adequate profits on new plant will hereafter be referred to as ''First Degree Competition'' and will be assumed to result in prices corresponding to balanced use of resources when resources are being used to the full though contributing nothing toward the maintenance of full use of resources.

When competition is sufficient not only to produce a long-run approximation between price and the sum of operating costs, taxes, depreciation, and adequate profits but also to provide a short-run flexibility of price which forces prices down toward direct operating costs whenever demand falls below an industry's capacity, it will be referred to as ''Second Degree Competition.'' This more intensive competition is assumed to contribute toward full use of resources and at full use of resources to result in prices corresponding to balanced use of resources.

A third concept is necessary for the analysis of current conditions, namely that of monopoly. This term will be limited here to refer to a condition where there is insufficient competition even to ensure prices corresponding to balanced use of resources. By this definition, unless a monopolized industry is regulated or government owned,[12] prices are likely to be set which yield a monopoly profit when the economy is operating to the full. Such exercise of monopoly control is presumed to produce an unbalanced use of resources since the product of the monopolized industry is not used as extensively as its production costs would warrant. When the whole economy is operating at less than full activity, buying power may be so low that no prices can be set which will yield monopoly profits though the prices set are likely to be above the prices which would correspond with balanced use of resources. It will be assumed that unregulated monopoly results in prices which neither correspond with balanced use of resources nor contribute to full use of resources. In a free-price economy, it is supposed either that second degree competition prevails in every industry or that such exceptions as exist in the form of monopoly are not significant to an analysis of the operations of the economy as a whole. In the Modern American economy, such a large part of the economy is subject only to first degree competition or is owned or regulated by government that the economy does not approximate a free-price economy.

First Degree Competition

The character of first degree competition can be seen more clearly by examining the typical price determining procedure in modern industry. In the bulk of American industry, the individual concerns do not produce to the full and pour their product into the market in the manner expected of a free-price economy. Rather they adopt price policies and set their prices so as to cover not only operating costs but also taxes, depreciation, and unit profits. Having set their prices, their major problem is then to sell the largest possible volume at those prices—a selling problem for the *individual* enterprise supposed not to exist in a free-price economy and not existing in the case of such free-price commodities as wheat, cotton, and scrap iron. The price administering procedure is clearly summarized in the latest annual report of the General Motors Corporation which states: "The policy of the Corporation over the years has been at all times—and this is true of the automotive industry as a whole—to establish such selling prices as might be expected to produce the greatest volume, giving consideration to a reasonable return on the capital employed in the business of the stockholders." There are few manufacturing industries in which some such procedure is not adopted.[13] In most of retail trade it is certainly adopted. Pricing in the regulated and government-owned industries follows a similar pattern.

The administered prices which result from this procedure are not entirely inflexible. Adjustments are made from time to time to meet new conditions and a long-run flexibility usually exists such that technological improvement is to a greater or less extent passed on to consumers and alterations in the price level such as occurred from 1914 to 1919 and from 1919 to 1921 are met. Thus in the automobile industry, technological improvement has been reflected partly in improved cars and partly in successively lower prices even though little drop in prices occurred between 1929 and 1932 when flexible-priced commodities suffered a general decline. In such industries competition may be sufficient to give a fairly good first approximation to the prices corresponding to balanced use of resources at full activity. But competition has not been sufficient to produce prices sufficiently flexible to contribute to the elimination of depression.

In the regulated industries and government-owned activities, the same relative inflexibility of price appears. Regulation has not been aimed to produce the price adjustments which would contribute to full use of resources but only prices or rates which would correspond roughly to balanced use. Government-controlled enterprises such as the post office have even raised prices in the face of depression rather than granting the lower prices which would make for fuller use of resources.

Finally, wage rates are relatively inflexible, partly as wage rates are set administratively by big-scale enterprise and partly as labor organization has been able to enforce rates not corresponding to those expected from second-degree competition. Prior to 1933 labor organization was of secondary importance in the bulk of American industry and practically nonexistent in the mass-production industries. The inflexibility of wage rates in the heavy industries before 1933 must be attributed in large measure to corporate policy. Since that time, labor organization has become increasingly important. Where industry is concentrated, strong labor organization, by bringing greater equality in bargaining position, is likely to bring prices and wage rates more in line with balanced use of resources but tends to reinforce the short-run inflexibility resulting from corporate concentration. Thus in correcting the unbalance in bargaining position between large corporate units and individual workers labor organization has still further increased the dissimilarity brought about by corporate concentration between the American economy and the free-price economy which is supposed to be made up of thousands of independent business, labor, and consumer bargaining units in each industry.

In the past when a deficiency of competition has been recognized, trust busting, regulation, or government ownership has been advanced as a cure. These will be examined below to see how far each can contribute toward the two basic ends of balanced use and full use of resources.

Trust Busting

In the past, trust busting, to the extent it has been effective, has been effective in the maintenance of first degree competition. When an industry became so concentrated that extensive monopoly profits were being made, antitrust procedures have often been successful in breaking up a monopolizing concern into several more or less independent concerns. The tobacco monopoly was broken into four major concerns, the oil monopoly into a larger number but less independent. But the courts would not order the United States Steel Corporation to be broken up even though it controlled nearly half of the steel business. Collusive agreements between independent concerns have been more readily upset by the courts but as long as one industry after another can be concentrated to the point that three or four major concerns do the bulk of the business, the ability to prevent collusive agreements becomes of secondary importance. In preventing absolute monopoly the antitrust procedure may have ensured a rough approximation to first degree competition in most unregulated industries. It has completely failed, however, to induce second degree competition.

In order for the antitrust procedure to be effective in producing second degree competition, it would be necessary to break up each of the more concentrated industries into a large number of separate concerns. No one has yet worked out the actual degree to which an industry would have to be atomized in order to ensure second degree competition. The 1,900,000 cotton farmers, the 1,200,000 wheat farmers, and the thousands of junk dealers are sufficient in number to produce free-prices in those commodities. How many automobile manufacturers would be sufficient to approximate a free-market in new automobiles? Twenty companies competing in the low price markets? Fifty companies? One hundred companies? The character of automobiles does not seem to facilitate a free-market type of production and distribution. A large enough number of producers to give free-prices would almost certainly eliminate low priced cars altogether. The evidence to date suggests that in a great many mass-production industries the breakup into a sufficiently large number of producers to approximate the results of second degree competition would force operation into inefficiency [sic] small units and eliminate the advantages of modern mass-production. For this reason, *the tentative conclusion seems warranted that modern technology precludes the development of second degree competition in a large part of industry.*

If such a conclusion is accepted, the basic function of antitrust activity becomes greatly clarified. Its function would be to ensure a close approximation to first degree competition in the unregulated industries, leaving the function performed by second degree competition to be accomplished in some other manner. In maintaining first degree competition, evidence that an industry was highly concentrated and that prices were consistently being set which were significantly above the production costs with the best new plant which could be built (including in costs, operating costs, taxes, depreciation, and adequate profits) would indicate the need for further increase in competition. Any industry in which at least first degree competition could not be maintained would be ripe for public regulation or government ownership. Reliance on antitrust procedure to maintain first degree competition would undoubtedly call for some measure of trust busting but not the wholesale breakup of industry implicit in an effort to obtain the results expected of second degree competition. At the same time the adoption of such a policy would mean that trust busting could not be relied on to contribute significantly to the solution of the basic problem of the day, the lack of any force pressing the whole economy toward full and maintained operations.

Public Utility Regulation

Just as trust busting has been mainly oriented to the maintenance of first degree competition, public utility regulation at best has sought to obtain by regulation only the results which first degree competition was supposed to produce. To the extent that it has been successful from the point of view of public interest, it has resulted in a crude first approximation to prices or rates corresponding to balanced use of resources. A few abortive efforts have been made to get utilities to adopt "depression rates" which would more nearly correspond with the results expected from second degree competition. In contrast, some utilities, notably the railroads, have sought rates in excess of those to be expected from first degree competition on the ground that under depressed conditions their rates were insufficient to yield profits however satisfactory they might be if the whole economy were running to the full. One can conclude that however satisfactory utility regulation may be as a tool for approximating the results of first degree competition, it does not lend itself to the rapid readjustments necessary to match the results to be expected from second degree competition.[14]

Government Ownership

As in the case of trust busting and utility regulation, government ownership has in the past been concerned with establishing prices which roughly correspond with those to be expected from first degree competition. Insofar as ownership lies in local government units there is no reason to expect that prices will be lowered in depression times to the "operating cost" level which would correspond with the results to be expected from second degree competition.[15] The federal government might operate so as to approximate the results of second degree competition but such a procedure seems difficult to put into operation and not likely to be particularly effective. In the case of the post office, mail rates were increased 50 percent from 1929 to 1933 whereas second degree competition would be expected to produce lower rates. Little more could be expected from government ownership of a particular industry than from trust busting or regulation so far as the maintenance of full economic operation is concerned.

Two major conclusions flow out of the above analysis—first, the need for more intensive effort, particularly through antitrust and regulatory activity, to ensure prices which correspond with balanced use of resources at full operation of the whole economy; and second, the need to create some force which will continuously press economic activity toward full operation. Methods for achieving the first of these ends are discussed below while the methods for accomplishing the second will be discussed in detail in a later memorandum.[16]

Balanced Use of Resources

Perfect balance in the use of resources is never likely to be achieved and the major goal in seeking the results to be expected from first degree competition is to establish conditions in which a rough and ready balance will develop. This task would be vastly easier if the whole economy were operating at approximately full activity. At full activity, significant monopoly profits would be a clear indication of unbalance. Likewise, at full activity, new plants are more likely to be built and put into operation thereby giving a basis for estimating costs on new plants inclusive of taxes, depreciation, and adequate profit. With less than full operation, the absence of monopoly profits would not indicate balanced prices since profits may be kept down by part-time operations. Yet studies of the costs for hypothetical and existing plants could give an approximate basis for determining whether prices for an industry in which prices appear fairly inflexible were significantly above the operating costs, depreciation, taxes, and unit profits which would be appropriate to the most efficient plant that could be constructed. At the same time it should be recognized that balanced use of resources is a long-time and moving objective. It involves more efficient use of resources but has relatively little relevance to problems of recovery and full use of resources. For this reason haste is not essential and a program can be built gradually.

This memorandum has only attempted to outline the characteristics of first degree competition and to suggest that such a degree of competition is all that can be expected from an antitrust approach. This readiness to exempt competition from the responsibility of ensuring full use of resources rests in part on the tremendous difficulties which appear to stand in the way of obtaining second degree competition in most mass-production industries, in part on the loss in productiveness which seems likely to result, and in part on the fact that even if all so-called competitive industries were broken up to the point that second degree competition prevailed, so much inflexibility would still exist in the regulated industries, in government activity, and in retail distribution that some force to supplement the market mechanism seems essential if full use of resources is to be approximated under conditions of modern technology.

Notes

1. Sometimes an ethical result is also claimed for the free-priced economy, namely that it operates in such a way that the income received by each factor of production just equals the particular contribution to production made by that factor. The validity of this claim is irrelevant to the present discussion.

2. Less than full capacity operation may be said to exist if there are unemployed men or machines. Unemployment of men may be said to exist if there are idle men who would gladly be employed at the wage rates currently being paid for the type of work they are capable of performing. Unemployment of machines may be said to exist if there are idle machines which the owners would gladly employ if there were a market for the product at current prices.

3. Balanced use of resources at less than full use could be defined as a condition such that no resource *being used* could be transferred to another use without lessening the product of the whole economy.

4. An outstanding exception is the industry in which demand is declining as rapidly or more rapidly than equipment is becoming useless from other causes. In such a case there is no need for new equipment and price is likely to be controlled by direct operating costs for long periods.

5. For instance, 40 to 50 billions of money medium is currently held by individuals and enterprises in this country. Thus a 20 percent decline in prices would increase the buying power of outstanding money by an amount equivalent to an increase of 10 billion dollars or more at the old prices.

6. It is worth noting that in a free-price economy a lowering of wage rates to a greater extent than prices of goods would be expected to aggravate rather than counteract an incipient depression growing out of a deficiency of buying power.

7. The more precise statement would be "when the differential out-of-pocket costs are less than the market price."

8. It should be recognized that "full capacity" is itself in part a function of price relationships.

9. There are, of course, many refinements which are customarily introduced but the picture stands virtually as given above.

10. The difficulties of defining capacity operation in no way invalidate this general principle applicable to the theoretical free-price economy.

11. Throughout this analysis "adequate profits" is used to mean profits sufficient to induce the new capital outlay necessary to maintain or expand the capacity of the industry.

12. Or cooperatively owned.

13. In some processing industries the margin between raw material and the processed product reflects administrative control rather than the price of the product itself.

14. The tendency for the courts to overbalance the protection of the rights of property as compared with the rights of consumers has tended to distort the results obtained in utility regulation. Greater emphasis needs to be placed on the rates which would contribute most to balanced use of resources at full operation of the economy and less on the maintenance of profits in a profit and loss economy.

15. This is due to the fact that a depression lowering of prices by government would involve public action in terms of the whole economy. While the federal government could adopt such a policy, the likelihood that a great many State and local governments will do so is almost as small as that business enterprises able to administer their prices will lower them to "keep the economy running."

16. The latter will take some time to prepare and I shall not have such time until the Structure Report is completed.

8

The Economics of Administered Prices: Introductory Explorations for an Atomistic Economy

In spite of the fact that prices fixed over periods of time have long been a common phenomenon, economic literature contains very little theoretical analysis focused on the possible economic effects of this price rigidity. The widespread prevalence of such administered prices and the increased role which they play in the American economy[1] suggests the need for intensive exploration into their implication for economic functioning. This and the following articles constitute introductory explorations in this field.*

Because the subject matter of these articles will be the ''economics of administered prices,'' it is important to give precise meaning to the term ''administered prices.'' This term is here used to refer to a price which is held for a period of time sufficiently long so that a series of transactions take place at this given price.[2] The definition has two essential elements: (1) that the price is ''held for a period of time,'' and (2) that a series of transactions take place at this price. If a house is offered for sale at a given price and this price is held for a period of time until the house is finally sold, this would not be an administered price even though the price is held for a period. There is only a single transaction. Likewise a series of transactions might, by chance, occur at exactly the same price but would not involve an administered price unless the price was set by some individual, organization, or combination. A series of transactions in a given commodity at identical prices would be presumptive evidence of an administered

January 29, 1940. From the Gardiner C. Means Papers at the Franklin D. Roosevelt Library, Series II, "Prices—Administered."

*The content and location of the ''following articles'' are unknown.—Eds.

price if the series was sufficiently numerous and covered a sufficiently long period to eliminate any practical likelihood that the prices were identical either (1) because of the lack of any change in the factors affecting demand or supply, or (2) because the influence on price of changes in the factors affecting supply are just offset by the influence on price of changes in the factors affecting demand and vice versa. A short or long series of sales of a given commodity by a particular seller at identical prices coupled with knowledge that the seller set and held his price would be conclusive evidence of an administered price.

Administered prices may arise as the result of the action of a single individual or enterprise, as for instance that of a street hawker or an enterprise producing a highly specialized article; they might arise as a result of individual enterprises independently following a price leader; they might result from collusion between enterprises or coercion by one or more enterprises over others; they might result from government regulation as in the case of railroads and other utilities; or they might be set by Congress as in the case of postal rates. This discussion of the economics of administered prices is not primarily concerned with the source of price administration but its effects on economic functioning.

Presumably administered prices can arise only under conditions of imperfect competition, but this does not mean that imperfect competition always results in administered prices nor does it mean that the problems arising from administered prices are the same as those usually discussed under the heading of the economics of imperfect competition. Most of the theoretical analyses in the latter field either assume that prices are sensitive to changes in demand and in cost conditions but conclude that the resulting prices would be different from those which could be expected under conditions of perfect competition; or else they deal only with long run adjustments, and the question of short run sensitivity or insensitivity to changes in demand or cost conditions is presumed to have no significance for the analysis.[3] In contrast to the economics of imperfect competition, the economics of administered prices is almost solely concerned with the short run insensitivity of prices to variations in economic conditions.

The economic problems associated with administered prices can be grouped, at least tentatively, under two heads: (1) the problems growing out of the immobility of price, and (2) the problems growing out of changes or prospective changes in price. Thus a price which is known to be so fixed that it is unlikely to be changed within the period which has to be taken into account in actual operation will present problems arising primarily from non-change. On the other hand, an imminent possibility of change in a price that has been rigid for a period has repercussions which give rise to another set of problems. If a price rise is imminent, current purchases may be increased so as to stock up ahead of any rise. Similarly, the rumor of a possible price revision downward may result in partial postponement of buying, while an actual cut in prices after a price has been fixed for a long time may be taken by a large enough number of prospective buyers to be an [indication] of further price reduction so that it leads, at least temporarily, to a reduction in sales rather than an increase. Other problems associated with the change of an administered price arise from the costs of making a change such as those of getting out new catalogs, notifying customers, and similar details of business practice or, in the case of regulated industries, the accounting and legal and other costs, both private and public, involved in bringing about a change of rates. Both the problems of fixed price and those of a change in a fixed price are outside the scope of the problems usually discussed under the head of imperfect competition and quite properly constitute the subject matter of a different field of analysis which is here being called *the economics of administered prices.*

In this first series of articles, attention will be focused on the problems arising from non-change and will aim to suggest how economic activity could be expected to develop under conditions of rigid prices, leaving for later discussion the dynamic problems arising from possible changes in an administered price. The procedure to be adopted will be that of setting up a series of abstract and greatly simplified situations involving first rigid prices and then a combination of rigid and flexible prices and tracing through the economic adjustments which might be expected to develop.

As a device for simplifying the process of tracing through the implications of rigid prices, four different abstract economics will be envisaged, each differing from the other in the type of enterprise within which productive activity is presumed to be carried on. In the first economy *all* production will be presumed to be carried on by individuals for sale to other individuals. For convenience this will be referred to as an atomistic economy.[4] In the second economy *all* production will be presumed to be carried on by workers hired by entrepreneurs[5] who own the instruments of production, receive the product, and sell it to other enterprises or individuals. Such an economy will be referred to as a factory economy. In the third or corporate economy, *all* production is presumed to be carried on by workers employed by business corporations whose stock is widely distributed. In the fourth or government economy, *all* production is presumed to be carried on by workers employed by governmental units.

For the present purpose the essential difference between these four abstract economies has to do with the different types of transactions and prices which they involve. If we assume that all economic transactions involve money on at least one side of the transaction then, by definition, the atomistic economy involves only transactions between money and goods (including both commodities and services) and goods prices are the only prices involved. Likewise the factory economy involves money-goods transactions and money-labor transactions so that it presents problems both of goods prices and wage rates. The corporate economy would similarly involve money-goods transactions, money-labor transactions, and money-security transactions (including the payment of dividends) and would present problems arising from security prices as well as from goods prices and wage rates. The government economy would introduce the problems of taxes. In each of these abstract economies it will be appropriate to introduce money loans so that each will involve problems of interest. By tracing through the possible effects of rigid prices in each of these abstract economies separately and then tracing them through a more complex and more realistic abstract economy in which production is carried on by all four different types of enterprise, it is hoped that significant light can be thrown on the short run influences at work in the actual modern economy.

Notes

1. Reference to Chapter VIII, Structure Report. [Means, *The Structure of the American Economy*. Washington, D.C.: USGPO, 1939.]

2. This is the same meaning and essentially the same definition as that given for the term "administered price" when it was first introduced in "Industrial Prices and Their Relative Flexibility," Senate Document 13, 74th Congress, 1st Session.

3. Cite Chamberlin, Robinson, etc.

4. This type of production has sometimes been referred to as the domestic system of production in contrast to the factory system of production. (See Edwin R.A. Seligman's introduction to Adam Smith's *Wealth of Nations,* Everyman Edition, N.Y. 1910, p. xiii.) An economy in which *all* production was on the basis of the domestic system might be called "a domestic economy" but such a term might be thought to imply an economy of home production for home use.

5. The term "entrepreneur" is here used to refer to an individual who owns, controls, and manages a business enterprise. By this definition, there would be no entrepreneurs in a pure corporate economy as defined above just as there would be no hired workers in a pure atomistic economy.

9

An Insensitive-price Mechanism of International Trade Adjustment and Its Policy Implications

Two recent proposals, the White Plan and the Keynes Plan, for setting up a world monetary standard have raised anew the theoretical problem of trade adjustment between nations when their currencies are more or less rigidly fixed to a common standard.[1] Classical economic theory delineated a mechanism of trade adjustment which could be expected to operate under conditions of *perfectly* sensitive goods prices and wage rates. An equally unrealistic mechanism of trade adjustment could be worked out for conditions of perfectly *in*sensitive goods prices and wage rates. For modern conditions, in which goods prices and wage rates range all the way from highly sensitive to highly insensitive, a more realistic mechanism could be expected to combine elements of both of these abstract mechanisms.[2] In what follows, these mechanisms will be outlined in terms of two countries whose currencies are rigidly linked to gold and the implications of these mechanisms for policy, particularly policy after the war, will be suggested.

The Classical Mechanism

The essentials of the classical gold flow mechanism of international trade adjustment are familiar and can be quickly stated. If there were an economy consisting of two countries, each with its own monetary unit based on gold and with the volume of its stock of money (currency and deposits) a direct multiple of its monetary gold, there would be a tendency for any unbalance in trade to be corrected as a result of a flow of gold between the two countries and the readjustments this would cause. The movement of gold would bring about monetary

---

July 1, 1943. From the Gardiner C. Means Papers at the Franklin D. Roosevelt Library, Series IV, "International Trade (1)."

expansion and an increase in goods prices and wage rates in one country and monetary contraction and lower goods prices and wage rates in the other. The lower price-wage level in the country losing gold would stimulate its exports while the higher price-wage level in the gold-receiving country would damp its exports. The gold movement and the changes in relative price-wage levels could be expected to continue until trade balance was restored or new factors intervened.

The mechanism of adjustment would be essentially the same if the money stocks in either or both countries did not vary in exact proportion to the monetary gold stock but varied in the same *direction.* So long as a gold flow produced monetary contraction and a lower price-wage level in one country and monetary expansion and a higher price-wage level in the other, it could serve to correct an unbalance in trade.

It should be noted that this classical mechanism of trade adjustment depends for its operation on goods prices and wage rates so sensitive to changes in demand that the net effect of changes in the money stock is that which could be expected if goods prices and wage rates were *perfectly* sensitive and the *whole* impact of the gold flow worked itself out through changes in the price-wage levels. For simplicity we can refer to this as "the sensitive-price mechanism of international trade adjustment."[3]

The Adjustment Mechanism with Perfectly Insensitive Prices

If, instead of assuming that goods prices and wage rates were perfectly sensitive, the equally unrealistic assumption is made that both price categories are *perfectly insensitive,* how would adjustment in trade be brought about? If there were an economy consisting of two countries, each with its own monetary unit based on gold and with the volume of its stock of money a direct multiple of its monetary gold, how would an unbalance in trade be corrected if goods prices and wage rates in each country were fixed? Under these conditions, the trade adjustment could not be brought about through changes in relative price-wage levels. Also, since the values of the monetary units of both the countries are, by assumption, fixed in terms of gold, a change in the relative values of the two currencies (such as could occur under inconvertible paper) would be out of the question. What form would the trade adjustment take?

The first major result of the unbalance in trade would presumably be a gold flow from one country to the other as in the case of sensitive prices. This would produce a contraction in the money stock of one and an increase in the money stock of the other. In the presence of fixed goods prices and wage rates, the contraction in the stock of money in the gold-losing country could be expected to result in a reduction in the total sale of goods and the development of unemployment in that country. In contrast, the country which received the gold and had an expansion in its money stock could be expected to have a boom in sales and increased production.[4] The depression in the first would presumably reduce that country's demand for goods from the second while the boom in the second would presumably increase the latter's demand for goods from the first. Thus the unbalance in trade would be cut down. In the absence of new factors, the movement of gold could be expected to continue until the unbalance in trade was entirely corrected by depression in one country and boom in the other. A new equilibrium would be established when the volume of money in each country was adjusted to the point where it would support a level of production, employment, and real income such that the respective demands of each country for the goods of the other were just equal. Thus, where goods prices and wage rates were fixed, the gold flow mechanism of international trade adjustment could be expected to operate through a change in the relative levels of employment and business activity in the two countries rather than through a change in the relative price levels. This type of adjustment can be referred to as a "rigid-price mechanism of international trade adjustment."

One peculiar characteristic of the changes in business activity and real income under the rigid-price mechanism should be noted. In the case of perfectly sensitive goods prices and wage rates, the trade adjustment could be expected to produce a *general* change in the price-wage level which would affect all prices more or less alike.[5] Essentially the *real* values of the two currencies in terms of goods would be altered while their gold values remained the same. But where goods prices and wage rates were perfectly *in*sensitive, the change in sales, production, and employment would not be general but would be greatest in the case of the most dispensable goods. Thus, in the country losing gold, *real* incomes would contract and consumers could be expected to reduce their purchases of things they could most readily get along without. This would mean greater contraction in the sales of consumers' durable goods and in luxuries. Indeed the contraction in real income might force a shift to less expensive types of goods to such an extent that the demand for some like wheat and oleomargarine at the fixed price would increase. Also in the field of capital goods, the decline in production of goods for consumption would leave productive capacity idle and thereby dampen the demand for new capital goods. Thus, the contraction in employment would be highly differential, hitting the durable goods industries most heavily and hitting the industries producing indispensable goods little or not at all. In the case of a country receiving gold, the effect would be the reverse. The greatest expansion could be expected in the most dispensable goods. This differential effect of the change in the level of business and employment is in sharp contrast to the general character of the adjustment through changes in the price level.

The mechanisms of trade adjustment under the two extreme conditions of perfectly sensitive and perfectly insensitive goods prices and wage rates outlined above apply, of course, to very unrealistic conditions. The realistic situation in the modern world during peacetime is that goods prices range all the way from highly sensitive prices like those of cotton, wheat, and scrap iron through the intermediately sensitive like steel sheets and shapes to the highly insensitive like postal rates, public utility rates, raw materials like sulphur, nickel, and iron ore, and fabricated products like agricultural equipment and hardware.[6] Wage rates show an intermediate degree of sensitivity while salary rates are relatively insensitive.[7] The actual price structure is thus intermediate between the perfectly sensitive and the perfectly insensitive. This suggests that the more realistic mechanism of trade adjustment might be a combination of the two types of adjustment outlined above.

Adjustment with Mixed Sensitive and Insensitive Prices

The mechanism of trade adjustment for a mixed price economy, while more complex than either of the simple mechanisms, would presumably not be significantly different in character. It could be expected that an unbalance in trade between two countries with prices ranging from the highly sensitive to the highly insensitive would tend to be corrected partly through a change in relative price levels and partly through a change in relative degrees of business activity and employment. The adjustment could be expected to take the following form—as before, an unbalance of trade between the two countries would lead to a movement of gold and a contraction in the money stock of one country and an expansion in the money stock of the other. In the gold-exporting country, the contraction in the money stock would lead to a decline in the sensitive prices, a decline in sales, production, and employment in the industries with insensitive prices, some decline in both prices and production in the industries with intermediately sensitive prices, and an intermediate decline in wage rates. To the extent of the decline in production, there would be a decline in real income and therefore a greater contraction in the demand for dispensable goods than for those which were less dispensable. Where the prices of dispensable goods were sensitive they could be expected to drop more than the prices of less dispensable goods whose prices were equally sensitive. Where the prices of dispensable goods were insensitive, the production of such goods could be expected to drop more than the production of insensitive-priced indispensable goods. The net effect of the adjustment in the gold-exporting country could thus be quite complex but its essential character would be simply a combination of lower prices and lower production.

The reverse effect could be expected in the gold-receiving country. Sensitive prices would rise, sales production and employment would increase in industries with insensitive prices and wage rates, and intermediate effects would develop in the intermediately sensitive industries and with goods having different degrees of dispensability.

Presumably the more insensitive the goods prices and wage rates were, the greater the part of the trade adjustment which would be brought about through a change in the level of production and employment; the more sensitive the greater the adjustment through changes in price-wage levels.

This complex mechanism of trade adjustment in an economy in which goods, prices, and wage rates are not all perfectly sensitive or perfectly fixed, might be referred to as "an insensitive-price mechanism of international trade adjustment." While this mechanism has been described in terms of gold, it would apply equally whatever the rigid world standard. Presumably it is this insensitive-price mechanism which would operate in the modern world if the currencies of different countries were tied rigidly to a world money standard.

The Theoretical Character of the Analysis

It should be recognized that the above analysis is both theoretical and relatively abstract. The theory presented in the classical mechanism of trade adjustment through gold flow has been tested in several factual studies, particularly in cases of large movements of capital such as took place in the Argentine between 1880 and 1900 and in Canada from 1900 to 1913.[8] In each case the shift in price levels which would be expected from the classical theory was found to take place and this was accepted as a validation of the theory. But in no case was an effort made to establish that the *whole* of the adjustment was brought about through the changes in price level. The classical theory is consistent with the evidence of changes in price level but so also is the theory that the adjustment was brought about partly through a change in price levels and partly through changes in levels of employment. Until factual studies are made with the alternative theory in mind the question would seem to be moot.[9] However, even in the absence of such studies, it is possible to explore the implications for policy which this analysis would have if it were proved to be or accepted as valid.

Policy Implications of the Insensitive-price Mechanism

There are three general implications of the insensitive-price mechanism of trade adjustment which have major importance for policy. For simplicity these will be considered first in terms of the rigid-price mechanism and in terms of gold flow.

The first of these three policy implications has to do with the gain which a country could hope to obtain through a "favorable" balance of trade. If the gold flow mechanism operated to bring about a change in the levels of business activity in two countries, a particular country having less than full employment could increase its level of activity and its real income by increasing its import restrictions or by subsidizing its exports. Thus, if one country set up quotas which cut its imports in half, it would have a "favorable" balance of trade which would result in an inflow of gold, expansion in its stocks of money and increased sales, production, and employment at the fixed prices and wage rates while the gold-losing country suffered depression. Of course, to the extent that the other country put retaliatory restrictions on imports, the gain to the first country would be less and the depression in the other country would be less. Such competitive restriction of trade could result in a stalemate with neither country continuing to gain at the expense of the other and each suffering from a reduction in gainful exchange of goods. However, if goods prices and wage rates were insensitive, the initiating country would be able to stimulate its business activity in an initial period through its restriction of trade.

This conclusion suggests that in trade between countries in which a considerable degree of price insensitivity exists and in which the respective currencies are rigidly linked to a common standard both in value and quantity, the raising of restrictions on imports or subsidizing of exports would yield a gain in prosperity to the initiating country until offset through retaliatory measures by other countries. The suggestion is consistent with the Mercantilist Theory of gain to a country from a net inflow of gold if that theory were applied to, say, a guild-dominated economy in which an important body of prices was rigidly fixed for considerable periods of time.

A second implication of the insensitive-price mechanism has to do with the spreading of depression between countries. Under fixed-price conditions the gold flow mechanism operating between two countries could be expected to spread depression from one country into the other, dividing the impact of the initial depressing factor between the two countries. Thus, if a depression arose in one country because of some internal development, its demand for goods from the other country would fall off and gold would flow. This would tend to reduce the depression in the first country and bring depression to the second. A new equilibrium might be reached with the level of activity in *both* countries lower than before the depressing factor arose.

This conclusion suggests that in a world economy of relatively insensitive goods prices and wage rates and with each country having its money rigidly linked to a common standard, both in value and in quantity, depressions and booms would tend to be world wide in character though with some lag between the initiating and the reacting countries.

The third major implication of the insensitive-price mechanism has to do with the limited control which a country could exercise over its internal level of production and employment through monetary and fiscal actions even if its volume of money could be adjusted independently of its monetary gold. If one of two countries incurred an adverse trade balance under such insensitive-price conditions that the normal operation of the gold flow mechanism would result in a continuing depression, that country would be powerless to avert the depression through its monetary and fiscal policies so long as the fixed gold standard was retained and the gold-receiving country chose to sterilize the expansionist effect of the gold it received. For example, if a country suffered an adverse balance of trade under such conditions, the outflow of gold would lead to depression unless its effects were offset in some fashion. The country could offset the depressing effect of the shrinkage in its gold holdings by monetary or fiscal expansion and thereby postpone the depression, but the conditions leading to the initial unbalance in trade would remain uncorrected except to the extent that there was a net expansion in the gold-receiving country. If the latter chose to demonetize the gold as fast as it flowed in, there would be no correction of the forces making for the initial unbalance in trade. The unbalanced trade would therefore continue to force a gold flow until the gold-losing country was willing to allow a depression or to revise downward the gold value of its currency or until the gold-receiving country was willing to allow a boom or revise upward the gold value of its currency. This means that, so long as the currency of both countries was tied to gold in a fixed ratio, the level of business activity in each would be to a considerable extent determined by the policies of the other. Neither country could be sure of controlling its internal level of employment and also staying on its fixed gold standard.

When this conclusion is applied to a world of relatively insensitive goods prices and wage rates, it suggests that a country which fixes its monetary unit rigidly to that of other countries is in part surrendering control over the level of business activity and employment within its borders. Even though it retains full control over its monetary and fiscal action and can expand its volume of money independent of its monetary gold or holdings of other forms of world money, an adverse balance of trade may force it to choose between a depression and departing from the fixed money standard. Similarly, a favorable balance may force it to choose between an excessive boom and a continuing inflow of gold or world money which can ultimately force other countries to depart from the world standards they have adopted.

While these policy conclusions implicit in the insensitive-price mechanism of trade adjustment have a general application, the immediate importance for policy of the insensitive-price theory of trade adjustment lies in its application to the problems of the post-war economy. In the White Plan for a world monetary unit to take the place of gold after the war, the value of the currency of each country would be quite rigidly tied to the world unit and would thus provide what is essentially a rigid world standard.[10] In the Keynes Plan, emphasis is placed on fixity of exchange rates but a central authority would be given power to alter rates. Thus at its least flexible, the Keynes Plan, if adopted, could lead to a rigid world standard. At its most flexible it would provide a system of exchange rates administered by a central authority and would thus provide what might be called an administered world standard. How each of these types of standard could be expected to operate in a world of mixed sensitive and insensitive goods prices and wage rates deserves investigation.

A Rigid World Standard

If the value of the currencies of the separate countries were to be rigidly tied to a world money unit, the insensitive-price theory of trade adjustment indicates that unbalances in trade between countries would lead to fluctuations in business activity which would be largely outside the control of the individual country. If, for example, the currency of a particular country were, at the outset, significantly overvalued in terms of the world money as compared with the currencies of other countries, that country would be seriously damaged by the workings of the world money system. It would have an "adverse" trade balance which it would have to meet by reducing its holdings of the world money. So long as the currency was overvalued and no artificial measures were taken to stop this drain, it would continue until the country's world money holdings were exhausted and it was forced off the world standard or it accepted a continuing depression as the means for adjusting trade. Artificial measures such as trade restrictions, special loans from abroad, or a forced downward revision of insensitive goods prices and wage rates would give a temporary or expensive corrective. But so long as there was a considerable degree of price and wage insensitivity, the basic choice in the case of an overvalued currency would be between a continuing drain of world money or a prolonged depression.[11] If the overvaluation continued long enough, the basic choice would be between departing from the rigid world standard and continuing depression.

Even if the currencies of the different countries were perfectly valued at the outset, both short-run and long-run developments could lead to unbalance in trade. This also could present the basic choice of departure from the world standard and depression. Thus, in adhering to a rigid world money standard, each country would appear to be accepting fluctuations in business activity within its boundaries as a part of the basic device for correcting unbalances in trade between itself and the rest of the world.

An Administered World Standard

An alternative to a rigid world standard would be one in which some world authority is given easily exercised power to change exchange rates. Such an authority could adjust exchange rates in such a way as to correct unbalances in trade as they develop. The Keynes Plan would provide a world authority with power to alter exchange rates but gives little attention to the principles on which such changes should be made. There does appear to be an expectation that if a country's "wage and price levels in terms of money are out of line with those elsewhere, a change in the rate of its foreign exchange is inevitable" (p. 14). It is not, however, clear to what extent it is expected that unbalance in trade would be corrected through changes in exchange rates and to what extent through inflationary or deflationary measures forced on the separate countries by the central governing body. What is clear is that the Keynes Plan places with a central governing body power to determine in a large measure the level of economic activity in each country and for the world as a whole. Thus, while exchange rates could be altered under the Keynes Plan, they would in essence be administered by a central world authority with the result that each individual country would have relatively little control over its internal level of employment.[12] How rigid this administered world standard would be in practice is uncertain, though in the current presentation of the plan, the main emphasis is on adjustment in balances without changes in exchange rates.

The Conception of a World Money Unit

The idea of a world money unit to which the different national money units are rigidly linked has a great appeal. We are familiar with the fact that within a nation, it is not necessary to have a separate money unit for each region. It is clear that there is no major need for adjusting unbalances in trade between regions within a country through a change in exchange ratios and that a single monetary unit for the several regions would not prevent the maintenance of reasonably full employment for a country as a whole. Why would not the same apply to the world as a whole?

The difference in trade adjustment between regions within a country and between countries is partly one of degree and partly one of kind. Within a country having a single money unit and relatively insensitive goods prices and wage rates, an unbalance in trade between regions could be expected to have a somewhat depressing effect on one region and a stimulating effect on the other but to the extent that the unbalance was between adjacent regions, it would tend to be reduced through the mobility of resources between regions.[13] The further apart the regions, the less the mobility of resources and therefore the less likely that an unbalance in trade would be corrected through geographical readjustments. An unbalance between continents would presumably be much more slowly corrected than one within continents even if there were no national barriers. This difference in degree between world trade adjustments and adjustments within narrower regions means that depression arising from unbalance in trade would be much more serious in the case of a rigid system of money for the world as a whole than in the case of a rigid money unit for a single country.

To this difference in degree is added the difference in kind which results from national barriers to the movement of resources between nations.[14] Of course, the national barriers to the movement of populations and real capital could be removed by international agreements but the differences in degree would remain. Thus, whether the barriers were removed or not, the depressing effect of adverse trade adjustment between a group of nations having a rigid money system could be expected to be more serious than the depressing effect of adverse trade adjustments between regions within each nation.

To these differences in trade adjustment must be added a second and perhaps more important difference between the effects of a rigid monetary unit for a single country and for the world as a whole. This lies in the problem of maintaining reasonably full employment. Within a nation having its own monetary unit, so long as its monetary unit is not rigidly fixed to that of any other country directly or through some common standard, it has the monetary and fiscal powers sufficient to determine its own internal level of employment. It can legitimately place on its government the responsibility for adopting fiscal and monetary policies which will bring about reasonable full employment. But if the country's currency is rigidly tied to that of other countries, it has in part surrendered the power to determine its own internal level of activity. Similarly it has surrendered such power if its exchange rates are not rigidly linked to a world monetary unit but are determined by some world monetary authority with administrative power to change its exchange rates. In either case a country loses power to determine its internal level of employment.

An Automatic World Standard

There is, however, a third alternative. It is well accepted that unbalances in trade could be corrected through a change in the relative values of the separate currencies in terms of a world standard without a change of internal price levels. An administered world standard such as that called for by the Keynes Plan could provide flexibility of exchange rates and *might* be so administered as to bring about trade adjustment primarily through changes in exchange rates, but on the other hand it might not. In either case, such a world standard would involve a tremendous centralization of power over the internal conditions in the separate countries. An alternative type of flexible standard would be one *which relied explicitly on changes in exchange rates as the principle on which trade adjustments between countries were to be brought about and set up a mechanism whereby changes in exchange rates were automatically made whenever a significant degree of trade unbalance developed.* Such an automatic flexible world standard would leave each country free to use its own monetary and fiscal powers to maintain full employment and develop a relatively stable price level within its borders while the adjustment of trade between countries was brought about through periodic adjustments in the relation of the separate currencies to the world standard. The difficulties in setting up such a system might be considerable but the danger of competitive devaluation which would exist in the absence of any world monetary system, the destructive effect of a rigid world standard, and the centralized power of an administered world standard would seem to justify the efforts to design an automatic world standard which would maintain a reasonable adjustment in international trade and yet leave each country free to determine its own internal level of economic activity.[15]

Notes

1. *Preliminary Draft Outline of Proposal for a United and Associated Nations Stabilization Fund*, U.S. Treasury Department, April 7, 1943. Popularly referred to as the "White Plan." *International Clearing Union*, British Information Services, April 8, 1943. Popularly referred to as the "Keynes Plan."

2. In suggesting that under modern conditions goods prices and wage rates range all the way from highly sensitive to highly insensitive, there is no implication that this is a new condition. Whether there was greater or less sensitivity in earlier days is irrelevant to the immediate discussion.

3. Since this classical mechanism was worked out, the oversaving theory has been developed as an explanation of mass unemployment. As this theory purports to explain an equilibrium at less than full employment under "A perfectly flexible competitive price system" (Alvin H. Hansen, *Fiscal Policy and Business Cycles,* p. 334, W. W. Norton & Co., N.Y.), it may be that the oversaving school would want to make some modification in this sensitive-price mechanism of trade adjustment. For the discussion above, however, the classical mechanism has been accepted as theoretically valid for a perfectly sensitive-priced economy under the conditions specified. Of course, even in a perfectly sensitive-price economy, some modification of the theory would presumably need to be made to take account of such factors as an expectation of gold movements and the correcting effect of shifts in expected buying power, but such modifications can be left out for the purposes of the present discussion.

4. If, at the outset, there was full employment in the gold-receiving country, the increased sales would lead to excessive employment, overtime work, etc., and might force some rationing of both goods and labor. For purposes of simplicity in the above analysis the limiting factor of the labor supply is overlooked, though in practice it could be quite important.

5. Some differential behavior might be expected between the prices of imported goods, exported goods, and other goods but this would be incidental to the general adjustment.

6. See *The Structure of the American Economy*, National Resources Committee, United States Government, Washington, 1939, Chapter VIII and Appendix 2.

7. See ibid.

8. Williams, John H., *Argentine International Trade Under Inconvertible Paper Money, 1880–1900* (Cambridge, Harvard University Press, 1920); Viner, Jacob, *Canada's Balance of International Indebtedness, 1900–1913* (Cambridge, Harvard University Press, 1924).

9. Of course, in a particular situation prices might be so sensitive that the great bulk of the whole adjustment was brought about through changes in price level. In the case of the modern industrialized state, goods prices and wage rates appear to be far too insensitive for the whole or even the great bulk of the adjustment to take the price form.

10. Altered only with a four-fifths vote of the governing body.

11. It is worth noting that in the 1920s, when England overvalued the pound in terms of gold, it suffered prolonged depression and some loss of gold. In the 1930s Australia reduced her depression through a forced reduction of her insensitive goods prices, wage rates, etc.

12. For example, if a country believed that it would only reach reasonably full employment at a level of real income of $120 billion while the world authority concluded that the country would reach full employment at $100 billion, the country would not be free to adopt the policies which would bring about the higher figure. Similarly a country whose level of economic activity was below that *believed appropriate by the central authority* would be under great pressure from the central authority to expand its activity.

13. Even between adjacent regions, the mobility of resources might not be sufficient to prevent prolonged depressions in particular sections of the country.

14. Of course, barriers to the movement of resources between regions within a nation may be set up but the decision to set such barriers lies within the nation. The presence of partially sovereign states within a nation further complicates the problem but not the principle.

15. The development of such an automatic world standard would have to combine a solution to the following problems: (a) the maintenance of short-run exchange stability for the conduct of ordinary business (or an adequate basis for hedging); (b) an exchange rate adjusting arrangement which would operate more or less automatically to maintain a reasonable balance of payments and without powers in any world authoritative body to prevent adjustment of balances through exchange rate changes; (c) the prevention of speculative disruption of the exchanges.

10

A General Formulation of Macro-Economic Equilibrium

It is the purpose of this article to present a general formulation of macro-economic equilibrium. The formulation is called general because it contains within itself three partial formulations of economic equilibrium, one of which leads to a liquidity-preference theory of interest, another which leads to a loan fund theory of interest with the Walrasian equilibrium as a special case, and a third which combines the liquidity-preference and the loan fund determinants of interest in a single formulation. The formulation is also called general because it is capable of dealing with rigid or administered prices as well as the flexible prices of classical economics.

In this article the general formulation will first be presented in financial terms so as to show why, in a given situation the liquidity preference and the loan fund theories of interest must produce identical results and how the Walrasian type of formulation relates to this general formulation. Then a more comprehensive formulation will be given making prices and physical quantities determinate.

I. A General Financial Formulation

This general financial formulation will be made in terms of a simplified economic model. In this model all transactions are assumed to be either goods-money or lending-borrowing transactions and the stock of money is assumed to be altered only by exogenous banking actions consisting of lending-money creating transactions or their reverse. Also transactions are between economic units which may be individuals or enterprises.[1]

January 31, 1957. From the Gardiner C. Means Papers at the Franklin D. Roosevelt Library, Series IV, "Economics—Macro (2)."

The Bookkeeping Constraint and the Allocation Matrix

The formulation starts with the bookkeeping necessity that money received minus money paid out equals the net change in money holdings. For a single economic unit (u) dealing in both goods and loans, this bookkeeping necessity can be stated for any given period as follows, using the customary symbols Y, C, and I for money income, consumption and investment and ΔB, ΔL, and ΔM for increases in borrowing, lending and money balances,

$$(1) \qquad Y_u + \Delta B_u - C_u - I_u - \Delta L_u = \Delta M_u$$

This bookkeeping requirement must apply to all monetary actions of a single unit and to the sum of the action of all units and will hereafter be referred to as the *bookkeeping constraint.*[2]

This bookkeeping constraint must apply to any *realistic* plans which a single unit might develop. If it plans to spend more money on goods it must be planning, at least by implication, to get the extra money from somewhere. Is its income going to increase? Will it borrow? Will it have loans repaid? Or will it reduce its money balance? In our model one or a combination of these actions must be a part of any realizable plan for the single economic unit to spend more. This means that in the simplified model the single unit, planning its economic course for any period, must allocate its resources—i.e., its money on hand, its income, and its potential borrowings—between spending on consumption or investment goods, the making of loans, the repayment of borrowings, and its money holdings at the end of the period in conformity with the bookkeeping constraint if its plans are to be realizable. The bookkeeping constraint must also apply to any actions or hypothetical actions of a unit regardless of whether it plans its allocation of resources realistically, or makes unrealizable plans, or makes no plans at all, and regardless of what stimuli induce its actions. This means that the allocation functions of a unit which represent how it would allocate resources in a given period under different hypothetical circumstances must also conform to the bookkeeping constraint.

The allocation of resources for a single unit (u) in the simplified model can then be stated in the following equation, the empty brackets representing the allocation functions, i.e., the unit's supply and demand functions:

$$(2) \qquad Y_u + \Delta B_u\,(\,) - C_u(\,) - I_u(\,) - \Delta L_u(\,) = \Delta M_u(\,)$$

One can go further than this and introduce the allocation functions for the individual unit. While there are various assumptions which could be made as to the appropriate content of these functions, the simplest formulation will be employed here by which each function contains only the factors Y and r (the level of interest rates). This formulation involves no particular problem for the demand functions for borrowing, consumption, investment, and lending. It may present a problem with respect to the demand function for changes in money balances and this requires examination.

Here we will assume that the demand for money is simply a demand for a highly liquid store of value regardless of how short or how long money is held, and that the holding of money renders a utility to the holder so long as he holds it regardless of the utility of the things on which he may finally spend it. For the holder the opportunity cost of immediate spending is greater than that of delayed spending and the advantage of liquidity overweighs the earnings and risk of lending. On this basis a demand function for money balances is qualitatively no different from that of other reservation demand functions and the demand function for an *increase* in money balances is no different in quality from the ordinary demand function. In the simplified conditions of the model the demand for an increase in money balance will be a function of income and interest rates like the other functions.

The Allocation Matrix

With the utility of money balances accepted, we can fill in the empty brackets in the system of allocation functions applying to a single economic unit as follows:

$$(3) \qquad Y_u + \Delta B_u\,(Y, r) - C_u(Y, r) - I_u(Y, r) - \Delta L_u(Y, r) = \Delta M_u(Y, r)$$

This general equation aims to reflect *all* the psychological factors which enter into the decisions of a single unit in the simple model in allocating its income and other resources and will be referred to as the "allocation equation." It represents an allocation matrix for the particular unit (u) indicating how the unit would allocate its resources during a given period under each relevant combination of its income and the level of interest rates. It assumes that the unit's initial holdings of money, its wants, its borrowing power, and its other resources are given.[3]

It should be particularly noted that the allocation functions in this allocation equation are subject to the bookkeeping constraint at all combinations of Y and r so that the five allocation functions are not independent. If any four are given, the fifth can be derived. This fact is essential to this analysis. It is the inclusion of all the functions and their subjection to the bookkeeping constraint which gives completeness to the general formulation and is one of the characteristics which distinguishes it from both the Keynesian and the Walrasian formulations.

Since the allocation matrix for each economic unit is a hypothetical statement of alternative patterns of behavior under alternative sets of conditions, the matrices for separate units are independent and can be summed for the total of all units. As a result, the general allocation equation for the economy as a whole could then be written:

(4) $$Y + \Delta B\,(Y, r) - C(Y, r) - I(Y, r) - \Delta L(Y, r) = \Delta M(Y, r)$$

The general allocation equation could also be written in terms of its constituents, the bookkeeping constraint and the separate allocation functions as follows:

$$Y + \Delta B - C - I - \Delta L = \Delta M$$

$$\begin{aligned}\Delta B &= \Delta B\,(Y, r)\\ C &= C\,(Y, r)\\ I &= I\,(Y, r)\\ \Delta L &= \Delta L\,(Y, r)\\ \Delta M &= \Delta M\,(Y, r)\end{aligned}$$

Thus the allocation matrix with its seven factors can be represented by six equations. However, since one of the allocation functions is redundant, the allocation matrix involves seven unknowns and only five independent equations. Presumably two more independent equations would state an equilibrium condition if they did not introduce additional variables.

Conditions for Equilibrium

Actually there are three conditions relating to the above variables which we recognize as necessary to equilibrium:

1. the sum of the demands for consumption goods and investment goods must equal income;
2. the demands for lending and borrowing must be equal; and
3. the net demand for a change in money balances and the change in the stock of money must be equal.

In the present analysis we are regarding increases (or reductions) in the stock of money and the concomitant addition (or reduction) in bank loans as exogenous and will represent it by the constant M_1. The three necessary conditions for equilibrium can then be written:

(5a) $$Y = C + I$$

(5b) $$\Delta B = \Delta L + M_1$$

(5c) $$\Delta M = M_1$$

These equilibrium equations add no new unknowns to the system, M_1 being given. However, all three equilibrium equations are not independent. If any two are given, the third is determined by the bookkeeping constraint. This leaves us with the necessary seven independent equations to determine seven unknowns.

The allocation matrix plus the three equilibrium equations thus state in general terms the condition of macro-financial equilibrium, including one redundant function and one redundant equilibrium equation.

Complete vs. Definitive Formulations

One of the advantages of this formulation is its completeness. So far as the particular economic model is concerned, it presents a complete set of factors and the relation between them necessary for financial equilibrium. The allocation equation can be presumed to reflect all of the psychological functions and it does so without giving overemphasis to or slighting any function even though any one function can be derived from the others. Also the set of equilibrium equations is complete even though, again, one is redundant.

This completeness is important. In the case of a logical construct, it is often possible to describe the construct definitively, i.e., so that someone else can precisely reconstruct it, without describing it completely.[4] And where there is more than one way to describe a construct definitively, each different method of description can lead to a difference in theory.

This can easily be seen in the case of a plane triangle. There are three different ways such a triangle can be definitively described. If we give measures for two angles and the contained side we emphasize angularity. If we give measures for two sides and the contained angle we emphasize sidedness. And if we give only the lengths of the three sides, all angularity drops out of the description. A complete description giving the length of each side and the magnitude of each angle would be giving more information than necessary to reconstitute the triangle but would also avoid any special emphasis.

In the case of the triangle, the three different definitive descriptions are not likely to be misleading because the triangle is such a simple construct. But in the more complex case of the economic model discussed above, the consequences can be serious. Here, there are three possible definitive descriptions implicit in the equilibrium equations. Any given equilibrium situation can be definitively described in terms of the allocation matrix and two equilibrium equations. If we describe it in terms of the equations, $Y = C + I$ and $\Delta M = M_2$, we get the Keynesian approach to equilibrium and a liquidity-preference theory of interest. If we describe it in terms of equations, $Y = C + I$ and $\Delta B = \Delta L$, we get a classical approach and a loan fund theory of interest with the Walrasian system of equations is a special case. If we describe it in terms of the equations, $\Delta B = \Delta L$ and $\Delta M = M_2$, we get a third approach combining the liquidity-preference and loan fund theories of interest.

The different emphasis given by different definitive descriptions can be sufficiently confusing, but there is another element of confusion. Different definitive [word unclear] descriptions of the same construct can be qualitatively different. The triangle gives a good example—the inclusion of angles in two of the descriptions and not in the third. This is an important *operational* difference. In order to be able to reconstruct any plane triangle whose three sides are given, the only instrument needed is a calibrated straight edge. If the definitive description includes one or more angles, a protractor or other angle-determining instrument or device is also needed.

In the case of our economic model, there is also an important qualitative and operational difference between the three descriptions. In the case of the second description, with the change in the stock of money given, all of the remaining variables have to be determined as a single system. But in the case of each of the other descriptions, there is a partial formulation which allows or even requires a determination of Y and r independently of certain other variables. Thus, the general and complete formulation given above contains not only three alternative definitive descriptions of equilibrium but two of these alternatives each involve a partial system of equilibrium which can be solved independently from the other. It seems likely that the presence of a partial system of equilibrium implicit in the total equilibrium has added to the confusion over the relation between the two competing theories of interest and also has made it difficult to relate the Walrasian system to the newer formulations. The next section will show the relation between the different formulations as they relate to interest theory while the following section will consider the Walrasian approach.

II. The Liquidity-Preference vs. the Loan Fund Theory of Interest

The liquidity-preference and the loan fund theories of interest can be simply stated in macro-economic terms for our simple model as follows[5]:

I		II	
Liquidity-Preference Theory		*Loan Fund Theory*	
(6a)	$\Delta M = M_1$	(6f)	$\Delta B = \Delta L + M_1$
(6b)	$\Delta M = \Delta M\ (Y, r)$	(6g)	$\Delta B = \Delta B\ (Y, r)$
(6c)	$Y = C + I$	(6h)	$\Delta L = \Delta L\ (Y, r)$
(6d)	$C = C\ (Y, r)$	(6c)	$Y = C + I$
(6e)	$I = I\ (Y, r)$	(6d)	$C = C\ (Y, r)$
		(6e)	$I = I\ (Y, r)$

The great difference between these two theories is apparent. Both theories require that in equilibrium the demand for goods $(C + I)$ and income (Y) should be equal. But one theory then makes the equilibrium and the rate of interest depend on the equality of the demand for money and the stock of money. The other theory makes the equilibrium and the rate of interest depend on the equality of the demand and supply of loanable funds. Certainly the two look like different theories.

This difference can be further emphasized if we assume that the demand functions are linear and give the constants hypothetical values as follows:

(7a) $$C = k_1Y + k_2r + k_3$$

(7b) $$I = k_4Y + k_5r + k_6$$

(7c) $$\Delta M = k_7Y + k_8r + k_9$$

(7d) $$\Delta B = k_{10}Y - k_{11}r + k_{12}$$

(7e) $$\Delta L = k_{13}Y + k_{14}r + k_{15}$$

Substituting in the equilibrating equations we get the following values for r and Y:

Liquidity-Preference Theory

(8) $$r = \frac{(1 - k_1 - k_4)\, M_1 - k_9\, (1 - k_1 - k_4) - k_7\, (k_3 + k_6)}{k_8\, (I - k_1 - k_4) + k_7(k_2 + k_5)}$$

(9) $$Y = \frac{(k_2 + k_5)\, M_1 - k_9\, (k_2 + k_5) + k_8\, (k_3 + k_6)}{k_8\, (1 - k_1 - k_4) + k_7\, (k_2 + k_5)}$$

Loanable-Funds Theory

(10) $$r = \frac{(1 - k_1 - k_4)\, M_1 - (k_{12} - k_{15})\, (1 - k_1 - k_4) - (k_{10} - k_{13})\, (k_3 + k_6)}{(k_{11} - k_{14})\, (1 - k_1 - k_4) + (k_{10} - k_{13})\, (k_2 + k_5)}$$

(11) $$Y = \frac{(k_2 + k_5)\, M_1 - (k_{12} - k_{15})\, (k_2 + k_5) + (k_{11} - k_{14})\, (k_3 + k_6)}{(k_{11} - k_{14})\, (1 - k_1 - k_4) + (k_{10} - k_{13})\, (k_2 + k_5)}$$

Thus the two theories are not only formulated quite differently, but appear to produce significantly different values for r and Y. Are they really different?

The answer is to be found in the allocation equation with its bookkeeping constraint. The essentials of either formulation can be derived from the other by substituting its special equations in the allocation equation. Thus, in the loan fund formulation we are given the demand functions for C, I, ΔB and ΔL. If they are substituted in the allocation equation, the demand function for additional money holdings can be derived. We then have the three functions of the liquidity-preference theory. Then if we substitute $\Delta B - \Delta L + M_1$ and $Y = C + I$ in the bookkeeping constraint, we have the remaining condition of equilibrium. Thus the loan fund formulation can be completely transformed into the liquidity-preference formulation.

However, the reverse transformation cannot be made completely but only in its essentials. The equilibrium equation $\Delta B = \Delta L + M_1$ can be derived from the liquidity preference formulation through the bookkeeping constraint but only the *net* value of the combined lending and borrowing functions can be derived. By substituting the demand functions for C, I, and ΔM in the allocation equation, we can obtain a *net* demand function for loanable funds which indicates all combinations of Y, r, and M_1. What we cannot determine is the absolute demand and absolute supply function. However, the *net* function for loanable funds is sufficient to establish an equilibrium and yield a loanable fund value for Y and r.

That the values for Y and r derived from the two different formulations must be the same can easily be shown in the case of the linear demand functions. If the linear demand function given in equations 7a–e are to meet the bookkeeping constraint for *all* values of Y and r, then the constants for Y must sum to one and the constants for the other factors must sum to zero. For this reason the constants in the linear functions above must bear the following relation[6]:

(12a) $$k_1 + k_4 + k_7 - k_{10} + k_{13} = 1$$

(12b) $$k_2 + k_5 + k_8 - k_{11} + k_{14} = 0$$

(12c) $$k_3 + k_6 + k_9 - k_{12} + k_{15} = 0$$

When we use these equations to substitute for k_7, k_8, and k_9 in the values for r and Y obtained through the liquidity-preference approach (equations 8 and 9), it will be found that they transform exactly into the values for r and Y obtained through the loan fund approach (equations 10 and 11). Thus not only can each formulation be transformed into the essentials of the other, but, in the case of linear functions, the two theories must lead to identical values for Y and r.

The identity of the two theories can be further reinforced by presenting the third partial formulation of equilibrium implicit in the general formulation, one which is entirely in financial terms:

III

Financial Theory

(13a) $$\Delta M = M_1$$

(13b) $$\Delta M = \Delta M(Y, r)$$

(13c) $$\Delta B = \Delta L + M_1$$

(13d) $$\Delta B = \Delta B(Y, r)$$

(13e) $$\Delta L = \Delta L(Y, r)$$

This formulation will also give a solution for Y and r, thus determining the rate of interest solely through consideration of the demand and supply of loanable funds and the demand and stock of money, and this formulation must produce the same results as the other two. Not one of these three formulations is a total formulation though each supplies sufficient information to determine Y and r. In the case of the liquidity-preference formulation, two additional equations are needed to determine ΔB and ΔL. The same is true of the financial formulation if C and I are to be determined. And, in the loan fund formulation, an additional equation is necessary to determine ΔM. Thus each of these formulations is partial as compared with the completeness of the allocation and equilibrium equations of the general formulation.

Prior Efforts at Reconciliation

This general formulation of equilibrium is useful in appraising other attempts to reconcile the apparently conflicting theories of interest. Only two such attempts will be considered here: (1) Hicks' attempt, based on the redundancy of an equation in the Walrasian system, and (2) a recent attempt by S.C. Tsiang.[7]

At first glance there appears to be a close resemblance between the reconciliation given above and that suggested by Hicks. In both cases a redundant equilibrium equation is involved and one gets a different theory depending on which equation is left out. But this is not all that is involved. If this were the whole explanation it should be a simple matter to reconcile the two theories by using a macro set of Walrasian equations. A little manipulation of such a set will quickly show that this is not possible because, while the definitive Walrasian system includes a demand-for-money-balances function, this function is not related to the other allocation functions and is expected to produce monetary equilibrium *independently* of the other functions. Therefore, if one excludes as redundant the equation equating the supply and demand for money in the Walrasian system, one has a loan fund theory of interest. But if one leaves out the equation equating the demand and supply of loan funds and includes the Walrasian money equation, one does not get a liquidity-preference theory of interest capable of producing the same values of Y and r except by chance. The transformable theories occur only if the bookkeeping constraint applies to the allocation *functions*, including money, as well as to the equation of exchange, a step Walras clearly did not take.

The problem is thus much more complex than Hicks' suggestion would indicate. It turns not only on the redundancy of one of the equilibrium equations but also on the effect of the bookkeeping constraint on the allocation functions. If this constraint did not operate on the allocation functions but operated only as a constraint at equilibrium there is no reason to expect that the liquidity-preference and the loan fund theories would produce identical results except by chance as can easily be shown by removing this constraint. Thus, while Hicks went part way toward the right answer by pointing to the equation redundancy, this alone does not give the basis for a true reconciliation.

The second attempt at reconciliation to be considered here is that of S.C. Tsiang. In his interesting analysis he employs various devices such as a special economic day, a special concept of idle balances, and the elimination of current income as a determinant of current behavior but these devices tend to obscure rather than help his analysis. Its real substance lies in the very special assumptions he makes with respect to the demand and supply functions for loanable funds. He does not treat these as functions independent of the investment and consumption functions. He, like Hanson,[8] makes borrowing equal to investment not only at equilibrium but at every combination of income, interest rates, and stock of money. It is as though he assumed that investment could only be financed by borrowing and all borrowing had to be used to finance investment. In this manner the demand for loanable funds is eliminated *by definition* from the independent variables. By a similar but more complex procedure the supply of loanable funds is eliminated from the independent variables. The supply (exclusive of net additions to bank loans) is defined as whatever stock of money is initially held less the amount it is planned to spend on consumption and less the amount that it is decided to hold as idle balances. Thus the non-bank supply of loanable funds is a function of a given and two other variables and is thus not independent. Whether this is a product of a peculiar bookkeeping constraint in the particular circumstances of Tsiang's model or is arbitrary need not concern us. What is important is that Tsiang's reconciliation applies only to a situation in which neither the demand nor the supply of loanable funds is an independent factor. In this special situation where ΔB and ΔL have been eliminated as independent variables, it is not surprising that the two interest theories produce the same results. But this is not a general reconciliation.

The conclusion seems justified that the liquidity-preference and loan fund theories of interest are in effect alternative formulations of the same set of relationships but that Hicks' effort at reconciliation, the most promising to date, is incomplete and that Tsiang's reconciliation applies only to a very special case.

III. The General Formulation and the Walrasian Equilibrium

The next question to be considered is the relation between the Walrasian formulation of equilibrium and the general formulation given above. Since the Walrasian system can state a condition of equilibrium in a money economy without introducing the demand function for money balances, it is obvious that the problem of testing this relation is most likely to succeed if we compare the Walrasian approach with the loan fund variant of the general formulation. We already have the loan fund formulation as applied to our simple model (p. 146). The Walrasian system can be applied to this macro-economic situation in the form of a three "commodity" and money model using the following additional symbols:

D_c, S_c, and p_c for the demand, supply, and price of consumption goods

D_i, S_i, and p_i for the demand, supply, and price of investment goods.

Also, since the stock of money is assumed to be fixed in the Walrasian system, it will also be assumed to be fixed in the loan fund formulation. On this basis the two formulations of equilibrium would be as follows[9]:

Loan Fund Formulation		*Walrasian Formulation*	
(14a)	$Y = C + I$	(15a)	$D_c = D_c\,(p_c, p_i, r)$
(14b)	$\Delta B = \Delta L$	(15b)	$D_i = D_i\,(p_c, p_i, r)$
(14c)	$C = C(Y, r)$	(15c)	$\Delta B = \Delta B\,(p_c, p_i, r)$
(14d)	$I = I(Y, r)$	(15d)	$S_c = S_c\,(p_c, p_i, r)$
(14e)	$\Delta B = \Delta B(Y, r)$	(15e)	$S_i = S_i\,(p_c, p_i, r)$
(14f)	$\Delta L = \Delta L(Y, r)$	(15f)	$\Delta L = \Delta L\,(p_c, p_i, r)$
		(15g)	$D_c = S_c$
		(15h)	$D_i = S_i$
		(15i)	$\Delta B = \Delta L$

When put beside each other in this manner, the two formulations look quite different. In each of the systems there are as many equations as unknowns,[10] but the systems have in common only three factors (ΔB, ΔL, and r) and one equation ($\Delta B = \Delta L$). For the rest, the Walrasian factors of supply and demand are stated in terms of quantities and the functions are in terms of prices and interest; the factors in the loan fund approach are in terms of money amounts and the functions are in terms of income and interest.

Fortunately, the Walrasian demand and supply functions can be restated in money amounts without introducing new variables by multiplying each side of the equation by the hypothetical price already in the function. Thus the consumption goods demand function can be rewritten:

$$C = p_c\, D_c\,(p_c, p_i, r) \tag{16}$$

and since price is already in the function, it can also be written

$$C = C\,(p_c, p_i, r) \tag{17}$$

Transforming each of the Walrasian demand and supply functions for consumption and investment goods in this fashion and designating the money value of the *supply* of consumption and investment goods as Y_c and Y_i, the Walrasian system can be written as follows:

(18a) $C = C\,(p_c, p_i, r)$
(18b) $I = I\,(p_c, p_i, r)$
(18c) $\Delta B = \Delta B\,(p_c, p_i, r)$
(18d) $Y_c = Y_c\,(p_c, p_i, r)$
(18e) $Y_i = Y_i\,(p_c, p_i, r)$
(18f) $\Delta L = \Delta L\,(p_c, p_i, r)$
(18g) $C = Y_c$
(18h) $I = Y_i$
(18i) $\Delta B = \Delta L$

Restated in this fashion it is clear that $C = Y_c$ and $I = Y_i$ can be combined to give $Y = C + I$ and that the real problem in relating the Walrasian to the general formulation is to establish the relation between the functions expressed in terms of prices and the functions expressed in terms of income. Can either set of functions be transformed into the other?

The Walras-to-General Transformation

If the demand and supply functions above are linear, they can be transformed into approximately the equation of the loan fund formulation and can be transformed exactly into the latter if one new and reasonable assumption is made.

Let the reformulated Walrasian functions be written as follows:

(19a) $Y_c = c_1 p_c + c_2 p_i + c_3 r + c_4$
(19b) $Y_i = c_5 p_c + c_6 p_i + c_7 r + c_8$
(19c) $C = c_9 p_c + c_{10} p_i + c_{11} r + c_{12}$
(19d) $I = c_{13} p_c + c_{14} p_i + c_{15} r + c_{16}$
(19e) $\Delta B = c_{17} p_c + c_{18} p_i + c_{19} r + c_{20}$
(19f) $\Delta L = c_{21} p_c + c_{22} p_i + c_{23} r + c_{24}$

By substitution between equation 19a and 19b, both prices can be written in terms of Y_c, Y_i, r and the constants as follows:

(20a) $$p_c = +\frac{c_6}{c_1c_6 - c_2c_5}Y_c - \frac{c_2}{c_1c_6 - c_2c_5}Y_i + \frac{c_2c_7 - c_3c_6}{c_1c_6 - c_2c_5}r + \frac{c_2c_8 - c_4c_6}{c_1c_5 - c_2c_5}$$

(20b) $$p_i = -\frac{c_5}{c_1c_6 - c_2c_5}Y_c + \frac{c_1}{c_1c_6 - c_2c_5}Y_i + \frac{c_3c_5 - c_1c_7}{c_1c_6 - c_2c_5}r + \frac{c_4c_5 - c_1c_8}{c_1c_6 - c_2c_5}$$

Substituting for p_c and p_i in equation 19c–f and regrouping, gives the following:

(21a)
$$C = \left(\frac{c_6c_9 - c_5c_{10}}{c_1c_6 - c_2c_5}\right)Y_c + \left(\frac{c_1c_{10} - c_2c_9}{c_1c_6 - c_2c_5}\right)Y_i$$
$$+ \frac{(c_9(c_2c_7 - c_3c_6) + c_{10}(c_3c_5 - c_1c_7) + c_{11}(c_1c_6 - c_2c_5))\ r}{c_1c_6 - c_2c_5}$$
$$+ \frac{(c_9\ (c_2c_8 - c_4c_6\ ) + c_{10}\ (c_4c_5 - c_1c_8) + c_{12}\ (c_1c_6 - c_2c_5)\ )}{c_1c_6 - c_2c_5}$$

(21b) I = (same as (21a) except substitute respectively c_{13}, c_{14}, c_{15} and c_{16} for c_9, c_{10}, c_{11}, and c_{12})

(21c) ΔB = (same as (21a) except substitute respectively c_{17}, c_{18}, c_{19}, and c_{20} for c_9, c_{10}, c_{11}, and c_{12})

(21d) ΔL = (same as (21a) except substitute respectively c_{21}, c_{22}, c_{23}, and c_{24} for c_9, c_{10}, c_{11}, and c_{12}).

This comes very close to transforming the Walrasian into the income functions. For example, the demand function for consumer goods becomes:

$$C = \text{constant} \times Y_c + \text{constant} \times Y_i + \text{constant} \times\ r + \text{constant}$$

instead of the loan fund function,

$$C = \text{constant} \times Y + \text{constant} \times r + \text{constant}.$$

The transformation can be completed by assuming that income from different sources will be spent in exactly the same way, regardless of source. This assumption seems reasonable since a worker does not spend his income differently because he works for the machine tool industry instead of the auto industry; nor does a stockholder spend his dividends differently because they came from the production of investment goods rather than consumption goods. In fact most recipients cannot tell whether their income is derived from producing capital or consumption goods. For example, they cannot tell whether their product was sold or went into inventory. Assuming the source of income generation does not affect the way it is spent, the coefficients of Y_c and Y_i would be the same within each function and we can complete the transformation by combining Y_c and Y_i in each of the functions into Y, giving it the sum of the coefficient of Y_c and Y_i.[11]

If income is subdivided into more sources of income (or supply), both the number of prices and the number of income (supply) and demand functions will increase so that there are always enough equations to state each price in terms of incomes and interest. And if the goods are designated as capital or consumption goods, the values of C and I can be arrived at by summation for any number of goods and without the use of ambiguous index numbers. Also, if the functions are not linear but are stated in terms of prices and r, each price can be stated as a function of the Y's and r. Then by substitution the price-demand functions can be transformed into income-demand functions. Thus, it would appear that this Walrasian formulation can generally be transformed into the general financial formulation.

The General-to-Walrasian Transformation

Can the general financial formulation also be transformed into the Walrasian? Even a cursory examination of the two sets of equations shows the unlikelihood of such a transformation. Detailed analysis will show that it is not possible. And this is to be expected since the Walrasian system assumes equilibrium only at full employment of resources while one of the great values of the general financial formulation and its partial formulations is that they can also provide conditions of equilibrium at less than full employment. The assumptions of the general formulation are obviously broader than the Walrasian and it should not be transformable into the Walrasian without some limiting conditions.

Actually there are two limiting conditions which distinguish the Walrasian from the general formulations. The former assumes (1) that prices are free to adjust, and (2) that supply and demand are fully equated, i.e., *that all that sellers wish to sell at the prices arrived at will be sold and all that buyers wish to buy at the prices arrived at will be bought.* In contrast, the general formulation makes no assumption that supply and demand are equated or that prices are freely adjustable. In our simple model these two Walrasian assumptions are implicit in the two income (supply) functions:

(18d) $$Y_c = Y_c\,(p_c, p_i, r)$$

(18e) $$Y_i = Y_i\,(p_c, p_i, r)$$

If we add these two equations as a constraint on the general formulation, it then becomes possible to transform the latter into the Walrasian. The sum of the two additional functions can be substituted for Y in the demand function of the general formulation (or separately for Y_c and Y_i if Y is subdivided) so as to state the demand function in terms of prices. With the two supply functions used to substitute for Y this gives the revised Walrasian type of functions. Division by the appropriate hypothetical prices will then give the Walrasian type of functions in quantitative terms. The conclusion thus seems justified that this Walrasian formulation is a special case implicit in the above loan fund formulation and therefore also a special case implicit in the general formulation given above.

IV. Non-Walrasian Pricing

So far this analysis has been concerned with setting up a general formulation of financial equilibrium, using it to relate the liquidity-preference and loan fund theories of interest to each other, and showing the relation between the Walrasian formulation and the general formulation. But it is obvious that a formulation of equilibrium in money terms is not also a formulation of equilibrium in terms of goods.[12] We have seen that the assumption of perfectly flexible prices and a perfect equating of supply and demand makes the general financial formulation convertible into the Walrasian formulation of equilibrium. But it is also obvious that the financial formulation is consistent with assumptions which are non-Walrasian since it is consistent with equilibrium under conditions other than those of full employment while the Walrasian system describes only a full employment equilibrium. It is the aim of this section to explore the non-Walrasian assumption that particular prices are administered and fixed for periods of time so that supply and demand are only equated by chance. The next section will attempt to reformulate the Walrasian system of equations so as to include administered as well as market prices in the formulation of equilibrium conditions. With this accomplished, the final section will then apply the results so as to reconstruct the *financial* formulation of macro-economic equilibrium in order to provide a *general* formulation of macro-economic equilibrium which establishes the money value, the physical quantities, and the prices of all categories of goods in a simple economic model in which some prices are made in the market and some are administered.

The introduction of administered prices involves a departure from the assumption of perfect competition and before making this introduction it will be well to examine the implication for equilibrium of monopoly pricing as such pricing has been conceived of in traditional economic literature.

The Classical Monopoly Price

The traditional picture of monopoly pricing is that of a monopolist who (1) sets his price so as to maximize his current profit, i.e., the difference between his current revenue and his current outlay (presumably also taking into account the discounted value of the effects on future revenue and future outlays), and (2) adjusts his price to changes in demand or costs as they become known to him so as to maintain the current profit-maximizing price. Such pricing would provide a flexible monopoly price which will hereafter be referred to as a "classical monopoly price."[13]

There is nothing in such a flexible pricing procedure to interfere with the conclusion that the only condition of equilibrium would be one of full employment. Any deficiency of employment would result in falling prices (including wage rates); and the monopolist's flexible prices could be expected to fall along with the others as falling demand and falling costs lowered the price, which would minimize his profits.[14] The fall in prices would increase the real value of the outstanding stock of money thereby increasing aggregate real demand and employment. In such circumstances, the only condition of equilibrium would be one of full employment. Presumably there could be a Walrasian-like system of equations which would include classical monopoly pricing. The equilibrium reached would differ from the Walrasian in that it would not represent the use of resources which maximized utility but it would be like the Walrasian equilibrium in that it could only be reached at full employment.

Alternative Pricing Procedures

However, classical monopoly pricing is not the only alternative. When a producer faces a downward sloping demand curve for his product and is sufficiently free of competition to have an *independent* price policy, there are several different procedures he might adopt.[15] He might employ the classical procedure already outlined to produce the classical monopoly price. He might make the price in each transaction a matter of specific and often prolonged bargaining as is customary under the imperfectly competitive conditions of oriental bazaars—thus making the resulting price a "bargained price." He might determine his production schedule and auction off the product of each period for what it would bring—thus making the resulting price an "auctioned price." He might set a price and hold it constant for a period of time in spite of moderate fluctuations in costs or demand, producing and selling as much as is ordered or demanded at that price but usually ready to supply more without changing his price—thus making the resulting price what I have elsewhere called an "administered price."

The difference between these procedures is important for economic analysis. It has already been suggested that the classical monopoly price is compatible with the equilibrium determining power of the Walrasian system. Presumably this would also be true of the bargained price which could be expected to be highly sensitive to changes in demand and costs. There can be some uncertainty as to whether the auctioned price is compatible with the Walrasian system but the question is not now important since this type of pricing is relatively rare. But is the widely employed administered price compatible with the Walrasian system?

The Problem of Semantics

Here it will pay to do a little semantic analysis to clear up the confusion between certain different concepts of price behavior. There is concept I—the classical concept of prices which are perfectly sensitive to changes in demand and supply (or costs). This type of price can be subdivided arbitrarily into Ia—prices which in experience move up and down a great deal under fluctuations in business activity because of large changes of demand or supply, and Ib—prices which move little either because there is little change in demand and supply for the particular good or because the changes are offsetting.

There is concept II—a concept not employed in general classical theory, that of prices which are set and remain unchanged for periods of time regardless of small changes in demand or costs and often of large changes. This type of price can be subdivided arbitrarily into IIa—prices which are set for periods of time but are fairly sensitive to changes in demand or costs and tend to produce a rough approximation to an equating of demand and supply in the classical sense; IIb—prices which are set for periods of time but are fairly insensitive to changes in demand or costs and do not approximate an equating of demand and supply in the classical sense; IIc—prices which are fixed and cannot be changed for a period without considerable difficulty because of a contract as in the case of wage contracts, or because of regulatory delays as in the case of utility rates or for some other reason.[16]

Just what names are attached to these concepts is not important so long as the names are consistently used and understood. In classical literature the terms "stable prices" or "inflexible prices" have sometimes been used to refer to concept Ib. More recently the term "inflexible prices" has been used as though it applied to Ib and IIb indiscriminately. The term rigid prices has often been applied to IIc or to the sum of IIb and IIc. For purely *analytical* purposes the important distinction is between concept I and concept II. For *practical* problems involving concept II it is IIb and IIc which are important. Also for practical problems the distinction between prices of type Ib and type IIb is important. Since no one has offered an alternative name for concept II, the term "administered prices" continues to seem appropriate while the term "market prices" seems appropriate for prices which are sensitive to changes in demand and supply (or costs). I will therefore employ the following terms:

Ia	unstable market prices
Ib	stable market prices
IIa	flexible administered prices
IIb	inflexible administered prices
IIc	rigid administered prices or rigid prices

In the present analytical piece it is the distinction between concepts I and II which is most immediately important, the distinction between market and administered prices.

A second semantic problem arises with respect to the term "supply" when employed in a situation involving an administered price. In the older classical usage "supply" was used to refer to the amount of a good *offered* at a price. Thus Mill says, "The supply of a commodity is an intelligible expression: it

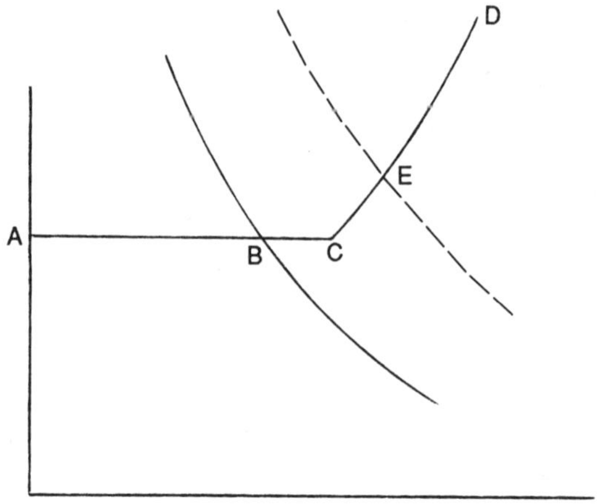

Chart I

means the quantity offered for sale, the quantity that is to be had, at a given time and place, by those who wish to purchase it.''[17] Marshall adopts the same meaning in discussing a temporary equilibrium of demand and supply, considering the amount each ''seller offers for sale'' at each price and speaking of an equilibrium price as one which ''would exactly equate demand and supply (i.e. the amount which buyers were willing to purchase at that price would be just equal to that for which sellers were willing to take that price)''[18]; neither was concerned with the situation in which the seller set an administered price and sold less than the amounts for which* at that price, adopted the convention of a ''supply schedule'' which was horizontal at the administered price, the seller being willing to sell any amount up to the full amount offered at that price. Such a ''supply schedule'' is shown in Chart I with a demand schedule cutting the ''supply schedule'' at less than the full amount offered at the administered price.

The schedule *CD* was presumed to represent the amount which would be *offered* at each price at or above the administered price while ''schedule'' *AC* represented the fact that at the administered price the seller would sell any amount up to that represented by *AC*. This, of course, redefined the term ''supply.'' To the right of *C* it continued to represent the amount offered; to the left of *C* it meant the amount sold at the price, not the amount offered. With this redefinition of supply, it was still possible to speak of an equilibrium in which supply and demand were exactly equal at the administered price since the demand schedule and the ''supply schedule'' intersected at *B*.

This device, however, did not take into account the administered price situation in which the demand exceeded the amount the seller was willing or able to

*The following line was entirely illegible—Eds.

supply at the administered price and the latter chose not to raise his price, as happens, for example, in the case of the Broadway hit or the steel industry operating at capacity and booking orders for months ahead. In such situations the amount demanded at the administered price is greater than the amount offered, a condition which the conventional "supply schedule" does not allow since the demand schedule would cut the "supply schedule" at a price above the administered price as indicated by the dotted line in Chart I.

In what follows, we will be frequently concerned with the fact of a difference between the amount of a good offered at an administered price and the amount demanded at that price, i.e., the possibility of a difference between *AE* and *AC* or between *AB* and *AC* in Chart I. Where the demand at the administered price is in excess of the amount offered at [that] price, there is no semantic problem. At that price, demand is clearly in excess of supply and the immediate equilibrium condition does not equate supply and demand.[19]

The semantic problem arises for the situation in which, at an administered price, the amount offered exceeds the amount demanded—where *AB* is less than *AC*. If we adopt the older meaning of supply, then clearly supply exceeds demand by the amount *BC* and the equilibrium in which the demand schedule intersects the "supply schedule" *ACD* to the left of *C* does not equate supply and demand. If we adopt the newer meaning for supply in the case of an administered price, i.e., the amount *sold* at that price, then the equilibrium condition is by definition one in which demand and supply are equal. But this latter procedure presents us with lack of symmetry in the treatment of supply and demand.

One way to reestablish symmetry would be to redefine demand to mean, in the case of an administered price, the amount *bought* at the administered price. The "supply" and "demand" would always be equal by definition and not as a result of any economic relationship. The other way to reestablish symmetry would be to return to the traditional meaning of the term supply as the amount offered at a price. Then, so long as an administered price remains unchanged, supply may exceed demand or demand may exceed supply. In the analysis which follows, the latter procedure will be adopted, using the term "supply" to refer to the amount offered at a price. If this return to the traditional meaning of the term "supply" troubles the reader, he can substitute the terms "offering" or "amount offered" whenever the term "supply" occurs.

With this semantic clarification, we can return to an examination of the Walrasian equations and administered prices.

Administered Prices and the Formulations of Equilibrium

It can be shown that administered prices are not compatible with the Walrasian formulation of equilibrium but are compatible with the general financial formulation and its three derivatives. Under an administered price, supply (in the sense of the amount offered at the fixed price) and demand are equal only by chance.

Yet it is the very essence of the Walrasian system that supply and demand are brought into equality by price. Clearly, administered prices do not fit into the Walrasian equations. On the other hand there is nothing in the general financial formulation to prevent the introduction of a given set of administered prices as a condition for converting the financial equilibrium into an equilibrium in terms of goods and employment.

The prevalence of administered prices in our economy needs no proving. Most of industry, most of distribution, and a large proportion of services operate on a basis of administered prices while wage rates are usually either set by the hiring agency or by a negotiated contract which determines the administered wage rate at which workers can be hired.[20] Since administered prices are such an important form of pricing procedure, the question arises—can the Walrasian equations be modified so as to state an equilibrium condition in an economy which operates in whole or in part on the basis of administered prices?

V. Expanding the Walrasian System

The Walrasian system was initially formulated in terms of a simple economy consisting only of the buying and selling of a few goods. It will help here to do the same. But because administered prices are usually associated with enterprises employing workers for wages, it will be useful to give examples of administered prices set by one-man enterprises. These can serve as prototypes for the construction of a simple administered price economy comparable to the simple Walrasian economy, leaving to a subsequent article the expansion necessary to make the model more realistic.

For this purpose, two examples should prove sufficient—a country doctor and a "homemade" candy store. When a new doctor comes to a town he is likely to put up his shingle, set a scale of prices for his services—so much for an office call, so much for a house call, and so much for each of a number of services—then wait for patients. At first he is likely to be underemployed, a probability which his initial scale has presumably taken into account—low enough not to scare off too many patients and high enough to afford at least survival until his practice is built up. And for a period the offering of services will be in excess of demand at his administered prices. An epidemic may reverse the situation so that he is overworking and would gladly refuse patients, in fact may turn away some. Here, to the extent that he turns patients away, demand exceeds supply. But a considerable surplus in supply or demand may have no effect on the rates he charges. For much the same reason a rise or fall in aggregate demand which alters the demand for medical services in general and his in particular would have to be quite large before he would be likely to change his rates.

A similar situation could develop for a one-man producer of goods such as a "homemade" candy store with candy made by the proprietor in the rear and sold in the front. Assuming he adopted price administration as a policy, one could expect that he would produce a variety of his wares and display them with appropriate price markers. Also one could expect that his sales at the administered prices would fluctuate with the seasons and the times. Before Christmas demand at his prices might be so high that, in spite of overworking, he is unable to fill all orders while in the slack season he would be underemployed. In spite of demand in excess of supply or offerings in excess of demand, the proprietor might make no change in price or perhaps introduce some high priced seasonal "specials," leaving his regular prices unchanged. Also fluctuations in demand due to changes in aggregate demand or changes in the price of sugar might have to be considerable before he was induced to alter his administered prices.

It is the common essential of these cases that the price is administered and supply and demand are not equated by price except by chance. The problem then is to develop a Walrasian-like set of equations which would determine equilibrium condition not only when prices adjust to equate supply and demand but also when some prices are fixed and supply and demand are not equated by price.

First let us adopt a simple Walrasian-like model in which there are only three goods (*a*, *b*, and *c*) and money (*m*) entering into transactions and in which each individual in the economy works for himself and can produce more or less of one or more of these goods for sale. Also assume that each individual carries over some money from a preceding period. The period of equilibrium is assumed to be short, say a week, and where prices are free to move, it is assumed that they will at once move to the equilibrium level. However, it is assumed that one or more prices may be fixed throughout the period. Anticipation of future price changes will also be neglected.

In these circumstances consider what an individual's allocation matrix might be like. One section of the matrix would presumably indicate how he would behave if all three prices were $1.00. The matrix might show that if the individual could buy and sell freely at these prices, he would sell $100 worth of *a* and buy $50 worth each of *b* and *c*. It might also show that, if the market would only absorb $90 worth of his product, *a*, he would spend over $45 on *b* and $48 on *c*, reducing his money balance by $3. Also it might show that if he could only sell $90 worth of his product and could only buy $40 worth of *b*, he would spend $50 on *c*. Also it might show that, if he could only buy $40 worth of *b* and $30 worth of *c*, he might feel it was only worth his while to sell $75 worth of his product, adding $5 to his money balance, even though the market would take all he wanted to sell. His allocation matrix would thus show what his allocation would be at the $1.00 set of prices for all the relevant combinations of limitations on his ability to buy or sell, including the classical case of no limits. The matrix would also show the same type of information at all other relevant combinations of prices.

The next step is to represent this matrix by a set of equations. Consider first his demand for *b*. If all prices were free, we could represent his demand for *b* as the usual function of the three prices. But if the price of *a* is fixed and supply exceeds demand at equilibrium, the individual's money income will be less than he would like and so his demand for b would be not only a function of the three prices but also a function of Y_a, his revenue from the sale of a. Also if the price of c was fixed and supply was less than demand, he could not buy as much c as he wanted and his demand for b would also be a function of c. To take account of these facts we could write the equation for his demand for b as follows, expressing his demand in terms of his expenditure on b instead of the usual quantity:

$$B = B(p_a, p_b, p_c, Y_a, C)$$

Thus his demand for b is made a function not only of the three prices but also of his income from the sale of a and his expenditure on c.

In similar fashion, we can represent his offering of a by the following equation:

$$Y_a = Y_a(p_a, p_b, p_c, B, C)$$

making his supply a function of prices and the amount he spends on b and c.

These functions imply that the individual will only produce a. But there may well be a combination of prices which would lead him to produce b or c and under some circumstances he might buy a. And he may get income from producing two commodities and buy the third. To make the demand and supply functions general, they can be written as follows:

$$\text{(a)} \quad A = A(p_a, p_b, p_c, Y_b, Y_c, B, C)$$
$$\text{(b)} \quad B = B(p_a, p_b, p_c, Y_a, Y_c, A, C)$$
$$\text{(c)} \quad C = C(p_a, p_b, p_c, Y_a, Y_b, A, B)$$
$$\text{(d)} \quad Y_a = Y_a(p_a, p_b, p_c, Y_b, Y_c, B, C)$$
$$\text{(e)} \quad Y_b = Y_b(p_a, p_b, p_c, Y_a, Y_c, A, C)$$
$$\text{(f)} \quad Y_c = Y_c(p_a, p_b, p_c, Y_a, Y_b, A, B)$$

From these functions, the individual's demand for additions to his money balance can be derived through the bookkeeping constraint to give,

$$\text{(g)} \quad \Delta M = \Delta M(p_a, p_b, p_c, Y_a, Y_b, Y_c, A, B, C)$$

This set of equations represents the complete set of allocation functions for any individual in the simple three-commodity model in which his power to buy or sell the quantities he desires may be limited.

Can these equations also represent the allocation functions for the sum of all individuals in the model? If all prices were flexible so that each individual could buy or sell as much as he wanted at the prices reached at equilibrium, this set of equations would represent the allocation function for the economy as a whole. When combined with the three equilibrium-condition equations ($A = Y_a, B = Y_b, C = Y_c$), they would yield the same equilibrium pattern of prices as that obtained from the simple functions which are stated only in terms of prices. Derived from the same set of allocation matrices and with the same set of unknowns, this more complex set of allocation equations is presumed to be transformable into the simpler set.

However, the problem is quite different where fixed prices are concerned. If the supply is limited, which individuals go without or does each individual who wants it get some of the limited supply and how is it rationed? A limit on purchases will affect different people differently. If an Irishman's purchases of bread are limited, his demand for potatoes is likely to go up. If a Mexican's purchases of bread are limited, it is more likely to affect the demand for beans. The same would also apply to limited demand. Thus it is clear that the allocation equations of individuals cannot be summed in so far as they deal with situations involving fixed prices.

On the other hand, if we know how much each person shared in the limited supply or demand of a good when there was an overall limitation, the allocation *matrixes* of the separate individuals would provide the basis for an aggregate allocation matrix which would state, for each combination of prices, the demand and the supply of each commodity under each of the relevant limitations. This matrix in turn could be represented by a set of allocation equations identical in character with the set already presented for the individual. This aggregate set would not be the sum of the individual equations but would contain all the information contained in them organized according to the pattern of rationing assumed. For present purposes, we can assume that this rationing is determinate and treat it as a "given" much as the production functions are treated as givens. In fact, we can properly refer to the rationing functions and treat them as a separate and worthy branch of special study not directly involved in the problem of equilibrium.

The aggregate allocation equations still present a special problem not met with when prices are flexible. If there is a limit on one or more commodities the system of equations becomes inconsistent. Thus, if the price of good *a* is administered and the supply is in excess of demand at equilibrium, then the supply of *a* does not equal demand for *a*. Rather the demand determines the amount sold and the supply function for *a* becomes extraneous to the equilibrium condition. On the other hand, the administered price provides an additional equation. When the new fixed price equation is substituted for the extraneous equation we get:

$$p_a = k_1$$
$$Y_b = Y_b\,(p_a, p_b, p_c, Y_a, Y_c, A, C)$$
$$Y_c = Y_c\,(p_a, p_b, p_c, Y_a, Y_c, A, B)$$
$$A = A\,(p_a, p_b, p_c, Y_b, Y_c, B, C)$$
$$B = B\,(p_a, p_b, p_c, Y_a, Y_c, A, C)$$
$$C = C\,(p_a, p_b, p_c, Y_a, Y_b, A, B)$$
$$\Delta M = \Delta M\,(p_a, p_b, p_c, Y_a, Y_b, Y_c, A, B, C)$$

Thus with the administered price of *a* given, and *a* known to be in excess supply, we have the same number of unknowns and the same number of equations as before and presumably this system plus the equilibrium equations produce an equilibrium solution. And in this solution, the amount of *a* purchased would depend on the demand at the administered price in the light of the market prices of *b* and *c*.

We can generalize this procedure for introducing administered prices by adopting the working rule that, in the case of fixed prices, the equation for the price of a commodity must be substituted for its demand or supply functions depending on whether, at the administered price, demand or supply is in excess.

In theory, it is not necessary to know beforehand whether at equilibrium, an administered price will result in a surplus of demand or of supply. If the price equation is substituted for the wrong allocation function, an "impossible" solution will be obtained for that particular commodity. Thus, if the demand function for *a* is discarded when actually there is an excess of supply, an equilibrium solution can be obtained, but when the equilibrium values are substituted in the discarded demand function for *a*, it will be found that the demand for *a* under those conditions would be less than the calculated equilibrium supply. This means that the wrong function has been discarded. By correcting this mistake and resolving for equilibrium, a closer approach to the true equilibrium would be reached. The second solution might so shift the relationships that particular functions properly included in the first calculation are found to be irrelevant in the second and that further changes have to be made. However, it is presumed that, by successive approximations, "impossible" solutions would be eliminated and a possible solution obtained.[21]

This system of equations is capable of being expanded to any number of commodities. It could also be modified to take specific account of lending and borrowing, employment, equity securities, government activity, and changes in the money supply. Here it has been developed sufficiently to provide a basis for formulating the equilibrium conditions for a simple macro-economic model which includes both market and administered prices.

VI. A General Macro-Economic Formulation

It has already been pointed out that the general financial formulation of equilibrium at the beginning of this article can be transformed into the Walrasian type of system if prices are assumed to be so flexible that they equate supply and demand. It has also been suggested that the general financial formulation is also consistent with the assumption of administered prices and with equilibrium at less than full employment. On the other hand the financial formulation, while it indicates equilibrium conditions for the financial flows, says nothing about prices or physical magnitudes at equilibrium. It is the purpose of this section to modify the financial formulation so that, with the level of administered prices given, it makes determinate at equilibrium not only the financial flows but also physical magnitudes and the level of flexible prices.

This objective will be carried out in terms of the simple model employed at the beginning of the article. However, one important change will be made. It would be possible to carry out the formulation in a way to maintain the distinction between consumption and investment. So long as the Pigou effect was disregarded, this distinction was of utmost importance. But the Pigou effect places the distinction in the same category as other important distinctions between categories of demand such as that between consumer durable and non-durable goods or between goods and services. A change in the demand function for any of these can be an important cause of changed activity, each can have a multiplying effect, and each deserves separate treatment in a more detailed analysis of macro-economic behavior. But for present purposes, aggregate demand is the crucial factor and it will simplify the analysis not to treat consumption and investment demand separately.

On the other hand, it is important to treat separately those goods whose prices are market prices and those which are administered and to divide the latter into those in surplus supply and those in surplus demand. For this macro-economic purpose we can designate these three categories of goods as m (market), s (supply in excess), and d (demand in excess) while revenue from these will be designated respectively Y_m, Y_s, and Y_d. Expenditure will be correspondingly designated E_m, E_s, and E_d, and the indexes of their money prices p_m, p_s, and p_d. Borrowing and lending will again be designated by ΔB and ΔL with the interest rate (r) assumed to be flexible and equating the supply and demand for loan funds. Also the demand for additional money balances will be designated ΔM, and changes in the stock of money are assumed to arise from exogenous banking action with the amount of increase ($\pm$) being represented by M_1. The problem then is to formulate the conditions of macro-economic equilibrium so as to include situations in which all prices are market prices, situations in which all prices are administered and fixed for the period of adjustment, and situations which include both market and administered prices.

The general allocation equation for this situation can be written as follows, the brackets representing allocation functions:

$$Y_m\,(\,) + Y_s + Y_d\,(\,) + \Delta B\,(\,) - E_m\,(\,) - E_s\,(\,) - E_d - \Delta L\,(\,) = \Delta M\,(\,)$$

In this allocation equation we have the condition that total income ($Y_m + Y_s + Y_d$) plus net new borrowing (ΔB) less total expenditures ($E_m + E_s + E_d$) and less net new lending (ΔL) equals the increase in money balances. But in the case of goods which are in excess supply, income (Y_s) is presumed to be determined at the administered prices by the equilibrium demand while, in the case of goods in excess demand, expenditure (E_d) is presumed to be determined at the administered price by the equilibrium supply.

The allocation functions all contain the same factors, the three indexes of price (p_m, p_s, and p_d), the rate of interest (r), the total revenue from goods in excess supply (Y_s) and the total expenditures on goods in excess demand (E_d). Finally, we can increase the scope of the system of equations by adding the influence of the initial stock of money (M) on behavior, thus allowing comparison to be made between different situations involving the same allocation functions but different initial quantities of money outstanding. On this basis the brackets in the allocation equations can all be filled in the following manner:

$$( ) = (p_m, p_s, p_d, r, Y_s, E_d, M)$$

Also, the allocation functions must conform to the bookkeeping constraint for all values of the variables so that any one allocation function can be derived from the other six.

In order to establish equilibrium it is necessary to have two additional sets of equations, four of the five [sic] equilibrium equations:

$$Y_m = E_m;\ Y_s = E_s;\ Y_d = E_d;\ \Delta B - \Delta L + M_1;\ \Delta M = M_1$$

and the two administered price index equations:

$$p_s = k_1;\ p_d = k_2$$

This gives 13 unknowns and 15 equations, two of which are redundant, a situation which is presumed to be soluble and to yield "possible" results so long as each good is properly classified according to its market condition.

A little examination of this formulation makes it clear that if there are no goods falling into the categories (s and d) and if $\Delta M = 0$, it transforms into the Walrasian system for two goods, loans, and money. Also it transforms into the general financial formulation (with consumption and investment combined) if all goods fall into the administered price categories and are in surplus supply, thus making the financial equilibrium *also* an economic equilibrium when all prices are given (not including interest as a price). Finally, it gives the equilibrium condition when some prices are market prices and some are administered, provided commodities are properly classified and the price indexes for the two administered price groups are given.

This system of equations represents the general formulation of macroeconomic equilibrium which has been a major aim of this article, but only for a very simple economic model. There is not room here to develop the corresponding formulation for a more realistic model which includes investment and consumption goods separately, adds equity securities, and provides for the role of government. Nor is there room to explore the various developments in the simple or more complex models which could lead to under- or overemployment and consider what condition would lead to equilibrium at full employment. What is important here is that the allocation equation, the five equilibrium equations, and the two price index equations represent a general and *complete* formulation of macro-economic equilibrium for the simple model. This formulation brings prices into the macro-formulation and allows prices to be either market prices or administered. And, because it covers both prices and financial flows, it makes the volume of physical activity also determinate. Finally, this formulation can not only explain equilibrium at full employment but can also explain at least a temporary equilibrium at less than or more than full employment. How long this equilibrium might continue is another matter.

Notes

1. This model is, of course, quite inadequate to deal with actual affairs. But I believe it contains all the essentials for dealing with the central logical problems with which this article is concerned and its simplicity will help in exposition.

2. It will be recognized that this "bookkeeping constraint" is identical with the term "budget restraint," sometimes applied to Walras' equation of exchange. My reason for not using the Walrasian term arises from the fact that the term "budget" implies planning whereas the term "bookkeeping" has no planning connotation. Walras applied the constraint to the *results* of equilibrium so that the planning connotation had no significance. Here the restraint is applied to functions which might reflect planning or might not. The term "bookkeeping constraint" seems to be satisfactorily neutral in this respect.

3. For many purposes more complex functions would be required which introduce differences in initial money balances, differences in other assets, etc. In real life the allocation functions can be very complex. For the purpose of this particular analysis the simple function is sufficient. It does, however, limit the analysis to a given set of starting conditions at the start of a period and the allocation of resources within a specified period, including resources to be carried beyond the period.

4. It should be noted that the concept of a complete description applies only to a *logical construct.* A *complete* description of any actual object would have to include not only the number and location of every electron and its spin but also the location of every star since it exerts a pull upon the object. And this is only a start on what a *complete* description would have to contain. In contrast, a logical construct, however complex, must be self-contained and therefore capable of complete description.

5. In the above analysis, the broad conception of the liquidity-preference theory of interest is adopted in which r is determined simultaneously by the relation between the saving and investment functions and the relation between the liquidity-preference function and the stock of money; not the narrow Keynesian conception in which r is determined by the relation between the liquidity-preference function and the stock of money. (See Alvin H. Hansen, *A Guide to Keynes*, McGraw Hill Book Co., 1953, pp. 140–158.) The loan fund theory is also portrayed in its broad classical form in which the rate of interest is determined by the supply and demand for loanable funds *in the general equilibrating process in which all prices, including interest rates, are simultaneously determined.*

I believe Hansen is able to say that the loan fund theory of interest is indeterminate only because he has given a narrow and partial statement of the theory. Confusion has also been added to the analysis by stating the loan fund theory in terms of the special case in which all investment is financed by obtaining loanable funds and all loanable funds find their way into investment. (Hansen, ibid., pp. 142 and 143.) In practice much investment is financed directly out of income (including undistributed profits of corporations) so that no loans or securities or loanable funds are involved. Also loan funds are often used to finance consumption. Thus, the demand and supply functions for loanable funds are only by chance the same as the investment and saving functions.

6. The negative signs for k_{10}, k_{11} and k_{12} arise from the fact that ΔB has the sign opposite to that of C, I, ΔL, and ΔM in the allocation equation.

7. J.R. Hicks, *Value and Capital* (Oxford, 1939), Ch. XII, pp. 153–162; S.C. Tsiang, *American Economic Review*, Vol. XLVI, No. 4 (September 1956), pp. 539–564. For an analysis of other attempts at reconciliation, see Tsiang, pp. 540–545.

8. See note 5 above.

9. It should be recognized that the Walrasian formulation given below is not to be found in Walras' *Elements of Pure Economics* but is rather an adaptation of the Walrasian micro-economic approach to the problem in hand. Since we are not concerned with the determinants of the allocation *functions*, the utility aspects of his system are not involved. Also, and even more important, the determinants of the capital *functions* drop out for the same reason. Thus capital goods can be treated like consumption goods as functions of all prices. Loan funds and interest are also treated in a manner different from that of Walras but, I believe, consistent with his treatment.

10. The money equations in both cases are treated as the redundant equations and are not included.

11. The assumption that the source of income generation does not affect the way money income is spent would place a constraint on the Walrasian equations, but if this assumption is valid, the constraint is implicit in the situation and the coefficients of the Walrasian equations would have to be modified to conform.

12. It should be noted that two assumptions are sometimes made with respect to the liquidity-preference formulation: (1) the price level and real volume of activity in a flexible price economy are determined when prices and the value of marginal product of labor are equal, *and* (2) that this condition can be reached at less than full employment. So long as the Pigou effect is neglected, as it was by Keynes, this double conclusion can be supported, but in the presence of the Pigou effect, the only condition of equilibrium with flexible price would be one of full employment. The assumptions of price flexibility and the requirement that price and the value of the marginal product of labor be equal convert the liquidity-preference formulation into a peculiar formulation of the special Walrasian case which can reach equilibrium only at full employment.

13. The term "classical" is used here in the Keynesian sense of that which has become standard in the teaching of economics, at least until quite recent times.

14. That a classical monopoly price would fall as much as a competitive price in the same circumstances may not be obvious but can easily be demonstrated. If there were a general fall in wage rates and other competitive prices of say 10% with a corresponding 10% decline in aggregate money demand, except as the rise in the real buying power of the money stock stimulated additional buying, the price of a particular competitive commodity could also be expected to fall approximately 10%—both its schedule of costs for different volumes being 10% lower and its demand at each possible price being 10% lower. Similarly in the case of a classical monopoly price, the aggregate cost schedule and the aggregate revenue schedule would both be 10% lower for each possible volume of production and sale. If the initial price were the classical monopoly price, the new classical monopoly price would be 10% less at the same volume except as the particular good was affected by the increase in the real buying power of the stock of money.

15. It should be noted that the above statement specifically excludes what might be called the dependent price maker, i.e., one who, in setting or revising his price, has to take into consideration the counter action of another price maker if he sets one price rather than

another. The problems of the dependent price maker are different and cannot be discussed within the scope of this article.

16. There are other possible subdivisions of II which could be important for particular purposes such as an escalator contract, but the above are sufficient for present purposes.

17. John Stuart Mill, *Principles of Political Economy*, Book III, Ch. I, Sec. 3.

18. Alfred Marshall, *Principles of Economics*, Book V, Ch. I, Sec. 2 (Eighth Edition, London, 1930), pp. 332 and 333.

19. It should be noted that the term ''immediate'' applies to a period in which the administered price is unchanged.

20. It should be obvious that the usual wage contract is not a purchase-of-labor agreement but only an agreement as to the administered price for labor, the amount of labor to be ''bought'' being left open.

21. There is, of course, no mathematical certainty that the Walrasian system of equations could be solved or have only a single solution. The same would hold in this more general formulation with the added possibility of an ''echo'' situation in which two or more goods were so related that a possible solution for one always involved an ''impossible'' solution for the other. However, when by chance demand and supply are just equal at an administered price and equilibrium, it is immaterial whether the demand or the supply function for that good is dropped since either would produce the same result and an echo situation would closely approximate this condition.

11

Letter to Jerry Cohen

March 20, 1964

Mr. Jerry Cohen
Senate Committee on Anti Trust and Monopoly
Senate Office Building
Washington, D.C.

Dear Jerry:

You ask "Why are administered prices important?" Let me give you this basic answer: The conventional economic wisdom and the clichés which dominate much of modern politico-economic thinking are based on the nineteenth century classical theory developed by such outstanding economists as Adam Smith, Mill, and Marshall. The principles and the policy implications of that body of theory rest on the assumption that prices and wage rates are *determined* by the interaction of buyers and sellers and move up or down in a highly flexible fashion to equate supply and demand. Until 1933, this body of theory was quite generally accepted as the basis for public policy. (At the University of Chicago it is still taught as the relevant theory.) And in this body of theory there is no room for administered prices. When administered prices are introduced as basic assumptions, the system of theory is *shattered.* It will no longer yield the classical conclusions that the free enterprise system is a cybernetic mechanism which (1) automatically tends to eliminate unemployment, (2) automatically tends to balance international payments, (3) automatically tends to minimize waste and direct resources into their most appropriate uses, and (4) automatically tends to reward workers and investors and managers in proportion to the value of their productive contributions.

The classical theory had its uses when our economy was primarily agricul-

March 20, 1964. From the J.M. Blair Papers in the National Archives.

tural and was dominated by flexible market prices. But today it is primarily industrial and is dominated by inflexible administered prices.

I cannot overemphasize the difference between an economy dominated by prices made in the market with supply and demand equated through flexible prices, and an economy dominated by administered prices with production controlled to meet the demands at fixed prices which are only adjusted from time to time. You, as a lawyer, have been trained in the principles of Anglo Saxon law. Suppose that you suddenly woke up and discovered you had to practice under the principles of Roman law. The contrast would be less great than that between the principles applicable to an economy dominated by classical market prices and one dominated by administered prices.

Below I will outline some of the basic differences but at the outset I want to make certain things clear.

First, I have defined an administered price as "a price which is set for a period of time and a series of transactions."

The great bulk of prices with which the individual comes in contact meet this definition. When your wife goes to the grocery store, she is faced with a whole series of articles with price tabs. She and others can buy at the indicated price or can refrain from buying. But she cannot bargain down the price. When you buy razor blades the price is usually set and you can buy as many packages as the dealer has on hand. If you want more packages than he happens to have in stock, he will tell you to come back tomorrow when he expects to have some more *but he will not raise the price because the immediate demand exceeds the supply.* Your doctor may charge you and others a standard $5.00 fee for an office call regardless of how many people come to his office. Such things as postal rates, railroad fares and telephone charges are, of course, forms of administered prices. And if you will review the expenditures you have made in the last month you will find that in most cases the money you paid out was for items with a fixed price and one in which the seller was making a series of sales at the fixed price. (The one major exception would be in the case of trading in an old car for a new. While at wholesale new cars are sold at administered prices, each car traded in is likely to be different so that a bargain has to be struck on the allowance to be made.)

At wholesale the great bulk of items are sold at administered prices. Fixed list prices with standard discounts and special discounts are often used but as long as the standard and special discounts are maintained fixed for periods of time and a series of transactions, the resulting sales are at administered prices. The most important categories of *classical market* prices are in the field of farm and forest products and certain metallic raw materials such as lead and zinc. But in modern industry the bulk of prices are administered prices.

Such administered prices dominate our economy. It has been guesstimated that as high as 80 percent of the value of commodity and service transactions at wholesale and retail take place at administered prices. And an even higher proportion of labor transactions are at administered wage rates either set by the employer or bargained between union and management for a period of time and a series of "transactions." Prices on the stock market are an outstanding exception. There, prices are "made in the market" to equate supply and demand.

The second point I would make is that I regard administered prices as *a good thing*. They make for economic efficiency. I doubt if we could have the efficiencies of modern industry without administered prices. The big mass-production corporations could not operate without administered prices. Sears and Wards could not operate without using administered prices. Business could not do its planning as effectively as it does and the super market would be impossible without administered prices. That administered prices make the main body of nineteenth century economic theory obsolete is the hard luck of those who only know how to teach that body of theory. But administered prices are a good thing from the point of view of the people of this country provided we understand and meet the problems which they create and which lie outside the scope of traditional economic theory.

The third point I want to make is that administered prices and their relative inflexibility are not a product of labor organization. Before 1933, labor unions played a very minor role in most of American industry and yet both prices and wage rates in such industries as steel and automobiles were administered and relatively inflexible. Both prices and wage rates were administered by management, presumably as a single policy. From 1929 to 1933 neither prices nor wage rates in steel and automobiles responded to the great drop in demand in the fashion called for by the principles of classical theory. Their price and wage declines should have been at least as great as those of agricultural prices and were in fact very much less. In contrast, in the more highly unionized garment industries, wage rates dropped much more from 1929 to 1933 than in the non-union steel and auto industries. The subsequent organization of labor may well have increased the inflexibility of administered prices but price administration grows out of the structure of our industrial economy and the character of its markets regardless of the degree of labor organization.

Finally, I want to make it clear that the presence of administered pricing does not mean the absence of competition. It obviously does mean the absence of *classical* competition, i.e., the competition among such a forest of producers that no one producer has the power to set a price and enjoy a series of transactions. But the absence of classical competition does not mean the presence of classical monopoly. Most American industries fall within these extremes, with active competition but with too few or too large producers to establish the conditions necessary for classical competition to prevail. Also, even if the anti-trust laws were *perfectly* enforced, we would not have classical competition in most of American industry. Administered pricing would still be the dominant form of pricing in this country.

Now for the ways in which administered pricing makes obsolete the classical theory. I will take up three classical conclusions which are concerned with the short run effects—employment, balance of payments, and inflation. Then I will take up the longer run problems of waste, income distribution, and effective use of resources.

The Problem of Persistent Unemployment

According to classical theory, a free enterprise system has built into it an automatic mechanism which tends to maintain full employment. If, for some reason, say a speculative collapse such as occurred in 1929, there is a general drop in aggregate demand which might result in unemployment, the theory said this would automatically be corrected by a fall in the price-wage level. The fall in demand would necessarily constitute an increase in the demand for money balances. This would be satisfied by the following adjustment: As markets and employment declined, (1) competition among producers would bring down prices, (2) competition among workers for jobs would drive down wage rates, (3) with the nominal money supply unchanged, the fall in the price-wage level would increase the real buying power of the money supply, (4) the increase in the real value of the money supply would make money redundant, i.e., there would be more money in circulation than the public would choose to hold at the current levels of employment and *real* incomes, (5) the effort to spend the extra money would mean a demand for goods in excess of that arising out of current incomes, and (6) the extra demand for goods would force the hiring of unemployed workers. Under this theory, the fall in the price-wage level would come to a halt only when there was full employment. Thus, the only condition of equilibrium would be one of full employment with the price-wage level adjusting to whatever extent was necessary to make the real money supply just large enough to satisfy the public's desire to hold real money balances at full employment. And at the new equilibrium *relative* prices and the *relation* between prices and wage rates would be essentially the same as before the price-wage drop. Workers would not only be fully employed but, though their *money* incomes would be lower, the cost of living would also be lower *in the same degree* so that workers' real wage rates would not be significantly changed. (For an outline of this mechanism see John Stuart Mill's discussion of the impossibility of general overproduction except as a temporary self-correcting condition.)

I see no reason to question the logic of this theory *provided one assumes flexible prices and wage rates* which quickly adjust to equate supply and demand. It was the cliché that the economy had such a built in automatic corrective which led President Hoover to take so little action in the great depression and to wait for the recovery which was "just around the corner."

It should be obvious that such a mechanism could not operate if all prices and wage rates were fixed. If there were an initial drop in aggregate demand (which would also be an increased demand for money balances), sales and production at the fixed prices would fall and unemployment would be created. This would reduce incomes and have a multiplied effect on employment. Equilibrium would only be reached when *real incomes* were reduced to such a point that the demand for money was just equal to the supply and with no change in the price-wage level, no change in the money supply, and no outside source of demand, there would be nothing to absorb the unemployed.

In our actual economy, where some prices meet the classical flexibility, some are quite inflexible at least for considerable periods, and some have an intermediate degree of flexibility, one has a more complex adjustment. An initial drop in aggregate demand (which would mean an increased demand for money balances) could be expected to produce (1) a drop in flexible prices, (2) a drop in employment where prices were inflexible, and (3) an intermediate effect where prices were intermediately flexible. But this would not be an employment correcting adjustment. The equating of the real money supply and the desire to hold real money balances would be brought about *partly* by the fall in the more flexible prices which would increase the real value of the money supply and *partly* by the contraction in employment and real incomes. The new equilibrium would be reached when a *combination* of (1) lower flexible prices and (2) reduced employment and real incomes had brought the real demand and real supply of money balances into equality. Once this condition was reached, there would be no short run factors making for an increase in employment.

The above is a greatly over-simplified picture of economic adjustment but does make clear that with administered prices, the classical mechanism of automatic employment adjustment could not operate and therefore is obsolete for an economy dominated by administered prices.

It should also be noted that the difference between the two types of adjustment is not a product of monopoly or imperfect competition *as such*. Classical theory assumed that monopoly prices would be just as sensitive to changes in demand as competitive prices. Under classical theory, a *general* drop in demand which induced a general drop in competitive prices and in wage rates would induce a monopolist to reduce his prices in about the same proportion. Such flexible monopoly pricing, if it actually occurred, would not interfere with the classical adjustment mechanism. (Classical theory at the economy-wide level pretty much ignored the situation most common in the United States in which there is neither classical competition nor classical monopoly.) The error in the classical assumption that, where classical competition did not prevail, prices would be flexible is made obvious by the prevalence of administered prices. It is the fact that pricing power results in *price inflexibility* which prevents the classical mechanism from working effectively. Thus the problem of unemployment is associated with administered prices. I would not expect it to arise if there were no administered prices or wage rates and all prices and wage rates were made in the market and adjusted quickly to equate supply and demand.

(I have not introduced the complexities of the Keynesian theory, first because the dominant role of administered prices is sufficient to explain the inapplicability of the classical theory to the problem of unemployment, and second because I believe Keynes' theory of unemployment applies only to a special case not likely to occur in practice. I am writing an article now to that effect.)

The Balance-of-Payments Problem

Administered prices also make obsolete the classical theory of an automatic corrective for unbalanced international payments. The classical picture of the gold flow mechanism was quite beautiful. If each of two countries, A and B, based its money on gold at a fixed ratio, then an unbalance in payments between them would be automatically corrected by a flow of gold between them. The steps in the mechanism were as follows: (1) If country A incurred an unfavorable balance with B, it would make payment of the difference with gold; (2) because it had lost gold, country A would have a contraction in its internal money supply while B, having received gold, would have an expansion in its internal money supply; (3) the decline in A's money supply would force a reduction in the aggregate demand for goods in A with a consequent reduction in A's price-wage level while the increase in B's money supply would lead to increased aggregate demand in B with a consequent rise in B's price-wage level; (4) lower prices in A would stimulate B to purchase more goods in A while higher prices in B would make A buy less in B, thus reducing the unbalance in payments; (5) this adjusting process would go on until the price levels in A and B had so changed that the unbalance in payments disappeared and gold ceased to flow.

It should be obvious that, if the economies of A and B were dominated by inflexible administered prices, this classical adjusting mechanism could not work—or rather it would work quite differently. A gold flow which decreased A's money supply and aggregate demand would create unemployment in A while the flow of gold into B would stimulate demand and create overemployment and perhaps demand inflation in B. Thus, where administered prices are a dominant factor, the old gold standard would operate primarily through relative changes in employment, not through changes in the price-wage level except possibly very slowly.

The disrupting effects of general changes in the money supply—particularly contractions—became so clear in the early twentieth century that after World War I the gold standard was rejected by the leading industrial countries and when stable monetary conditions were reestablished after the war, this was done on the basis of the gold *exchange* standard. Under this standard, each country could control the volume of its internal money supply, using gold as a backing but not keeping the quantity of money in a fixed relation to its gold holdings. The primary function of gold was then to meet unbalances in payments. But there was no longer a simple price-wage level adjusting mechanism which would correct any persistent unbalance in payments. Thus, I would attribute the rejection of the gold standard and the emergence of balance of payments problems to the disrupting effect of administered prices and wage rates on the classical mechanism of adjustment. A theory which does not rest on an assumption of administered prices simply cannot explain international economic behavior in recent years.

The Problem of Administrative Inflation

Administered prices also make obsolete the classical theory of inflation. According to classical theory, there was only one basic kind of inflation. When the money supply was greater than the public would choose to hold at an initial level of prices and incomes, demand for goods in general would exceed supply and both prices and wage rates would rise, thus reducing the real value of the money supply. If the rise was not too violent, it would come to an end when the *real value* of the money supply had been reduced by the rise in the price-wage level to such an extent that it was just equal to the *real* amount of money the public would choose to hold at full employment. If the rise in the price-wage level was sufficiently violent or its causes deep seated, it could develop into a run-away inflation, involving both an uncontrolled rise in the nominal money supply and a contraction in the willingness to hold money so that there would be no limit to the rise in the price-wage level. In either case, the classical inflation theory involved a *general* rise in the price-wage level with all types of prices and wage rates participating in about equal degree.

Where administered prices dominate an economy, a wholly new type of inflation is possible which would not be possible according to classical theory. An administered price indicates that its price-setter has some degree of pricing power and pricing discretion. Under ordinary conditions of stable demand the price administrator is likely to keep his prices fixed except as his costs change. But under some conditions, *even though no change in demand occurs or is expected,* an upward revision of administered prices can occur. This could arise either because business sought to widen its profit margins or because labor forced wage rates up more than could be absorbed by increased productivity. In both cases the price rise is associated with price administration and would not be possible under the assumptions of classical theory. It is for this reason that I call it administrative inflation. It is sometimes called seller inflation or "cost-push" inflation (though the latter term would seem to apply only where wage increases were the source of the inflation). It can occur, even when demand is not sufficient to induce full employment.

I believe just such an administrative inflation was forestalled by President Kennedy's vigorous action against an arbitrary steel price increase in the spring of 1962.

Administered prices also cause an inflation arising from excessive demand to take quite a different course from that envisaged in classical theory. Instead of a general more or less simultaneous price and wage rise, a general excess of demand will first produce a rise of flexible prices and where prices are administered will produce over-employment and a much slower upward revision of administered prices corresponding to the rise in unit costs until there is a balance between the money supply and the willingness of the public to hold money. Then flexible prices will fall while administered prices continue to rise until the two groups are in approximate balance.

(For examples of administrative inflation and demand inflation, see my testimony before the Kefauver Committee in January and March 1959.)

When we turn from the short run problems of full employment, balance-of-payments and inflation to the longer run problems of industrial efficiency, income distribution, and the direction of the use of resources, administered prices play an important role but their effects are intertwined with the effects of pricing power as such and some of the effects might occur if the same degree of pricing power existed but prices were not administered (though the empirical evidence indicates that pricing power without price administration is not likely to arise in practice, classical theory notwithstanding—the de Beers diamond auctions are an outstanding exception).

The longer run effects of administered prices and pricing power have to do with concentration in relation to the market and the entrance of new competition. Quite different results can be expected where it is easy for new competition to come into the market and where entry is difficult. I will take up these situations separately.

Easy Entry and Competitive Waste

It is an essential part of classical theory that competition in an industry forces each producer to be as efficient as possible in his particular use of resources and that this results in efficiency for the industry and tends *over a period* to bring prices down into close relation to the economic cost of capital, labor, and materials. If prices persist at levels which yield excessive profits, new competitors will enter the industry and take over a part of the market, bringing down prices. And conversely, if prices and profits are too low over a period, individual competitors will leave or be driven out of the industry, thus reducing output and raising prices and profits to a competitive level.

Where sufficient pricing power prevails to allow administered prices and entry is easy, quite a different development can occur. Let us say that in a particular market there are only ten producers, that their products are sufficiently similar so that they must all sell at the same price in that market and that without collusion but through the natural operation of price leadership they are all selling at prices which yield an excessive rate of return on capital. But also assume that entry is easy. What can be expected?

If classical theory applied, an additional competitor would appear offering more product, prices would fall, etc. But where prices are administered, it is quite likely that the eleventh and twelfth competitor etc. will open up for business *at the existing administered price* and try to take business away from the existing competitors by advertising and other forms of promotion. (After all, the same considerations which lead the existing competitors to hold to a given highly profitable price are likely to apply equally to the newcomer unless his costs are radically lower.) The old competitors will expand their promotion to offset that of the newcomer. The customers will be supplied at the old administered price, their business will be divided up among a larger number of producers. But notice that the unit costs of production will have risen, partly because of the increased expenditure on promotion (assuming that the addition is mostly for competitive offset and has no great effect on the total volume sold by the industry) and partly because each separate producer has a smaller volume of production over which to spread his overhead. This will mean that each producer's profits go down, partly because of the rise in unit costs and partly because of the smaller number of units it sells. If profits are not brought down to a competitive level, more new entrants can be expected. A stable condition will be reached only when costs have risen and production has been so divided that no one makes an unreasonable profit at the unchanged administered price. Excessive profits have been eliminated, not by lower prices but by increasing waste of resources both through excessive promotion and through excessive use of capital and management skills.

In this example the whole of the competitive process of eliminating excessive profits is brought about with no change in price. In many cases, the new producer may have a much cheaper process of production which makes his most profitable price lower than for the rest of the industry. Then some reduction in prices may take place at the same time that the costs of other producers are increased and their profits reduced partly from the lower price and partly from their lower volume, while the newcomer will make excessive profits. Then, assuming the new methods are not patented, others in the industry or newcomers will adopt the cheaper methods until production is subdivided to the point that there is enough wastage to eliminate excessive profits.

It is not yet clear under what conditions, *if any,* the competition from easy entry will reduce profits to competitive levels by reducing administered prices. But many examples can be given of the reduction of excessive profits by increased waste. Thus, with administered prices and easy entry, competition can be expected to control excessive profits but is quite as likely to do this by increasing costs toward price as by reducing price toward costs.

Difficult Entry and Excessive Profits

Where classical competition is absent and entry is difficult, administered prices are likely to be set at levels which produce profits in excess of those necessary for a competitive rate of return on capital. The result of this is to distort the distribution of income and to limit unduly the use of resources of both capital and labor in these industries. How far these distortions are the result of pricing power as such and to what extent they are facilitated by the use of administered prices is not clear and is probably not important, at least if one accepts the proposition that administered prices are essential to efficient modern business.

Here endeth the reading of the lesson. I think I have said enough to make a case for the importance of administered prices for problems of national policy. You will find a more detailed discussion of some of these points in my books, *Pricing Power and the Public Interest* (particularly the last half of the book) and in *The Corporate Revolution in America.* (Sent by separate package.)

I hope this will convince any reader of the importance of administered prices.

With best regards,

Gardiner C. Means

12

Industrial Prices, as Administered by Dr. Means—A Reply

The humorous character of the title of the above attack in the September 1973 issue of the *Review* leads me to suggest that the whole attack is pretty funny. Eleven cases of misrepresentation, five cases of serious historical error, a crucial double non-sequitur, a serious error of omission, the testing of a straw theory and a clearly false conclusion; all in four and a half pages. Truly a "Comedy of Errors."

The Definition

The fun starts in the first scene with the definition of an administered price and a nice play on words. We have a senior author who has persistently and properly insisted that for economic analysis the term "price" means a *transaction* price unless the term is specifically modified. Then we have Means' 1935 definition of an administered price as "a price which is set by administrative action and kept constant for a period of time." And finally we have the criticism of this definition as "palpably vague" because it includes "asked price" whether or not there are any transactions ([Stigler and Kindahl], 1973, p. 718).

To avoid such an unsophisticated interpretation, Means in 1939 introduced the term "transactions" without changing the concept (1939, p. 109). And in Means' 1972 article which is the main subject of the attack, the definition is explicitly given as "a price set for a period of time and a series of transactions" (1972, p. 292), an unambiguous definition not mentioned by the authors. This scene might well be titled "Much Ado About Nothing."

From the Gardiner C. Means Papers at the Franklin D. Roosevelt Library, Series V, "Prices."

Means' Early Work

The next scene explores the relation between Means' early work and the "economics profession." It includes the remarkable double non-sequitur and amusing cases of misrepresentation and of historical error. We have the authors saying:

> In his actual practice during the 1930's Means defined administration as infrequency of price change, and measured it simply by frequency of price change per price reporter.
>
> * * *
>
> The literature of economics did not faithfully follow Means in this respect; it introduced two different criteria which were absent from his early work:
>
> i *Oligopoly* or high concentration was identified with administration; Means expressly disavowed this connection.
>
> ii Frequency of price change received less emphasis, partly as a result of the increased attention to concentration, in favor of amplitude of price change. [1973, p. 718. Emphasis added.]

The amusing double non-sequitur arises when the authors give as the *only* evidence of "disavowal," Means' statement in 1935 that: "Administered prices should not be confused with monopoly. The presence of administered prices does not indicate the presence of monopoly—" (1973, p. 718).

The first non-sequitur comes in using a statement about *monopoly* as evidence about *oligopoly*. Most scholars can recognize the logical difference.

The second non-sequitur comes in taking a statement that "the presence of administered prices does not indicate the presence of monopoly" and treating it as if it read, "the presence of administered prices indicates the absence of monopoly." Again logic does not allow such a conclusion.

It is also sheer misrepresentation to claim that Means disavowed the connection between high concentration and administration. The whole thrust of his analysis is to identify *concentration in relation to the market* as the source of the market power to administer prices. In the very paragraph from which the authors lift the above "monopoly" quote, Means says: "In general monopolized industries have administered prices, but so also do a great many vigorously competitive industries in which the number of competitors is small" (1935, p. 1). The automobile industry is cited as an example.

The authors' statements quoted above contain three other important falsifications, two of them serious historical errors.

First, Means never "defined administration as infrequency of price change." He used frequency of change as a crude measure of market power.

Second, the authors are historically wrong in saying that the criterion of high concentration was introduced by others and absent in Means' early work. In

Means' 1935 Price Pamphlet, this criterion was discussed and, in the 1939 report on the *Structure of the American Economy,* Means and his staff classified the item in the B.L.S. wholesale price index by all three of the crude measures of market power:

1. Frequency of price change.
2. Degree of concentration in relation to the market.
3. Amplitude of price change in recession and recovery.

Indeed, it was at Means' request that the Census Bureau made its first measurement and compilation of concentration ratios and the ratios could not have been used in the literature until published in the Structure Report.

The third misrepresentation and second historical error parallels the preceding. It was by Means, not in subsequent literature, that the amplitude of price change was first introduced as a crude criterion of market power. In the 1939 report practically all the items in the B.L.S. wholesale index were classed according to "depression sensitivity" and charts were given showing the distribution of the B.L.S. items according to this measure of amplitude in recession and recovery (1939, p. 131).

These are not excusable errors.

Commodities to Test the Means Thesis

The third scene focuses on the selection of commodities to be used in testing Means' administered price thesis. This scene, like the second, is enlivened by misrepresentation and historical errors.

In the NBER report by the same authors, 66 products were selected for the purpose of making such a test though complete data is given for only 63. There the authors say: "we chose commodities (really classes of commodities) which have figured prominently in the discussion of 'administered prices' " (1970, p. 5). They also say in 1973 that one of the two conditions for selection of these commodities was that "the prices were generally considered to be administered prices" and that "we deliberately omitted all industrial prices where the phenomenon of administered prices had not been urged with some plausibility" (1973, p. 717).

In making use of this new and valuable data collected from buyers, Means rejected 13 of the 63 items as not relevant to the administered-price thesis. Five were rejected on the ground that their prices were made in classically competitive markets and were not subject to significant administrative control. The remaining eight were excluded on the ground that a substantial part of their cost consisted of raw materials having market prices dominated by classically competitive world markets. Prices falling in these two groups were classed as market-dominated and the remaining 50 as administration-dominated and suitable to a test of the administered-price thesis. Also excluded were two items for which no price data were given.

The authors criticized these exclusions, saying, "In his most recent article Means offers still another criterion of administered prices. He omits fifteen as being market-dominated. . . . This is an almost new criterion of nonadministration, wholly absent from his works in the 1930's'' (1973, p. 718).

Again we have historical error. The concepts ''*market-dominated prices*'' and ''*administration-dominated prices*'' were introduced, defined, and used by Means in the Structure Report of 1939, more than 30 years ago.

The authors are also wrong in saying that these concepts provide another criterion of administered prices. Rather they provide two important categories, new at that time, neither of which is co-terminous with the category ''administered price'' as Means defined it.

The dividing line between market-dominated and administration-dominated prices is less easy to draw than between market and administered prices. It turns on market power which varies like the gradations from black to white. The dividing line between is necessarily arbitrary and the classification is in some degree subjective. But so also is the classification used by the authors when they decided whether a price has ''figured prominently in the discussions of administered prices'' or is ''generally considered to be administered.'' At least one can get data on concentration, depression sensitivity, and frequency of price change.

Often, other empirical evidence can determine the classification. For example, it is easy to see that there is no justification for classifying lumber and plywood as administration-dominated prices or even as administered prices. Both are traded in organized markets with daily high, low, and closing transaction prices regularly reported in the press and sometimes changing as much as 4 percent in a single day. Their inclusion in the 63 test prices as prices ''generally considered to be administered'' and as prices whose administrative character had been ''urged with some plausibility'' is truly strange.

This scene also has an amusing by-play involving two historical errors. The authors take exception to Means' suggestion that the removal of trend and seasonal price fluctuations is appropriate in the classification for the purpose of examining the cyclical effect of general changes in aggregate demand. On trend they say, ''this is a novel departure from previous practice'' (1973, p. 719) and on seasonal they say, ''This again is a wholly new interpretation'' (1973, p. 719). Yet both were discussed in the 1939 Structure Report and trend was partially adjusted for there in classifying prices according to ''depression sensitivity.'' As the authors themselves said in their NBER report, ''When there are strong trends in the price indexes, the cyclical responsiveness of price may be swamped or exaggerated by the trend component'' (1970, p. 44). The relevance of removing seasonal is too obvious to deserve discussion here.

The Thesis to be Tested

In the fourth scene tension begins to build up as attention focuses on the meaning of the administered-price thesis and how it can be tested. It is clear that the thesis is only concerned with industrial prices and only with their behavior in recession and recovery. The authors correctly quote Means as saying, "Basically, the administered-price thesis holds that a large body of industrial prices do not behave in the fashion that classical theory would lead one to expect" (1973, p. 719).

The authors refer to this statement as "so broad as to be almost uselessly vague" (1973, p. 719). Yet in their NBER report, the authors have clearly stated what they think classical theory would lead one to expect. There they said:

> Classical theory leads one to expect prices to fall in competitive industries during a business contraction, because both demand and marginal production costs fell, and that reverse movements will occur in expansions. [1970, p. 60]

For monopoly they give the same general classical expectation saying: "Here too, marginal costs would fall and there was no strong reason to expect marginal revenue to rise" (1970, p. 61).[1] Since this conception of classical theory is also that held by Means, there is agreement on the general classical expectation. This provides the ground rules for the test. In general, a price movement down in recession or up in recovery is to be classed for the purpose of the test as tending to support the classical thesis. A price which makes no significant change or moves perversely is to be classed as tending to support the Means thesis.

This scene is enlivened by two more cases of misrepresentation. They are both contained in the authors' statement: "Means insists upon limiting 'classical' price theory to the large-number auction of perishable goods" (1973, p. 719). First, Means does not limit the conception of classical price theory to perishable goods. Metals, lumber, and other durable goods are also included. Nor is it limited to large-number auctions. In classical macro-theory, monopoly prices were expected to be practically as flexible to changes in demand and cost as were classically competitive prices.

The serious error of omission also occurs in this scene. The authors fail to mention the *relative* character of the administered-price thesis, a characteristic which was stressed in the article which they are criticizing. The thesis, first presented under the title *Industrial Prices and Their Relative Inflexibility,* holds that administration-dominated prices show a strong tendency in a recession not to fall as much as market-dominated prices if they fall at all. Thus the true thesis would include as non-classical behavior not only prices which showed no change or a rise in recession but also prices which showed *relatively* little drop as compared with market-dominated prices. It would hold the reverse in recovery. For present purposes it is sufficient to make the test run on whether the bulk of administration-dominated prices fall with recession and rise with recovery or behave in an unresponsive or perverse fashion so long as it is recognized that prices which go down little in recession relative to market prices or rise little in recovery also tend to support the thesis.

The test is delayed and tension is further built up by three amusing bits of by-play.

The authors return to the subject of classification, saying that the commodities excluded by Means were excluded because they were ''raw-material dominated'' (p. 719). Five of the thirteen were not. Rather they were made in markets in which competition was among the many.

The authors also object to the exact periods of contraction and expansion used by Means on the ground that they do not conform to NBER cycle turning points. They say, ''We adopted the reference cycle dates of the National Bureau of Economic Research'' (1973, p. 719). But this is not true. For the fourth period they rejected the NBER trough and chose a ''trough'' which was not a trough at all but started the ''recovery'' *after* expansion had already been underway for over three years. For a study of *industrial* price behavior, the FRB index of *industrial* production used by Means would seem to be a better guide to fluctuations in *industrial* demand than the now somewhat obsolete NBER cyclical turning points which the authors themselves found not wholly satisfactory.

The authors also object that Means ''leaves the last six months of 1959 in the limbo of neither expansion nor contraction'' (1973, p. 719). Since the industrial production index, having reached a peak, dropped 8 index points in the first three of these six months and recovered an equal amount in the next three months before starting down, even King Solomon would have difficulty deciding whether this six months was a period of expansion or contraction.

The Great Test

Finally we come to the Great Test Scene and a beautiful table is wheeled center stage showing how many of the 50 mutually acceptable price series had increased, how many had stayed the same, and how many had decreased in each of two contractions and in each of two recoveries.

Actual examination of the table shows that in the 200 opportunities to change, price moved in the *same* direction as production in only 62 cases; in 59 cases, price showed little change; and in 79 cases price behaved in a perverse fashion, rising in recession or falling in recovery.

But in their interpretation of this table, the authors, suddenly and without warning to the reader, change the rules of the test. They do not attempt to test the Means thesis that a large proportion of administration-dominated prices behave in non-classical fashion. Rather they test a substitute thesis in which they classify all changes in *either direction* as *classical* behavior and in conflict with the Means thesis. This straw-man makes prices which perversely go *up in recession* or *down in recovery* behave in the fashion classical theory would lead one to expect. With this straw-man thesis to test, the authors find only 59 cases or less than 30 percent of the observations in support of the straw thesis. No mention is made of the fact that in 138 cases out of 200 or in 69 percent of the observations, the price behavior was not that to be *generally* expected according to classical theory and therefore tended to support Means' actual administered price thesis.

The Curtain Conclusion

This "Comedy of Errors" reaches a superb and strange climax in its curtain lines. For their curtain conclusion the authors drop the straw-man thesis and return to the Means' thesis but apply the straw findings to it. They conclude that:

> The thesis that modern economics has received from Means . . . is that *perverse or unresponsive* price behavior is widespread. Our study . . . contradicts that thesis. [1973, p. 721. Emphasis added.]

Clearly the facts in the test table do not contradict the administered price thesis. Rather they clearly support it with 69 percent of the observations showing "perverse or unresponsive" behavior. The support would rise to 80 percent with the inclusion as supporting the thesis of those cases in which prices changed in the classical direction but by less than a third of the average movement of the market-dominated prices in the NBER sample. It is truly strange that such preponderant support for a thesis contradicts it. One can only say that the authors' facts do not support their conclusion and do support the administered price thesis.

We could be amused by this parody of scholarship if the implications of price administration for macro-economic theory and policy were not so serious. Currently we have been experiencing the third and worst case of simultaneous recession and inflation since World War II.[2] Under the paradigm of classical macro-theory in which the prices of all goods and services continuously adjust to equate marginal cost and marginal revenue, recession and inflation at the same time are theoretically impossible. Recession could come from too little demand; inflation from too much demand; but not both at once. On the other hand, a paradigm which includes the non-classical behavior of administration-dominated prices as a major factor can easily explain simultaneous recession and inflation with the question of whether the inflation is wage push or profits push a matter for investigation. It can also explain a short run equilibrium in the presence of excessive involuntary unemployment. Further, the administered-price paradigm points to the likelihood that, with optimum employment of men and machines, and with no excess in demand, the average of administration-dominated prices would tend to rise, a development which lies wholly outside the realm of classical macro-theory. (See Means et al., *The Roots of Inflation,* 1975, Chapter I.)

Notes

1. The authors add a *special* exception in the case of monopoly to the effect that a price reduction is not a *necessary* result of a leftward shift in demand and cost functions. Since it is quite doubtful that a recession drop in demand shifts the functions *to the left* and since this explanation of behavior contrary to the *general* classical expectation is not relied on in either the NBER report or in the 1973 article, it will not be discussed here.
2. Also in 1957–58 and 1969–70.

References

Means, G.C., 1935. *Industrial Prices and Their Relative Inflexibility*. U.S. Senate Document 13, 74th Congress, 1st Session, Washington.

Means, G.C., 1939. *The Structure of the American Economy, Part I, Basic Characteristics*. National Resources Committee, Washington.

Means, G.C., 1972. ''The Administered-Price Thesis Reconfirmed.'' *American Economic Review*, June, 61, 292–306.

Means, G.C., et al. 1975. *The Roots of Inflation*. New York.

Stigler, G.J., and Kindahl, J.K., 1970. *The Behavior of Industrial Prices*. New York.

Stigler, G.J. and Kindahl, J.K., 1973. "Industrial Prices as Administered by Dr. Means," *American Economic Review*, September, 63, 717–721.

13

Collective Capitalism and Economic Theory

The modern corporation has undermined the preconceptions of classical economic theory as effectively as the quantum undermined classical physics at the beginning of the twentieth century. An equally drastic reconstruction of economic theory is due and is, perhaps, now in process. It is my purpose here to present a background for this reconstruction. This I propose to do by examining the relation between recent events and economic theory.

But first let us consider the role of theory in human action. In a basic sense man is a systematic animal. We live by systems of thought which guide our actions. Whether the particular system of thought is that of the witch doctor or the modern scientist, a system built around concepts of freedom and democracy or around a single God and the Ten Commandments, we could not live our lives effectively without such systems of thought. The real world is altogether too complex to be grasped. We build simplified systems of thought in order to aid our action. And these simplified systems are our theories about the real world.

Now it is a fundamental characteristic of our systems of thought that they never fit reality exactly. We can expect at best only a rough fit. A theory may be highly complex and logically consistent, and yet it is beyond wisdom to make it take account of *all* the real facts. As an approximation, a theory may serve us well. Newton's theory of gravity is sufficiently accurate for everyday purposes. But we should recognize that a theory can never be so complete as to give a perfect fit to reality.

In the field of the social sciences the crudeness in the fit of theory to reality is of particular importance because the social reality can itself be changing relative to the theory. It is for this reason that I think of society as moving in a curve of

Reprinted with permission of Collier Books, an imprint of Macmillan Publishing Company from *The Corporate Revolution in America: Economic Reality vs. Economic Theory* by Gardiner C. Means. Copyright © 1962 by The Crowell Collier Publishing Company.

change and a social theory as a straight line which may or may not be tangent to the curve at a particular time. When the theory is tangent to the curve, at that time the theory fits the reality well enough so that good policy can be made in terms of the theory, even though the theory does not exactly fit the facts.

But then the social reality may change. The tangent of theory and the curve of reality get farther and farther apart. Policies made in terms of the theory fail to produce good results.

I believe that we are now in a period in which society has moved out from under our older economic theories and that a new or revised set of theories is now in process of development. It is my purpose here to show why new theories are needed to guide policy, and also to suggest some of the directions the new theories seem likely to take.

The "straight-line" character of social theory arises from the basic assumptions of any given theory. A given theory can be elaborated within the framework of its own logic, but it is confined to the limits of its own assumptions. More cannot be derived from a theory than is put in by assumption. Let us see how this works in the case of economic theory.

Types of Control over Production

For economic theorizing, we can distinguish between at least four basic types of nongovernmental production which differ as to who controls production and can imagine economic models, each made up of just one type of production.

We might assume a subsistence model in which each economic unit produces only for its own consumption and in which there is no buying and selling. In approximation, such a model describes the economic condition of the Virginia settlements before tobacco exports became a significant factor, it describes most of our early pioneer settlements as our population moved west, and it still applies to some mountain homesteads. But, more importantly, this model applies in considerable degree to more than half of the present-day population of the world—to the Indian village, to the African tribesmen, and to people in many other parts of the world. For such people the market plays a negligible role, and production is organized within the village or tribe on a collective basis to meet the needs of the producers who are also the consumers. In such subsistence economies, consumers are in control of production or, what is more significant for our present analysis, consumer, worker, owner, and management are combined in a single economic unit. As a result, production policy and the instruments of production are controlled by units which combine the interests of consumer, worker, owner, and management.

Or we might assume an economic model in which individuals produce goods for sale in the market and buy goods in the market for consumption but in which no one works directly for anyone else. In such an economy, price and the market serve to organize the production of separate economic units. This form of production is typified by most American farms—a single producer raising cash crops, selling the product into the market, and taking out of the market what he needs for production and for consumption. If all production were carried on by such one-man enterprises, we would have a pure atomistic economy, with the consumer no longer in direct control of production but influencing production only through the market. In such an economy, direct control over production policy and the instruments of production would rest with individuals who combine the interests of worker-owner-manager, while the interests of consumers would depend on market forces. It is the great achievement of Adam Smith that he presented a theory of market behavior for such an atomistic economy. I will come back to this in a moment.

A third type of economy which we might assume is one in which production is carried on under the factory system with individual factory owners managing production but hiring workers to do the main producing. In such an economy, not only the consumer but also the worker is separated from control over production policy and the instruments of production, except as consumer and worker affect production through the market. This system of production has properly been called private capitalism, and it was factory production which provided the basic assumption of Marxian theory, while the separation of the worker from control over the instruments of production provided the basis of his class struggle.

A fourth type of economic model which we might assume is one in which all production is carried on by great corporate units in which ownership is so widely dispersed that owners, as well as consumers and workers, are separated from control over production policy and the instruments of production. In such an economy, management would be in control, subject, of course, to the influence of the markets for goods, for labor, and for securities. And with the separation of ownership and control comes the possibility of great aggregations of productive activity. We now have single corporate enterprises employing hundreds of thousands of workers, having hundreds of thousands of stockholders, using billions of dollars' worth of the instruments of production, serving millions of customers, and controlled by a single management group. These are great collectives of enterprise, and a system composed of them, or dominated by them might well be called "collective capitalism."

It would be possible to elaborate other types of economy such as the Soviet Government ownership and control, or an economy of cooperatives, but those outlined here will serve the present purpose.

Actually, the history of Europe and America in the last four centuries roughly fits the pattern of these four economies, though at no period was the economy exclusively of one type or another. The feudal economy of Europe and the pioneer economies of America were primarily of the subsistence type; Adam Smith's eighteenth-century economy was dominantly atomistic; the nineteenth-century economy was dominated by the factory system; and today the big corporation gives its particular character to our modern economy. Let us then trace economic theory in relation to the curve of our changing economy.

Economic Theory and the Real Economy

We can begin with classical economic theory, which for present purposes starts with Adam Smith and comes down through Mill and Marshall. This body of theory, *in its essentials,* relates to an atomistic economy and never really grapples with the problems which make a factory economy different from an atomistic economy. This assertion may surprise some since, certainly, the determination of wage rates was one of the classical problems. But consider that in classical theory, labor was treated as a commodity. In an atomistic economy, the shoemaker bought leather and shoe pegs and twine, combined them into a pair of shoes, and sold the shoes. And in classical theory the shoe manufacturer bought leather and shoe pegs and twine *and labor,* combined them into a pair of shoes, and sold the shoes. The factory system brought no change in theory except the delineation of a special commodity, labor, for which there were especially interesting problems of demand and supply. At the same time, the worker himself was treated as an entrepreneur seeking to market his ''product''—labor.

A single example will help to underline this fact. Ever since I became aware of the limited basis of classical theory, I have sought cases where a classical scholar has made a *significant* theoretical point which would apply to a factory economy and could not apply to an atomistic economy. So far, prior to Keynes, I have found only a single case. It occurs in D. H. Robertson's brilliant little book, *Banking Policy and the Price Level.* Robertson points out that if price and production policy in a company or an industry were made by the owners, one policy would result, whereas if policy were made jointly by owners and workers, a different policy would result, with lower prices and larger volume, since instead of seeking to maximize profits, the joint policy would seek to maximize the sum of profits and wages. Such a statement would make no sense in a pre-factory system in which there was no separation of the worker from control over production policy.

Although there may be other examples of such a departure from the assumption of an atomistic economy, I believe they are few and far between and have not produced modifications in classical theory. They do not stand in the way of the conclusion that, for practical purposes, classical theory is built on the basic assumption of an atomistic economy; we apply the classical analysis and classical conclusions to a factory or corporate economy at our peril.

Karl Marx took a big step forward in building his economic theory on the assumption of a factory economy and private capitalism. He recognized the separation of worker from control over the instruments of production and rejected the idea of treating labor as a commodity. In this he was more realistic than the classical theorists. On the other hand, he built a body of theory which has clearly been proved wrong in this country and certainly has not been supported so far by events in the Soviet Union. In this country, instead of progressive exploitation, there has been remarkable improvement in the workers' lot—the poor have become richer—while in the Soviet Union the workers are being exploited for the purposes of the state, with a real question whether the people are better off as a result. For Marx' theory, the superiority of his basic assumption of a factory economy does not make up for the weakness in his theoretical analysis.

As for collective capitalism, no comprehensive economic theory has been developed in terms of such an economy, in spite of the fact that the collective enterprise of our great corporations sets the tone of today's economy. As a result, we stand with a great deal of economic theory, but a major part of it was built on an obsolete base, and another part has been disproved by events. It is clear to me that a major reconstruction of economic theory is in order. We must create a body of theory which applies to collective capitalism and modify it to the extent necessary to allow for the fact that not all enterprise is collective enterprise.

Steps toward the Reconstruction of Economic Theory

The first step in a reconstruction of economic theory is to define its scope in modern terms. As long as economics dealt only with a pure atomistic economy (or with the theoretical equivalent, a factory economy with labor treated as a commodity), the scope of economic theory could be limited to the market mechanism and to a consideration of the ways in which individual behavior affected and in turn was affected by the market. For such an economy, an analysis of the market is also an analysis of the way in which the activities of separate individuals are coordinated in using resources to satisfy human wants. Some economists would like to limit the scope of economic theory today to the operation of the market mechanism. But today, with the great role played by corporate management in coordinating the activity of separate individuals within an enterprise, it is obvious that the market mechanism is not the only coordinating device. If we limit economic theory to the market, we are leaving out a major part of economic coordination. I believe that economic theory must be given the broader scope and that it must deal with economic coordination within enterprises as well as between enterprises. It must be concerned with the coordination of individual action in using resources to satisfy human wants, however that coordination is brought about.

If we accept this broad scope for economic theory, the second step is to investigate the various means by which economic coordination is brought about. So far, I have been able to discover four distinct and important ways by which the economic actions of individuals can be coordinated. The first and most obvious is the market mechanism. I do not need to point out how the market can coordinate the productive activity of thousands of individuals. A second and equally obvious method of coordination is by administrative direction. The manager tells *A* to do one thing, *B* another, and *C* a third, and, because the manager planned it that way, the separate actions of the three fall into a common pattern.

But there are two other devices of coordination which are not so obvious, and yet they are particularly important for a democratic society. These devices are what might be called canalizing rules and the acceptance of common goals.

We are all familiar with the canalizing rules—the laws, rules, and customs—which help to coordinate daily living. The rule that one drives on the right side of the road or the custom that bills are sent out at the end of the month helps to bring order into individual behavior. Or consider two people getting into an elevator. It is much easier for a man and a woman to enter than it is for two polite men to do so. These are perhaps trivial examples. More important are the custom of accepting money in exchange for goods, the laws enforcing contracts, and the rules and regulations set up by a corporation to facilitate its activity. The canalizing rules play a major role in coordinating the activities of separate individuals.

The fourth coordinating influence is the acceptance of common goals. We had an outstanding example of this during World War II. There was a nation-wide acceptance of the aim of winning the war. And, in the light of this common goal, any number of people did things or put up with things in ways to contribute to the war effort without being told. Or take a more homely example. A family decides to go on a picnic and, without specific instructions, various members in the family start to prepare. Some make sandwiches, some get the car ready, and others get out the picnic hamper. Once the picnic goal has been accepted, coordination can come simply as a result of the thinking and action of each individual as he sees how his effort can be coordinated with that of others. Business enterprise is constantly using goals both to stimulate and to coordinate production and sales. We will come back later to the coordinating role of common goals.

For our present analysis, what is important is that there are at least four ways in which the action of individuals can be coordinated to a greater or lesser degree, and, in any concrete situation, coordination may involve two or more of these different methods. I believe that economic theory must take account of all four.

With this background, let us consider the various areas of economic theory and the direction in which they are developing or should develop because of the facts of collective capitalism. For this purpose I will distinguish between the following four major areas of economic theory: the theory of employment; the theory of the firm; the theory of allocation; and the theory of economic planning.

Employment Theory

The term *employment theory* is relatively new, but classical theory dealt with the problem of under-utilization of resources under the heading of Say's law and in the equilibrium equations of Walras. According to both, the only condition of equilibrium in an atomistic economy is one of full use of resources. As Mill pointed out, according to classical theory general overproduction was impossible—except, of course, temporary overproduction, which would quickly correct itself.

Actual events—the long American depression of the 1890's, Britain's long depression in the 1920's, the world-wide depression of the 1930's, and the long history of business fluctuations—finally broke the hold of Say's law and the belief in a self-correcting mechanism that would maintain reasonably full employment. Keynes came forward with a new theory of employment which he believed would explain the possibility of equilibrium at less than full employment in a competitive and flexible-price economy.

For many years this theory found wide acceptance and helped to make theoretically respectable the rejection of Say's law. But in spite of the brilliance of Keynes' analysis, it rested on an assumption that is no longer generally accepted by economists—the assumption that the only way a change in the real stock of money could affect the level of demand and employment is through changes in the level of interest rates. I cannot go into detail here. It is sufficient to say that the statistical evidence does not support Keynes' assumption. Keynes has not supplied an explanation of unemployment for an economy of flexible prices and wage rates. For such an atomistic economy, the only condition of equilibrium would appear to be one of full employment; Say's law would still seem to hold for an atomistic economy.

But our present-day economy is not an economy of flexible prices and wage rates. The factory system and the modern corporation have brought changes which must be taken into the basic assumptions of theory. Labor is not a commodity, and wage rates are not flexible but a form of administered prices. In addition, administration of enterprise has extended into the goods market, and we also have administered prices for goods. When economic theory is rebuilt on the basis of administered prices and administered wage rates, I believe the inapplicability of Say's law and the Walrasian full-employment equilibrium will be obvious.

First let us consider wage rates. Classical theory had no difficulty picturing a commodity market for wheat or oranges with suppliers and demanders brought into adjustment by price. But have you ever run across a theoretical description of a market for labor in which the wage rate equates the demand and supply of labor? I never have, and I have never been able to envisage such a market. Would each worker come into the market each day and offer a basket full of "labor," and would employers "buy" a fresh lot of labor each day? This just does not make sense. A worker cannot sell his labor apart from himself; an enterprise cannot use labor apart from the persons who constitute it. And an essential part of the value of "labor" to an enterprise is the familiarity of the persons constituting "labor" with the equipment or affairs of the enterprise employing them. This means that a free market and flexible prices for labor are not feasible if big factory or corporate enterprise is to be efficient.

In actual fact, as I have said, wage rates are a form of "administered price."

Before labor became organized, the typical procedure for establishing wage rates was administrative. In starting up a factory, the manager decided on what wage rates he would pay for each type of work and sent out word that jobs were available. If the supply of job seekers at those wage rates was larger than the number he wanted to hire, he would turn some away. If the supply was not as large as he wanted, he would send word farther afield, or perhaps he would send out recruiting agents to bring in workers. Thus the wage rates set by the manager would equate supply and demand only by chance. In most cases, either demand or supply would be in excess. And, what is most important for employment theory, the fact of a discrepancy between the supply and demand for labor would not lead the manager to alter his wage rates unless the discrepancy was considerable. Similarly, once a factory was in operation, if the manager needed fewer workers, he would lay off a part of his labor force. But he was unlikely to reduce his schedule of wage rates unless there was a very large increase in unemployment or unless his own firm was being seriously squeezed by competition. Thus, under the factory system, and even without labor organization, wage rates were administered and tended to be relatively inflexible, seldom closely equating the supply and demand for labor.

Whether or not the organization of labor has increased the inflexibility of wage rates is not clear. During the Great Depression of the early 1930's, wage rates dropped more in the clothing trades in which labor organization was strong than they did in such durable-goods industries as automobiles and electric equipment where unemployment was greater, labor was weak, and wage rates were administered by the corporate management. On the other hand, negotiated wage contracts certainly limit the power of management to change wage rates for periods of time. For present purposes it is immaterial whether the organization of labor increases the inflexibility of wage rates or simply confirms a behavior which management would have adopted in any case. What is important is that the factory system and the corporate system involve wage rates which do not behave like the classical commodity prices.

Administration of prices has also come to be a dominant characteristic of our factory and corporate economy. A company will set its price for a product and hold it constant for a period of time, selling whatever amount is demanded at the administered price. Demand at the administered price may be in excess of supply, as was recently the case with steel. Or demand may be less than the company is willing to supply at the administered price. As a result, an administered price will equate supply and demand only by chance, while an excess of supply or demand of considerable magnitude may develop without resulting in a revision of an administered price.

The classical theorists were familiar with administered prices, but, so far as I know, administered prices were never introduced as a basic assumption in classical economic theory. Their effect was treated as a matter of "friction" which slowed up but did not prevent the process of automatic adjustment. But today a large proportion of all labor and commodity transactions in this country take place at administered prices. Certainly most retail distribution, including a large part of food distribution, is at administered prices. So are most manufactured products and most of the services. Only in farm products and raw materials is the classical market price the general rule, and even here there are many exceptions. Thus, the factory and corporate systems provide us with administered prices, as well as administered wage rates, both of which lie outside of classical theory.

Once one introduces administered prices and wage rates as basic assumptions in employment theory, it is not difficult to explain equilibrium at less than full employment. Keynes did this, not as a theory, but as a device of exposition. When he analyzed the effect on employment of changes in the propensities to consume and invest, he first assumed that prices and wage rates were fixed. This was only a device to make it easier to follow his analysis, and he has made it clear that his conclusions on employment did not depend on this temporary assumption. Yet perhaps his greatest claim to fame will be this inadvertent introduction of a formulation of equilibrium with fixed prices and wage rates.

Of course, administered prices and wage rates are subject to change, and the new theory of employment must take account of the successive re-adjustment of prices and wage rates as the discrepancy between supply and demand exceeds some threshold of administrative action. The theory must be concerned both with the magnitude of this discrepancy and with the magnitude of the price revision when it is made. What is immediately important is that, when administered prices and wage rates are assumed, it is easy to construct economic models which reach short-run equilibrium at less than full employment and in which automatic forces operate toward full employment so slowly that they are not important. Thus, in one plausible model which I constructed, the automatic forces would restore full employment only after an infinite regression in time.

Here, then, is a major reconstruction of economic theory required by the actual characteristics of our economy. Fortunately, our practice in seeking to maintain full employment has run ahead of dependable theory. But a dependable theory of employment could greatly clarify the essential role of government and greatly increase the efficiency of practice in this field.

The problem here is to develop a statement of short-run economic equilibrium on the assumptions that some prices are of the classical type and that some are administered. We have the Walrasian formulation of equilibrium for an economy of perfectly flexible prices. We have the Keynesian formulation with its ambiguity about price, but it is capable of stating an equilibrium with prices fixed. What we need is a Walrasian-like formulation which will state the condition of equilibrium if some prices are administered and some prices are flexible, and indicate how changes in the equilibrium-determining factors will alter the equilibrium result.

Theory of the Firm

A second area of economic theory which needs reconstruction because of the modern corporation is the theory of the firm. This presents a many-issued problem, one that is at the heart of economic theory, since assumptions about the behavior of the firm enter into all other areas of economic theory.

Classical economics has given us a highly elaborated theory of the behavior of a firm—and here I include not only the classical line through Marshall but also the somewhat arid analyses of Chamberlin and Robinson. This theory is concerned with the firm as a buyer, combiner or producer, and seller of goods. And because labor is treated as a commodity, it applies primarily to an atomistic economy. The theory itself starts with the assumption that the entrepreneur is seeking to maximize his profit and works out the different patterns of behavior which would maximize profit under various known conditions.

This theory, when it is applied to imperfect competition, has always given me a good deal of trouble, even as applied to an atomistic economy. But let us assume that the classical theory of the firm does apply to the small entrepreneur in an atomistic economy or is so modified that it does apply, and ask what modifications are needed to make it fit the corporate firms of collective capitalism.

The first change is implicit in our discussion of employment theory: the new theory of the enterprise must account for the well-nigh universal presence of administered prices and wage rates and their respective behavior. There is nothing in the classical theory of the profit-maximizing firm which would lead one to expect administered prices or administered wage rates.

A second change was pointed out by Adolf Berle and me in our book, *The Modern Corporation and Private Property,* in which we indicated how the separation of ownership and control in most of our big corporations undercuts the function of profits to owners as a stimulus to more efficient operation of the enterprise. Consider first the profits going to those stockholders who do not in fact control the enterprise or make policy. Such profits cannot act as an incentive to better operation of the enterprise. And if, instead, profits over and above the amount necessary to induce investment were to go to the controlling management so they would induce more efficient operations, as profit theory would require, the courts would find this illegal, because the profits "belong" to the stockholders.

On the other hand, how much do profits from ownership act as a stimulus to those in control of a big corporation whose stock is widely dispersed? It is often said that, even though a controlling group may own only a small proportion of a company's stock, their ownership interest and the incentives arising from it can still be large because of the size of the company. Let us look at this for a minute. Consider, for example, a memorandum recently circulated by the Atchison, Topeka, and Santa Fe Railway Company giving the stockholdings of the directors of the company who are, in effect, in control of that corporation. In combination, the directors hold one-tenth of 1 percent of the outstanding stock. The average stockholding per director has a current market value of approximately $50,000, and the largest holding by a director is just under $200,000. These are sizable amounts of investment. But do they really supply a significant inducement to strive vigorously to increase the company's profit? Suppose that, by more vigorous direction, the company could be made to yield 20 percent higher profits. Assuming that this would mean a 20 percent higher dividend, the average director would get $600 more in dividends, while the director with the largest stockholding would get four times this amount. And since most of the directors, if not all, are already paying income taxes at the more robust rates, only a part of the $600 would be a reward. My own belief is that the directors of such a well-run railroad as the Santa Fe try to run it well for the same reasons that the trustees of a great university seek to run the university well. In the case of the Santa Fe, profits are a symbol of successful operations, but I question how far the receipt of profits by the controlling directors *through their ownership* is a dominant stimulus to efficient operation.

I am not here suggesting that profits do not play an important role in big corporate enterprise. I am suggesting that their role may be quite different from that attributed to profits in the representative small firm of classical theory. As a minimum, we can say that profits cannot perform their traditional role where ownership and control are separated, for this traditional role depended on the assumption that ownership and control were combined. We should start fresh and ask just what are the motivations of top corporate management—to increase their personal incomes, to serve the stockholders, to expand management's power, to foster the status of the corporate collective, to serve the public interest? Clearly, a new theory of the firm to apply to the corporate collective must start with an analysis of motivation in the big business bureaucracies. Such an analysis must be based on actual observation. This will not be easy, because motivation is itself elusive. Perhaps such investigations will require the joint action of economist, political scientist, psychologist and anthropologist. Until such studies are made, our basis for assuming motivation is inadequate.

In the meantime, I offer the suggestion that a study of motivation in the top management of a great university would throw more light on the motivation of top corporate management than any amount of study of small private enterprises. Like a university, the great corporate collective is a "going concern" with its own momentum and its own internal drives and internal conflicts. Literature is beginning to reflect this in such books and plays as *Executive Suite* and *The Solid Gold Cadillac*. How far is the task of top management in the corporation that of generating and sustaining group thinking and group decision-making? And what factors actually enter into top management decisions?

There are also problems of motivation in the lesser ranks of management. Are the pressures for conformity and compromise in the group activities of management reducing initiative and enterprise, either by suppressing it or by selecting away from it? Are the great corporations creating a new "economic man"—the "organization man"—with new characteristics which the economist will have to understand, analyze, and take into account? And can the "organization man" be adequate to fill the shoes of top management?

The bureaucratization of industry requires still another extension of the theory of the firm—the study of the bureaucracy itself. How are the great corporations actually run? How are the activities of 100,000 persons coordinated within a single enterprise? What kind of organization makes for effective use of resources; what kind, for wasteful use? With so much of the coordination of individual activity brought about through administrative action within single units, how does this affect the use of resources in the satisfying of wants? In some degree this aspect of enterprise theory must deal with the same problems of administration as those dealt with by political theory in its analysis of government bureaucracy, but in other respects, particularly in its focus on the impact of administration on the use of resources, this will be a new kind of allocation theory in which the unseen hand of Adam Smith is replaced by the visible hand of business bureaucracy.

The reconstituted theory of the firm will also have to take account of corporate politics as well as corporate economics. The modern corporation is more than a legal framework of enterprise. It is an institution for interrelating the interests of security holders, workers, consumers, and management. As such, it is a focus for conflicting, as well as common, interests, and it is the focus of power conflicts. Just where in these power conflicts economics leaves off and political science begins is not at all clear. Perhaps what we need is a new joint science which gives new content to the old term *political economy* and applies it to the politico-economic formation of policy in the great corporate enterprises as well as in government.

Finally, the theory of the corporate firm will have to consider the public responsibility of corporate management arising from size and from the separation of control from consumer, worker, and owner alike. In our book on the modern corporation, Berle and I suggested that, if the controlling management of the big dispersely owned corporations adopted the role of arbiter between stockholders, workers, and consumers, the courts might accept such a role. Certainly there is considerable evidence that the larger corporations are accepting some degree of social responsibility as a step toward their own long-run status and survival. The theory of the collective firm must therefore consider under what conditions, if any, an enterprise can operate to serve the public interest without itself assuming any social responsibility; and also under what conditions an enterprise is so large or so relates investors, workers, and consumers that it must take into account, or be made to take into account, considerations of social interest as well as those of corporate profits.

When we have an adequate theory of the collective corporate firm, we will be able to picture an economic model of big corporate enterprise. Such a theory, combined with adequate theories of the firm for an atomistic and for a factory economy, should give us the basis for understanding most firm behavior in our actual complex economy.

Allocation Theory

The third great branch of economics I propose to discuss is allocation theory. Classical allocation theory rests on or includes the traditional theory of the firm and is concerned with the process by which scarce resources are allocated to different uses. It starts with the assumption of full employment and deals with the way in which prices and the market mechanism operate to direct resources into the production and distribution of the goods most in demand. Marshall's *Principles* represents the greatest formulation of this theory. It has been much elaborated since Marshall's time, but a great deal of the elaboration is to be found, at least in embryo, in Marshall's footnotes.

Certain basic assumptions of this theory are clear. Besides the assumption of full employment, the theory postulates Marshall's representative firm with ownership and control combined in a single owner or partnership. It treats labor as a commodity. And it assumes flexible prices which adjust to equate supply and demand. With these postulates, Marshall purports to show that, in general, prices (including wage rates) will so adjust that price and marginal cost will tend to be approximately equal, resources will tend to be used in the most productive manner, and the rewards to the factors of production will tend to be close to their respective marginal contributions to production. This theory is of great importance today because a great deal of private and public policy is built upon it, either consciously or unconsciously.

Now I do not wish to raise here the question of whether the conclusions of this theory logically flow from its postulates. The significant question is whether these same conclusions would flow if we postulated, not Marshall's representative firm, but the modern corporation with its vast size and the separation of ownership and control; if we postulated, not labor as a commodity, but labor as a group of human beings; if we postulated, not flexible prices which equate supply and demand, but administered prices under which supply and demand can be different. As far as I know, there is no one who has developed a coherent theory which rests on such modern postulates and develops their implications.

I have not done much work in the field of allocation theory, having been primarily concerned with employment theory, but I can at least lay down some questions which should challenge attention.

Let us consider an economic model in which all economic production is carried on by four hundred huge corporations. Let us also say that, at the outset, while each company produces many products, there are only four companies producing each particular commodity and that each has its own particular brands with their own characteristics; that labor, unlike a commodity, has created labor unions, and that wage rates are made by collective bargaining between unions and individual companies; and that the individual companies offer and promote the sales of their products at administered prices which are seldom changed except as quite large changes in costs or demand occur; and finally, that we start with full employment. How would such an economy run?

You will notice that I have excluded price wars by assumption. With only four producers of a commodity and with a considerable degree of product differentiation, competition can express itself in greater advertising expenditures, increased product differentiation, product improvement, and other means which seek to take business away from competitors or to expand the market. But the knowledge that a price cut will be met or surpassed by a competitor will inhibit price cuts, except to adjust to a considerable change in cost or demand.

I would also raise the question whether even a major change in demand would affect price. At a recent meeting of businessmen and economists, the head of one of our big retail and manufacturing enterprises argued that demand had no influence on prices and challenged the economists present to show how an increase in the demand for the products of his company would lead to his charging higher prices. In his thinking, prices were determined by costs and probably, for his particular firm, he was essentially right. Of course, it was easy to suggest that many raw materials have flexible prices which are sensitive to changes in demand and that, when the demand for his products increased, he increased orders and thereby increased the demand for raw materials somewhere back along the line and that this ultimately raised his costs. But suppose that raw materials were produced only by a few companies and these companies also operated with inflexible, administered prices. Under what conditions would changes in demand have an effect on prices? How large a change in demand would be necessary to trigger a change in price? And what relation could be expected between marginal cost and price?

Then consider the question of profits or rate of return on capital. Traditional theory suggests that with only four producers and no price wars, the rate of return on capital would tend to be abnormally high in relation, say, to interest rates or to the current costs of capital. Is this in fact true? What would place a roof on excessive earnings? Would strong labor unions prevent too high rates of earnings? Or would labor and capital gang up on the consumer? And if this happened equally for *all* industries, would it make any difference, since the high money prices could be met out of high money incomes? Would competitive advertising and promotion so increase selling costs as to absorb excessive profits, keeping costs and prices in line not by reducing prices but by increasing costs? Would the threat of new entrants into a given market keep profits in bounds? And if profits were not kept in line, who would benefit from high rates of earnings, stockholders who do not control the enterprise or management that does? Also, would it be possible to maintain full employment in such an economy and avoid inflation?

An even more fundamental question is whether, in our economic model of a few great collectives, resources would be well allocated. Here we have to deal not only with the determinants of relative prices which help to guide the flow of resources into different uses but also with the direction of resources within the great collectives. It is often said that consumers direct the use of resources by what they purchase. Yet how great is consumer choice? If you want to buy a new American car this year you have, as far as I can see, very little real choice. What you are offered is a longer, heavier car with fins. I am reminded of a recent cartoon in which two men are looking down at the rear of a new high-finned car and one says to the other, "You don't like fins and I don't like fins. What would happen to the American economy if nobody liked fins?" In some ways, our big American producers are the most efficient in the world. But if finned cars are a temporary matter and are not really wanted by the people who will have to buy them second-hand, the resale value of finned cars will be low and the reduction will reflect inefficiency in the use of resources which could offset a good deal of efficiency in production. The problem of the allocation of resources through corporate enterprise is both a matter of efficiency in production and importantly a matter of what is produced. A consumer veto over wasteful use of resources is by no means the same as consumer control over their use.

Here I have raised questions about how allocation in an economy made up of big enterprises could be expected to take place. I could go a lot further in asking specific questions. But what is important here is that the questions are of a sort which cannot be answered by any amount of study of Marshallian theory, including Marshall's footnotes. Clearly a new, coherent body of allocation theory is needed if we are to understand our actual economy and make wise decisions in such matters as anti-trust policy, government regulation, and economic planning. Such a new, coherent body of theory would derive many of its parts from older theory. Other pieces for such a theory which cannot be derived from Marshallian theory are already developed or in the process of development. But, as far as I am aware, no coherent theory has been produced which would effectively describe allocation in a model economy of collective capitalism or for our actual economy, which is so largely composed of big collective corporate enterprises.

I could go on into other fields of economic theory and point to other changes in theory required by the factory system and collective capitalism: the inapplicability of the classical mechanism of international trade adjustment, the irrelevance of a wage theory which relates wage rates to the marginal product of labor, and the minor importance of a growth theory which builds on private individual invention. But to go into them would take too much space.

There is, however, one major field of theory which has been added by the development of collective capitalism and which was quite absent from traditional theory—the theory of economic planning.

Need for a Theory of Economic Planning

There has been a great deal of confusion about economic planning—particularly its relation to dictatorship. This is understandable, since economic planning has been most highly developed in the USSR and is directly tied to government operation of industry. But economic planning itself can be an important tool in a democracy. It can facilitate more effective use of resources without dictating those uses.

Consider for a moment our recent transition from a war to a postwar economy. For the first time in a long history of business fluctuations, a postwar depression was avoided. How did it happen that demand and employment were sustained after the war? Partly it was the result of the pent-up demand and monetary expansion which have always accompanied major wars. But I believe it was partly the result of economic planning (in which the Committee for Economic Development played an important role), as a result of which both government and industry were already prepared to make a quick shift from war to civilian production, and the potential goals of production were set for a full-employment economy. How this was done is a long story, but that it was done and that it did contribute to the prevention of a postwar depression, I am certain.

We find economic planning being encouraged by businessmen in connection with our foreign economic aid. Thus, one well-known business leader recently suggested that, in providing economic aid to the less-developed countries, we should require that any country to be aided should prepare a well-worked-out plan for economic development.

And, of course, we are undertaking a form of economic planning in our governmental agencies concerned with the maintenance of full employment, particularly in the Council of Economic Advisers and the Federal Reserve Board.

We also need to consider the potentials of economic planning in bringing about a better use of resources. I believe that when an adequate theory of allocation is worked out for collective capitalism, it will show a very considerable degree of indeterminacy in the allocation of resources insofar as purely economic forces are concerned, and that if we are to have a high degree of effectiveness in the use of resources and avoid the pressure for government direction, we must have a clearer picture of what seems likely to constitute effective use of resources as a background against which private, corporate, and government decisions can be made. This would be economic planning without compulsion.

Conclusion

Finally, I want to express my enthusiasm for collective capitalism. I believe that it is, to a major extent, responsible for the high levels of living which we enjoy in this country. I believe that we are still some way from understanding how it really works and what its imperatives are. We have started meeting some of these imperatives in our social security programs, in government action to clear the way for the organization of labor, and in our acceptance of government responsibility for full employment. Our problem now is to understand its operation so well that we can make it provide not only full employment and high productive efficiency but effective use of resources, equitable distribution of income, freedom to the individual to develop his resources, and the continued growth which is a potential of collective capitalism. I do not believe that this can be achieved if we base our policies on economic theories built on the postulates of Marshall's representative firm, flexible prices, and labor treated as a commodity.

As I said at the outset, I believe that our position today is very much like that of the physical scientists fifty years ago when the reality and importance of the quantum had been accepted but was not a postulate of current theories. We need an economic Niels Bohr, a de Broglie, a Heisenberg, and a Dirac to reconstruct or revolutionize economic theory as these men revolutionized physical theory. Such new theory seems to me likely to be quite different from classical theory, because so many of its underlying parts would be new. It would have to take full account of the implications of administered prices, the new status of profits, the concept of countervailing powers. I believe that such a theory would indicate the great economic and social advantages of the great corporate collectives but that it would also bring out the ways in which the economic results fall far short of being satisfactory and suggest ways in which improvement could be made. But, even more important, I believe that it would greatly clarify the character of the responsibilities which the managers of our great collectives have assumed and are only now beginning to be aware of and would provide an improved basis for public policy under our system of collective capitalism.

14

Thoughts on Concentration

At the outset, I want to make it clear that this paper has no statistical significance. It was prepared in haste, its coverage is incomplete, the sample is badly skewed and it is dominated by the subjective.

I have called the paper "Thoughts on Concentration" so that I would not have to give it organization or structure or too much content. It was only a week ago that the emergency of John Blair's prospective absence arose and placed me in the position of pinch hitter. Press of other business did not allow me to start work until the day before yesterday.[1] I make explanation but no apology for the randomness of this sample.

Different Measures of Concentration

First, I want to talk about the significance of different measures of concentration for different purposes.

My first adventure in the field of concentration was, as you know, concerned with property rights, the change in the character of property rights due to the separation of ownership and control in the big corporations and the concomitant concentration of control over the instrument of production. For this purpose I used assets or wealth controlled as the primary measure of concentration and compared the wealth of the two hundred largest non-financial corporations in the U.S. at the end of 1929 with all non-financial corporate wealth, with total business wealth, and with total national wealth.

I was immediately attacked by Professor Crum of Harvard, not on the reliability of the estimates, but on the ground that I was adding apples and pears by adding together two quite different things, public utilities and railroads which were known to be big and regulated, and manufacturing and

Reprinted with permission from the *Proceedings of the American Statistical Association: The Business and Economic Statistics Section* (September 1962), pp. 118–126.

other enterprises which were supposed to be controlled by competition.[2]

I defended the use of wealth for the particular purpose in hand—the consideration of the changing character of property rights and conceded to Professor Crum the position that for discussing problems of competition, the regulated activities should be excluded.

But as I look back today, I believe I conceded too much. At that time, the prevailing picture of the economy *as a whole,* the tableau economic, was classical (or if you prefer, neo-classical) and was epitomized in Walras' brilliant system of equations. This was the competitive system.

Now to present figures of concentration that bear on whether or not the Walrasian competitive tableau applies to the modern economy, I believe that concentration figures which include public utilities and railroads are more relevant than those which exclude regulated industries. For macro-economic analysis, the utilities and railroads are just as important as manufactures. They are an integral part of the whole.That they don't fit into the Walrasian competitive system is too bad for that system. It doesn't apply to the modern economy. I find it intriguing that Walras' book has only recently been translated into English when it has ceased to be relevant. It is a brilliant museum piece.

For building up the new tableau economic at the macro-economic level, I believe we need figures for concentration which cover all types of enterprise activity. We should have figures for say the largest 200 and the largest 1,000 corporations as compared with all corporations, all enterprise and the economy as a whole. Only then can we picture the actual structure of the American economy.

Also, we should have such figures by various measures. To me, the three most important measures are wealth, value added and employment. For some purposes, such as that involved in the *Modern Corporation and Private Property,*[3] wealth is the more relevant measure. For other purposes, such as labor-management relations, employment would be the more relevant measure. Probably the most generally useful measure for macro-economic purposes would be value added which reflects both labor and capital. Other measures such as value of product would be useful for particular purposes.

In this connection, the major difference to be expected from these different measures arises from the clearly discernible tendency for activities requiring large amounts of capital per worker to be more concentrated except as there is some strong element of inefficiency in large scale activity as there is, for example, in the case of most farming. On the whole, we can expect a higher percentage concentration figure when wealth is the measure than when value added is used and the degree of concentration would be least where employment is used.

Even from the macro-viewpoint we also need to have figures on concentration by industrial segments. What is the degree of concentration in manufacturing, in utilities, in banking, in railroads, in distribution, in farming? Here also it seems to me wealth, value added and employment are the most important measures.

When we turn to micro-analysis and concern ourselves with the role of competition in determining price, I am less clear on just what concentration figures can be useful. Here I can agree with Professor Crum that regulated industries are not relevant. But, as many have pointed out, the focus of pricing analysis must be the particular product and the particular market. If markets for a given product are local, figures for the concentration on a national scale may have little relevance. And even where markets are national, concentration figures on an industry-wide scale may not disclose the presence of a high degree of concentration if there is much specialization.

Perhaps the two most important values of industry figures of concentration for pricing problems are, first, that high concentration tags an area for more detailed investigation, and second, that a trend of increasing concentration suggests that competitive forces are changing if not weakening in the particular industry and need to be examined. Of course, where it is established that a high or increasing concentration exists in a highly homogeneous industry with a national market, this concentration is certainly relevant to pricing problems.

Between the macro-economic problems and those of pricing and competition, there are a range of problems for which concentration data have value. Professor Adelman draws the distinction between the political and the economic aspects of concentration.[4] But there are also other aspects. A society made up for the most part of self-employed workers such as exists in many farm areas has different social problems from those of a society in which most workers are employed by small business enterprises and a society in which a substantial proportion of workers work for huge corporations has still other problems. Problems of health, education and of religion may be quite different in the three cases. For some of these purposes the relevant concentration figure may be the absolute size of the enterprise and for others it may be the relative concentration. Thus, concentration data has relevance to a much wider field than that covered by the economic and the political alone and should be developed in many forms.

So much for the measures of concentration. Let no man attempt to patent the term "concentration" to make it apply to some specified measure or scope.

Macro-economic Concentration over the Years

Next I want to adopt the macro-economic viewpoint and present my views as to what has happened over the years with respect to concentration.

Let us go back to 1870 when more than half of the gainfully employed were engaged in agriculture; only a quarter of our present railroad system had been built and most of it was unconsolidated (Professor Ripley says that in that period a railroad of 100 miles was considered the maximum for efficient operation[5]; public utilities were a minor factor; manufacturing was for the most part carried on by independent plants and distribution and the services were carried on mostly by small enterprises). On the whole, we had an economy of one-man enterprises and small establishments. By the turn of the century, the proportion of the gainfully employed engaged in farming had shrunk from one half to one third; nearly 90 percent of the present railroad system had been built and sixty percent of the railroad mileage was in 48 companies each with a thousand miles or more of track; utilities were growing but not yet a major factor; manufacturing had experienced a growing merger movement which erupted into the burst of trusts created from 1897 to 1900 and culminated in the creation of U.S. Steel in 1901; chain store and mail order distributors were just getting under way. We do not have statistics on the extent of concentration in either 1870 or 1901. But it is difficult to look at the decline in proportions of gainfully employed in agriculture, the growth and consolidation in railroads and the trust movement in manufacturing and not reach the conclusion that the economy as a whole was much more concentrated at the end than at the beginning of this period.

Professor Mason has held that increased concentration has come almost entirely from the increased industrialization as the one-man enterprises of farming became a smaller proportion of the total and industry with its multi-worker enterprises became a larger proportion. I doubt very much if this is a valid statement as applied to the period from 1870 to 1901. Certainly, the relative decline of agriculture contributed to the increase in concentration but surely a part was contributed by railroad consolidation and the trust movement in manufacturing.

In the twenty years after 1901, the relative decline in agriculture continued; large public utilities became important; and retail distribution began to consolidate. On the other hand, railroad consolidation was slowed up or halted, particularly by the Supreme Court decision in the Northern Securities case in 1904 in which the court applied the Sherman Act to the consolidation of competing railroad lines; and the consolidation of manufacturing was temporarily halted and probably reversed for a time. This halting of manufacturing concentration appears to have been partly a result of the failure of many of the companies produced by consolidation to make the expected earnings and partly the government anti-trust actions. It was in this period that a number of major anti-trust cases were instituted and some break up of companies occurred much as the dismemberment of Standard Oil and American Tobacco. And even where charges were not brought, the increased public and government pressure undoubtedly had a repressing effect on new mergers.

When we look at the economy as a whole in this twenty year period from 1901 to 1921, there are offsetting factors but it again looks as if there had been a considerable increase in concentration even though there may have been no increase in concentration in manufacturing or even a decline from the high level reached at the turn of the century. In the latter part of this period, that is from 1909 to 1921, the figures I presented in the *Modern Corporation and Private Property* suggest that the proportion of the wealth of all non-financial corporations held by the two hundred largest increased from 41 percent to 52 percent.[6]

The value for 1921 is a fairly satisfactory figure but that for 1909 is much more subject to error. However, when it is recognized that in those twelve years the relative importance of agriculture declined, the proportion of non-agricultural activity carried on by corporations markedly increased and the amount of water in the stocks of the big companies was markedly reduced, the finding of a significant increase in concentration for the economy as a whole would seem to be justified. And again, I doubt if most of it can be attributed to the shift in the relative importance of agriculture.

Whether there was a sufficiently sharp decline in total concentration between the turn of the century and 1909 to offset the rise from then to 1921 we do not have the data to say, but it seems to me most unlikely since in that period also there was continued relative decline in agriculture, growth and concentration in utilities and concentration in railroads. The average rate of concentration may have been slower than in the preceding period but that there was some growth in concentration seems probable.

For the next period, that from 1921 to 1929, there seems to be general agreement that there was a marked rise in concentration so I will not go into that except to say that in this period, there can be no question. A major part was not due to the shift from agriculture to industry.

Then, in the great depression from 1929 to 1933 there was a further sizable increase in concentration. I believe most of this increase was a product of the depression. On the one hand, there was no big merger movement in the period though undoubtedly there was some buying up of smaller companies in distress. But I believe the main increase came from two factors.

First, at the end of 1929 the big companies were committed to very sizable programs of investment in fixed capital, whereas the smaller companies with their greater flexibility were able to curtail their investment operations. As a result, the fixed assets of the 200 largest companies were much higher in 1930 than in 1929 and, even though depreciation charges ate into these assets, these companies had larger fixed assets in 1933 than in 1929. On the other hand, the fixed assets of corporations other than the 200 largest declined steadily and were 20 percent less in 1933 than in 1929. This decline in fixed assets was partly the attrition of depreciation but it was even more the bankruptcy or closing out of smaller companies which could not stand the strains of the prolonged depression. To a considerable extent this behavior could be reversed in a recovery as new smaller companies were created and the more flexible smaller companies that survived expanded their fixed assets to meet the renewal of demand.

The second factor has to do with inventories. The big companies tend to have smaller inventories relative to their fixed assets than do smaller companies. As a result, if the fixed assets of both large and small companies remained the same and prices remained the same but each group cut its inventories, say 30 percent to adjust to reduced sales, this would produce a larger *percentage* reduction in the assets of the smaller companies and thus increase the concentration ratio. The actual decline in prices would also work in the same direction as would the disappearance of the inventories of enterprises forced out of business.

When recovery came, the expansion of sales would presumably require expanded and higher priced inventories as would the newly created companies, thus reversing much if not most of the depression increase in concentration. In my opinion as I pointed out frequently at the time, much of the increase in concentration from 1929 to 1933 was a reversible depression phenomenon and not a part of the long run trend of concentration.

If we take the longer period from 1929 to the present, these depression effects should be largely canceled out by the recovery and so it is better to skip the depression and ask what has happened since 1929?

First, we have the fact that the proportion of gainfully employed that is engaged in agriculture has dropped from around 20 percent to around 8 percent. But we have little information on the change in concentration within the total corporate sphere as a whole.

Under the New Deal, a strong drive developed to limit concentration. Many of the holding companies in the utility field were broken up and an attitude against mergers was created. The war played peculiar tricks with concentration. While a high proportion of the value of the war contracts went to a relatively few companies, many of these were not big companies. Also many of the big companies did not share significantly in the war growth. As a result, the net effect of war contracts was probably some deconcentration rather than concentration.

I have made no effort to appraise developments since 1929 from this macroeconomic point of view but in the last decade there would seem to have been some tendency for increased concentration. What these mixed developments mean for overall concentration I have no idea. It may well be that from 1929 to the present concentration has come only from the big relative reduction in agricultural employment. Or perhaps there was also increased concentration in the non-agricultural part of the economy. Indeed, I wait with fascination for the results of the study Dr. Dessel is about to discuss.

Now let me turn to a much more controversial subject, the question of whether *manufacturing as a whole* has become more concentrated. In 1951, Professor Adelman presented (in the *Review of Economic Statistics*) two sets of figures on the trend of concentration in manufacturing taken as a whole, one comparing 1901 with 1947 and the other comparing 1931 with 1947.[7] From these he reaches striking conclusions about the lack of increase in manufacturing concentration. I will examine these two sets of figures.

Manufacturing Concentration, 1901–1947

Let us take first the 1901 to 1947 comparison according to which an index of concentration dropped from approximately 33 percent in 1901 to 24 percent in 1947 or a drop in the concentration index of more than 26 percent.

Since I am going to question its significance, I want to point out that I have no axe to grind with respect to it. I have never made estimates of changes in concentration in manufacturing as a whole except those for the years 1929 and 1933 which appear in the Structure Report and are incidental to corporate concentration as a whole.[8] Nor have I made a commitment as to trend in manufacture as such.

When I was working on my first study of concentration, I was familiar with Moody's writings on the trusts at the turn of the century and often wondered whether concentration in manufacturing might not have been greater at the peak of the trust movement than it was in 1929. When Professor Adelman's estimates came out, I was delighted to have an answer. It confirmed my belief that in manufacturing there is an underlying pressure to concentrate but that whether this pressure works itself out in practice depends on how vigorously government pursues its anti-trust policy. When government resists concentration as it did after 1901 and from 1933 to 1952, it can halt or even reverse concentration. (Don't forget the Standard Oil decision of 1911 or government's role in the creation of a second and third aluminum company at the end of World War II.) And when government is less vigorous in applying the anti-trust policy, concentration in manufacturing proceeds rapidly as it did in the 1920's and in the 1950's.

But in preparing this paper, I examined Professor Adelman's figures critically for the first time and came to the unfortunate conclusion that the method he employed can throw *no* light on whether manufacturing as a whole was more or less concentrated at the peak of the trust period than in more recent years.

Let me make clear just what the issue is. In Professor Adelman's article, the section just preceding that on the 1901 to 1947 period is entitled "The Trend of concentration, 1931–1947" and is concerned with measuring the change in that period in the proportion of total manufacturing corporation assets which were held by the 139 largest manufacturing corporations in the respective years. Then comes the section entitled "Concentration in manufacturing, 1901–47." It is clear that concentration is being used in the same sense in both sections. In neither section is the article concerned with concentration in relation to the market. Presumably, if data had been available to estimate the proportion of manufacturing assets held by the 139 largest manufacturing corporations in 1901 such an estimate would have been used to compare with the corresponding estimate for 1947. In the absence of such material, an indirect approach is used to make what purports to be essentially the same comparison.

We can therefore state the issue in terms of the relative importance of a small number of the largest manufacturing corporations in the respective years. The question is what light does this indirect approach throw on whether the largest, say, 100 or 139 manufacturing corporations in 1901 played a larger or small[er] role than the corresponding number of largest manufacturing corporations in 1947.

The indirect approach involves a complex blend of micro and macro considerations. It uses 4 digit census industry data which might be appropriate for micro-economic analysis to draw conclusions as to macro-economic developments. It is the applicability of an index for micro-economic concentration to the macro-problem which I want to discuss. But first let me outline the method by which Adelman arrives at his index—what I will call the micro-index.

Most immediately, the index is aimed to measure the change from 1901 to 1947 in the proportion of manufacturing carried on by industries which were relatively concentrated in the respective years. The method used can be stated in general terms as follows:—the 4 digit census industries were classified into the more and the less concentrated industries according to whether or not they showed a concentration ratio of more than 50 percent for the largest 4 producers in the particular industry; then the value-added for the more concentrated industries was summated and this total compared with the total value-added for all manufacturing industry.[9] The micro-concentration index thus represents the proportion of the total value added by all manufacturing which is produced by the more concentrated 4 digit industries. According to this index the proportion of total value added in manufacturing which was produced by the more concentrated industries dropped from around 33 percent in 1901 to 24 percent in 1947. This result is not surprising in the light of the trust-busting in the early part of this century and the more or less continuous anti-trust pressure since which has been specifically aimed against monopoly and micro-economic concentration. But this leaves still open the question of what significance the micro-index has for macro-economic concentration. Does it mean that the 100 or the 139 largest manufacturing companies produced a smaller proportion of value added in 1947 than the corresponding number of companies in 1901?

I am going to suggest that the micro-index casts no light on what has happened at the macro-economic level. This is so for two reasons. First, the micro-analysis treats the *producers* classed as the largest four in each 4 digit industry as if each were a separate *company* and thus takes no account of inter-industry integration. And second, the companies whose value-added underlies the micro-index are mostly small companies.

Consider what it means when we shift attention from "producer" in a single 4 digit industry to "company" which, if big is almost certain to contribute to the value-added in a number of 4 digit industries. The micro-index can reflect a change in *intra*-industry concentration but it could not possibly reflect a change in *inter*-industry concentration. If steel companies buy up steel fabricating plants, or fluid milk companies buy up cheese factories, butter factories and milk concentrating plants, or auto companies buy up refrigerator companies or go into making farm machinery, farm tractors and airplanes, this would have no effect on which of these specific 4 digit industries was classed in a particular year with a concentration ratio of more than 50 percent and no effect on the proportion of total value-added produced by such industries in that year. And so, no effect on the micro-index. Yet each represents a step in the concentration of manufacturing taken as a whole. And this would be true whether the increased concentration was due to diversification or to vertical integration.

In his article, Adelman pays *no* attention to the possibility of increased diversification, and seems confused on the effect of vertical integration. Thus he says "An increase in concentration via greater vertical integration might not be fully reflected in the concentration ratio" and gives two examples of inter-industry vertical integration, one of which he says would produce a spurious decrease in the concentration ratio and one of which he says would produce a spurious increase in concentration.[10] But census experts assure me that neither type of vertical integration would alter the 4-producer concentration ratios for the separate industries and would not alter the total value-added for each industry. Thus, inter-industry vertical integration would have no effect on the micro-index, spurious or otherwise.[11]

We have no clear statistical evidence on whether or not there was a significant amount of inter-industry integration between 1901 and 1947. Adelman *says,* "The available evidence points to no increase in vertical integration by manufacturing *establishments;* in the absence of any other evidence, this would indicate no increase in concentration by *firms.*[12] He cites no evidence for the first proposition and the second proposition would seem to be sheer nonsense.[13] Ironically, he adds to the above statement, "but the matter cannot be regarded as settled."

On the other hand, there is a good deal of reason to believe that there has been a large amount of inter-industry integration since 1901. The trust movement from 1870 on was primarily focused on *intra*-industry concentration. The aim, as was so often publicly stated, was to obtain a practical monopoly. This could be achieved through buying up one company after another in the particular industry and any *inter*-industry concentration tended to be incidental. Likewise, the antitrust activities have been aimed at breaking up or preventing too high a degree of intra-industry concentration. But there has been no law against vertical integration or against diversification and there is a good deal of evidence that both have taken place.

Also, we have evidence being presented to you this afternoon by Dr. Dessel in connection with the paper he is reading, that a very substantial part of the employment provided by the big manufacturing companies lies in other industries than the particular industry in which it is classified. He is presenting a sample section of Table 6 in the forthcoming census publication, *Company Statistics.* For this Table, all companies are classified into single and multi-industry companies and, for the multi-industry companies, the employees are distributed by the industry in which they work. For this purpose, the more than 450 4 digit industries are grouped into 90 industries and the sample section of the Table covers 19 of these industries. For the companies covered in this tabulation, 23 percent of the manufacturing employees of multi-industry companies and 49 percent of their total employees belonged to industries other than the particular industry in which the particular company was classified. If the same type of tabulation were made for the four-digit manufacturing industries, the proportion of manufacturing employment of multi-industry companies which lay outside the particular four-digit manufacturing industry would have been much greater. Also, the biggest manufacturing companies could all be expected to be multi-industry companies under the four-digit classification and to show an even larger inter-industry integration than the *average* of all inter-industry companies. This suggests the *present* magnitude of the inter-industry integration, perhaps well over 50 percent. Because the micro-index is limited to measuring intra-industry concentration, it is quite incapable of indicating how much of this large amount of inter-industry concentration occurred between 1901 and 1947.

Of course, how much of this great integration did occur between 1901 and 1947 is another matter. In my opinion, there was a significant amount of increase in vertical integration between 1901 and 1947 (there was no law against it) and an even greater diversification as the managements of the big companies sought to apply their very real management skills to the greater areas allowed by law. If a large part of the present inter-industry integration occurred between 1901 and 1947, the micro-index would not even approximate the change in concentration for manufacturing taken as a whole. Indeed, if the micro-index could be modified to take account of inter-industry concentration, though I don't see how this could be done, it is a real possibility that it would show a rise, not a decline.

How important this might be can be shown by a simple set of calculations. Let us first arbitrarily assume that the 1901 figure of 30 in the micro-index represents the percent of all manufacturing value-added which was produced by the 100 largest companies in 1901 and that in 1947 each of the then 100 largest companies produced half of its value-added in the 4 digit industry in which it was classed and the remainder scattered among several other 4 digit industries. Then let us make two extreme assumptions, first that in 1901 the inter-industry integration was *the same* as in 1947, i.e., that only half of each company's value-added arose in its particular census industry; and second that there was *no* inter-industry integration in 1901. Under the first extreme assumption, the concentration figure for 1947 comparable with the figure of 30 would be the micro-index figure of 24; under the second extreme assumption, the figure comparable with 30 would be 48. I am willing to grant that if 30 is a fair index of macro-concentration in manufacturing in 1901, the comparable figure for 1947 would lie somewhere between 24 and 48. But whether it lies below or above 30, Adelson's data do not suggest.

There remains, however, my second major criticism of the micro-index as an index of macro-economic concentration. This index is concerned with a mixture of small and large companies. For example, the 1947 figure of 24 represents the 150 4 digit industries in which the concentration ratio was more than 50 percent, yet more than half these industries were so small that the total assets of the whole industry amounted to less than $100 million. In so far as the largest four producers in these industries confined their activity to their particular 4 digit industry, even the four companies combined could not get into the big company class by the $100-million-assets-or-more criterion. What have the largest companies in the "beauty and barber shop equipment" industry, the "china decorating for the trade" industry, the "cigar box" industry and the "reed and rattan furniture" industry got to do with macro-economic concentration?

Frankly, I do not see how an index which so thoroughly scrambles small and large companies and takes no account of the large amount of *inter*-industry integration that has occurred can throw light on whether macro-economic concentration occurred between 1901 and 1947. It can point to the very considerable *intra*-industry deconcentration which has occurred since the peak of the trust movement in 1901. As far as I can see, this is all it can do. I am still most uncertain whether manufacturing was more concentrated in 1901 than it was in 1929 or 1947.

Manufacturing Concentration, 1931–1947

When we turn to Adelman's figures for manufacturing concentration from 1931 to 1947, we are faced with two problems. There is first the question of the comparability of his concentration estimates for the two years and second we are faced with the abnormality of the two years.

The actual estimates he presents show the largest 139 manufacturing corporations in 1947 holding a smaller proportion of total manufacturing corporation assets than the 139 largest in 1931. The decline indicated by his figures is from 49.6 at the end of 1931 to 44.4 percent at the end of 1947.[14]

I would like to suggest that the method used for adjusting for incomplete consolidation does not result in comparable figures.

For 1947, the adjustment for consolidation is quite simple. The Bureau of Internal Revenue supplies relatively unconsolidated figures for the total assets of all manufacturing corporations and for the total assets of the largest companies. The Federal Trade Commission and the Securities Exchange Commission have developed a more thoroughly consolidated but less complete set of figures for approximately the same general categories. To obtain the BIR degree of coverage and the FTC-SEC degree of consolidation, the higher concentration ratio from the latter is applied to the former and appropriate adjustments are made to bring the 132 companies up to the 139 companies for which 1931 data was available.[15]

The main difficulty arises in the 1931 estimate. The BIR provides data for all manufacturing and for 139 largest companies. To the asset data for the 139 Adelman applies the same ratio of adjustment as in 1947. This would be justified if the degree of under consolidation were the same in the two years. But in 1931, corporations filed consolidated returns to a very much greater extent than in 1947. In 1931 there was no penalty for consolidating and any direct or indirect subsidiary could be consolidated if 95 percent or more of the voting stock was controlled. In 1947 the same degree of consolidation was allowed but there was a 2 percent surtax on the taxable income reported in consolidated returns. As a result, nearly half of the compiled receipts of all manufacturing corporations were reported by companies filing consolidated returns in 1931 while in 1947 less than 7 percent of compiled receipts were in consolidated returns. In 1947, only 351 manufacturing corporations filed consolidated returns, covering 1,499 affiliates; in 1932, 2,542 manufacturing corporations filed consolidated returns covering perhaps six times as many affiliates. My own investigation into the actual tax returns for the 1929 to 1933 period indicated that practically all the subsidiaries which the law allowed were consolidated. On the other hand, only 78 of the country's 561 largest corporations filed consolidated returns in 1947. This means that the application of *the same* adjustment for consolidation to both years produces non-comparable results.

It is quite possible that the degree of consolidation in the 1931 BIR data is of about the same magnitude as that in the FTC-SEC data. The 1931 data lack consolidation where less than 95 percent of stock is owned. The 1947 data are only consolidated to the extent that the particular corporation customarily consolidates in reporting to its stockholders and this is usually far from complete. I doubt if any adjustment is needed for consolidation to make the 1931 figure comparable with that for 1947 *after adjustment*. In that case, the comparable comparison should be between 1931 and 1947. It would not be between 49.6 and 44.1 but between 46.5 and 44.1, a much smaller decline.

Also, if one makes the comparison on the basis not of total assets which involve a considerable amount of double counting, but on the basis of tangible assets which involve no double counting, there is a slight rise in concentration indicated. In 1931, the largest 139 manufacturing corporations reported by the Treasury held 45.6 percent of the tangible assets of all manufacturing corporations. In 1947, using exactly the same method used by Adelman, the 1947 ratio exclusive of any inventory adjustment is 46.2 percent.[16]

I suspect that the data used are not sufficiently comparable to reach a positive conclusion as to whether there was a small rise or a small fall in the relative importance of the largest 139 manufacturing corporations in 1947 as compared with 1931.[17] On the other hand, we are probably safe in saying that there was no great difference in the relative importance of the largest corporations in 1947 as compared with 1931.

But does this justify Adelman's explicit conclusion that, "The extent of concentration shows no tendency to grow, and it may possibly be declining"?[18] In starting his discussion of the 1931–1947 data, he properly points out that in 1931, there was a "high wind" of depression blowing in one direction; in the later period there was "a strong wind blowing in the other direction."[19] As a result of these winds, both 1931 and 1947 were abnormal but in opposite directions. Concentration in manufacturing was abnormally high in 1931 because of depression influences; it was abnormally low in 1947 because of the aftermath of war and inflation. And in each case I use normal to mean the absence of high winds.

First, consider the depression year 1931. The National Resources Committee provided fixtures on concentration for 1929 and 1933 which are generally regarded as reliable. Indeed they are probably the most reliable figures on macro-concentration which we have since a more complete job of assembling parents and subsidiaries was done for those years than has been undertaken since. According to these estimates, the proportion of all manufacturing corporation assets held by the 82 largest of these corporations jumped from just under 40 percent in 1929 to just under 46 percent in 1933.[20] All of this increase in concentration appears to have occurred in the two years from the end of 1929 to the end of 1931 and most of it can be attributed to special depression forces of a reversible character. With economic recovery, it would not have been at all surprising if for a period there was no change in the actual degree of concentration. The deconcentration due to recovery could *offset* the underlying trend toward concentration. In that case when full recovery had been achieved, say by the end of 1941, the concentration ratio in terms of assets could be expected to be the same as in 1931 but 6 points higher than in the previous full-employment year of 1929. This would represent an underlying trend increase in concentration of 15 percent in 12 years, once the abnormality of 1931 was eliminated.

The abnormality of 1947 works in the opposite direction. Not only were inventories a distorting factor, and Adelman has made some adjustment for this, but the distribution of war contracts had a war-time deconcentrating effect. As I have pointed out, a disproportionally large proportion of contracts went to medium sized companies such as airplane makers while the big manufacturers of 1941 *as a whole* seem to have received much less than their proportionate share of contracts (net of sub-contracting). The result was to give an abnormal war structure to manufacturing and this would not have been fully corrected by 1947. Thus, I would expect the figures for manufacturing concentration in 1947 to be abnormally low.

This hypothesis finds support in the recently published Commerce Department figures for manufacturing concentration. These figures, using value-added as a measure, show a surprisingly rapid increase in concentration from 1947 to 1954. The concentration ratio by this measure for the top hundred rose from 23 percent to 30 percent.[21] I strongly suspect that an important part of this sudden increase was due to the return to a more normal post war structure. If this is true, it may well be that between 1941 and 1947, there was an underlying trend of concentration but this was overlain by the effects of this abnormality. In that case, the concentration ratio could have been about the same in 1947 as in 1941 in spite of an underlying trend of concentration.

Thus it would not be at all impossible to have an underlying trend of concentration in manufacturing from 1931 to 1947 and yet no significant change in the concentration ratios. Adelman's figures are not at all incompatible with a substantial rise in concentration between the more normal years of 1929 and 1958.

Indeed, we can use the figures provided by the Structure Report, Adelman and the Census Bureau to construct an approximate picture of concentration for manufacturing as a whole since 1929.

Figure 14.1. **Manufacturing Concentration**

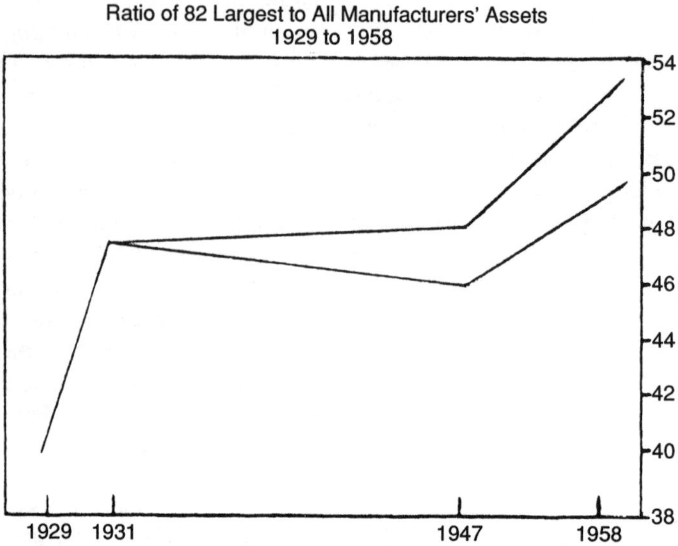

The anchor for such an analysis is 1929 when 82 corporations held 39.7 percent of the assets of all manufacturing corporations. By 1931 the 82 largest held 45.9 percent. Between 1931 and 1947 Adelman's figures when adjusted for error, show no substantial change in concentration between 1931 and 1947, allowing us to use the 1931 figure as an approximation to the 1947 figure, giving us say a range of 45 to 47 as the measure for that year. Then from 1947 to 1958 the census figures show an increase of 30 percent in the proportion of the total value-added in manufacture which was produced by the 100 largest companies in the respective years. How this relates to the change in relative asset position is not clear but it does suggest some increase in the proportion of assets held by the largest companies. If we arbitrarily assume that concentration by assets for the largest 82 companies increased half as fast as concentration by value-added, by the hundred largest, then the concentration ratio for the 82 largest by assets would fall within the bracket of 51 to 53. I think we would be safe in expecting that, if the same careful job of combining parents and controlled affiliates which was done for the Structure report for 1929 were repeated for 1958, it would show a concentration ratio for the largest 82 manufacturing enterprises of over 50 percent to compare with the under 40 percent in 1929. These figures are plotted in the chart below [Figure 14.1] with bracket for 1958 doubled in width.

We must wait for a more complete consolidation of the 1958 data before we can be reasonably sure of the trend of change in concentration between 1929 and 1958. But again I want to say that I don't think Adelman, at the time he wrote in 1951, had any statistical basis for reaching his widely quoted conclusion that "The extent of concentration shows no tendency to grow, and it may possibly be declining."

Notes

1. It should be noted that, while the body of this paper had to be prepared in the two days before the meeting, in the final section on manufacturing the statistical material has subsequently been confirmed, tightened up, and in a small degree elaborated as a result of an examination of source material not available to me at the time of drafting.

2. W.L. Crum, "The Alleged Concentration of Economic Power" (and "A Reply"), *American Economic Review*, Vol. XXIV, No. 1 (March 1934).

3. Adolf A. Berle, Jr., and Gardiner C. Means, Macmillan Co., New York, 1933.

4. M.A. Adelman, "The Measurement of Industrial Concentration," *The Review of Economics and Statistics*, Vol. XXXIII, No. 4 (Nov. 1951), p. 287.

5. William Z. Ripley, *Railroads*, Longmans, Green and Co., New York, 1915, p. 456.

6. Op. cit., p. 36.

7. Op. cit., pp. 288–291.

8. National Resources Committee, *The Structure of the American Economy*, Washington, 1939.

9. Actually, two different sets of concentration ratios were used. For 1901, an industry was classified with a concentration ratio of over 50 on the basis of *value-added*; in 1947 on a basis of value-of-product. No justification or even mention of this difference is given in the article yet it could make a significant difference.

It seems likely that higher value would have been obtained for the micro-index for 1947 if the 4 digit industries had been classed by value-added instead of value-of-product. This is so because of the abnormal distribution around the 50 percent dividing line. There were 12 industries with value-of-product concentration ratios lying between 50 and 52.5 and having a combined value of product of around $800 million. Likewise there were twelve industries with value-of-product concentration ratios of 47.5 to 50, but these industries had a combined value of product of more than $3,000 million. If a reclassification according to value-added shifts six companies from each group into the other group, which could easily happen, the micro-index figure for 1947 would be raised from 24 to more than 26.

10. Op. cit., p. 291.

11. *Intra*-industry integration would, of course, tend to increase the concentration ratio for a single industry. This would be properly reflected in the micro-concentration index and would not be spurious.

12. Op. cit., p. 291. Emphasis added.

13. The null hypothesis is an important tool in decision making; it would seem to be out of place in scientific research.

14. Adelman actually supplies two figures for the largest 139 in 1947, 44.4 and 45.1. The latter involves an adjustment for the abnormality of inventories in the two years. I prefer the unadjusted figure, since inventories were not the only or the most important abnormalities of the two years.

15. Even the figures for 1947 involve some difficulties. The large discrepancy between *total assets* of all manufacturing corporations as compiled by the BIR ($111.4 billion) and that compiled by FTC-SEC ($97.6 billion) is explained in part by the fact that when subsidiaries are consolidated with parents, some of the duplication in the "all corporation asset" figure is eliminated. But it is hard to explain the $4.2 billion discrepancy between the BIR derived figure for total tangible assets ($63.0 billion) and the FTC-SEC figure ($58.8 billion). The extra degree of consolidation should not affect the total for tangible assets since no duplication is involved. Also, a mathematical error in arriving at a figure for the estimate of the number of corporations covered by the FTC-SEC "over $100 million asset" category makes that figure too large perhaps by as many

as 2 or 3 corporations so that the assets for this group would have to be adjusted for more than 7 corporations. And no account is taken in making adjustment for the fact that consolidation must reduce the "total assets" figure for all corporations. Such corrections are small in themselves, but could increase the 1947 concentration ratio from 44.4 to over 45.

16. The above figure for 1947 cannot be derived from Table 11 in Adelman's article because of a mathematical error and a copying error in the Table. In line 3 of the table the ratio for the proportion of the tangible assets of all corporations (as given in the table) that are held by the largest 133 corporations should be 41.0 not 44.3. Also the figure for the net capital assets of all manufacturing corporations (line 1) is approximately the correct figure for all manufacturing corporations *reporting net income* but does not include the capital assets of manufacturing corporations reporting no net income. The correction for this adds $2,008 million to the "net capital assets" figure and to the total tangible assets figure for all manufacturing corporations. This makes the ratio for the BIR figure for total tangible assets $63,013 million, not $60,985 million and the ratio of the largest 132 corporations 39.7 percent, not 44.3 or 41.0.

After these corrections, the calculation for 1947 is as follows.

		Total Tangible Assets
1	All Mfg. Corps (BIR)	63,013
2	Mfg. Corps with assets exceeding $100 million (BIR)	25,034
3	Line (2) as percent of line (1)	39.7
4	All Mfg. Corps (FTC-SEC)	58,794
5	Mfg. Corps with assets exceeding $100 million (FTC-SEC)	26,268
6	Line (5) as percent of line (4)	44.7
7	Line (2) adjusted by line (6) $\left(\frac{44.7}{39.7} = 1.126\right)$	28,188
8	7 additional mfg. corp $(7 \times 100 \times 60\%)$	420
9	Line (7) plus line (8)	28,608
10	Line (9) adjusted for wartime amortization (+ 2,010)	30,618
11	Line (1) adjusted for wartime amortization (+ 3,304)*	66,317
12	Line (10) as percent of line (11)	46.2
13	Line (12), adjusted for abnormal inventories**	47.8

*In Table 12A (line 5) this figure is given as 3,338,000 but this cannot be derived from line (4) × line (2) even after the typographical error is corrected.

**In Table 12B (line 4) total mfg. inventories are reduced by $11.3 billion and big corp. inventories (line 6) by $4.3 billion to make adjustment. The same absolute amounts have been used calculating line (13).

It should be pointed out that there are numerous mathematical errors in the section of the article with which this discussion is concerned (pp. 288, 291 and 292). In these three pages there are 51 mathematical operations involving multiplication, division or the addition of a column of figures. In 16 of these, or nearly one-third, there are errors greater than could be explained by rounding or the use of a slide rule. In a large number of cases there is internal evidence suggesting that the error is not likely to be typographical. Only one error was clearly typographical.

17. Adelman states that the FTC-SEC data for the end of 1947 "are on a completely

consolidated basis. (The data for the largest corporations rest not on sample estimates but on a complete count.).'' Both of these statements are incorrect. The consolidation is partial and depends on the choice of the parent company. Presumably the degree of consolidation given is that used in annual reports to stockholders. While all the unregistered corporations *believed* to have assets over $100 million were *asked* to report, a number failed to do so and those not reporting had to be estimated by indirect and less reliable means. For the registered corporations also there had to be some estimating. And finally, subsequent investigations disclosed some corporations with assets over $100 million in 1947 that were not included in either list.

18. Op. cit., p. 295.

19. Op. cit., p. 289.

20. *Structure of the American Economy,* op. cit., p. 285. The actual figure for 1929 was 39.7 percent of total assets held by 82 corporations and 45.5 by 78 corporations in 1933. If 4 corporations with $60 million assets are added to the 1933 figures, this gives 82 corporations with 45.9 percent.

21. Concentration Ratios in Manufacturing Industry in 1938, Bureau of the Census, Washington, 1962, p. 8.

15

Conglomerates and Concentration

I. Introduction

In his column of June 2, 1966, in the Washington Post, Mr. Buchwald wrote the following:

> Every time you pick up the newspaper you read about one company merging with another company. Of course, we have laws to protect competition in the United States, but one cannot help thinking that, if the trend continues, the whole country will soon be merged into one large company.
>
> It is 1978 and by this time every company west of the Mississippi will have merged into one giant corporation known as Samson Securities. Every company east of the Mississippi will have merged under an umbrella corporation known as the Delilah Company.
>
> It is inevitable that one day the chairman of the board of Samson and the president of Delilah would meet and discuss merging their two companies.
>
> "If we could get together," the president of Delilah said, "we would be able to finance your projects and you would be able to finance ours."
>
> "Exactly what I was thinking," the chairman of Samson said.
>
> "That's a great idea and it would certainly make everyone's life less complicated.
>
> . . . .
>
> "But if you merge," someone pointed out, "there will be only *one* company left in the United States."
>
> "Exactly," said the president of Delilah. "Thank God for the free enterprise system."[1]

This country is, of course, a long way from the final merger, but we are also considerably closer to that event, as compared with the simple small-enterprise

---

Reprinted from the *University of Miami Law Review* 25 U. Miami L. Rev. 1 (1970) which holds copyright on this article.

economy of a hundred years ago. Needless to say, the conglomerates, including bank conglomerates and railroad conglomerates, are taking us headlong toward that end. In the four years preceding 1970, nearly seven percent of the assets of all mining and manufacturing corporations were merged into other corporations. At the merger rate which took place in the first half of 1969, it would take only a score of years to absorb most of the manufacturing assets into a couple of hundred huge companies. The railroads and utilities are even more concentrated than manufacturing and are not only merging further, but some railroads, through holding companies, are becoming conglomerates. In the banking industry, one-bank holding companies are being used to break down the line between banking and nonbanking activity which public policy had previously established. The long-run trend toward economic concentration has presented serious economic problems and this recent wave of conglomerate mergers has increased the importance of these problems.

This article will first examine the available statistics on concentration, and then consideration will be given to the problems of public policy which concentration engenders.

II. The Trend toward Concentration

The trend toward concentration will be considered first by going back to a time when there was little concentration, then the several merger movements will be discussed, and finally the statistics of concentration will be examined for the manufacturing industry alone and for the economy as a whole.

A. An Economy with Little Concentration

To find a period of slight concentration in the United States economy it is necessary to go back only a hundred years. Just before the Civil War, two-thirds of the labor force was engaged in agriculture. The family farm was the usual form of organization and flexible farm prices were determined by the interaction of a large number of buyers and sellers in the market. There were no telephone or electric power companies, and the railroads were just beginning to be consolidated. In 1853, the New York Central was formed by consolidating the ten short sections of railroad, mostly end to end, which spanned the 300-mile distance between Albany and Buffalo. At that time, according to Professor Ripley, one hundred miles of railroad was considered to be the maximum which could be operated efficiently.[2] Most manufacturing production took place in small local plants or in small shops. The clothing industry was just coming out of the home with the invention of the sewing machine, and the shoe industry was in the process of being brought into the factories. American ironmasters had only recently shifted from the old method of hammering out bar iron in a forge fired by charcoal to the newer method of rolling. The Bessemer steel furnace, invented in

1856, had not yet been put into practical operation, and the open-hearth furnace was still to be developed.

In that period, the United States economy was indeed an economy of small-scale enterprise. For practical purposes, there was little concentration. Even for theoretical purposes, such concentration as existed could be disregarded for most purposes of public policy. National economic policy could be decided on the basis of a body of economic theory which assumed that all production was carried on under conditions of classical competition; that is, competition between such a large number of buyers and sellers that no producer or buyer had significant pricing power and prices were *determined* by the law of supply and demand.

This unconcentrated economy, and the classical theory based upon it, dominated public policy through the 19th century and the first third of the 20th century. In fact, the Sherman Act was passed in 1890 with the aim of preserving this type of economy.

B. The Drive for Monopoly

After the Civil War, industry became increasingly important in the economy as a whole, and toward the end of the century there was a merger movement aimed, often explicitly, at obtaining monopoly control over prices. This movement is reflected in Chart I[3] [Figure 15.1A] which shows the number of mergers year by year reported in the Commercial and Financial Chronicle from 1895 to 1914. As can be seen, there was a burst of mergers from 1898 to 1902. Some of the industries which were substantially monopolized are listed below with the proportion of the market held by the single largest producer indicated.[4]

	Proportion of industry by largest company (%)
Cigarettes	100
Cane sugar refining	100
Tin cans	90
Petroleum refining	85
Agricultural implements	85
Copper	85
Explosives	80

This merger movement culminated in 1902 in the merger of mergers which produced the U.S. Steel Corporation with control over two-thirds of all steel ingot production and a higher degree of control over many steel products. A parallel wave of concentration took place among railroads, culminating in the acquisition of control of the Great Northern and the Northern Pacific by the Northern Securities Company in 1901. The public reaction to this merger movement was strong and the powers of the Sherman Act were brought to bear. First, the *Northern Securities*[5] decision by the Supreme Court in 1904 outlawed the holding company as a device for achieving monopoly. Then other court decisions brought the break-up of monopolies in manufacturing, such as the Standard Oil Company and the American Tobacco Company. Still other merged enterprises failed to achieve or retain monopoly under the new attitudes of the public and the court decisions, and thus the rate of mergers dropped back to a low level as is indicated in Chart I.[6] In this manner, the first great wave of mergers was not only halted but turned back so that big *monopoly* as such was largely eliminated and there was probably less concentration in manufacturing by the beginning of the First World War than there was in 1902.

C. The Drive for Bigness

A second wave of mergers occurred in the decade after the First World War, reaching its peak in 1929. In this period, the drive behind the merger movement was clearly not a drive for monopoly but a drive for bigness. To what extent this was a drive for market power, as contrasted to an attempt to gain productive efficiency, has been hotly debated and is an unsettled issue. This issue has been confused by the frequent use of profit rates as a measure of productive efficiency even though profits could also be a measure of market power.

The merger movement in manufacturing and mining from 1919 to 1939 is shown in Chart II[7] [Figure 15.2A]. The figures in this chart represent a counting of mergers more complete than that of Chart I so that the absolute number of mergers cannot be compared but the story is the same; a short period of very high merger rates followed by a period of low rates.

In this same period, an even more vigorous wave of mergers occurred among public utilities, as great numbers of independent local utilities were brought under a single control. This wave was not only brought to a halt by popular reaction but there was also some break-up under the Holding Company Act of 1935.

Mergers among railroads were largely prevented by the I.C.C., but stock acquisitions in the 1920's continued to bring many railroads closer together.

Altogether, the decade of the 1920's was one of mergers which contributed to concentration, while the post depression decade was the reverse. In the latter period, government stood ready to apply its antitrust powers against mergers and its other powers against holding companies. Mergers in the manufacturing and mining field from 1935 to 1939 averaged just over one hundred a year, as compared to an average of over 1,000 a year from 1926 to 1929.

D. The Conglomerate Drive

The third major wave of mergers, which took the primary form of creating huge conglomerates, has only recently been brought to a halt by a decline in the stock market and a concomitant drop in the value of many conglomerates. Chart III[8]

[Figure 15.3A] shows, for each year since 1948, the number of mergers of manufacturing and mining firms in which the acquired firm had assets of $10 million or more. From 1948 to 1952, the annual rate of big mergers was 7 a year. From 1953 through 1966, the annual rate was 70 a year. In the last three years, the annual rate of big mergers has been over 165 a year with $30 billion of assets thereby acquired by other companies. This represents around 7 percent of the assets of all manufacturing and mining corporations and a much larger percentage of the assets of corporations not included in the 200 largest.

The current merger movement has also affected other fields. Dr. Mueller, Economist for the Federal Trade Commission, recently made the following statement to a Congressional Committee:

> mergers in wholesale and retail trade, services and miscellaneous industries have risen even more rapidly than have mergers in manufacturing and mining. Moreover, in recent years, railroads not only have been merging with one another but increasingly have absorbed manufacturing and other concerns through newly created holding companies. Mergers also are occurring with increasing frequency in other areas of transportation as well as in the utility and broadcasting industries. Most recently one-bank holding companies have been formed by many large banks for the purpose of expanding the scope of these institutions and, in some cases, absorbing business enterprises outside banking.[9]

This wave of mergers has tended to be increasingly a matter of conglomerate mergers. The FTC classes as conglomerate 80 percent of the substantial manufacturing and mining mergers of the last five years and 89 percent of those occurring last year.[10] Of course, the acquisition of industrial companies by railroad and bank holding companies creates conglomerates. This is in sharp contrast to the merger wave at the turn of the century, when the focus was on horizontal mergers aimed at achieving monopoly, and also with the second wave which sought bigness and market control mostly through vertical and some horizontal mergers within the limits of the antitrust acts. Whether the antitrust acts place significant limits on conglomerate mergers remains to be seen.

E. The Underlying Trend toward Concentration in the Economy

It is clear that there has been an underlying trend toward making the United States economy more concentrated. The small enterprise economy of a hundred years ago has given place to the modern economy of big business. The questions are, how fast has this increase in concentration been taking place, and how far has it actually carried?

To answer these questions it is necessary to consider the various sources of concentration. Mergers have contributed a spectacular part to the increasing concentration. However, there have been other developments contributing to concentration. Perhaps, even more important than mergers is the shift from a predominantly agricultural to an industrial economy. In the earlier period, two-thirds of the gainfully employed persons were in agriculture. Today less than 5 percent of the gainfully employed are in an agricultural industry in which nearly two-thirds of farm marketings are still made by family farms.[11] Today, the major proportion of employment is in industry where large units prevail. This shift alone without any mergers would have greatly increased concentration for the economy as a whole.

Another source of concentration is the internal growth of single enterprises. For example, the assets of the American Telephone and Telegraph Company have increased 275 percent in the last 16 years, primarily from internal growth, and much faster than the assets of all nonfinancial corporations. The increase in concentration from this source is more difficult to measure because a company can choose between expansion by merger and expansion by internal growth. This complicates the determination of concentration since corporations classed as the largest in any year will depend on a combination of the two.

In measuring concentration, account must also be taken of the increased proportion of industry and trade which is carried on by corporations. A hundred years ago, there were relatively few industrial corporations. To illustrate, in Pittsburgh in 1860 there were 17 foundries, 21 rolling mills, 76 glass factories, and 47 other manufactories, but not a single one was incorporated. Only in the early New England cotton industry were corporate enterprises a significant factor. By 1900 only two-thirds of manufacturing was incorporated, while today over 99 percent is incorporated.[12] Trade and services were still largely unincorporated in 1900, while today two-thirds of retail sales are made by incorporated enterprise.[13] Thus, as the proportion of *corporate* enterprise which is carried on by a few enterprises increases, the proportion of *all* enterprise carried on by the few corporations increases even faster.

F. Overall Concentration in Manufacturing

The most comprehensive data on concentration is in the field of manufacturing. Reasonably reliable data is available on the proportion of corporate assets controlled by the hundred largest manufacturing corporations in 1929 and at intervals from 1950 onward for both the 100 largest and the 200 largest. Chart IV[14] shows the proportion of all manufacturing corporation assets and the corresponding proportion of net capital assets (land, buildings and equipment) controlled by the 100 largest manufacturing corporations in each year since 1947.

As can be seen from Chart IV[15] [Figure 15.4A], the hundred largest manufacturing corporations in 1929 controlled 40 percent of the total assets of all manufacturing corporations.[16] By 1962, the hundred largest manufacturing companies controlled nearly half the assets of all manufacturing corporations. In 1969, the preliminary estimates suggested that 100 manufacturing corporations controlled 52 percent of all manufacturing corporation assets.

More important than concentration of total assets is the concentration in net capital assets; the land, buildings, and equipment which provide the material basis for production and, along with business organization, give a corporation its market power. In 1929, the hundred largest manufacturing corporations controlled 44 percent of all manufacturing corporate assets, and by 1952 or 1953, the hundred largest corporations of that year controlled 50 percent of the net capital assets of all manufacturing corporations. Today the hundred largest corporations control approximately 62 percent of the net capital assets of all manufacturing corporations.[17]

Besides the foregoing, there are other means of measuring concentration. If the proportion of manufacturing corporation profits made by the hundred largest manufacturing corporations were used, the degree of concentration shown would be greater. The big corporations not only tend to use more capital per worker, but also tend to obtain a higher rate of return. If "value added" or "workers employed" were used to measure concentration, the degree of concentration would be substantially less. Figures for total assets and net capital assets have been given here because of the power that arises from concentrated assets.

The assets of the second hundred largest manufacturing corporations in the respective years have also been increasing more rapidly than the assets of all manufacturing corporations. In 1950, the second largest hundred controlled approximately 8.7 percent of the assets of all manufacturing corporations, and in 1962 this figure increased to 9.3 percent.[18] Only crude estimates for 1969 are available but they suggest that the second hundred in that year controlled at least 10 percent. Adding these percentages to the more reliable figures for the largest hundred suggests the following conclusions: the largest 200 manufacturing corporations in 1950 controlled nearly 52 percent of all manufacturing corporation assets; the 200 largest in 1962 controlled 58 percent; and the 200 largest in 1969 controlled 61 percent. In terms of the more important figures of capital assets (land, buildings, and equipment), the proportion controlled by the 200 largest manufacturing corporations in the respective years rose from around 57 percent in 1950 to around 66 percent in 1962, and eventually to nearly 70 percent at the present time.[19]

The *rate* of increasing concentration for manufacturing as a whole, including unincorporated manufacturing, is somewhat greater than these figures suggest. In 1950 over 5 percent of manufacturing assets were held by entities other than corporations, while today barely one percent of manufacturing assets are unincorporated. Thus, the proportion of *all* manufacturing assets controlled by the largest 200 corporations in the respective years has gone from just under 50 percent in 1950 to just over 60 percent in 1969, and net capital assets of all manufacturing enterprises controlled by the largest 200 corporations have risen from 55 percent in 1950 to more than 70 percent in 1969.

A simple extrapolation of the increase in concentration of the last score of years to the year 2000 would give a figure of 92.5 percent as the proportion of net manufacturing capital assets controlled by 200 corporations. If the recent more rapid rate of concentration were to continue, this high degree of manufacturing concentration would come much sooner. Effective enforcement of the antitrust acts could prevent any final merger and could slow up the increasing concentration, but how effective it can be will depend to an important extent on the treatment of conglomerates.

G. Concentration for the Economy as a Whole

The most reliable figures for concentration in the economy as a whole are those for 1929. In that year, 200 corporations controlled 48 percent of the assets of all nonfinancial corporations, including not only manufacturing but also transportation, trade, and service corporations. These same 200 corporations also controlled 58 percent of the net capital assets of all nonfinancial corporations.[20]

Since 1929, no adequate statistical study of concentration by all nonfinancial corporations has been made. We have seen the increase in manufacturing concentration. Big railroad mergers such as the Penn-Central and the Norfolk-Nickel Plate mergers have clearly increased railroad concentration, while air transportation is carried on in large part by huge air transport companies. The chain supermarket and other chain-stores have increased in relative importance. But until a competent study of corporate concentration has been made, it is not possible to state with certainty how much the concentration for nonfinancial corporations as a whole has increased, although it is relatively certain that it has not decreased. It is concentration in the economy as a whole as well as concentration in manufacturing which pose the problems of public policy arising from concentration which will be discussed in the next part of this paper.

III. Problems of Public Policy Created by Concentration

The shift of the U.S. economy from one predominantly characterized by small scale enterprise to one made up predominantly of big corporate enterprise has created problems of public policy with which the society is only beginning to grapple. In this article, some of the more important problems will be considered under three headings. First, consideration will be given to three related problems created by concentration which affect the economy as a whole—unemployment, inflation, and the balance of international payments. Second, attention will be given to the changed character of competition and the resulting effects both on the way resources are used and on the distribution of income. And, finally, attention will be given to the welfare of the people who live and work in an economy of big business enterprises and experience both its affluence and its effluence.

A. Employment, Inflation, and the Balance of Payments

The economists of the 19th century did a brilliant job of analyzing how a world economy made up of individual buyers and sellers and of small business enterprises could be expected to operate. They concluded that, in such an economy, the working of the market mechanism in which supply and demand were equated by price would automatically prevent excessive unemployment, would automatically prevent serious inflation in the absence of monetary manipulation, and, under the gold standard, would automatically maintain a reasonable balance in international payments. For such an economy, the appropriate policy of government was one of laissez-faire so far as employment, inflation, and the balance of payments were concerned. In these three fields, the function of government was met when each government assured sound stocks of money directly related to the monetary stock of gold in that country and maintained a free flow of gold with other countries.

The automatic mechanisms by which full employment would be maintained, inflation avoided, and international payments kept in balance all depended on a very high degree of price flexibility and the determination of price by supply and demand. It required a degree of competition among such a large number of buyers and sellers that no single buyer or seller had any power to choose to buy or sell currently at one price rather than another. The individual seller could either sell at the market, as shares are sold in today's stock market, or could hold off selling in the hope of a price rise. A seller could not have a *price* policy: he could not *set* a price for a type of product and expect a series of sales at that price over a period of time. The same applies to buyers.

Today, the great bulk of commodities are sold at prices which are set for periods of time and involve a series of transactions. Such prices, which have been called administered prices in contrast to the market prices of 19th century theory, reflect some degree of market power—the power to set one price rather than another.

A monopoly can, of course, set its price and is likely to adopt price administration as its procedure in marketing. Regulated monopoly usually operates with prices administered by the interaction of the seller and a government commission. The government itself operates with administered prices as in the case of postal rates which are set by Congress for periods of time. With monopoly, administered prices are to be expected.

However, price administration is also the normal marketing procedure where competition is active but sellers are few. The prices of standard steel products are set for periods of time and revised from time to time with set differentials for different special characteristics, and the bulk of steel transactions take place at these fixed prices. Although supply and demand influence steel prices, they do not determine them. The determination is a matter of the administrative decision of single companies in the light of supply and demand conditions, usually with the behavior or anticipated behavior of specific recognized competitors in mind.

This type of pricing is essential for modern, efficient industry, and with the increased concentration in the economy, it has become so much the normal pricing method that the great bulk of commodity and service transactions take place at administered prices. Concentration has also led to the administration of wage rates either by management, as was true of the heavy industries before 1933, or by negotiated agreements between management and organized labor. Thus, instead of economy with flexible prices set predominately in a free market, as 19th century theory assumed, we have an economy in which prices are administered and are inflexible, at least for short periods of time. In the next section, the effect of price administration on the use of resources and income distribution will be considered. Here, the immediate concern is the relation between price administration and employment, inflation, and the balance of payments. As will be seen, even a very moderate degree of market power, which allows price administration, if widespread, can prevent the operation of the three automatic mechanisms relied on in the policies inherited from the 19th century. In the following text, each of these automatic mechanisms will be outlined as they apply to an economy of market prices, then the distortion resulting from price administration will be indicated, and finally, the problem thereby created will be discussed.

B. The Classical Theory of Employment Adjustment and a Concentrated Economy

It was a conclusion of the 19th century theorists that the market mechanism would automatically tend to produce full employment, *i.e.*, that general overproduction or underemployment would automatically be corrected through price-level adjustment.[21] The operation of this classical mechanism is quite simple. If there were a recession involving excessive unemployment, prices would fall because of the decline in demand for goods and wage rates would decline because of the competition of workers for jobs. With prices and wage rates falling together, the recession, however, would not be corrected. But the fall in the price-wage level would increase the real buying power of each unit of money. If the nominal stock of money remained constant, its real buying power would increase, and soon the public would find itself with larger cash balances than they would choose to hold—in Ricardo's terms, money would become redundant. The public's effort to spend the extra money would create the extra demand necessary to absorb the involuntarily unemployed. Thus, in theory, any recession would be quickly and automatically corrected by a general adjustment in the price-wage level, provided the stock of money was not allowed to shrink as fast as the fall in price level. According to this theory, recovery from an initial recession would be "just around the corner."

It is difficult to see why this adjustment mechanism would not work, if prices and wage rates were perfectly flexible or even highly flexible. The price-wage level would constantly be fluctuating down or up to correct any tendency toward underemployment or overemployment, and the relatively quick correction would prevent any movement one way or the other from gaining such momentum that a *general* expectation of further fall (or rise) might affect the process. This cybernetic mechanism would operate to produce reasonable stability at full employment.

It is equally obvious that, if all prices and wage rates were administered and inflexible, this mechanism would not work. An initial shrinkage in aggregate demand would produce a decline in the employment of both men and machines and there would be no automatic correction.

In the early 1930's, when agricultural prices and wage rates filled the classical requirement for market prices, while most industrial prices other than raw materials were administered, the recession brought a continuing decline in agricultural prices and wages to farm labor but not a comparable decline in industrial prices and industrial wage rates. In agriculture, the initial shrinkage in aggregate demand followed the classical pattern of falling prices and no shrinkage in farm employment. In industry, on the other hand, the primary effect of the fall in demand was a fall in employment with the consequent further fall in aggregate demand. Under such conditions, with the nominal money stock constant, the only condition of short run equilibrium resulting from an initial recession would be one of low agricultural prices and low employment in industry. The 19th century theory of an automatic correction simply would not apply.

Today, there is general agreement among economists that there is no automatic correction for excessive unemployment. There is also general agreement that aggregate demand can be increased through government's monetary and fiscal policies. The Employment Act of 1946 placed on government the responsibility for maintaining the aggregate demand necessary for full employment, but there is still a conflict among economists as to the reasons for the failure of a laissez-faire policy and as to the role of money in altering aggregate demand. Does money only affect aggregate demand through interest rates as Keynes held, or does it also operate directly on demand as experience since World War II would seem to indicate? In either case, monetary and fiscal instruments for maintaining the desired level of aggregate demand have not yet been designed to play the new role which is now assigned to them. Thus, the first policy problem created by concentration has been recognized and the outlines of the new policy have been accepted. However, effective practice for maintaining the necessary aggregate demand remains a problem. What should be the relative role of monetary policy and of fiscal policy? What changes, if any, are needed in monetary and fiscal institutions in order to carry out these policies designed to maintain full employment?

C. Classical Inflation and a Concentrated Economy

According to 19th century theory, only one source of inflation was possible—that arising from too much money chasing too few goods; a type of inflation which is properly called demand inflation. If the initial condition of an economy were one of full employment and the money stock were increased in excess of that amount of its wealth the public would choose to hold in the form of money at the initial price level, money would become redundant and aggregate demand would increase, which would bring about a rise in prices and wage rates. This type of inflation could be expected to continue as long as the stock of money continued to be greater than the public chose to hold. It could be converted into run-away inflation if the public as a whole came to expect rising prices and therefore chose to reduce still further its money holdings. In the absence of run-away inflation, the inflation arising from an initial excess in the stock of money would automatically be corrected by the reduced real value of each unit of money as the price level rose. Thus, a small rise in the money stock in excess of the money the public would choose to hold could be expected to lead to only a moderate price rise with no further repercussion. Also, such an inflationary rise in prices could not, in theory, occur except under conditions of full employment.

In a concentrated economy with the bulk of prices and wage rates administered, a quite different kind of inflation is possible and it can arise even when employment is considerably below the level considered to be full employment. This type of inflation results from a somewhat arbitrary exercise of market power. In an industry where competitors are few, the exact level of prices is by no means determinate, even though firms are in active competition with each other. There is usually some pricing discretion on the part of a price leader. Even with no change in demand or costs, an enterprise may seek to widen its profit margin by a small price increase and be followed by others in the industry. This type of price increase could occur in many industries, and if sufficiently general, could lead to both a rise in the general level of prices and in unemployment. Meanwhile, the rise in price level would provide labor with a basis for a legitimate demand for higher wage rates, the granting of which would in turn reduce profit margins. The result of the arbitrary price increases could thus be to increase unemployment without changing the level of profit margins. Then, if government brings about an increase in aggregate demand in order to absorb the new unemployment, conditions would be established for another arbitrary rise in prices and the process could be repeated.

This type of "administrative inflation" could also be created by labor pressure to force wage rates up faster than the increases in national productivity. An excessive rise in wage rates would provide a legitimate basis for price increases. Because of the increase in costs, the rise in prices could be used to justify further wage increases.

It is clear that such an administrative inflation can occur even though there is extensive unemployment. Thus, in the period from 1953 to 1959, the wholesale price index rose 8.5 percent, even though unemployment throughout the period averaged 4.8 percent of the civilian labor force. During this period, an index dominated by flexible market prices showed no important change, being lower in

1959 than in 1953.[22] The rise in the wholesale price index in this period was almost entirely in the more concentrated industries. It was triggered by rising steel prices and appears to have resulted primarily from an effort to widen steel profit margins, which were already ample, and only in a minor degree from a legitimate reaction to increasing costs.[23] This same phenomenon has been occurring in 1970 with recession and inflation at the same time: a development which simply could not occur under conditions of classical competition.

There is considerable evidence that as full employment is approached, the likelihood of administrative inflation, the arbitrary increasing of prices or wage rates or both, also increases. Thus, if just that degree of aggregate demand needed to support full employment were maintained, an initial situation of stability could be expected to shift into administrative inflation. Whether triggered by management or labor, the price rise with no further increase in aggregate demand would generate unemployment. Thus, the problem of preventing inflation not only requires techniques and institutions for preventing excessive demand, but also techniques and institutions for preventing administrative inflation. Both the problems of maintaining full employment and the problems of preventing inflation are complicated, and in turn, they complicate the problem of maintaining a balance in international payments.

D. The Classical Theory of Trade Adjustment and a Concentrated Economy

According to classical theory, payments between countries which were on the gold standard would automatically be maintained in reasonable balance. The mechanism maintaining balance was beautifully simple in principle, and under the market-price conditions assumed in classical theory, there is no reason to think that it would not work as theory indicated. In fact, it did work throughout much of the 19th century.

Under the gold standard, if one country had an unfavorable balance with the rest of the gold standard countries because it was buying more from abroad than it was selling, it would pay the difference in gold. Since under the gold standard, the quantity of money in a country was directly related to the country's monetary gold holdings, the money stock of the gold-losing country would contract, thereby reducing aggregate demand. With all prices and wage rates assumed to be highly flexible market prices, the country's price-wage level would fall, thus encouraging other gold-standard countries to buy from it. Simultaneously, the money stock in the gold-receiving countries would increase, thereby expanding aggregate demand. Since prices and wage rates were assumed to be highly flexible, the price-wage levels would rise, thereby discouraging the gold-losing country from buying from them. Thus, the gold-losing country would buy less from abroad and sell more abroad while the gold-receiving country would do the opposite. The gold flow and price-wage changes resulting from these purchases could be expected to continue until the unbalance in payments disappeared.

Of course, such an automatic mechanism could not be expected to operate in a concentrated economy. If a concentrated country had its money stock directly related to its monetary gold and an adverse balance in payments arose, the outflow of gold and the contraction in its stock of money would reduce aggregate demand as classical theory prescribed. But, in the presence of inflexible administered prices and wage rates, the fall in demand would create unemployment. Even though some market prices fell, the incomes in the country would shrink until it was unable to buy as much abroad. Simultaneously, the gold-receiving countries, if concentrated, would experience a boom and with increased incomes would be buying more from the depressed country. Thus, the unbalance in payments would automatically be corrected as the gold-losing country bought less and sold more abroad. However, the automatic adjustment would have been brought about by a *depression* in one country and a boom in others, instead of through changes in relative price-wage levels.

In practice, the gold standard was abandoned in country after country during the first part of the 20th century, presumably because it was working progressively worse as the industrial countries became more concentrated and prices and wage rates became less flexible. In place of the gold standard, under which the money supply of a country expands or contracts in line with the country's monetary supply of gold, the central banks focused monetary policy on the problems of maintaining internal employment and price-wage stability. Unbalances in external payments have thus become a chronic problem, sometimes for one group of countries, sometimes for another. Concentration has made the old gold standard unacceptable. Various measures have been adopted for postponing the need for correcting an unbalance in payments in the hope that by good fortune it will disappear. Nevertheless, there is no automatic corrective. Can techniques be found for correcting unbalances in international payments without subjecting particular countries to depression or boom and without the strains of drastic devaluation and revaluations?

Here we have three major and interrelated sets of problems arising from the effects of concentration which involve the economy as a whole. Until these are satisfactorily solved, the more specific problems of competition, use of resources, and the determinants of income, though important, will be more difficult to solve in a satisfactory fashion.

E. Competition, the Use of Resources, and Income Distribution

At the time the Sherman Act was passed, two basic market concepts dominated economic thinking, "competition" and "monopoly." The act was aimed to preserve the first and to prevent or eliminate the second. So long as there was competition, it was assumed that prices were determined by supply and demand or what can be called "classical competition." The act was expected not only to eliminate monopoly outside of regulated industries, but also to maintain or to reestablish classical competition.

It was not until three studies appeared in 1933–35, one concerned with imperfect competition, one with monopolistic competition, and one with administered prices, that nonclassical competition entered into general economic theory. The first two of these studies pointed to the theoretical possibility that active competition between a few companies could be expected to produce pricing results quite different from those to be expected from classical competition. The third study indicated the prevalence in the American economy of prices which are clearly *competitive* but which do not behave at all as prices could be expected to behave under conditions of classical competition. As already indicated, most of American industry operates with administered prices. This means that, where competitive, they operate under a condition of the newly recognized type of competition, which will hereafter be referred to as "administrative competition."[24]

When one looks at the successes and failures of the antitrust legislation, keeping in mind these three concepts—classical competition, administrative competition, and monopoly—two things stand out.

First, operations under this legislation have been outstandingly successful in preventing industrial monopoly. Today, there is no major unregulated industry in which there is only one significant company. In practically every industry, there are three or four or more companies actively competing with each other. There may be some instances of price collusion, but the legislation provides the basis for dealing with them as was done for example in the case of price-fixing in electrical equipment. Preventing monopoly is a never-ending task for the agencies enforcing the antitrust laws, but action under the antitrust laws has eliminated the industrial monopolies which developed at the turn of the century and has prevented their recurrence on any major scale.

On the other hand, the antitrust laws have been a complete failure in preserving classical competition. The Sherman Act seems to have been written in the belief that, if monopoly were prevented, competition in the classical sense would be maintained. This confusion of competition with classical competition means that no attention was given to administrative competition, therefore, the tradition was established that somehow the prevention of monopoly would be sufficient to maintain the full benefits of classical competition.

The difference in the results to be expected from the two different types of competition are complex and not widely understood. To bring out the most important difference, it is necessary to go back to first principles and simplified cases. Here, the results to be expected from classical competition will be outlined first, and then those to be expected from administrative competition will be considered.

F. The Results to Be Expected from Classical Competition

The theory of classical competition is well-established, and there is much evidence that where the conditions for this type of competition exist, the actual results tend to confirm the theory. The best examples of classical competition are in agriculture. The individual wheat farmer is competing with such a large number of other wheat farmers that his own decision to plant more or fewer acres of wheat or to produce one kind of wheat rather than another will not significantly alter the prices of the different grades of wheat. He has no market power. He is a price accepter. He can make his production and marketing decisions on the basis o[f] what he expects prices will be without taking into account the effect of his own decisions on prices. This is the key difference between classical competition and administrative competition. In the latter, the producer does have to take into account the effect of his own production policy on price, or, more often, he has his own price policy.

We could examine the results of this type of competition in terms of wheat or cotton or tobacco production. However, it is difficult to imagine a comparative condition in which all, or practically all, wheat is produced by one or the other of "the big four" or "the big six" wheat producers. For this reason, a simplified example will be taken from the textile industry where it is possible to imagine a condition of classical competition and to compare it with a possible condition of administrative competition.

For the analysis of classical competition, assume that there are 400 cotton spinning mills: each is able to make every standard type and count of cotton yarn; each is separately owned and operated; each buys its cotton in the competitive cotton market; each sells its output in a cotton yarn market; and each draws its labor from an area without union organization but in which wage rates are fairly uniform for all employers. We can assume that some of the mills are relatively new, others are old, some are efficiently run, others are poorly run, and that production costs will be different for different mills. Also, assume that at the outset, some mills are shut down and others are operating.

For the management of a closed mill, a decision must be made whether to open. The central calculus could be expected to turn on the current and expected price of yarns, the price of cotton, the availability and cost of labor, and the cost of other production factors making up the operating cost of the mill. If there were a sufficient margin between the out-of-pocket costs of operating the mill and the in-pocket revenue to be expected, the mill would presumably be opened and add its output to the total supply of yarn available in the market.

There are two characteristics of this calculus which should be noticed. First, it does not take into account the past capital cost of the mill itself. The owner already has the mill. Unless he sells it or operates it, he will presumably derive no revenue from it. If he can operate it and derive *some* revenue in excess of his out-of-pocket costs, he would be better off than if he kept it closed. Thus, the decision to operate or not to operate an *existing* mill would turn primarily on future costs and rest not at all on what was paid in the past for the mill itself. In the calculus to operate or not, the capital cost of the existing mill would be "water over the dam."

The second characteristic of this calculus is that the decision would turn only on whether to keep the mill closed or operate it *at capacity*. There would be no question of operating part-time or at a low rate in order not to flood the market or because of insufficient orders. Under the condition of classical competition, the owner could sell all the yarn he could make within the capacity of his mill without significantly affecting prices. The exact capacity of his mill would, of course, vary with the type of yarn he chose to make and on relative prices. But once the decision to open was made, there would be no holding back production because of the effect such holding back might have on price.

In considering whether to close an operating mill, the same type of calculus would apply. Were out-of-pocket costs being covered by revenue when operating at capacity? If they were, operating at capacity would presumably be continued.

Under these conditions, and with this type of calculus, one could expect that the more efficient mills would be open with each operating at capacity and the less efficient would be closed. The supply of yarn flowing into the market would meet the market demand and yarn prices would adjust to just clear the market. If demand increased, prices would rise relative to costs and more mills would have an inducement to operate. A fall in demand would reduce prices, providing some mills an inducement to close. Thus, so long as we consider only the 400 mills, the supply would vary with price as more or fewer mills were operated, each at capacity, and demand and supply would be kept in line by changes in prices.

The cost of capital would enter into the market process primarily through the decisions to build new mills. It is obvious that simply a margin of revenue over out-of-pocket costs would not provide an inducement to build new mills. A potential new producer would have to have a reasonable prospect not only of recovering his capital (reflected in depreciation charges), but also of obtaining a competitive return or better on the capital he invests. If the margin between revenue and out-of-pocket costs is expected over a reasonable period to be large enough to cover both expected depreciation and at least a competitive return on capital, new mills will be built and operated at capacity.

In oversimplified form, the above paragraphs outline the essence of classical competition. With a slowly growing industry or a stable industry with slowly improving technology, prices in any short period would be dominated by the relation between demand and the out-of-pocket costs of the least efficient mill which needed to be operated at capacity in order to supply the demand at the market price. But over a longer period in which new mills could be built, prices would be dominated by demand, the out-of-pocket costs plus depreciation, and a competitive rate of return on capital for the capacity operation of the most efficient mill which could be built.

In a declining industry where the existing mills could more than supply the demand, out-of-pocket costs of the least efficient mill needed to fill demand would dominate prices. And in a rapidly growing industry, appreciably more than a competitive rate of return on capital could be expected to develop and continue for a time as new mills were being built at an insufficient rate. But in general, prices in such a classically competitive industry could be expected to gravitate around the total cost of production at capacity of the most technically efficient mill which could be built, including total production costs, depreciation, and a competitive rate of return on capital.

If there were no economics of size and if each industry were operating under conditions of classical competition, classical theory would dictate that the resources of a society could be most effectively used in meeting the individual wants of the society. Prices would be in line with economic costs, individual producers would be under constant inducement to be efficient, natural and human resources would be directed into different uses in the fashion which would best serve the society, and capital would be directed into different industries until each industry tended to yield a competitive rate of return. Each individual would receive income in proportion to his contribution of labor and capital.

These classical conclusions as to the results of classical competition have been successfully challenged on at least two major grounds: first, that there are important economic costs which are not reflected in business costs, such as air and water pollution; and second, that the income distribution resulting from classical competition might fall short of socially acceptable goals. These are problems which will be taken up in the next section of this article. For the remainder of this section, the essentials of what can be expected if classical competition prevailed throughout the economy will not be questioned. What will be explored is the difference between what can be expected from a classically competitive industry as opposed to one operating under conditions of administrative competition.

G. The Results to Be Expected from Administrative Competition

In order to explore the results to be expected from administrative competition, let us assume that there has been a big merger movement and the 400 independent cotton spinning mills have been absorbed into four big cotton yarn companies, each owning 100 separate mills. We can name these four companies the American Spinning Company, the National Spinning Company, the U.S. Spinning Company, and the Consolidated Spinning Company. Competition among them will appear as follows: First, collusion between them on prices and rates of production can be ruled out. Such collusion might occur, but it would be illegal under the antitrust laws, and the problem would be more vigorous prosecution under the law. How could law-abiding managements be expected to act with only four competing spinning companies?

The theories of administrative competition are not as well-developed or tested as those of classical competition. The pioneer theories presented by Robinson and Chamberlin stimulated theoretical discussion and clearly established the theoretical basis for a kind of competition lying between classical competition and monopoly. However, these theories of business behavior have failed in important respects to conform to actual business practice. The discrepancies are reflected in the inflexibility in administered prices, in administrative inflation, and in the use of target pricing; none of which are deduceable from these pioneer theories of nonclassical competition.

In considering the competitive behavior to be expected from the four spinning companies, it will be convenient to apply certain elements of these pioneer theories and then show specific modifications.

The pioneer theories suggest that if there were only four spinning companies, each owning one hundred mills, the yarn prices arrived at would be very close to monopoly prices, even if there were no collusion or agreement between the companies. Each company could be expected to survey demand and their own costs and arrive at a base price (with differentials for each type of yarn) which would be the most profitable price, if it were able to retain its proportionate share in the total market. If, by chance, all four arrived separately at the same base price, as the most desirable price, this price would presumably be announced by one and adopted by the others. In that case, it might well be the base price that a monopoly owning all 400 mills would adopt, which presumably would be a "monopoly" price. But the more likely development would be one in which the four companies differed somewhat as to the most desirable price. Then, the more likely effect would be for the companies with the lowest "most desirable price" to set the price for all, either initially or later by undercutting a higher price. This also would be substantially above a classically competitive price for mills having the same costs, although not quite as high as those set by a *monopolist* with the same mills and costs. It was recognized that sometimes price wars might break out and rage for a period. Also, the fear of starting a price war could inhibit price changes and thus make for inflexibility in prices. But the self-interest of the four firms in the most profitable price was presumed to be so great that the normal price to be expected would be close to a monopoly price.

This pioneer theory proved to be faulty in at least four important respects: the effect of uncertainty on pricing; the time span involved in pricing; the effect of potential entrants; and the effect of public and government attitudes. When modified in these respects, the theory of administered competition takes on a substantially different and more realistic cast but points to fundamentally different results from those to be expected from classical competition.

Uncertainty as to the most profitable price makes for inflexibility and arbitrariness in administrative pricing. In classical monopoly theory upon which the pioneer theories of administrative competition are based, it is assumed that the single seller can estimate the demand for his product at different prices with a good deal of precision and can also estimate his costs for different amounts of output. With this information, arrival at the most profitable price is a matter of simple arithmetic. On this basis, it would be expected that as demand or costs change, that most profitable price would usually change. It was assumed that the monopolist would adjust his price accordingly. As a result, monopoly prices would tend to be almost as flexible in the short run as those made under conditions of classical competition. The essential difference would be greater profit, not inflexibility. In other words, flexibility was implicit in the pioneer theories of administrative competition.

Yet, in practice, the monopolist cannot usually estimate the demand for his product with precision, and there is likely to be a range of prices which may be almost equally profitable. Thus, there is a zone in which the monopolist is relatively indifferent to the exact price. Uncertainty as to the most profitable price plus the existence of this zone of relative indifference means that the initial price set by a monopolist is likely to be somewhat arbitrary. Once set, however, considerable changes in demand or costs can take place without inducing a change in price. Furthermore, a moderate and arbitrary change in price can be made in the absence of any change in demand or costs. Instead of a monopoly price being determinate as a result of precise profit calculus, there is likely to be a considerable degree of arbitrariness in a monopoly price. The monopolist, in pricing, usually operates within an area of considerable discretion in which precise market considerations do not determine the price which he sets.

This uncertainty can have the same effect in creating an area of pricing discretion where competition is among a few producers. Assume for example that in the textile example of four spinning companies given earlier, that the U.S. Spinning Company is the recognized price leader. Its management can be expected to go through a pricing calculus similar to that of a monopolist and arrive at a relatively broad zone within which its most profitable price is likely to lie. It will then have to consider what price each of the other three companies will accept. It will then decide upon and announce a price. If its analysis has been correct, each of the other companies will find the price lying within or below its zone of relative indifference and will accept it as its own. Occasionally, the price leader guesses incorrectly and one of the other companies comes out with a lower price which may be accepted by the other companies.

The large degree of pricing discretion also means that once a price has been adopted, moderate changes in demand and costs will not provide an inducement to price change. This, when combined with other advantages of a fixed price, goes far to explain the relative inflexibility of administered prices which the pioneer theories would not lead one to expect.

The second modification of the pioneer theories has to do with the time span which must be taken into account when pricing. When there are only a few big competitors, the focus of pricing is not to make the maximum profit in the current market. Rather, the pricing policy is focused on long-run profit. The possibility of greater profit in the immediate future is sacrificed for greater profit over a longer period. Thus, a big surge of demand for a particular product, which would lead to a sharp rise in a classically competitive price, might be met by a forced-draft operation with overtime production to supply the extra demand and no increase or only a moderate increase in price. Similarly, a drop in demand would be met primarily by a cut in production and employment rather than in price.

The emphasis on long-run rather than short-run profits contributes to the inflexibility of administered prices, but its more important effect results from two long-run considerations which are brought into the pricing calculus. The first is the danger of new entrants into the industry. The second is the public reaction to excessive profits. Both of these can be expected to result in prices lower than those usually expected from short-run profit maximizing.

If we start with only four spinning companies, they share the whole market. Nevertheless, each must fear that other companies will build spinning mills and take away some of the market. The price leader in setting price can be expected to take into account the fact that too high a level of profits on the part of four companies will soon bring new entrants into the industry. If this happens, future profits could be severely curtailed. Over the years, profits of each of the four companies could be expected to be greater if prices were set to keep current profits low enough so that new entrants would be discouraged.

If it were perfectly easy to enter the industry, prices would have to be set in such a manner that there would be little more than a competitive rate of return on capital. Thus, in the spinning mill example, if the yarns from the four companies were essentially interchangeable, entry would presumably be easy. All that would be necessary would be to call up Charles T. Main & Co. or one of the other textile engineering firms and arrange for the construction of a new spinning mill. This danger would tend to make the prices of cotton yarn set by the industry so close to cost that the return on capital for the four companies would be close to the competitive rate. With the same number of mills and the same costs, the prices set by the four companies could be expected to vary less than with the 400 separate companies but their level of prices could be expected to be about the same as the longer period average of the classically competitive prices.

Under administrative competition, the danger of new entrants becomes the chief instrument through which prices are kept in reasonable relation to costs. With impossible entry, administered prices could be expected to be close to monopoly prices. With perfectly easy entry, prices would tend to be administered and inflexible but could be expected to bear much the same average relation to costs as could be expected under classical competition. Between these extremes lies a whole range of situations in which entry is more or less easy, and the pricing results lie between the longer run results of classical competition and those to be expected from monopoly.

The difficulty of entry into an industry is partly a matter of technology. It is difficult to imagine efficient production and classical competition in the production of pig iron. The Chinese drive for backyard blast furnaces might have created enough separate enterprises to allow classical competition but not efficiency. Only a relatively few blast furnace plants are required to supply this country's pig iron requirements, and, even if each plant were independently owned, the small number would not insure classical competition.

A second impediment to entry into an industry can be created by vertical integration. As long as the four spinning companies confined themselves to spinning, entry could be easy. Yet, if the merger movement had combined all cotton spinning, weaving, and finishing into four integrated companies, it would be more difficult for a new company to break into the finished cotton cloth market. To create a new integrated company would require more capital, a spinning mill would have difficulty finding a market for yarn, and a weaving mill would have difficulty obtaining yarn. If only four companies divided up the market for *all* textile cloth products, a break-in would be even more difficult.

A third impediment to entry can be created through product differentiation, advertising, and organization of the channels of trade. Four integrated textile companies might, through advertising, so condition buyers that only expensive advertising could allow a new company to break into the market. Apparent differences in the details of the product, as in the case of typewriters and automobiles, can make advertising and promotion more effective. And, where exclusive dealers are used, the cost and time required to build a new organization makes entry more difficult.

Whatever the degree of ease or difficulty in entering an administratively competitive industry, the important and recognized fact is that under conditions of administrative competition, the threat of new entry is the major and probably the most important influence tending to limit a serious discrepancy between actual profit rates and the competitive cost of capital. Anything which makes entry more easy can be expected to result in prices closer to costs plus a competitive rate of return on capital. Conversely, anything which reduces the likelihood that new entries will be stimulated by the making of more than a competitive rate of profit can be expected to result in higher profit rates.

Whether and to what extent pricing administration is influenced by public and government attitudes is a matter for debate. The leading companies in highly concentrated industries are, to some degree, vulnerable to public opinion. Promotion to obtain a favorable public image may not be enough if pricing policy is antipublic. When pricing power is great, actual pricing policy may be somewhat tempered, bringing prices somewhat closer to those yielding only a competitive return on capital.

The rigors of pricing under administrative competition have led some progressive companies to adopt a relatively new technique in pricing which has come to be known as "target pricing." It involves a procedure which lies quite outside classical theory and outside the pioneer theories of administrative competition. Instead of starting with estimates of costs and demand, it starts with two basic estimates. The first is an estimate of how high a rate of return on capital can be achieved without drawing new entrants into the industry or stimulating adverse government reaction. This would be the target rate. The second is an estimate of the average rate of operating which reasonably can be expected over a period of years in light of the ups and downs of demand. This would then be adopted as the rate of operation at which the target rate of return should be earned. Prices would then be set so that *if* operations were at the average rate, say 85 percent of capacity, the prices would just yield the target rate on the capital invested. These prices would mean that if demand at the set prices did not reach the level necessary to operate at 85 percent of capacity, the earning rate on capital would fall below the target rate. If demand were higher, earnings would exceed the target rate. But over a period of years, the target rate would be achieved.

The target rates employed in the period 1947 to 1955 are given below for the price leader in ten major concentrated industries along with actual returns on investment[25]:

	Target Rate of Return after Taxes (%)	*Actual Rate of Return after Taxes 1947–1955*	
		Average (%)	*Range (%)*
General Motors	20	26.0	19.9–37.0
DuPont	20	25.9	19.6–34.1
General Electric	20	21.4	18.4–26.6
Union Carbide	18	19.0	13.5–24.3
Standard Oil of N.J.	—	16.0	12.0–18.9
Johns-Manville	15	14.9	10.7–19.6
Alcoa	10	13.8	7.8–18.7
International Harvester	10	8.9	4.9–11.9
United States Steel	8	10.3	7.6–14.8

Target pricing makes the prices involved relatively inflexible to changes in demand but sensitive to changes in costs. Also, the formula for target pricing is more of a company guideline than a rigidly adhered to price determinant. An unexpectedly low demand can lead to pricing below the target price, while expectation of inflation can lead to prices higher than current cost would prescribe.

H. Administrative Competition and Public Policy

Whether or not the device of target pricing is employed, the results to be expected from administrative competition are significantly different from those to be expected from classical competition, and serious problems of public policy arise.

One such problem concerns those situations in which competition is among a few big producers and technology makes entry difficult. Both theory and observation indicate that in such a situation, a drive to maximize profits is likely to result in rates of return on capital well above the competitive rates for capital. Profits would then be excessive; resources, including capital, would not be used as extensively in the industry as would be economical and income distribution would be distorted. What public policy should be adopted in this case?

A somewhat different problem arises when entry is presently difficult but could be made easier. It could be expected that with difficult entry, the industry, in the interest of profit, would not push production to the point required to make effective use of resources. But easier entry is technically possible and could be expected to correct this to a greater or lesser extent. What public policy should be adopted in this case?

I. Mergers and Concentration

Of even greater importance for future concentration is the set of problems concerning mergers. While the Sherman Act focused on preventing monopoly, the Clayton Act, as amended in 1950, outlaws mergers which tend toward monopoly or to substantially lessen competition. Thus, the amended Clayton Act deals with administrative competition, even though no monopoly is in prospect. Here, the problem of mergers which substantially lessen competition can best be discussed separately for each of the three merger types; horizontal, vertical, and conglomerate.

1. Horizontal Mergers

A horizontal merger which had the effect of eliminating a competitor would clearly be against public policy if there were only two competitors to start with. The real problem presented by horizontal mergers occurs when they will not result in a single seller. What constitutes a substantial reduction in competition? If one wheat farmer buys out another and operates both farms as one, there is, in some sense, a reduction in competition, but it is certainly not "substantial" as it affects the price of wheat. However, if there are only five producers in an industry, does a merger of two of them substantially reduce competition? If there are twenty, would a merger of two represent a substantial reduction in competition? Furthermore, when competition is administrative, under what conditions would mergers not involve a substantial reduction? These are the policy questions with respect to horizontal mergers.

2. Vertical Mergers

Vertical mergers involving administrative competition raise quite a different kind of problem. Ease of entry becomes an important objective of public policy, and any merger which reduces potential entrants becomes a matter of public concern. A vertical merger in which a company acquires a company in the same stream of production, using its product or supplying its raw material, can reduce the company's danger from potential entry. It has already been indicated that entry into an integrated industry can be more difficult than entry into the same industry without integration. The integrating effect of a vertical merger on ease of entry is so important that it deserves to be spelled out in more detail.

The effect of vertical integration on ease of entry can readily be seen in the textile example. Assume an initial condition of administrative competition between four independent spinning companies doing all the cotton spinning, and assume all cotton weaving is done by four independent weaving companies. If yarn prices are kept too high, *i.e.*, if the profits of the yarn companies are substantially above a competitive return to capital, one of the four weaving companies, seeking lower yarn prices, can be expected to threaten to set up its own spinning mills. This threat could serve to keep yarn prices in fairly reasonable relation to costs, even though none of the weaving companies actually built spinning mills. Also, the threat would presumably be much more effective than the possibility of an outside company coming into the spinning business. The latter would also have to ''break into the market'' for yarns, while the weaving company would have no such problem.

Similarly, if the prices arrived at for cotton cloth by the interaction of the four weaving companies resulted in excessive rates of return on capital, it would presumably be much easier for one of the four spinning companies to build weaving plants than it would be for an outsider to do so.

Furthermore, it is reasonable to suppose that if there were four integrated companies, each starting with raw cotton and ending with finished cotton cloth, it would be much more difficult for an outsider to enter the industry than if there were four spinning companies, four weaving companies, and four finishing companies.

Thus, under administrative competition, vertical integration can substantially reduce the threat of entry and allow an increase in the margin between prices and costs. As a result, one can be reasonably sure that, if the price leader among the four independent spinning mills adopted the target pricing procedure, it would adopt a lower rate of return as its target in pricing than would the price leader among the four integrated companies.

Of course, there are other considerations involved in dealing with vertical mergers, such as the financial power of size and the withdrawal of potential markets from other producers. But the competitive pressure of potential entrants is so important for administrative competition that it presents a major problem of public policy where vertical mergers are concerned. In the presence of administrative competition, vertical mergers can reduce the likelihood that prices will be kept reasonably in line with costs. Thus, they operate to reduce competition. The main problem is to draw the line between cases of vertical integration which substantially lessen competition and those which do not.

3. Conglomerate Mergers

In 1927, duPont acquired a substantial block of U.S. Steel Corporation stock and became one of its largest stockholders. It already held nearly 23 percent of the stock of General Motors which gave it working control of the latter. The antitrust agencies were critical of this acquisition and in 1928 duPont informed the government that it had disposed of its steel stock. Subsequently, the courts forced it to dispose of its holdings in General Motors. If the three companies, leaders in chemicals, automobiles and steel, had come under common legal control the result would have been a conglomerate. The latter could be defined as a combination of companies whose primary activities make the combination neither a horizontal nor a vertical combination. This does not mean that there may not be some measure of horizontal or vertical relation between the combining companies but only that this relation is not the dominant relation. Whereas a cotton yarn mill and a weaving mill are obviously in a single line of production, a steel company, such as U.S. Steel, and an auto company only partially overlap. Much of the steel goes to other industries and much of the raw material or parts for autos come from other than steel companies. Practically all large conglomerates involve some degree of overlap, either with some competition between the separate companies or with some buying and selling between them. To this extent, the principles of horizontal or vertical merging apply. The major policy problems are as follows: whether the merging will substantially reduce competition between constituent units and whether it makes entry into the industries of the constituents substantially more difficult?

A conglomerate can and usually does involve other substantial problems affecting competition. If the conglomerate only acquired enterprises which were engaged in classically competitive industries, it is difficult to see what problems of public policy would arise. For example, if the United Farm Corporation acquired a wheat farm in the south, a corn-hog farm in Iowa, a tobacco farm in Virginia and a cattle farm in Texas, classical competition in the pricing of the various products could be expected to continue. But the usual conglomerate acquisition is operating not only under conditions of administrative competition but also under conditions of difficult entry. The conglomerate promoters will seldom see potential extra profit in acquiring a company operating in an industry in which entry is quite easy. Such companies do not fit into the conglomerate syndrome. Thus, the main problems arising from conglomerates concern a combination of administrative competition and difficult entry.

The wave of conglomerate mergers is relatively new, and neither the actual behavior of conglomerates nor theoretical analysis has brought substantial agreement as to their effects on competition.

Claims are regularly made that conglomerate management can raise the efficiency of the combined companies by bringing to bear financial resources and superior central management skills which the separate companies do not possess.

However, it is also pointed out that the problems of management become more complex with the possibility of decreased efficiency. The experience of large conglomerates would appear to be mixed, with some of them having serious management difficulties. Unfortunately, the financial reports of most conglomerates do not allow a before-and-after comparison of operations. Revising accounting procedures, reshuffling underlying properties, and consolidating accounts make it impossible even to compare before-and-after profits and to distinguish between profits arising from changes in accounting, profits from inflation, and profits from improved management. Even if there were profits from improved management and the figures were available, there would still be the problem of distinguishing between profits from increased efficiency and profits from increased market power.

Until there is substantial evidence to the contrary, there is good reason to be skeptical of the claims of increased efficiency alleged to result from bringing under one central control, the operations of diverse separate companies which usually make up a big conglomerate. Many of the management skills which a central conglomerate management is supposed to supply could be obtained by the constituent companies from independent management consulting firms. Furthermore, the proposition that the new financing provided by the conglomerate is cheaper than that which the constituent companies could obtain has yet to be firmly established.

There is substantial agreement, though, that a conglomerate has opportunities to increase short-run profits through tax and accounting procedures not open to the separate companies. If a conglomerate acquires a company by exchanging bonds for outstanding stock, income taxes are saved on earnings paid out as interest, an action not open to an individual company. There may be opportunities for setting losses off against gains. Profits can be temporarily increased by altering depreciation policies, and in other ways profits may be increased for a time without any change in operating efficiency.

There also seems to be agreement that a two-billion dollar conglomerate has greater financial and market power than the separate companies which it has taken over. Though just how much greater power is involved and how it affects competition has not been definitely ascertained.

Part of the market power of a big conglomerate comes from its ability to finance losses in one activity from earnings in others. This ability can distort the workings of competition in at least two different ways. It allows the conglomerate to carry on nonprice rivalry through advertising, sales effort, model changes, services to buyers, and similar means so that sales go to the conglomerate because of its financial resources and not because of lower costs. This type of rivalry tends to increase industry costs and result in higher prices and less efficient use of resources. In a particular market, a conglomerate can carry on destructive price competition or take other measures to damage a rival with the knowledge that the rival is likely to be hurt more than the conglomerate. Although, in the short-run, this may benefit customers, in the longer run, a weakening of the rival may result in higher prices.

Even if neither of these actions were taken, the mere existence of the power to take them could be expected to reduce competition. The other enterprises in the particular industry would know that these actions *could* be taken and would be less willing to initiate competitive moves which they would otherwise employ to intensify competition. Likewise, potential entrants into the industry would be less willing to enter the industry when they know that one of the few companies in the industry was controlled by a conglomerate with its considerable market power. This could significantly increase the difficulty of entry.

A merger of a company in a concentrated industry into a big conglomerate could also affect competition quite apart from the conglomerate's market power. The conglomerate, without merging a company already operating in the industry, is itself a potential entrant into the industry. If it had to build its own new plants to enter, competition would be strengthened. The merger would eliminate this potential entrant.

Finally, if there were two conglomerates, each carrying on activity in a number of the same markets, competition is likely to be lessened. If Conglomerate A is competing with Conglomerate B in both the market for gadgets and for widgets, it might forbear to push competition in the market for gadgets because of the danger of retaliation in the widget market. The more markets served by conglomerates, the greater this competitive forbearance is likely to become.

The ways in which a conglomerate merger can reduce competition raise two major questions of policy. In appraising a conglomerate takeover of a company from the point of view of the public interest, how should the various ways in which competition is likely to be reduced be weighed in deciding whether there is likely to be a "substantial reduction of competition"? If there were a small amount of horizontal competition between the merged company and one or more of the conglomerates plus other activities and some cross-buying between it and them, so that the merger involved an element of vertical integration, and additionally, if each of the other ways that the merger would affect competition was small although the aggregate of these was large, would the merger involve a "substantial reduction" in competition? Or would the reduction have to be substantial in at least one of the ways discussed? And to what extent, if any, should the antitrust laws be modified to deal with the problems raised by conglomerate mergers?

J. The Larger Problem of Competition

There still remains the question of the extent to which such administrative competition under the antitrust laws can be expected to keep prices in reasonable relation to cost. Present-day theory suggests that in industries lacking easy entry, profits are likely to average appreciably higher than a competitive rate. The statistical evidence also suggests that this is the case. Income tax statistics show a higher average rate of return on capital for large companies than for medium or small companies, and presumably this is true for the more concentrated industries than for the less. If this is the case, then the level of present-day competition must be falling short of maintaining prices in a reasonable relation to business costs. To this extent, resources are not being channeled into the most effective use, and income distribution is to this extent distorted. This presents a real problem. When concentrated enterprise operates under conditions of administrative competition, can it be expected that the market and competition alone can ensure business operation in such a way that within the limits of business costs and business activity resources are effectively used and incomes fairly distributed? This is what classical competition was supposed to bring about.

Since this article is concerned with corporate concentration, little attention has been given to labor organization and its effect on prices and the distribution of income. This could be the subject of a separate article. In this regard, only three things need to be said. First, when an industry makes more than a competitive rate of return on capital, this can be expected to make labor relations more difficult. Second, under conditions of administrative competition and difficult entry, labor pressure for higher wages is not likely to eliminate a discrepancy between prices and a competitive rate of return. Instead, increases in wage rates in excess of increased productivity are likely to increase costs which will be made the basis of price increase. Third, fairness of wages as between different industries and the direction of resources into different uses will each depend in part on the extent that labor organizations work to bring about such fairness.

None of these propositions alter the analysis of the effect of corporate concentration on competition, on the use of resources, and on income distribution but they do highlight the importance of labor concentration to the use of resources and the distribution of income.

IV. Corporate Concentration and a Way of Life

In the preceding text, attention has been focused on the problems created by corporate concentration within the general framework of a business economy. Attention will now be focused on the society and the problems of the good life that concentration and the corporation have generated which lie outside the scope of a business economy but which relate to it. Only four of these problems will briefly be touched on here: the discrepancy between business costs and social costs; the distribution of income in a good society; living with the big corporations; and the political role of the big corporations.

A. Business Costs vs. Social Costs

It has long been recognized that there can be a serious discrepancy between business costs and social costs. The factory inspection laws have reduced the social cost of factory operation which was not included in business costs, and the compensation acts have made a social cost into a business cost. The current concern with pollution is leading to similar action, either to eliminate a social cost or to convert it into a business cost. The intermittent or irregular employment of workers has in part been converted into a business cost through unemployment insurance but it is still carried to an important extent by individuals. Social costs not now included in business costs present a real problem in the use of resources. To the extent that these social costs can be eliminated, there is a solution, but to the extent that they are converted into business costs, resources can be expected to be directed by business into different uses in relation to social as well as business costs. In some cases, the discrepancy between social and business costs may be more effectively handled by charging it directly to the government, as in the case of education.

This discrepancy between social and business costs has always existed, but the success of big corporate enterprise in creating an affluent society has heightened the problem: it has made the measures to eliminate social costs or to convert them into business cost no longer a luxury but a necessity for the good life. The problem is to determine what these uncovered social costs are and to determine how they should be handled and who should pay for or suffer them.

B. The Distribution of Income

The concentrated economy presents three types of income distribution problems. The first problem arises from discrepancies between corporate earnings and the competitive rate of return on capital where competition is administrative and entry is difficult. This has already been discussed. It presents a real problem of how corporate earnings can be kept in reasonable relation to costs.

The second income problem evolves from other imperfections in the working of the system as the concentrated economy fails to make the adjustments which were to be expected in an economy of classical competition. In the classical economy of atomistic enterprise, involuntary unemployment was expected to be of such short duration that there was no great hardship on individuals, and those employed were expected to receive income in proportion to the value of their contribution. However, in a concentrated economy operating under conditions of administrative competition, there can be substantial discrepancies between reward and potential contribution, which are only partly alleviated by social security programs. In this area, the problem is complex. It is partly a matter of organization, partly one of fitting jobs to people, and partly one of fitting people to jobs. The unemployment of two million persons willing and capable of working is the equivalent of throwing away approximately ten billion dollars of income.

The third problem of income distribution concerns those individuals unable to make a substantial contribution and to obtain a substantial income under the concentrated-economy system of production. This includes not only "the lame, the halt and the blind'' of traditional analysis but the psychological misfits that the system rejects or for which it does not make a place. It also includes those who are only capable of low productivity. Again, social security programs deal with this problem to some degree. Since the affluence arising from the concentrated economy makes the establishment of a minimum level of incomes not only feasible but almost mandatory, the central problem here is how and at what level this can most effectively be done.

C. Corporate Concentration and the Good Life

Economists used to treat labor as a commodity and analyze the role of a worker in the economy much as they would analyze the role of a sack of wheat or a bale of cotton as a raw material input in the production of output. Today, working for a big corporation has become a way of life for a large proportion of workers. Apart from sleeping and eating, nearly half of a worker's time is likely to be spent at the job or going to and from it. The affluent society, therefore, must reflect that affluence in the conditions surrounding the work. Labor unions have pushed for better working conditions and corporations have contributed to better conditions. But the rise in affluence has altered the magnitude of the problem. The good life is a problem during working hours as well as outside them.

D. Corporate Concentration and Government

Corporate concentration has also posed a major problem in the relationship of government to business. As long as production was carried on by relatively small business, political theory could be built on the assumption of an atomistic electorate. Pressures from constituents on elected representatives and public officials which, though individually biased, would in the aggregate serve to guide them toward the public interest. Concentration of much production into the hands of a relatively few giant corporations conflicts with the assumptions of traditional political theory and presents a set of problems which have been recognized but are far from being thought through or dealt with adequately. Such measures as those which prevent corporate contributions to political parties and which require registration of corporate lobbyists are moves in that direction. But the power of corporations on government far exceeds the bounds suggested by these measures. To some extent, it is offset by the pressures from labor organizations and other organized groups. But it still represents a major pressure. The problem is to determine the ramifications of this pressure and to develop the balances which will result in government in the public interest.

V. Conclusion

This article has sought to appraise the degree of corporate concentration and the major problems of public policy which this concentration has engendered. It has examined the changes brought about by concentration for the economy as a whole and the problems this has created in the economy-wide policies with respect to total employment, inflation, and the balance of external payments. It has examined the changes in the dominant form of competition and the major problems these have created with respect to the use of resources and the distribution of income. It has sketched other major problems arising from corporate concentration or associated with it, but lying outside the areas of overall economic policy and competition. Any effort of an individual to classify major and minor problems is necessarily subjective. Others attempting the same task would undoubtedly include other problems as major and exclude some the author has included, or would state them differently, or would find a different relation between the problems and corporate concentration. In any event, although it is important to clarify the major problems of public policy created by corporate concentration, an even more important task is to find solutions.

Notes

1. *Washington Post,* June 2, 1966.

2. W. Ripley, *Railroads* 456 (1915).

3. *See* Appendix.

4. J. Fred Weston, *Hearings on Economic Concentration before the Subcomm. on Antitrust and Monopoly of the Senate Comm. on the Judiciary,* 88th Cong., 2d Sess., pt. 1 at 140 (1964).

5. Northern Securities v. United States, 193 U.S. 197 (1904).

6. *See* Appendix.

7. *See* Appendix.

8. *See* Appendix.

9. W. Mueller, *Hearing on Economic Concentration before the Subcomm. on Antitrust and Monopoly of the Senate Comm. on the Judiciary,* 91st Cong., 1st Sess. (1969).

10. *Id.* at 7a, fig. 2. "Substantial mergers" include all mergers in which the acquired corporation had assets of $10 million or more.

11. In 1964, 64 percent of the value of farm marketings were made by family farms, *i.e.,* farms employing no more than one hired worker (or the equivalent) per year, up from 63 percent in 1959.

12. U.S. Dep't of Commerce, *Historical Statistics of the United States* 413 (1960) (for 1900 measured by value of products in 1899).

13. *Statistical Abstracts for the United States* (1969).

14. *See* Appendix.

15. *Id.*

16. *Hearings on Economic Concentration before the Subcomm. on Antitrust and Monopoly of the Senate Comm. on the Judiciary,* 88th Cong., 2d Sess., pt. 1, at 18 (1964) [hereinafter cited as *Senate Hearings*].

17. *See* G. Nutter, *Extent of Enterprise Monopoly in the United States* (1951); Adelman, "The Measurement of Industrial Concentration," 33 *Rev. of Econ. & Statistics* 287 (1951).

The Nutter monograph is concerned with the relative importance of monopoly and concentration *in relation to the market;* rather than overall concentration. It attempts to measure market concentration around 1900 and again in 1937. It concludes that there was somewhat less *monopoly* in the latter year than at the turn of the century.

This conclusion depends in part on a peculiar definition of monopoly, which includes railroads as a monopolized industry in 1900 and as a competitive industry in 1937. A more practical definition which treated railroads as regulated monopolies in both periods would have reversed the finding and shown an increase in monopoly even under Nutter's definition of monopoly for other activities. The subjective character of Nutter's other classifications has also been brought out in Lebergott's criticisms. *See* Lebergott, *Senate Hearings, supra* note 16, at 343. *See also* G. Nutter, *Senate Hearings, supra* note 16, at 345.

Nutter's questionable finding has often been treated as a finding that *overall concentration* declined in this period. But there is nothing inconsistent between a decline in monopoly, which is concerned with *concentration in the market,* and an increase in *overall concentration.* If a steel company acquires a structural steel fabricating company, this may add to overall concentration, but it does not alter the degree of concentration in the production of steel. If an automobile company adds electric refrigerators and railway locomotives to its activity, market concentration may go down while overall concentration goes up. Whether overall concentration in manufacturing, or for the economy as a whole, occurred between 1900 and 1937 cannot be deduced from the Nutter analysis. The question of concentration in relation to the market will be examined in a later section when competition is being discussed.

The second monograph by Adelman purports to show among other things, that there has been no tendency for concentration to increase from 1931 to 1947. But the analysis is so crude that the estimates have no significance for the following reasons.

First, the depression year, 1931, is used as the base of measurement, in spite of the fact that the assets of the 200 largest nonfinancial corporations had increased 3 percent from 1929 to 1931 while the assets of all other nonfinancial corporations had shrunk 24 percent in the two years of depression. *Senate Hearings, supra* note 16 at 311. Clearly a depression year is unsuitable as a base.

Second, Adelman uses unadjusted Treasury figures with no attempt to adjust or even discuss the important changes in the basis of competition, with no adjustment for the serious under-consolidation of subsidiaries which changed markedly over the period, with no adjustment or mention of the double counting of assets which arises from the holding by one corporation of the stocks of another which it does not control, and with no attempt to deal with net capital assets which involve no duplication and are more fundamental to the problem of overall concentration.

Third, Adelman disregarded completely the most reliable estimates of concentration available for a nondepression year, those for 1929, which were made directly from tax returns of the larger corporations with reasonable complete consolidation of all legally controlled companies. *See Senate Hearings, supra* note 16, at 287.

Finally, Adelman's general findings are at direct variance with the findings of others, including the staff of the Federal Trade Commission, the staff of the Senate Antitrust Committee, and my own.

For a more detailed critique of Adelman's estimates see G. Means, *Thoughts on Concentration, Proceedings of the Business and Economic Section of the American Statistical Association* 123–26 (1962).

Professor Adelman presented similar figures with essentially the same flaws, covering the period from 1931 to 1960, to the Senate Committee on Antitrust and Monopoly. They show no attempt to meet the above criticisms. *Senate Hearings, supra* note 16, at 234–40.

18. *Senate Hearings, supra* note 16, at 121.

19. Estimates made by the author on the basis of reliable data given above for the largest 100 manufacturing corporations plus crude estimates for the second hundred largest form the basis for these figures.

20. G. Means, *The Structure of the American Economy* 107 (1939).

21. Keynes indicates that the classical economists *assumed* full employment and that their theory "is best regarded as a theory of distribution in conditions of full employment." J. Keynes, *General Theory of Employment, Interest and Money* 16 (1936). *See also Id.* at 6. As a result he presents no argument to show that the classical mechanism could not be expected to work under the flexible market-price conditions they assumed or that the introduction of liquidity preference to the flexible market-price economy would inhibit the working of the classical corrective mechanism.

22. Source for wholesale price index and unemployment is *Economic Report of the President* 252, 282 (1969); source for flexible market prices is G. Means, *Pricing Power and the Public Interest* 63 (1962) [hereinafter cited as *Pricing*].

23. See *Pricing, supra* note 22, at 112–50.

24. The designations, "imperfect competition" and "monopolistic competition" are rejected here, partly because classical competition was probably never "perfect" as that has been defined nor does the newly recognized type of competition involve monopoly, and partly because the theoretical analysis of business behavior presented under these heads does not appear to apply to most actual business behavior.

25. *Pricing, supra* note 22, at 240.

Appendix

Figure 15.1A **Recorded Mergers in Manufacturing and Mining**
1895–1914

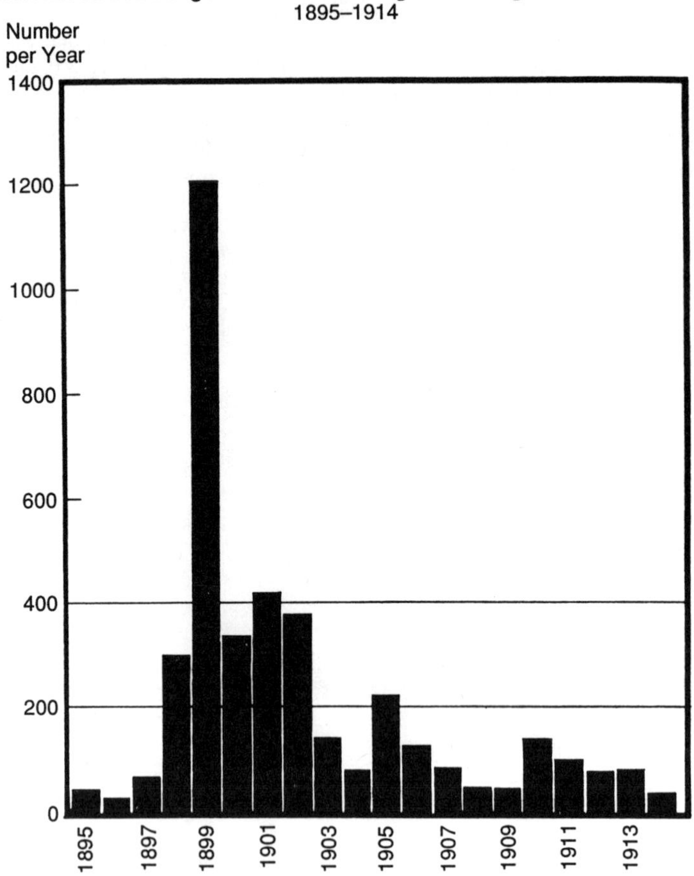

Source: R. Nelson, *Merger Movements in American Industry*, ch. III, Appendix B (1959).

Figure 15.2A **Number of Mergers and Acquisitions in Manufacturing and Mining**
1919–1961

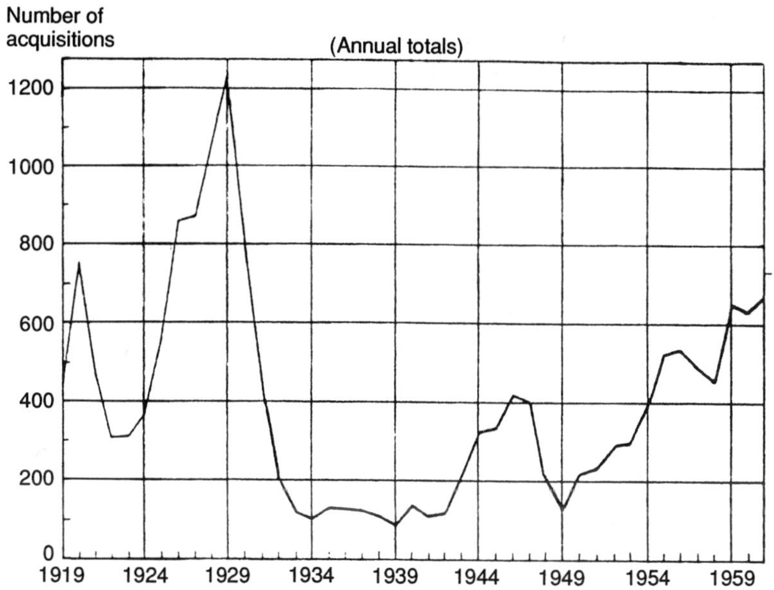

Sources: Temporary National Economic Committee, Monograph No. 27, 1919–1939; Federal Trade Commission, 1940–1961.

Figure 15.3A **Manufacturing and Mining Firms Acquired**
1948–1969

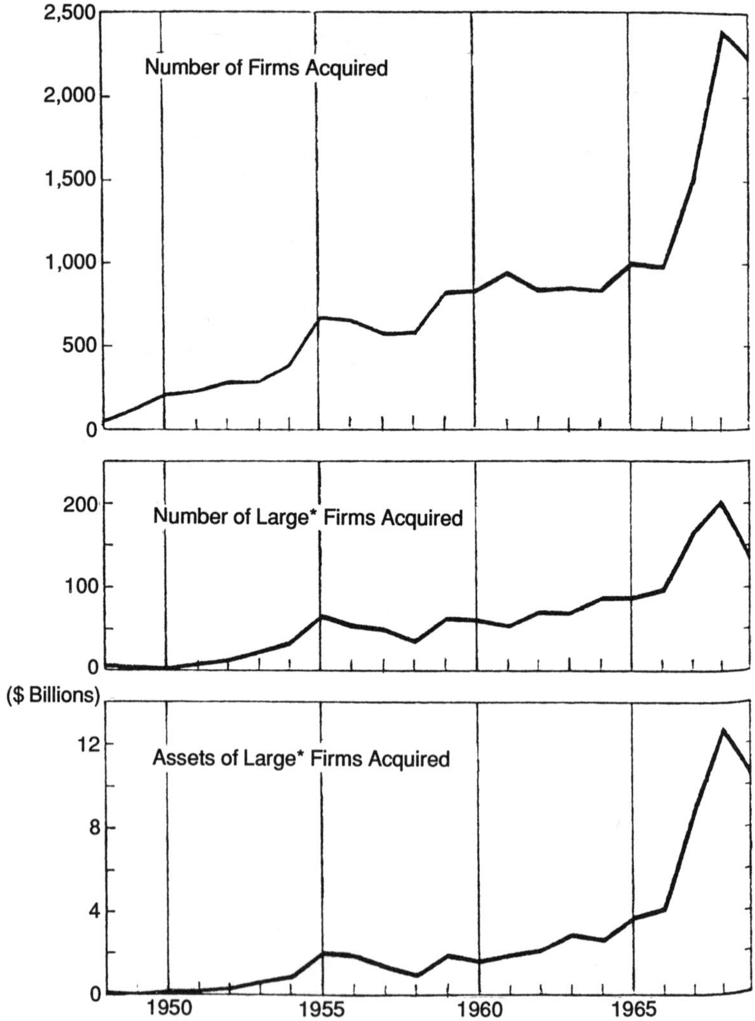

*Firms with assets of $10 million or more.

Source: Bureau of Economics, Federal Trade Commission, *Current Trends in Merger Activity*, 6 (1970).

Figure 15.4A **Shares of Total Assets and Net Capital Assets in Manufacturing Held by 100 Largest Manufacturing Companies**
1947–1968

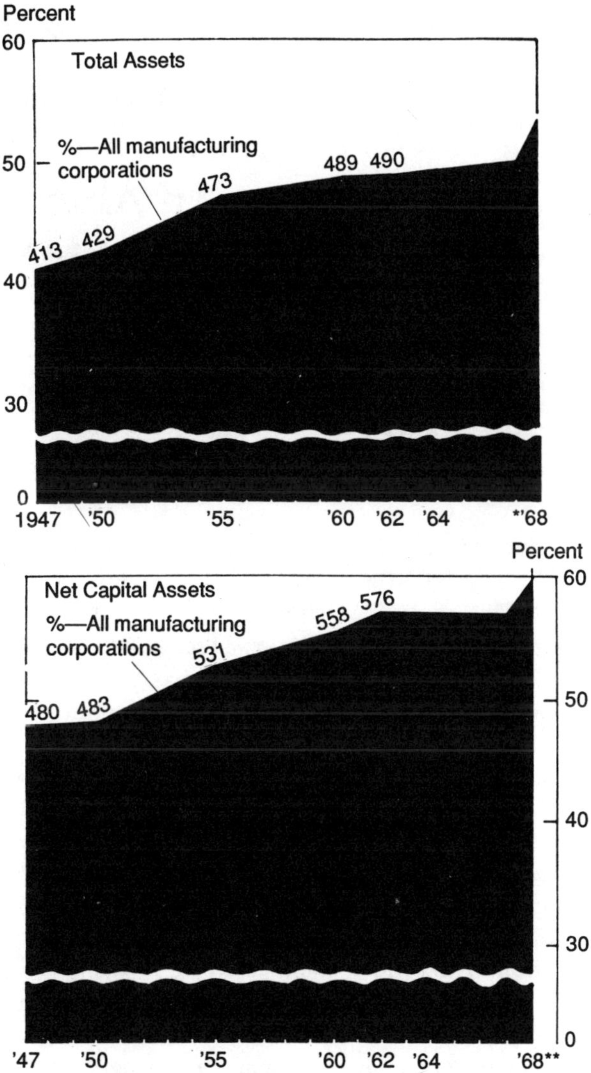

Source: Bureau of Economics, Federal Trade Commission, *Economic Concentration,* pt. 1, p. 206.

*Corporations, proprietorships, and partnerships.

**Annual rate based on first 6 months for the year 1968.

16

How to Control Inflation in the United States: An Alternative to "Planned Stagnation"

A Faulty Diagnosis

For five and a half years the Nixon administration sought to control inflation and failed. The index of wholesale prices rose 50 percent and the consumer index rose 40 percent. This great failure in policy has come from a faulty diagnosis. The inflation has been treated as a traditional type of inflation, a general demand inflation coming from too much money chasing too few goods. Yet at no time in those five and a half years was there such a general excess in demand.

Most of the inflation of the last five and a half years has involved a new type of inflation, one new to the theory of inflation and not experienced in this country prior to World War II. It grows out of the market power of big business and big labor. In the concentrated industries, the market forces of demand and cost do not determine prices but only limit the range within which price can be set. Within this range, management has an area of discretion in pricing which can lead to inflation. And no excess in demand is necessary to bring it about. This new type of inflation will be referred to here as "administrative inflation" because it arises so largely from the private power to administer prices within a substantial range of discretion. The instant article will briefly review the emergence of this new type of inflation, examine the bungling effort of the Nixon administration to control it, explore its anatomy, and finally propose a positive program to bring it under control.

Reprinted with permission from the *Wage-Price Law & Economics Review* 1, 1 (1975), pp. 47–74.

The Emergence of Administrative Inflation

The first appearance of administrative inflation came in the Eisenhower years. In the five years between 1954 and 1959, the wholesale price index went up 8 percent in spite of the fact that unemployment averaged more than 5 percent and in no year averaged as low as 4 percent. This is to be compared with the absence of inflation in 1953 when unemployment was 2.9 percent and the Korean War price controls had just been removed. This 8 percent rise in wholesale prices during 1954–59 was almost entirely in the concentrated industries, with at least half attributable to the direct and indirect effect of a 36 percent steel price increase. If the rise in the wholesale price index had resulted from demand inflation, it would have appeared primarily in the non-concentrated parts of the economy.

The Federal Reserve Board regarded this mild inflation as a case of traditional demand inflation and adopted a tight money policy which brought a contraction in the money stock and in general demand. While this effort to control administrative inflation by a general contraction of demand produced the recession of 1957–58, it did not halt the administrative inflation. Fortunately, however, the inability of tight money to halt administrative inflation ultimately came to be recognized at the Federal Reserve Board and its restrictive policy was finally reversed. As Dr. Woodlief Thomas, then a chief economist of the Board, wrote in a letter to the *Washington Post* (March 12, 1959): "[T]here are unstabilizing forces in the pricing actions of the private economy—on the part of both management and labor—that cannot be effectively controlled by governmental actions in the area of fiscal and monetary policies."

The Kennedy Guideposts

The Kennedy forces took over in 1961 at a time when nearly 7 percent of the labor force was unemployed and only 73 percent of manufacturing capacity was being utilized. It set out to achieve high employment without inflation. Its economic advisers had learned the lesson of administrative inflation and adopted a program to resist its push through price and wage guideposts combined with persuasion, while fiscal and monetary measures were used to expand general demand. From 1961 to 1965, general demand was increased by a third with a rise in the wholesale price index of only 3 percent. The wage and price guideposts, plus persuasion, were indeed over-successful in holding down wage rates and moderately successful in holding down prices in the concentrated industries. As a result of the great increase in general demand and the resistance to administrative inflation, industry was operating at 89 percent of capacity by the end of 1965 and unemployment was down to approximately 4 percent. Unfortunately, however, the Kennedy guidepost for wages had been badly designed. It appropriately called for wage increases to take account of increases in national productivity but it left no room for the natural increase in the cost of living, an essential part of recovery from 7 percent unemployment to 4 percent. A normal recovery would call for increased sales, production, and employment in the more concentrated part of the economy and increases in prices in the least concentrated, such as farming. Thus some "reflation" should have been expected and a cost-of-living factor should have been included in the wage guidepost.

Labor's Losses of 1961–65

This factor was intentionally excluded from the wage guidepost, however, because it was believed that it would create a dangerous upward spiral. A "living-cost" increase in wages would be passed on in higher prices and these, in turn, would justify further wage increases. What was not realized was that this spiral would have been self-limiting, with each round of it producing only a fraction of the price increase justified by the previous round. This would be true because labor is only part of the overall cost of goods and because concentrated industry is only part of the total economy. This normal price rise in the unconcentrated part of the economy did occur and the resulting cost-of-living rise took away nearly half of the productivity gain which workers should have received over those five years, 1961–65.

This inadequate wage guidepost also allowed profit margins in the concentrated industries to be increased somewhat without adding to price increases, thus producing, in the division of income between capital and labor, a shift against labor. In the previous decade capital had received as interest, dividends, and undistributed profits approximately 12½ percent of the income generated by non-financial corporations and divided between capital and labor. Labor had received 87½ percent in wages, salaries, and fringe benefits. By the end of 1965 the compensation to capital had risen to 16 percent of the joint income and compensation to labor was down to 84 percent. The failure to include some cost-of-living adjustment was manifestly unfair to labor.

The Labor Revolt

Up to mid-1965 labor had in very large degree adhered to the wage guidepost, an action made easier by management's resistance to wage increases in excess of those indicated by the guideposts. But then the unfairness of the wage guidepost soon became so clear that labor rebelled and insisted on wage increases greater than the guidepost allowed. The result was administrative inflation during the next two years as labor sought to catch up on living costs and management sought to retain its widened profit margins. The wholesale price index went up at the rate of 1.7 percent a year in the two years from mid-1965 to mid-1967. While these two years of administrative inflation have often been regarded as a general demand inflation resulting from the requirements of the Vietnam war, there is little evidence of any such general excess in demand. In farm prices, an area where a general excess would be expected to show itself first, there was only a 1.0 percent a year price rise, which must be attributed to the decline in crop yields in 1966. Most of the two-year rise was in the more concentrated industries. In manufacturing, for example, there was a reduction in the amount of over-time hours worked and a smaller proportion of industrial capacity was used in 1967 than in 1965. These figures do not suggest an excess in general demand.

Inflation from Excess Demand

In the latter half of 1967 and early 1968, however, there *was* true demand inflation combined with some administrative inflation. While the money stock was increasing at only a normal rate (6.6 percent in 1967 and 7.8 percent in 1968), the economic budget was $12 billion in deficit ($25 billion deficit in the administrative budget). Unemployment averaged 3.5 percent and during the fiscal year manufacturing operated at 85 percent of capacity. But there was a rise in the wholesale price index of 2.3 percent. How much of this was demand inflation and how much administrative is difficult to say. Certainly the demand-inflation part was short-lived. At the beginning of 1967, President Johnson, foreseeing the inflationary effect of the Vietnam expenditures, requested a surtax, a request that was repeated in the summer of that year and at the beginning of 1968. Finally, in August 1968, the 10 percent surtax was passed and by the end of 1968 was bringing in a budget surplus at an annual rate of $10 billion. This, plus a slower rate of growth in the money stock, eliminated the general excess in demand. Wage rates had also caught up with the cost-of-living increases by early 1968 and the long-run balance between compensation to labor and compensation to capital had been re-established. With cost-of-living adjustments included, the guideposts, plus persuasion, again became a reasonably effective way of controlling administrative inflation. Combined with a budget surplus and moderate monetary growth, inflation at the wholesale level was limited to 1.1 percent in the eight months before the election in November 1968.

The Bumbling Nixon Policies

It is abundantly clear that Nixon and his economic advisers did not understand administrative inflation. Our economy was in excellent condition at the time he came into office. The surtax was producing a Federal surplus at the rate of $10 billion a year. The money stock was growing at the moderate rate of 4 percent a year. There was no excess in demand. The balance in external payments was favorable. Demand inflation from the Vietnam war had been brought under control and administrative inflation was being controlled by a moderate program of price-wage guidelines. Manufacturing industry was operating at 87 percent of capacity. Employment was high, with the seasonally adjusted unemployment rate under 3.5 percent. The wholesale price index had risen only 1.1 percent in the eight months before the election. And the balance between the compensation to capital and the compensation to labor was good. The stage was set for a period of high employment without serious inflation. But Nixon's economic advisers were tied to the traditional conception of inflation as *demand* inflation with too much money chasing too few goods. They had not learned the lesson taught by the abortive tight-money effort to control administrative inflation in the 1950s, the partial success of the guideposts in the early 1960s, or the final success in 1968. Their thinking was dominated by the traditional idea of inflation as the result of a general excess of demand and a tight money policy as the accepted way to prevent further inflation. This conception dominated Nixon economic policies.

The Five Nixon Game Plans

Nixon adopted five different economic game plans to control inflation in the five and a half years of his incumbency. Yet the index of wholesale prices rose by more than 50 percent, the rate of plant utilization was low, and unemployment was high. Some of the price rise resulted from crop failures, the Arab cut-off of oil, and from other foreign developments. But even leaving out farm products and food and fuel, the wholesale index went up 32 percent in his five and a half years, an average rate of approximately 6 percent a year. It is only necessary to look at the five Nixon game plans and the faulty interpretation of actual conditions they reflected to see how little that administration's advisers understood of the actual workings of our economy.

Planned Stagnation

On achieving office, Nixon *immediately* canceled the guidepost program, announcing that he would rely entirely on free market forces to determine prices and wage rates. Further, he adopted a program of planned stagnation to "bring inflation under control," one based on the belief that the 8 percent rise in the wholesale price index during the preceding four years was entirely of the traditional demand inflation. Thus in his first *Economic Report,* President Nixon said that "the growth of total spending, public and private," was the "driving force" of the inflation that "had gathered powerful momentum" by the time his administration took office. His first game plan was thus to eliminate this assumed "momentum" by halting the growth in total demand for a year, thereby intentionally increasing unemployment to more than 5 percent and, while allowing some growth, generally holding this stagnation level for two more years.

"Unleashing" Market Power

This ruthless program was carried out but, in spite of a large budget surplus, almost complete cessation in monetary growth, and a substantial decline in real demand, wholesale prices rose in 1969 and 1970 *faster* than in any of the preceding five years. Instead of reducing inflation, this program stimulated it and created a recession as well, bringing utilization of manufacturing capacity down to 74 percent of capacity—a 15 percent drop—and raising the unemployment rate to 6 percent. The wholesale price index rose 7.2 percent in two years, an annual rate of 3.6 percent in spite of a recession. Clearly the diagnosis was wrong. Why? The answer is simple. At the beginning of 1969 there was no demand inflation. The real problem was the *new* type of industrial inflation, one that arises from the market power of big business and big labor and that cannot be controlled by the traditional prescription of limiting demand. What Nixon did on taking office was to adopt a program which could not control administrative inflation and publicly eliminated the guidepost program that *had* held such inflation in substantial check. *He unleashed the "unstabilizing forces" of market power.*

The "Conversion" to Keynes

When it became clear after two years that his "stagnation" program was a failure, President Nixon announced his conversion to what he called the Keynes doctrine. Both fiscal and monetary policy had been made somewhat expansive in the spring of 1970, as planned in the original stagnation program. But in the winter of 1970–71, unemployment seasonally adjusted averaged 6 percent and manufacturing was operating at less than 75 percent of capacity. In these circumstances, the President in his 1971 *Economic Report* adopted what he called the principle of the "full employment budget." This called for a budget which would balance at full employment but would automatically provide a substantial deficit when employment is low, partly because revenues would tend to be lower and partly because government expenses, especially unemployment insurance payments, would tend to be higher. Following this principle, the Nixon administration proceeded to develop budgets which produced the largest economic deficits since World War II. But this second game plan, like the first, relied on free markets to control prices and *practically the whole of the increase in buying power that was generated by the expansionist fiscal and monetary measures was absorbed by price increases.* In the eight months to August 1971, wholesale prices rose at the annual rate of 5.3 percent, partly because of poor harvests in 1970 but primarily because of the large increase in the industrial price index. This index rose at an annual rate of 4.5 percent during that period in spite of the fact that less than 75 percent of manufacturing capacity was being utilized and unemployment was still over 6 percent. No effort was made to control administrative inflation despite the fact that the rise in prices in the presence of the large volume of unused manpower and equipment made it clear that something other than excess demand was causing the inflation. Again the diagnosis was wrong.

The New Economic Policy

The failure of this second game plan was evident by the summer of 1971, with inflation rampant in a depression, a condition theoretically impossible according to the traditional theory of the free market on which the advisers to the President relied. On the 15th of August, 1971, he suddenly announced a third game plan, one he called "The New Economic Policy." This one, which included a price-wage "freeze" to be followed shortly by Phase II with more flexible controls, finally faced the fact that traditional policy could not control inflation (though it is doubtful that the *reasons* for this fact were well understood). The essence of this plan was to resist inflation directly while a huge deficit and a more rapid expansion in the money stock expanded demand, production, and employment. It was announced as a general inflation control program and made no clear distinction between the objective of controlling *market* prices and that of controlling *administered* prices. It was remarkably successful, however, in limiting *administrative* inflation. In the 16 months of Phases I and II, the index of industrial prices rose at the annual rate of only 2.8 percent (compared to 4.5 percent in the year before the freeze) and much of this rise was in non-concentrated industrial products such as lumber, textiles, and leather. In the corporate sector of the economy where most of the market power of big business and big labor resides, the inflation rate dropped from 4.0 percent in the year before the price freeze to 1.3 percent in the year after it. This limiting of inflation was accomplished without markedly changing the relation between the compensation to labor and the compensation to capital.

Phases I and II a Success

The very substantial degree of this success in controlling administrative inflation was hidden, however, by three developments which raised prices in the non-concentrated sectors of the economy. The first was crop failure, mostly abroad, which contracted the world food and feed supply and engendered the big grain exports to Russia. The second was in the international field where a combination of dollar devaluation and heavy demand inflation abroad raised import prices and stimulated exports. The third was the normal rise in the prices of the non-concentrated products such as food, lumber, and scrap steel, a rise that was to be expected from an expansion in real demand that raised real GNP at the rate of 7 percent a year, brought industrial utilization up to nearly 82 percent of capacity, and brought unemployment down from 6 to 5 percent. As a result of these three developments, farm prices rose in the 16 months of Phases I and II by 21 percent, hides and leather products by 24 percent, lumber by 11 percent, fuel by 6 percent, and textiles by 5 percent. These and similar competitive items accounted for most of the 7 percent rise in the wholesale price index and the 4.3 percent rise in the consumer price index in that period. None of these represented an exercise of market power by big business or big labor. And they should not be allowed to disguise the very substantial success of the Phase II program in resisting *administrative* inflation. The rise in farm prices due to the world-wide reduction in farm supply and the rise in flexible market prices from the partial recovery would have happened whether or not administrative inflation had been controlled and does not indicate a failure of the control program. It emphasizes, rather, the inability of price controls alone to limit a rise in traditional market prices.

A Failure of Understanding

The true failure here was again the failure of the Nixon administration to understand the character of the inflation in question. It should have accepted the small reflation as a necessary and temporary part of the process of bringing prices into balance during recovery. It should have recognized the price rise from crop failures as a misfortune that hopefully would soon be reversed by normal crops. It acted wisely in adjusting the external value of the dollar and in expanding farm acreage. It should have recognized the success of the control program in limiting administrative inflation and kept it in operation.

Dismantling Controls

Having concluded that Phase II was no longer needed, President Nixon set up his fourth game plan in January 1973, one designed, however, to dismantle the controls over a period of months. It was not only based on inapplicable theory but was so badly designed that it ended in chaos. This new plan rested on the *major assumption that there had been a "momentum" of inflation when he took office in 1969 which had been largely eliminated by Phases I and II.* This is shown in the President's *Economic Report* of January 1973, which said that, by the end of 1972, not only had there been a suppression of price increases but "a more durable change had taken place in the conditions underlying wage and price increases. Expectations of rapid inflation," according to this *Report* (p. 68), had "diminished." In other words, the "momentum" of inflation had been largely overcome at that point. This diagnosis in terms of traditional theory and the failure to understand the role of administrative inflation produced the confusion and chaos of Phase III. The Phase II control organization, one that had been working well in limiting the arbitrary use of market power by big business and big labor, was suddenly dismantled and a new and less well-designed operation was set up. Controls were abolished or made self-administered for most nonfood commodities and services but kept on for foods where they could not be expected to work without rationing. The President's abhorrence of price controls was made clear without any equally clear recognition of their role in limiting administrative inflation.

A Widening of Profit Margins

Phase III was widely interpreted as a signal that price restraints had come to an end and industrial prices shot up, rising in five months at an annual rate of 14 percent compared to the 2.8 percent rate of Phases I and II. While a part of this rapid increase was an adjustment for increased labor and material costs, to an important extent it was a *widening of profit margins.* For manufacturing corporations, profits per dollar of sales increased at an annual rate of more than 40 percent during these months while hourly wage rates in manufacturing went up at an annual rate of less than 6 percent. The developments in this period are highly confused because of the several sources of inflation that were present, particularly the continuing effect of inflation abroad and rising meat prices at home. But it appears that a considerable part of this burst of inflation was administrative and not directly related to either a contraction in supply or an expansion in specific demand. And certainly it was not a product of a *general* excess of demand. Manufacturing in the second quarter of 1973 was operating at little more than 83 percent of capacity and unemployment in that quarter was nearly 5 percent.

A Loss of Credibility

Faced with this sudden price surge, the Nixon administration again instituted a freeze on prices for two months and, in August of 1973, introduced Phase IV, a game plan that expired with the law at the end of May in 1974 and left industrial prices (other than fuel) up 17 percent since the end of Phase II. The in-and-out policy of that administration, the lack of a clear realization of the non-traditional character of much of the inflation it had attempted to deal with, the sharp rise of prices in the last year and a half of its leadership, and the continued high unemployment had combined to destroy any credibility in its grasp of the inflation-employment problem.

More Planned Stagnation

Nixon then introduced his final stagflation game plan. As it was explained by the President on July 25th, it calls for more planned stagnation: "In the short run we must focus on measures to restrain demand," this restraint being described as follows: "As far as the federal government is concerned we will cut the growth of Federal spending. We will hold down the growth of money and credit to check private spending. And I will call on state and local governments, on businesses and consumers to hold down their own spending and increase their own saving as their contribution to the fight against higher prices." Most families, he added, "could reduce or defer some expenditures, building their savings instead." This takes us back to square one, the planned stagnation of the first game plan, with three important differences: (1) The wholesale price index is 50 percent higher and the industrial price index is rising at a double-digit rate. The rate of inflation before the 1968 election was almost negligible by comparison. (2) National production is well below our full potential, with unemployment at the rate of 5.8 percent instead of 3.5 percent and industrial plant operation at only 80 percent of rated capacity instead of the 87.7 percent that prevailed in

1968. (3) A dangerous degree of illiquidity has been created through the tight money policy of these last few years. The money stock *in constant dollars,* for example, has been reduced in the last year by between 4 and 8 percent, depending on the price index used to deflate, an illiquidity that is reflected in the highest short-term interest rates in a century.

The program announced by President Ford continues the essentials of this most unsuccessful game plan. The call is for less spending by consumers and continued tight money. His advisers are still confusing the problems of demand inflation and those of administrative inflation.

A Shocking Misinterpretation

The administration's truly shocking misinterpretation of the basic forces making for inflation can be brought out by comparing the recent behavior of the group price indexes for the more competitive industry groups in the BLS wholesale price index with the behavior of those for the more concentrated groups. Between June 1973 and June 1974, for example, the wholesale price index rose 14 percent, with perhaps half of this being attributable to the direct and indirect effects of the 58 percent rise in the index for fuel prices. But the other half appears almost entirely in the indexes for the more concentrated groups of industries. Of the 15 group indexes that make up the wholesale price index, 5 are properly classed as competition-dominated, including farm products, food, lumber, textiles, and leather. A weighted price index for these groups increased by only 2 percent during this period and so contributed little to the 14 percent inflation. In contrast, a weighted price index for the 6 group indexes which can properly be classed as dominated by concentrated industries rose 22 percent and accounted for most of the inflation at the wholesale level other than that due to fuel price increases.

To interpret the inflation of this period as a general demand inflation and attempt to control it by tight money and recession is the extreme of folly. It is obvious that there was no general excess in demand or it would have been reflected in a substantial rise in prices in the competitive industries. To try to control the rise in fuel prices by contracting general demand, for example, is to cut the face to spite the nose. Labor did not push up wage rates enough in this period to maintain its real income. And, as will be seen when the anatomy of administrative inflation is examined below, stagnation or recession simply cannot control this latter type of inflation.

Expansion of Demand Needed

The Ford plan to limit demand might be appropriate if the present inflation were caused by a general excess of demand. But at no time in the last five and a half years has there been such a general excess of demand or a demand inflation. For this reason, a program to limit demand would mean continued stagnation or, worse still, further recession, an aggravation of a dangerous degree of illiquidity, and a continuation or stimulation of administrative inflation. Because the current inflation is largely administrative in character and because we can produce much more goods and services than we are now producing, the immediate problem is to *expand* demand and make sure that this additional demand is not absorbed by price increases in the more concentrated industries. Clearly Ford's economic advisers have not yet learned the lesson of administrative inflation, a lesson that was learned with much trial and error in the Eisenhower-Kennedy-Johnson era.

The Anatomy of Administrative Inflation

In order to reach full employment and to control administrative inflation, it is first necessary to understand more clearly how the latter comes about. According to traditional theory, administrative inflation is not possible. Prices are *determined* by supply and demand. Specific price increases can arise from unplanned reductions in supply such as crop failures or an oil cut-off and these can add to the level of prices. But the only source of general inflation is an excess in demand, one that can be controlled by appropriate monetary and fiscal measures.

Pricing in the Competitive Sector

There would be no reason to question this theory if each product in the economy were produced by a multitude of enterprises. No producer would have a significant degree of market power, a condition under which wheat and cotton and hogs and scrap steel are produced. With a general fall in demand, their prices fall. With a general rise in demand, their prices rise. The government can limit the supply in order to support the price but it cannot for long prevent price increases when demand rises without some form of rationing. And if price control is temporarily successful, prices rise when the controls are removed. If such products were typical of the whole economy, the only form of general inflation would be that from a general excess of demand and this type of inflation could indeed be controlled by limiting general demand.

Role of 'Entry' Conditions

Traditional theory would also apply if there were only a few suppliers in each market for goods but it was easy for newcomers to break into the market. Then the few sellers, even though they had enough market power to set their own prices, would be closely controlled in the prices they set by the market considerations of demand and costs. With easy entry, any attempt to set prices significantly above a competitive level would tend to bring in new competitors, thus reducing the share of the market held by each and cutting profits per enterprise even though profit margins were increased. Once prices were adjusted to demand

and costs, in other words, those in a position to administer prices would have little pricing discretion since the fear of bringing in new competition would tend to keep prices close to costs plus a competitive profit. In these circumstances, demand inflation would be the primary type of inflation and it could, as noted, be controlled by limiting demand.

It is when we examine situations involving big business, big labor, and difficult entry that we find traditional theory does not apply. It is in industries such as steel, automobiles, and many other highly concentrated industries that the traditional principles of pricing become unreal and actual pricing can lead to administrative inflation. We will first consider the very difficult problem faced by management in setting prices where there is a protective wall of difficult entry and only a few producers. Then we will examine the respective contributions of management and labor in generating administrative inflation.

Management's Pricing Problem

Traditional theory gives management a relatively simple problem in setting the price for a particular product, one that is simply stated in the economist's jargon: "Set the price which will equate marginal cost and marginal revenue." The economist can show you with simple diagrams why this will result in the maximum profit. It is also easy for him to show you that, if all enterprises adhered to this formula, administrative inflation would not be possible.

Here we do not need to understand this formula because a big business which priced on this basis would be most unbusinesslike. The traditional economist is only talking about the price which would maximize the profit *in the very short run,* e.g., in the coming week or the coming month. But the successful corporate management is not trying to set a price which will maximize profits "this week" or "this month." It is trying to adopt, instead, a current price as a step in developing pricing policies which will bring in high profits over a period of years. The current price which would maximize short-run profit would almost invariably defeat this larger purpose.

Pricing to Restrict Entry

The basic problem of management with substantial pricing discretion is therefore to set a current price which will bring in good profits now and not prevent good profits *later.* A current price which brought in *too high* corporate profits now could be expected to induce other enterprises to climb over the wall of difficult entry and take away part of the market even if they did not force lower prices. Loss of market share means lower long-run profits. Therefore the price which would be most profitable in the short run could reduce the opportunity for future profits. In this and other ways the management in its pricing has to balance greater profits now against the prospects of greater profits later. As a result, *the prices actually set tend to be significantly below those which would bring in the maximum profit in the current week or month.*

Demand and Cost Uncertainty

The necessity of balancing more short-run profits against more longer-run profits also means that there is a *range* of possible current prices which are just about equally good. A higher current price can mean greater current profit but a greater risk of lower profits later, whatever the price that will be charged then. A lower current price, on the other hand, can mean less current profits but a better prospect of future profits. Thus even if management *knew* what its demand and costs would be, there would still be a range of prices among which it would be difficult to choose and between which the management would likely be relatively indifferent. In practice, moreover, there is in fact a great deal of uncertainty about demand and costs over any considerable period of time. This tends to increase the ''zone of indifference'' as to the exact price which is the most profitable in the longer run.

Pricing by Formula

Because of the great difficulty of setting prices, managements have simplified the pricing process in two major ways. First, they have adopted one or another of a variety of pricing formulas, such as pricing for a target rate of return, full-cost pricing, standard mark-up pricing, index pricing, and break-even pricing. Second, they tend to hold prices constant for months at a time, changing them only when changed conditions call for a very substantial price shift, one that is beyond the zone of relative indifference. For example, basic steel prices are so seldom changed that, when a change is made of, say, 5 or 10 or 15 percent, it becomes front page news. Similarly, the factory price of an auto is usually set for a year at a time. Just what triggers a price change thus becomes of vital importance in considering the problem of inflation.

The Upward Bias in Administrative Pricing

Neither the use of pricing formulas nor the practice of infrequent large price changes is in itself a cause of administrative inflation but there is a tendency under them for management to be more sensitive to cost increases than to cost declines for a number of reasons. Cost increases, for example, tend to be ''passed through'' because they usually come from outside the enterprise and can be blamed on outside forces. Cost reductions, on the other hand, are likely to be the result of management's own constructive activity in seeking greater efficiency and management naturally takes credit for them. Unless the cost reduction is large, management is not likely to reduce the price. The magnitude of the cost change needed to trigger a price rise thus tends to be somewhat smaller than that needed to trigger a price reduction. There is a further tendency, moreover, to make an upward price change a little *larger* than a particular cost increase calls for and to make a price reduction a little smaller than such a cost reduction calls for. Management's reaction to changes in costs is not a balanced one. In each case, there tends to be a small departure from the dictates of demand and costs and in both cases the departure is up, thus reinforcing the upward creep.

The Price Creep from Increasing Productivity

This small tendency toward an upward price creep is further reinforced by increasing productivity. There is nothing inherent in higher output per worker-hour which is inflationary. When national production per worker-hour goes up because of improved technology, it is to be expected that both labor and capital would share in the gain, certainly in a small-enterprise economy. But in a big-business economy, the process by which the sharing is brought about can lead to an inflationary creep. Under traditional theory (the one applicable to a small-enterprise economy), if the total real income produced jointly by a given body of workers and a given real amount of capital were to increase, the real compensation to workers could be expected to go up because real wage rates would rise. At the same time, the compensation to capital would be expected to rise, not because profit margins increased but because, as the quantity sold increased, the same profit margin per unit would bring in a greater total profit. This could be expected to occur where there was no pricing power. In the presence of substantial pricing discretion, however, and the upward bias in administrative pricing, the adjustment for increased productivity would be expected to produce an upward creep in prices in two ways. This creep would come in part from the reaction of an average producer to the rise in wage rates required by the improved technology. It would also come in part from differences in the rate of increase in productivity in different industries.

Productivity Gains 'Overlooked' in Pricing

Consider, for example, a product for which productivity has increased by just the amount of the increase in national productivity, e.g., national productivity has increased 3 percent and wage rates have appropriately increased 3 percent. Assume further that, in the case of this particular product, output per worker has also gone up 3 percent. In this case the *labor cost* per unit of output would not change and hence there would be no economic justification for a price increase. But with the upward bias in administrative pricing, the 3 percent rise in wage rates is more likely to trigger a price increase than is the 3 percent reduction in the hours of labor used per unit of output to *prevent* such a triggering. The wage increase is likely to come all at once and be very visible. The productivity increase, on the other hand, is likely to be spread out over time, to be the net result of many factors, and to be minimized or overlooked in the pricing process. Thus the perfectly offsetting rise in cost from increased wage rates and fall in costs because of increased productivity are not just offsetting in their practical effect on pricing.

Price 'Creep' by Formula

This source of creep is sometimes even built into a price-adjusting formula. This is the case, for example, where a corporation, once having set its price, makes subsequent price adjustments by maintaining a weighted index of the prices of the raw materials plus the cost of labor *per hour* going into its product. Prices are raised when this index has risen by a certain amount. But since the index takes no account of the difference between labor cost per hour and labor cost *per unit* of output, it is automatically inflationary when there is an increase in labor cost per hour and no increase in labor cost per unit.

Different Rates of Change in Productivity

Probably more important is the upward creep coming from the different rates of increase in productivity for different products. If there is no increase in productivity for product A and wage rates generally go up by say 3 percent as a result of a rise in national productivity, the labor cost per unit in producing this product goes up and this can trigger a legitimate price increase. If productivity in producing product B has gone up 6 percent, on the other hand, and wage rates have gone up only 3 percent, the labor cost per unit will go down and this calls for a price reduction. Since the likelihood of a reduction in the price of B is much less than the likelihood of a rise in the price of A, the net effect of a 3 percent average increase in productivity combined with a 3 percent increase in wage rates is likely to be a *rise* in the average of prices. This tendency, together with the general upward bias in pricing, noted above, thus make the rising productivity resulting from improved technology a significant source of creeping inflation in those sectors where there is substantial pricing discretion. It is ironical that improving technology, which is one of the prides of a free enterprise system, should also be a source of creeping inflation.

Leaping Administrative Inflation

We have assumed so far that there is no general *expectation* that there will be further inflation. Yet after inflation has continued for a period with no end in sight, economic decisions tend to be made not only in the light of the usual consideration of demand and costs but also in the expectation of continued inflation. The effect of this expectation in an economy of big business is quite different from that to be expected in an economy of small enterprises. In the latter situation, the expectation of inflation leads to speculative buying of commodities, thus adding temporarily to total demand from users seeking to protect their future supply and from pure speculators who foresee the price rise and hope to cash in on it. While this temporary extra demand helps to push up the prices for a period, the speculative holdings overhang the market and cause a price drop when the speculators think the price is unlikely to go higher. The users who bought ahead use up their extra stock and so, for a time, buy less. The pure speculators sell out, with the successful ones making money at the expense of those who did not expect inflation. But the temporary speculative demand has little *net* effect on prices after the speculative period is over.

'Beating the Gun' on Inflation

Where there is substantial market power and pricing discretion, on the other hand, the results of an expectation of inflation can be quite different. Users can still be expected to buy ahead with much the same temporary results as under traditional conditions. But the pure speculator is seldom in a position to deal in administered-price products. Sales organizations and promotion are usually required for that. We have, instead, a wholly new phenomenon in which the producers arbitrarily raise their prices without any change in demand or costs. The initial prices of these firms usually represent a rough balance between the short-run and longer-run considerations already discussed. Adding in an expectation of continued inflation tends to shift the balance toward the short-run and toward higher prices. Producers know that extra profits made from "beating the gun" of inflation will not add to the danger of new entrants and future loss of markets. Their competitors, being few in number and expecting further inflation themselves, will tend to go along with big price increases.

Reducing Aggregate Demand Won't Help

Such arbitrary price increases tend to be a one-way street. They do not involve the build-up of extra stocks which overhang the market and later reverse the price rise. And once the price increases have been made, they tend to resist reduction. Furthermore, if general demand is maintained at the higher prices through monetary and fiscal measures, the expectation of further inflation leads to further arbitrary price increases with no offsetting effect such as the accumulation of speculative stocks to damp it down. There is nothing in the natural forces of the market or the free enterprise system as it is now operated to prevent a continuation of this process, one that provides the basis for leaping administrative inflation. Price leaders make large price increases, 10 or 15 percent at a time. These increases are accepted by their followers because they, too, expect more inflation. And this kind of leaping inflation, unlike the demand variety, *cannot be controlled by a tight money policy short of business collapse.* Thus a simple reduction in general demand would not halt either the price creep noted above or the more dangerous leaping administrative inflation emphasized here.

Labor's Contribution to Administrative Inflation

There is little evidence that labor contributes directly to *leaping* administrative inflation. Once that stage of administrative inflation is reached, labor is perpetually in the process of catching up. Living costs go up drastically and large wage increases become legitimate. The appropriate wage increases can then trigger another round of excessive price increases, thus prolonging the period of leaping inflation.

On the other hand, the bargaining power of labor could be used to contribute to creeping administrative inflation. If there were no administrative inflation from the management side, i.e., if price changes by management were only those justified by changes in demand and costs, it would still be possible for labor unions in their collective bargaining to force wage increases greater than those that could be justified by increases in national productivity and increases in living costs. These extra-large wage gains, in turn, would increase production costs per unit and thus lead to larger price increases than would have been required by more legitimate wage increases.

Such excessive wage increases could arise from three major sources, namely, a misinterpretation of the indexes of productivity and living costs, a belief by labor that management had raised profit margins excessively (thus leading to a labor drive to get its share), and the simple use of market power to get more income, an effort that would be comparable to management's action to increase its income level. Each of these can result in creeping inflation but could not be expected to produce the leaping variety.

Most Administrative Inflation on Management Side

While creeping inflation in a particular period may come from only one side or from a combination of both, management has been the major source. Apart from periods in which labor has been catching up with increased prices or unbalanced profits, most of the administrative inflation of the last 20 years has come from the side of management, with price increases periodically taking away some of labor's rightful gains from increases in national productivity, followed by a period such as the present in which labor seeks to recover its lost ground.

Other Factors at Work

This analysis of the anatomy of administrative inflation can only hope to give an outline of the forces at work in bringing it about. The process is much more complex and many other factors enter into it. Nothing has been said, for example, of the market power of labor in the few industries in which labor is well organized but in which entry to new enterprises is so easy that management has little market power. Nothing has been said of the way increases in the prices of imported raw materials can trigger price increases greater than the increased costs warrant. What we have tried to do here, instead, is to show how economic concentration and market power can bring about this new type of inflation so different from demand inflation and so little controlled by the measures which can control inflation arising from an excess in demand.

A Program for Full Employment without Serious Inflation

Before leaving office, President Nixon's chief economic counsellor, Dr. Herbert Stein, recommended three or four years of stagnation as the way to control inflation. Such a program would cost at least $60 billion a year in lost production and place the main burden of controlling inflation on those seeking work and unable to find it. And there is no reason to expect that such a $200 billion program would succeed in bringing our current administrative inflation under control.

An alternative program is to attack the arbitrary use of market power directly while expanding general demand to achieve full employment of men and machines, thus providing more real income to both labor and capital. It would put the main burden on those in a position to wield market power, a burden that need not be a heavy one. And experience has already indicated that the abuse of market power can be successfully limited, at least for short periods of time.

In broadest outline, this program should consist of three parts: (1) A price-guidance program applied only to the more concentrated industries; (2) the expansion of general demand through increasing the money stock while the budget is balanced or produces a small surplus; and (3) the maintenance of a floating exchange rate to minimize the effect of foreign inflation on the domestic economy. The first of these, the price-guidance program, will be the most difficult and will be discussed after the role of the other two has been considered.

Inflation Other than Administrative

While much of the current inflation is administrative in character, some comes from abroad or from the specifics of supply. For the first, a freely floating exchange rate tends to reduce the domestic effects of foreign inflation but is unlikely to eliminate them all. To the extent that it does not, an effort to control the internal effects by contracting the level of general demand in this country would be self-defeating. The appropriate government policy for the items involved is to stimulate production and accept the changed price relationships involved, leaving it to the free market to make the adjustments at the cost of a small rise in the average of prices. When inflation abroad is overcome, there would tend to be a return to more normal price relationships.

The same stimulus to production and adjustment to temporarily higher prices would apply to crop failures and energy shortages. A reduction in the supplies of food and oil is no reason why there should be planned stagnation to increase unemployment and produce more idle machinery.

Expanding General Demand

The required expansion of general demand could be brought about by either a budget deficit or an expansion in the money stock but only the latter would deal with the danger of a liquidity crisis. The high short-term interest rates and the low values of equity securities arise from a combination of not enough capital funds for financing new plant, equipment, inventories, consumer buying, and a money stock that is too small to meet the public's desire to be more liquid by holding larger money balances. To the extent that general demand is increased through a government deficit, the resultant borrowing takes capital funds out of the market and raises interest rates. To the extent that the government runs a surplus, this tends to increase the funds available for industrial and consumer borrowing, thus reducing interest rates.

Increasing general demand by expanding the money stock, on the other hand, would not only increase the capital funds available to industry and consumers, thereby reducing interest rates, but would also increase the stock of that most liquid asset, money, thereby reducing or eliminating the danger of a liquidity crisis. A reduction of interest rates could be expected to bring a price rise in the stock markets, thereby making it easier for industry to obtain equity capital. For these reasons, an expansion of general demand through monetary measures would be very much superior in the present circumstances to the use of a government deficit. But an expansion of general demand could be absorbed by more general inflation unless there is an effective program to control administrative inflation.

Controlling Administrative Inflation

The short-run problem of controlling administrative inflation is to minimize the inflationary abuse of market power. How far this can be done through persuasion and how far it will require government sanctions remains to be seen. Here a program will be presented which can use persuasion as far as that can be effective and, beyond that, government sanctions.

Price and Wage Guidelines

Whether or not government sanctions are used, the first step to inhibit the inflationary abuse of market power is to draw a line between pricing actions which constitute non-inflationary use of such power and those which constitute abuse.

Traditional theory gives no solid basis for such guidelines since its dictum that price should be that which equates marginal cost and marginal revenue is irrelevant to longer-run pricing. The problem is not a simple one for either prices or wage rates, a fact that is emphasized by the need to refine the crude guidelines of the earlier attempts at intervention.

We need to reconsider, for example, the simple guide for labor compensation which allows for increases in national productivity and for changes in living costs. The increase in productivity which is available for general division between capital and labor is that which arises from improving *technology.* When output per worker goes up because a larger part of the work force is more skilled and occupies higher-paying jobs, the higher pay of those particular workers absorbs a part of the gain in productivity and only the remainder is available for general division. And the consumer price index may not be an accurate instrument for making the necessary adjustment. To the extent that wage rates in different industries or activities are out of reasonable balance and are brought into better balance by raising the laggards, this again absorbs some of the productivity gains and reduces still further those available for general division. There is some question whether higher living costs due to crop failure, for example, in themselves justify wage increases. Again, the guideline for the compensation of labor needs to take into account a number of other factors, not just an index of national output per hour and the consumer price index.

The guideline for prices should focus on *gross profit margins* and, like the wage guideline, should take account not only of the relation of prices to costs but should also include a cost-of-living adjustment for capital, i.e., an adjustment for changes in the buying power of the dollar.

This is not the place to spell out suitable price-wage guidelines but only to suggest that they need to be sweated out by experts who reflect the viewpoints of business, labor, and consumers. Two cautionary notes might be added here, however. First, it should be emphasized that the guidelines are concerned with *changes* in prices and wage rates, not with whether the rates of return on capital are fair. Secondly, an allowance would have to be made for hardship cases but the immediate inflation control program should not be made to deal with the longer-run problem of actually *reducing* market power or minimizing its harmful longer-run effects.

The Persuasive Influence of Fair Guidelines

Administrative inflation is a bad thing for both business and labor. If one could offer the management of most big enterprises a contract embodying a fair set of guidelines and give it, in addition, binding assurance that "if you sign this contract to abide by these guidelines and do in fact adhere to them, all other big enterprises plus big labor will also sign and adhere," management would sign it as a "good piece of business." There is clear evidence that, while management and labor in the concentrated industries tend to blame each other somewhat more than themselves, they both recognize some degree of responsibility for administrative inflation. These is also clear evidence that both management and labor do want to exercise some responsibility in the way they wield the market power they have. At the beginning of the Great Depression, for example, President Hoover called on big business not to cut wage rates and for a year and a half most big business enterprises adhered to this guideline even though profits were disappearing. When President Kennedy called on big labor not to push for wage increases greater than gains in productivity, this guideline was largely adhered to for nearly four years even though its unfairness was increasingly apparent. There is a substantial reservoir of responsibility on the part of management and labor which could be drawn on if a fair set of guidelines could be developed and agreed on through the joint activity of management, labor, and consumers, a sense of responsibility that could also be reinforced by public pressure to adhere to such guidelines.

Private Sanctions

With a fair set of guidelines generally accepted, certain private sanctions could be expected to come into play, the most important of them being the one exercised by management in the process of collective bargaining with labor. If labor sought to obtain wage increases greater than those made legitimate by the wage guideline, management would have an important tool to use in resisting. This is, of course, a tool which could be abused and there might be need for a labor appeals board, not to set wage rates but to interpret the application of the wage guidepost to the facts of the concrete situation as supplied by management and labor.

Another such private sanction would arise in regard to transactions between big buyers and big sellers, particularly those involving open-ended contracts. The big buyer faced with a price increase that exceeded the price guideline would have a comparable incentive to use the guideline as a tool of resistance.

In the case of the ultimate consumers, traditional theory makes them kings, giving them the sanction of not buying. But in practice the consumer is not king. Refraining from buying may not hold down price. Indeed, where the practice of full-cost pricing is used, a reduction of demand would mean that the producer must spread overhead costs over a smaller volume, thus increasing full unit costs and producing, in many cases, a *higher* rather than a lower price. In the absence of collective bargaining between management and consumers, only government can provide the sanctions on pricing where management fails to abide by the guidelines.

Limiting the Scope of Government Intervention

Government sanctions to enforce the adherence to guidelines should be limited to those enterprises which have substantial market power. The existence of such power can be deduced from past price behavior, from the degree of concentration in relation to markets, and from the relative importance of the products being priced. Where there is no private market power, e.g., where there are a multitude of producers of essentially the same products for the same market or where there is easy entry into the market in question, there is usually no pricing problem. And if the product is unimportant, interference in pricing might not be necessary even if it is sold by firms with substantial market power.

Since the core of the problem thus lies in the market power of big business, the relevant legislation might specify that the pricing of all unregulated corporations controlling assets of more than, say, $1 billion are deemed to be vested with a public interest and *automatically* subject to government sanctions with respect to the prices set by those firms and, though probably unnecessary, the labor contracts negotiated with them. The question of what smaller corporations should come within the scope of such intervention could be left to a government agency responsible for making that determination, subject to a lower limit of, say, $100 million in assets, with firms under that size being exempt from the intervention authority. Limitations of this kind would focus attention on the few hundred corporations that produce more than half of the country's manufactured goods and, in doing so, would make the scope of the program very much narrower than that of Phase II of the Nixon controls. Of the corporations not covered, some, if not most, could be expected to voluntarily abide by fair guidelines.

The Powers of a Price Guidance Board

In order to develop fair price and wage guidelines and exercise such government sanctions as are essential, the government would need to set up a price guidance board with adequate powers. While the price and wage guidelines should have general application, the sanctions to enforce adherence should not only be limited to a relatively small number of enterprises and unions but should also be as limited in character as events might make possible. If there were widespread voluntary adherence to the guidelines, for example, the problem of sanctions would apply only to the few cases in which market power was being abused. If departure from the guidelines was widespread, however, more extensive sanctions would have to come into play.

We can anticipate at least three different levels of sanction that could be employed. First, the Guidance Board would presumably have, at a minimum, the power to publicize departures from the guidelines. This would require regular *reporting and justification* of price increases by the big enterprises subject to the Board's scrutiny. The likelihood of a public announcement of any abuse of power found by the Board could act as a deterrent in some degree and persuasion might sometimes succeed in producing a rollback of an excessive price increase. Secondly, this Guidance Board should have a somewhat stronger sanction available to it, the authority to require *prior notification* of price changes. This would give it more time and opportunity to exercise persuasion and bring to bear the force of public opinion, thus avoiding the more difficult process of actual price rollback. The mildest of these two sanctions, the reporting requirement, should apply, as noted, to all of the few hundred enterprises designated by statute or found by the Board to be within the scope of its guidance powers. The second one, prior notification, might be limited to some narrower subgroup of those covered firms.

The Guidance Board should also have, however, a third sanction, the power to *prevent* price or wage increases that are found to be excessive. This more extreme sanction might be limited even further than the prior notification authority, perhaps to the small group of firms that sell products of major importance in the economy.

An 'Administrative Inflation Index'

The power of the Board to induce adherence to the guidelines could also be limited by tying them to the rate of administrative inflation. It would be possible to develop a rough index of administrative inflation by compiling an index of prices at wholesale for the products of the more concentrated industries and a price index for the raw materials for these products. With a proper weighting for raw materials and due adjustment for an appropriate cost of living factor in the compensation to labor and capital, it would then be possible to derive an index which tended to reflect changes in prices due to a widespread abuse of market power by management or labor, one that would roughly reflect the rate of administrative inflation.

The powers of the Guidance Board could be linked to movements in the administrative inflation index. If that index rose at a rate of less than 1 percent a year, for example, the power of the Board could be limited to price reporting. If it rose at the annual rate of, say, 2 percent for each of two successive quarters, the Board could automatically be given the power to require *prior* reporting but not the power to limit or roll back prices. If the administrative inflation index increased in two successive quarters at the annual rate of, say, 4 percent or more, then and only then could the Board exercise a direct power to control prices on the ground of price abuse. It would of course be up to the Board to decide how extensively it should *use* its power as thus limited.

The Location of a Guidance Board

Where such a Price Guidance Board should be located in the structure of the government is a serious problem. If the President and his economic advisers really understood the anatomy of administrative inflation and were not so committed to treating the current inflation as a demand inflation, the appropriate location would be in the executive branch. But the executive arm of government is now so mentally set against price controls that it is not psychologically equipped to control administrative inflation. Its Council on Wage and Price Stability represents a coming at the problem from the wrong end with no real grasp of the problem. And there has still been no repudiation of the idea that three or four years of planned stagnation is the way to control inflation. One major alternative would be to follow the pattern of the Federal Reserve Board, creating a temporary Price Guidance Board and making it responsible to the Congress rather than the President. Its membership, appointed in part by Congress and in part by the President, should reflect the three interests most concerned with pricing, namely, business, labor, and the consumer. If the Board is located in the executive branch, the members should be appointed subject to confirmation by the Senate and the latter should establish before confirmation that each member understands the characteristics of administrative inflation and believes in the purpose of the program.

Initiating the Program

There is a serious imbalance at the present time between the compensation to capital, the compensation to labor, and living costs. In the concentrated industries, real wage rates have gone down in the last year while real profits and dividends have gone up. There is thus a question as to whether that imbalance should be corrected through a rise in wage rates or a rollback in prices. If the former, one has the difficulty of preventing prices from rising along with wages. And even stronger intervention would presumably be required to carry out a price rollback.There is another problem as well. A program to reflate the economy back to a reasonable level of production and employment will necessarily involve some degree of price increase in the less concentrated part of the economy. All of this means, of course, that all inflation cannot be halted immediately. But a vigorous program to minimize administrative inflation while demand is expanded to a substantially higher level could nonetheless be accomplished, thus achieving a greatly reduced rate of inflation and bringing it about in a way that would not cost us $200 billion in lost production.

More Than a 'Postponement' of Inflation

Nor is there any reason to expect that a price-wage guidance program to limit administrative inflation would simply create the kind of explosive situation that is produced by a price control program to deal with an inflation that is being caused by a general excess of demand. In the case of demand inflation, a holding down of prices and wage rates by government only *postpones* the effect of the excess demand. But in the case of administrative inflation, a price program which prevents the abuse of market power does not create an excess of demand. If the program of intervention is halted after a successful period, further administrative inflation will arise only if there is further abuse of market power. Whether there will be need for continued price guidance will then depend partly on how well the wielders of market power accept the responsibility which goes with that power and partly on any intervening structural changes which might reduce such power.

Intervention in the Free Enterprise System

It will be said, and with justification, that a direct effort to limit the abuse of market power is an interference with the freedom of individual enterprises in the free enterprise system. But the free enterprise system has never given the individual enterprise complete freedom. The law interferes with freedom when it says one corporation shall not steal from another corporation and most don't. The law interferes with freedom when it says a corporation shall abide by contracts which it has entered into and most do. The government regulates the prices of public utilities which have the extreme of market power in the form of single-firm monopoly. In each of these cases, the interference with the absolute freedom of enterprise arises from the substantial public interest in limiting the particular power of the individual enterprise in order to make the free enterprise system work better than it would otherwise work. The issue of interference with free enterprise thus turns not on some theoretical concept of absolute freedom but on whether the free exercise of substantial market power threatens the working of the free enterprise system itself. In weighing this interference with the freedom to set price through the exercise of substantial market power, it should be recognized that the market power of corporations does not arise from "natural right." The right to combine the capital of many individuals and organize it in the form of a corporation is a right granted by government. And since enterprises would have little market power if there were no corporations, the abuse of market power is the abuse of a grant from government. Interference with the free use of the substantial market power of the big corporations would thus in no sense be an interference with the natural rights of individuals.

Major Changes in Economic Policy

Twenty-eight years ago the Congress made a major change in economic policy when it passed the Employment Act of 1946, a law that gave the federal government the new function of maintaining the high employment made necessary in part by the changes wrought in the national economy by the modern corporation. Today we are faced with the need for a second basic change in national policy due to the corporation, that of limiting administrative inflation. The kind of program outlined above would seem to be the most suitable for the immediate future. Over a longer period, however, other ways of limiting administrative inflation may be found and much effort should go into the search for them. Certainly it does not seem impossible for our society to achieve both full employment and price stability. Planned stagnation and continued rapid inflation do not provide a satisfactory alternative to the moderate degree of government intervention that would be required to limit the abuse of market power and permit the country's economy to resume its forward march.

17

Simultaneous Inflation and Unemployment: A Challenge to Theory and Policy

Inflation is an age-old problem. So is underemployment, though it seems to have become more acute in the twentieth century. But simultaneous inflation and excessive unemployment is something relatively new.

According to traditional theory, simultaneous inflation and underemployment are not possible. Inflation can occur if an excess in aggregate demand develops. Deflation can occur if a deficiency of aggregate demand develops, and experience indicates that deflation can result in excessive unemployment. But the received theory provides no possible explanation of a general rise of prices in the presence of excessive unemployment.

Yet in recent history, many examples can be found of inflation which has occurred in the presence of heavy unemployment of both men and machines. In the United States, both wholesale and consumer prices have nearly doubled in the last twenty years, but in only two of those years, 1967 and 1968, has there been an excess in overall demand, and these two years accounted for less than 4% of the total price rise. For most of the period, there was a deficiency in demand, while unemployment averaged 5% of the civilian labor force. Clearly, experience is in conflict with traditional theory, and new theory is required.

This chapter is concerned with the new inflation as it has arisen in the United States and the issues of theory and policy it raises. To understand this new phenomenon, it is necessary to distinguish between five types of inflation, three to be found in the classical literature and two nonclassical types.

Reprinted with permission from *The Roots of Inflation* (New York: Burt Franklin & Co., Inc., 1975), pp. 1–31.

Classical Types of Inflation

The classical theorists have recognized and taken into account three types of inflation: (1) demand inflation arising from an excessive increase in aggregate demand; (2) price increases due to crop failures or a comparable shrinkage in supply; and (3) a rise in the domestic prices of both imports and exports due to monetary devaluation or foreign inflation. None of these could explain simultaneous inflation and excessive unemployment. But it is necessary to understand each in order to distinguish them from the nonclassical types of inflation.

Classical Demand Inflation

Most important in the classical literature is the familiar inflation which arises from excessive demand. In popular terms, it comes from too much money chasing too few goods. Technically, it occurs when there is already full employment and aggregate demand expands beyond the output which can be supplied at full employment. Then prices and wage rates rise more or less together.

This is the type of inflation discussed in the traditional textbooks under the head of inflation. It is properly called "demand inflation." It occurred in the United States both during World War I and following World War II. If this classical demand inflation were the only type of inflation, traditional theory would be correct in holding that simultaneous inflation and excessive unemployment are incompatible.

Supply Shortages

The second source of price rises accounted for by classical theory, supply shortages such as crop failures, does not alter this classical conclusion. Bad harvests could raise not only farm prices but, to a lesser degree, other prices as well since living costs are reflected in the price of labor. The same could be expected from a temporary cutoff of crude oil supplies. In both cases, the price rise would not only be temporary but, according to classical theory, the market would continue to absorb all that could be produced consistently with the classical condition that marginal cost and marginal revenue are equated by price. Unemployment would not be involved in this type of inflation.

Foreign Trade

The third type of classical inflation, that originating in foreign trade, would likewise not involve unemployment. Inflation abroad would raise the prices of a home country's imports directly, while the prices of domestic exports would, in turn, rise as foreign countries bought more from the home country since domestic prices would be lower in terms of "their" (foreign) currency. This rise in the prices of goods in foreign trade could result in a rise in other prices as well, partly as imports entered as raw materials in the production and costs of domestic goods, and partly as they affected living costs and the price of labor. Essentially the same result could be expected for a country which devalued its currency. But in neither case would the postulates of classical theory allow the result of the price rise to be the creation of unemployment. The two would be incompatible.

The Basis of Traditional Theory

The classical incompatibility between inflation and unemployment rests on the postulate of price and wage flexibility, with prices moving in the same direction as demand. Traditional theory assumed that prices and wages were highly flexible, constantly adjusting to equate supply and demand. The haggling and bargaining in the marketplace was expected to clear the market just as, in the wheat market or a stock exchange, the bids and offers are matched and the price adjusts. All who are willing to sell at the current market price sell all they want to, and all who are willing to buy at the current market price buy all they want to, thus clearing the market. Whether markets were formally organized or not, prices were expected to respond quickly to changes in aggregate demand, falling with a decrease in demand and rising with an increase. Even monopoly prices were expected to be flexible as the monopolist constantly adjusted his price to equate "marginal cost" and "marginal revenue." Any inflexibility was treated as a "friction" and not taken into account in the theoretical models on which traditional theory based its policy conclusions. Prices which behaved in this classical fashion can properly be called "classical market prices" or more simply "market prices." If the great bulk of market transactions took place at such flexible market prices, general inflation and general unemployment would be incompatible.

Nonclassical Price Behavior

When actual transactions in the modern world are examined, it is found that prices (other than those of farm products and some raw materials) are seldom highly flexible and that supply and demand in the traditional sense are seldom equated by price. For most goods, the price has been set, usually by the seller, and kept constant for a period of time and a series of transactions. At the price set, more is likely to be offered than is currently demanded, and the seller would usually be delighted to sell more at the same price. Sometimes demand exceeds supply, and some form of rationing occurs other than through a change in price. Only by chance are supply and demand equated and the market just cleared by the price which has been set. Such a price has been called an "administered price"—and is the type of price at which the great bulk of commodity and service transactions take place in a modern industrial society.

Market vs. Administered Prices

The contrast between "market" and "administered" prices is clear in the field of retailing. Haggling and bargaining is still the standard procedure for arriving at prices in oriental bazaars. But prices in a modern chain store are set by the store management and kept constant for a series of transactions. Sometimes a given item will be offered at the same price for weeks or months at a time. In a well stocked store, supply is usually in excess of demand, with stock immediately available to fill whatever demand arises at the fixed price. Occasionally demand exceeds supply, and a customer is told, "Sorry, we are all out of that item. Come back next week." Even the oriental bazaars have been turning to price administration. A Turkish shop selling at administered prices is likely to post a sign "Prices à la Franca."

Most industrial prices are administered prices, not classical market prices. The bulk of such prices are set by the administrative action of the seller. In the steel industry, prices are not only set for periods of time, but for such long periods that a price change often becomes front page news. Many prices are set in open-ended contracts negotiated between buyers and sellers for a year or more at a time, with the actual purchase transactions not occurring until the buyer decides how much to buy from time to time at the agreed-upon price. This procedure has also become traditional for wage rates, with the "price" set either by the employer or by an open-ended contract negotiated between management and labor. The actual amount of labor employed is then usually determined by the requirements of the employer.

The Relative Inflexibility of Industrial Prices

Studies of actual behavior of industrial prices show great inflexibility of prices. A study concerned with the Great Depression of the 1930's shows that for a fifth of the weight in the wholesale price index of the U.S. Bureau of Labor Statistics, the average frequency of price change reported by individual sellers was once every two years. For another fifth, individual sellers reported on the average only one change about every eight months.[1] A recent study by the National Bureau of Economic Research indicates that for a sample of twenty-seven important industrial products, the price paid by an individual buyer reporting in each month over a four-year period changed on average less frequently than once every seven months.[2]

The only concrete examples of this infrequence of price change given in the National Bureau study are contained in a chart for bulk ammonia which is reproduced below. The series in the chart were chosen in the Bureau study "to display the varieties of price data reported: unchanging prices, irregularly changing prices, broken price series, and frequently changing prices," and ammonia is referred to as ". . . our illustrative commodity. . . ." The chart gives the whole-

Figure 17.1. **Ammonia: Selected Individual Price Series**

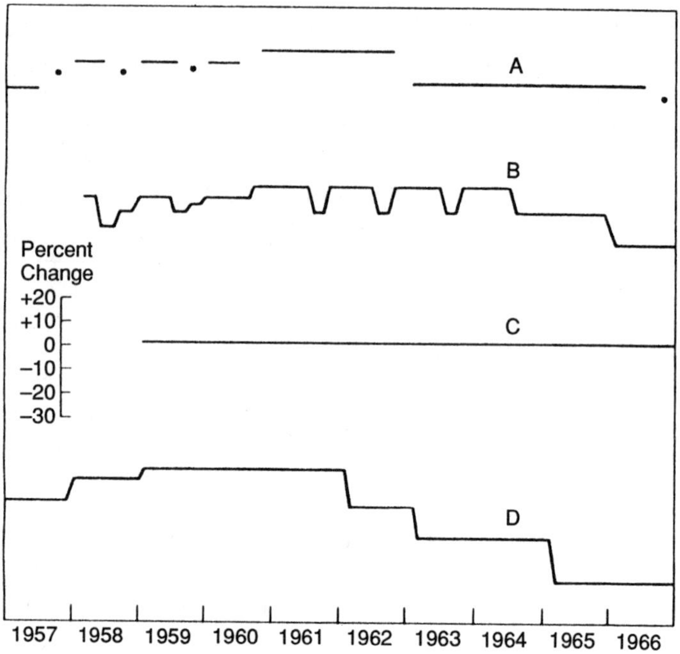

sale price paid by each of four substantial bulk buyers of ammonia who reported the prices actually paid in successive months in the period 1957 to 1966.

Examination of Chart I [Figure 17.1] shows a high degree of inflexibility. Buyer C reported that it paid *exactly* the same price each month for eight years. Buyer A, though it did not buy in every month, paid only four different prices in a ten-year period. Buyer D reported only five price changes in ten years. And Buyer B reported fifteen changes in nine years, but many of these were temporary seasonal changes. If one leaves out the seasonal changes, the four series show eleven changes in a combined life of thirty-six years, or an average change of once every three-and-a-quarter years.

The chart also shows that when the prices did change, the change came in quantum jumps. The three changes reported by buyer A averaged 8%. For buyer D, the average change was 9%. For buyer B, even including the seasonal changes, the average change was 6%.

These National Bureau data collected from buyers reinforce the evidence collected by the Bureau of Labor Statistics from sellers that for many industrial products, prices are administered and held constant for very considerable periods of time; and that when changes are made, they take quantum jumps.

Clearly the behavior of administered prices does not fit the expectation of traditional theory. It is not credible that for a seller of a given product, marginal cost and marginal revenue are constant for a matter of months at a time and then, suddenly, change so that a price 8% higher or lower is the price which just clears the market by equating marginal cost and marginal revenue. It would be even less creditable that marginal revenue and marginal cost both changed over a prolonged period in such a fashion that the price at which they were equal was constant and then, suddenly, was 8% higher or lower. Such price behavior implies not only significant market power in the determination of prices but also the use of pricing discretion in ways not expected from traditional theory. And most important here, it gives rise to two types of inflation, one which occurs when there is less than full employment, and the other, which can occur whether or not there is full employment—neither of which is consistent with the received theory.

The Reflation of Prices

The first of these nonclassical types of inflation grows out of the quite different reactions of market prices and administered prices to business fluctuations.

In a recession, the general drop in demand produces a fall in market prices, although production tends to remain level, as classical theory would lead one to expect. At the other extreme, administered prices tend to drop little, while the fall in demand for such products works itself out in reduced sales, production, and employment. Other administered prices behave in an intermediate fashion, particularly those in which flexible, market-priced commodities constitute an important raw material. In such intermediate cases, both prices and production tend to drop to an intermediate degree. Thus, excessive unemployment develops along with reduced production in those sectors with relatively inflexible administered prices, while the classical reduction in market-determined prices comes mostly from competition. The net result is not only excessive unemployment, but also a severe unbalance in price relationships.

In a recovery from depression, the rise in demand operates primarily to lift employment where prices are inflexible, to lift flexible-market prices without much change in supply, and to lift both prices and production to an intermediate degree for the intermediate items. Because the rise in prices is a natural and necessary part of the process of recovery, it is "a good thing" and deserves a separate name. Here it will be called *reflation.*

A spectacular case of deflation and reflation occurred in the United States during the Great Depression of the 1930's. Chart II [Figure 17.2] shows the behavior of five price indexes during the depression for products at wholesale which differ in the frequency of price change and therefore tend to reflect differences in the extent to which market power and administrative discretion are exercised over price. The chart shows the movement of the five indexes from the relatively full-employment years 1926 to 1929 as well as the depression and

Figure 17.2. **Deflation and Reflation** Wholesale Prices for Five Frequency Groups 1926 to March 1942 (Price Freeze 1926–1929=100)

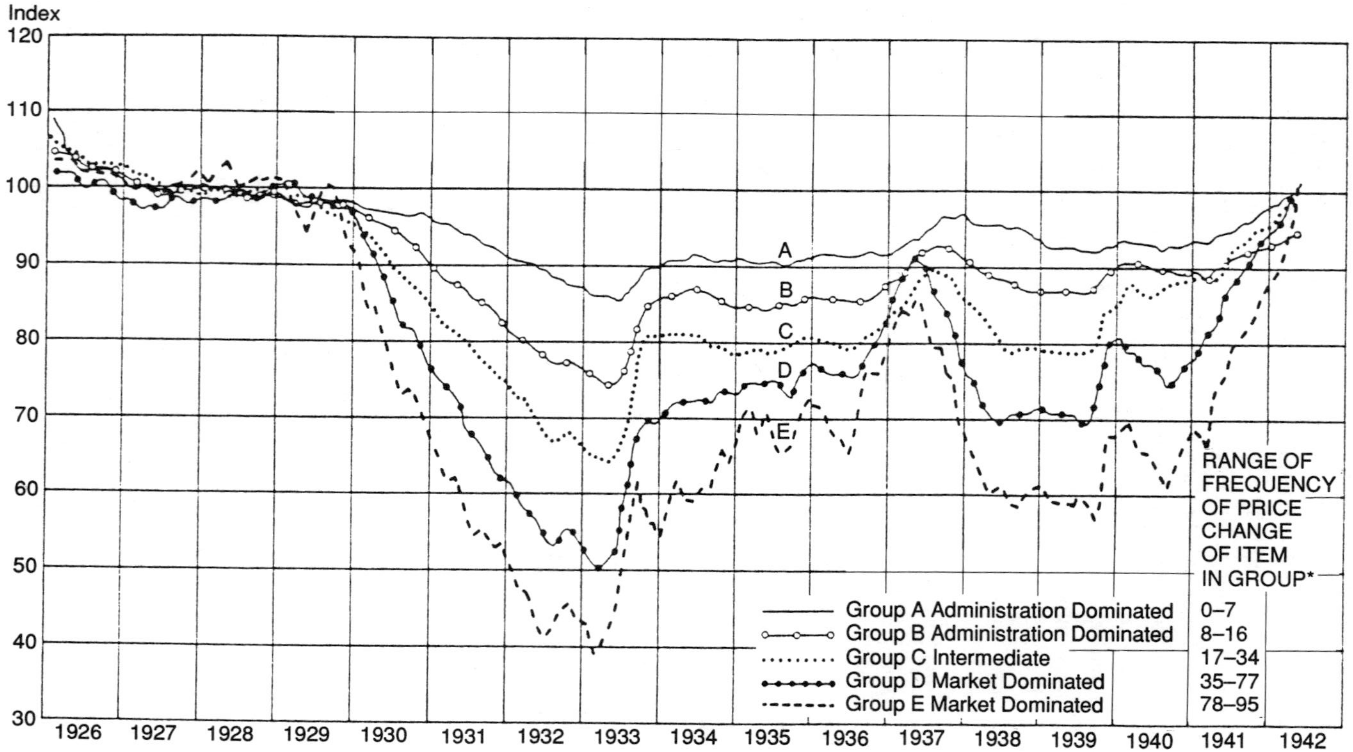

*Price indexes are for 731 items included in the B.L.S. wholesale price index grouped according to frequency of price change in the months of the period 1926–1933.

recovery years from 1929 to early 1942 when full employment was again achieved and the price-wage structure was frozen under wartime controls.

As can be seen from Chart II, the market-dominated index E, made up of such items as wheat, cotton, beef cattle, hides, lead, zinc, lumber, and scrap steel, fell over 60% and recovered an equal amount so that at the time of the price freeze in 1942, it was back to approximately the level of 1929.

Index A, the most administration-dominated, comprising such items as agricultural implements, iron ore, hand tools, plate glass, and sewing machines, fell less than 10% and recovered by about nearly the same amount.

The intermediate indexes behaved in an intermediate fashion.

As a result, the five indexes which had diverged during the recession came somewhat together in the partial recovery of early 1937, diverged again in the 1937–38 recession, and came together again by early 1942 when prices were frozen under the war powers. As can be seen, the five indexes bore nearly the same relation to each other at full employment in 1942 as at full employment in 1929.

During this period, the fall in production and employment and the recovery of both occurred primarily in the industries whose prices had dropped least in recession and recovered least during reflation. This can be seen in Table I [Table 17.1], which gives the drop in the prices and production for each of ten major industries from 1929 to 1932 and their recovery to 1937.

Thus, the rise in aggregate demand during recovery lifted the sensitive market prices and increased employment where prices were least sensitive, thereby restoring the pre-depression price balance and full employment.

This same differential behavior of prices occurred in the recession and recovery of 1957–58 and in that of 1960–61 according to the new price data collected by the National Bureau of Economic Research from buyers of products.[3] There was this significant difference, however: in the National Bureau sample, a substantial number of administered prices, not only did not go down in recession, but actually went *up,* while a substantial number went *down* during recovery.

This nonclassical type of inflation would not be possible if all prices, including wages, behaved in a manner that satisfied the classical postulates of price flexibility, market clearing, and the equating of marginal cost and marginal revenue.

The reflation of prices in a recovery from a preceding recession should be regarded as a natural part of the recovery process and, in this way, is wholly different from an inflation due to a general excess in demand. Both come from an increase in aggregate demand. But only the recovery rise in prices is constructive since it is an integral part of the recovery process and tends to restore price balance. Because it is a "good thing" it presents no major problem of policy, except that of recognizing its appropriateness and not trying to prevent it. However, in the period of recovery before full employment is reached, it does involve a rise of prices in the presence of excessive unemployment.

Table 17.1

Price and Production Behavior in Recession and Partial Recovery

	Decline 1929–1932 in percent of 1929		Rise 1932–37 in percent of 1929	
	Prices	Production	Prices	Production
Motor vehicles	12	74	2	64
Agricultural implements	14	84	9	84
Iron and steel	16	76	20	67
Cement	16	55	20	24
Automobile tires	25	42	27	24
Leather and leather products	33	18	29	27
Petroleum products	36	17	21	37
Textile products	39	28	24	24
Food products	39	10	24	–1
Agricultural commodities	54	1	36	8

Source: The Structure of the American Economy, National Resources Committee, Washington, D.C., 1939, p. 386

Administrative Inflation

The second type of nonclassical inflation also arises from the exercise of "market power," but can occur whether employment is full or less than full and can occur in a period of recession, in a period of stagnation, or in one of recovery. It can appear, as well, during a period when prices are also rising as a result of excessive demand.

This type of inflation may be initiated by management in an effort to widen profit margins and could then be properly called "profit-push" inflation. It could also be initiated by labor in an effort to obtain unwarranted wage increases which would, in turn, be called "cost-push" inflation. To avoid any implication of its specific source, it will be called here "administrative inflation," leaving the complex issue of the initiating source open for further investigation in each specific case.

The first clear example of administrative inflation in the United States occurred in the 1950's. In the five years from 1953 to 1958, there was an 8% increase in the wholesale price index, while at the same time, unemployment of both men and machines was excessive and higher at the end than at the beginning of the period.

The present writer brought this new phenomenon to the attention of the Senate Anti-Trust and Monopoly Committee in July 1957, and in January 1959, presented the committee with Chart III [Figure 17.3]. It covers all items in the

Figure 17.3. **Administrative Inflation**
Wholesale Price Changes by Product Groups 1953 to October 1958
(average increase 8.1 percent)

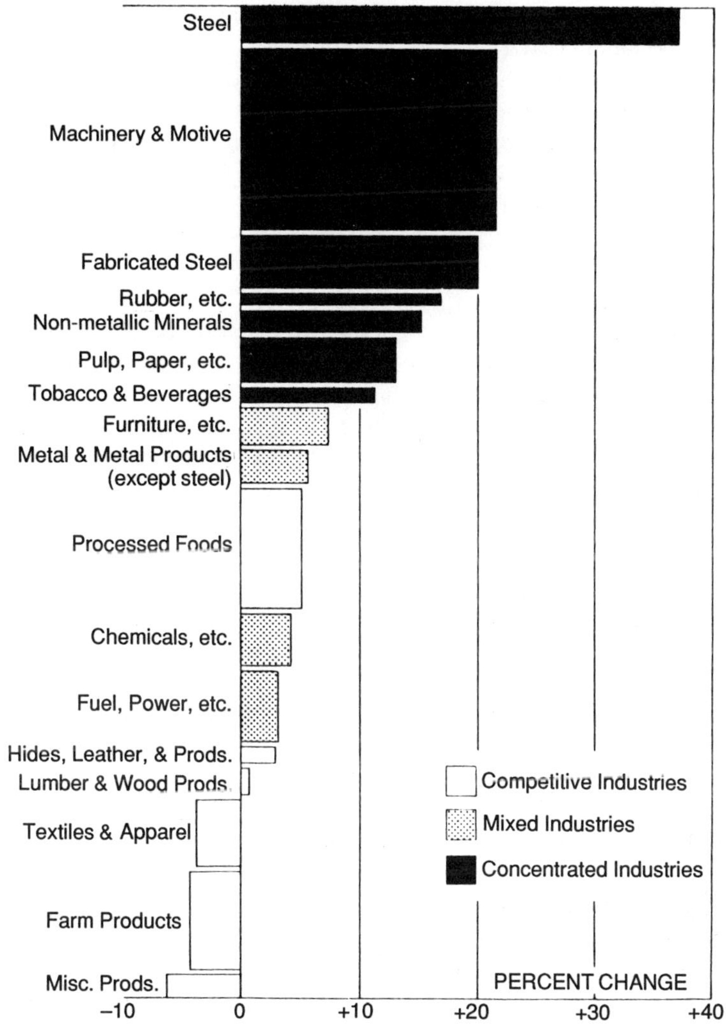

Source: B.L.S.

Note: Width of columns represents weight of item in the Index.

wholesale price index grouped into seventeen industries.The height of each column shows the change in the index for the respective industrial group from the average for 1953 to October 1958. The width of each column indicates the relative weight the group carried in the total wholesale index. This chart shows that the bulk of the increase in the wholesale price index was in the more concentrated industries (indicated in black) while prices in the more competitive industries (indicated in white) went down or rose little. This finding was confirmed by the investigations of the Joint Economic Committee.[4] If all wholesale prices had behaved like those in classically competitive industries, there would have been no inflation. If all had behaved like the more concentrated prices, the administrative inflation would have been nearly twice as great.

It is clear that in this period the major source of the inflation was the 36% rise in steel prices and the substantial price increases in the steel-using industries. Together these accounted for more than half the rise in the total wholesale price index. Subsequent information has made it clear that the steel price rise involved a very considerable widening of steel profit margins, so that this particular administrative inflation was initiated as a profit push.[5]

The administrative inflation from 1953 to 1958 was clearly not due to an excess of aggregate demand. It did not involve either of the other two classical types of inflation—or a reflation. It could not have taken place if administered prices had behaved in the classical manner.

Administrative inflation appears to be endemic under the conditions of modern industry. It occurs in periods of full employment when there is no excess in aggregate demand. It occurs when there is excessive unemployment. And it even occurred in the recession of 1969–1970 when administered prices rose, while those prices subject to market forces and the level of employment both dropped.

Unlike reflation, administrative inflation presents major problems of economic theory and economic policy. Why do administered prices rise in a period when there is no excess in aggregate demand and classical market prices are not rising? How can it be that administered prices rise when aggregate demand is declining? And most important, how can administrative inflation either be prevented or kept to a minimum during a period of expanding demand leading to full employment, as well as after full employment has been achieved?

Efforts to Control Administrative Inflation

Much light can be thrown on administrative inflation by considering the six qualitatively different attempts at inflation control which have been employed in the United States in the last twenty years.

Monetary Contraction

The first attempt came in 1956–57 when the Federal Reserve Board sought to control the *administrative inflation* of the 1950's through a tight money policy. This more than halted the growth of the nominal stock of money and produced a 10% drop in the *real* stock of money.[6] It also precipitated the recession of 1957–58.

This effort to control administrative inflation was a complete failure. Farm and other market-dominated prices fell with the recession and rose with the recovery when the tight money policy was reversed. But industrial prices continued to rise and, by 1959, were 5% above their 1956 level. The 13% decline in industrial production and the extra two million persons out of work had little effect in reducing the administrative inflation.

The failure of this effort at controlling inflation arose from the fact that while a sufficiently tight money policy can control a demand inflation, it cannot control an administrative inflation. This was acknowledged by the chief economic advisor to the Federal Reserve Board, Dr. Woodlief Thomas, when he wrote to the *Washington Post* in March, 1959:

> Recent discussion of the influence of administered prices, stimulated by . . . the Kefauver Committee, has made a significant contribution to a better understanding of the problems of inflation and fluctuations in economic activity and employment. This contribution is in pointing out that there are unstabilizing forces in pricing actions of the private economy—on the part of both management and labor—that cannot be effectively controlled or corrected by governmental actions in the area of fiscal and monetary policies.

The Kennedy Guideposts

The second major attempt to control administrative inflation was the Kennedy guidepost program which was the first to directly face this problem. When the program was being drafted in 1961, unemployment was above 6%. The problem was recognized as one of preventing administrative inflation while expanding demand through fiscal and monetary measures so as to achieve full employment.

The guidepost program was both an outstanding success—in holding down administrative inflation while expanding demand through fiscal and monetary measures—as well as a partial failure. By the end of 1965, full employment had been substantially achieved, while unemployment fell to 4%. Labor had adhered to the wage guideposts so closely that the labor cost per unit of manufacturing output was down 3%. Management had not adhered as closely, and industrial prices rose a little. This in itself was not serious and alone might have been corrected. Nearly full employment had been achieved with a total four year rise of less than 0.6% a year for wholesale prices and close to 0.4% for industrial products.

But this goal had been achieved at the expense of a serious distortion in the relation between prices and wage rates because the guidepost program took no account of the *reflationary* rise in the prices subject to market competition which was appropriate for a period of recovery. The increase in demand which reduced unemployment from above 6% to a level of 4%, in conjunction with only a small increase in the most administration-dominated prices, could have been expected to raise substantially the average of farm prices and other flexible market prices.

And in fact this is what happened, creating some overall increase in the average of prices and living costs. Between the end of 1961 and the end of 1965, the wholesale price index for processed foods rose 8%, while the index for industrial products rose only 2%. In the same period, the consumer price index rose to an intermediate degree. Yet the wage guideposts took no account of this appropriate rise in living costs.

As the result of the failure to include a cost-of-living factor in the wage guidepost, the program suffered a partial breakdown. By 1965, the rise in living costs had absorbed more than a third of labor's legitimate productivity gains. During the same period, industry had significantly widened profit margins. When this unfairness in the guideposts became obvious, labor refused to cooperate any longer and forced wage increases larger than gains in productivity in order to catch up with living costs. Management, striving to maintain the widened profit margins, passed along the increases in labor costs. This struggle lifted the wholesale index of industrial products by another 4% from the end of 1965 to the end of 1967, but also brought wages and profits more nearly in line with each other.

Even with the partial breakdown of the wage guidepost, nearly full employment was maintained throughout 1966 and 1967 without signs of excessive demand prior to the fall of 1967. The average unemployment in each of these years was 3.8%. Farm prices did not rise, a normal indication that excess demand was not building up. Profit margins in industry, which had increased substantially over the long run, declined somewhat, but were still abnormally high. It is clear that the immediate source of inflation in 1966 and 1967 was administrative and came primarily from the effort of labor to realize its share in the productivity gains generated during the whole guidepost period—gains which the guideposts had denied to labor.

When the whole period from 1961 to the end of 1967 is taken into account, it is apparent that most of the inflation was a reflation. In moving from a 6.8% rate of unemployment in the first quarter of 1961 to the 3.8% level of 1966 and 1967, a normal reflation would have been expected to lift the wholesale index substantially. The actual increase in prices—under 6% for the total six years—does not indicate much administrative inflation. Instead, it primarily indicates a delayed reaction of wage rates to the normal reflationary rise in living costs. One must give high, though not perfect, marks to the guidepost program.

It seems likely that with an appropriate living-cost provision in the wage guidepost, the full recovery and reflation could have been accomplished by 1965 and held for another two years with negligible administrative inflation. Whether or not full employment could have been maintained for a much longer period without further inflation is another matter. But the many claims that the guidepost program was a failure—because the total index of prices rose—fail to take account of the reflation which was a necessary part of the recovery.

War Inflation

The third recent attempt to control inflation arose out of the Vietnam War and was an effort to prevent a *demand* inflation. In calendar year 1966, the federal budget was in balance according to the National Income Accounts. But military expenses were expected to increase rapidly and produce a heavy deficit unless taxes were raised. With the economy already at full employment, the extra demand for military supplies could have been expected to produce an excess in demand, causing a demand inflation unless nonmilitary demand was restricted.

This danger of demand inflation was well recognized by the administration. In January 1967, President Johnson recommended a 6% surtax to be made effective by mid-1967. But the Congress failed to act. The President repeated his request in the summer of 1967, raising the requested surtax rate to 10%, but again the Congress took no action. And again in January 1968, the President repeated his request. It was not until mid-1968 that a 10% surtax was finally passed, a year-and-a-half too late. It brought the budget into balance by the last quarter of 1968 and insured a substantial surplus in calendar 1969. A prime source of demand inflation was thus finally removed.

In the meantime, demand inflation had pushed the wholesale price index up more than 3% from the 1967 level, with the increase approximately equal for the market-dominated and the administration-dominated indexes. It seems probable that if the surtax had been passed in early 1967 and the guidepost policy stressed, full employment could have been maintained and the war program financed without either demand inflation or serious administrative inflation.

Planned Stagnation

The fourth recent attempt to control inflation began in 1969 and was a complete failure due to a faulty diagnosis. On taking office, President Nixon announced that prices and wage rates would be left to be controlled by the free market, and inflation would be controlled in the classical fashion by fiscal and monetary means, thus rejecting *any* price-guidance program. A large budget surplus was maintained throughout 1969 as a result of the surtax imposed the year before, and such a tight money policy was adopted that expansion in the money stock was halted. Throughout 1969 there was no clear evidence of an excess in demand. Yet in the same year, the wholesale price index rose 4.8%, twice the annual rate of the years from mid-1965 to the end of 1968 when guidelines were to a greater or lesser degree in operation.

In his 1970 Economic Report, President Nixon explained the price rise by saying, "The inflation unleashed after mid-1965 had gathered powerful momentum by the time this Administration took office a year ago." He designated *the growth of total spending* as "the driving force of the inflation" and outlined the plan being followed to "slow down the rapid expansion of demand firmly and

Figure 17.4. **Planned Stagnation**
Actual Gross National Product through 1969
Planned and Potential Gross National Product after 1969

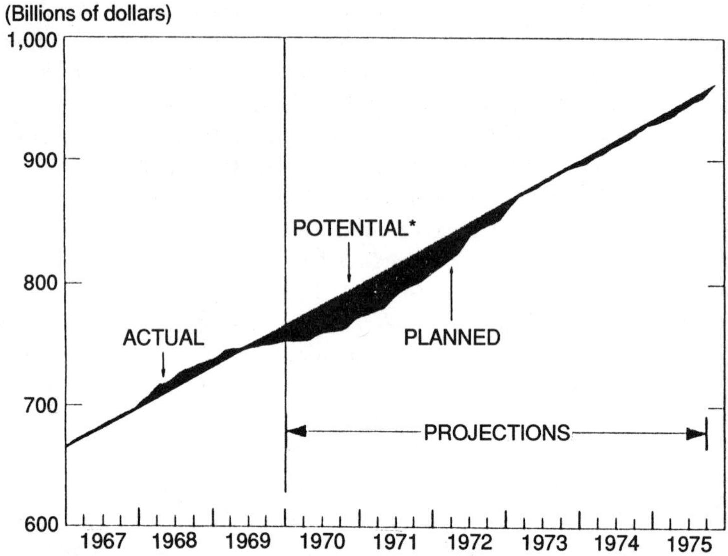

Note: Ratio scale – seasonally adjusted annual rates
*Trend line of 4 percent from 1965 IV to 1969 IV, 4.3 percent from 1969 IV to 1970 IV, 4.4 percent from 1970 to 1971 IV, and 4.3 percent from 1971 IV to 1975 IV.

persistently.'' The actual program being followed was set forth in the body of the President's Economic Report. It was to take the heat out of the inflation by creating two-and-a-half years of planned stagnation. This is clearly shown in Chart IV [Figure 17.4] which reproduces, on an enlarged scale, the relevant part of Chart 8 in the President's report. The chart shows the actual growth of GNP in constant prices from 1967 to mid-1969, then the halting of growth in the last half of 1969 and the planned halt to mid-1970 followed by two years in which GNP was, *by plan,* to be kept some $30 billion a year below the estimated potential of the economy. This called for an increase in unemployment by two million persons in an effort to increase the rate of unemployment to around 6%.

This brutal plan was indeed successful in creating stagnation. The continued budget surplus became a restraining force, and the money stock, measured in constant purchasing power, was reduced. Real aggregate demand declined, industrial production started down in the summer of 1969, and unemployment increased as planned. By the end of 1970, the goal of 6% unemployment had been reached and a recession had been achieved.

But stagnation did not halt the inflation. The reason is simple. The driving force of the inflation in 1969 was not ''the growth of total spending.'' Rather, the President had unleashed the forces of administrative inflation by pointedly

Figure 17.5. **Administrative Inflation in Recession**
Wholesale Price Changes by Product Groups June 1969 to December 1970
(average increase 4.0 percent)

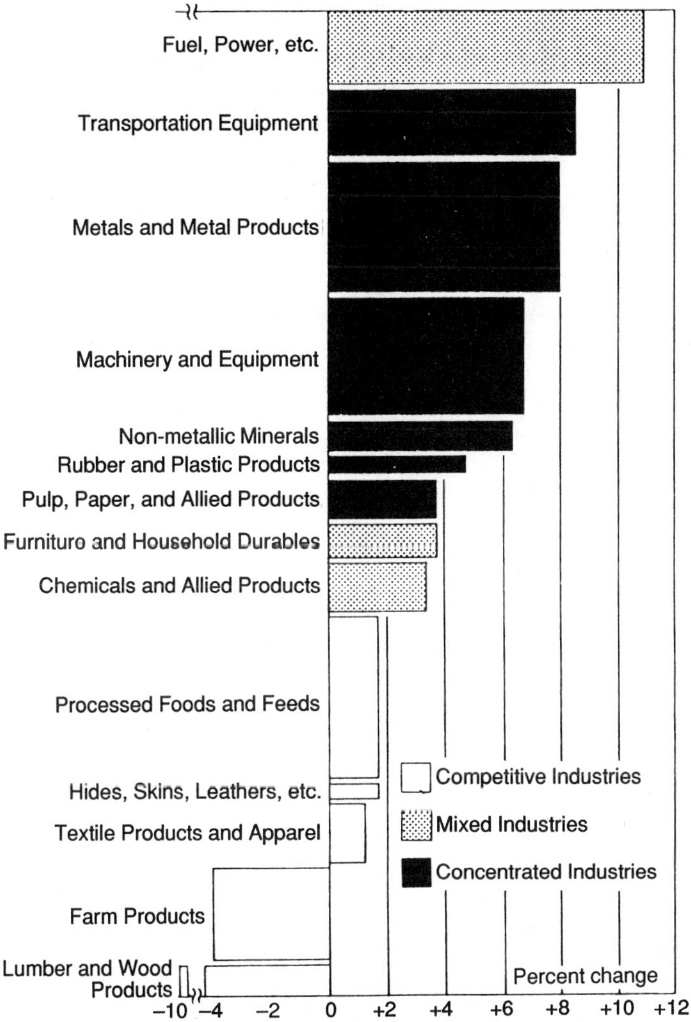

Source: B.L.S.
Note: Width of column represents weight of item in the Index.

rejecting the guidepost program. The inflation in the 1969–70 recession was almost entirely administrative inflation.[7] It was the kind of inflation that Dr. Woodlief Thomas had said could not be controlled by fiscal and monetary measures.

The administrative character of this inflation-in-recession is easily shown by examining the main sources of the rise in the wholesale price index. Chart V [Figure 17.5] makes clear the parallel to the administrative inflation of the

1950's. As in Chart III, the more concentrated groups are shown in black, the most competitive in white, and the mixed groups in light gray, while the height of each column indicates the price change, and the width shows the weight which each group carried in the total index.

As can be seen, the great bulk of the increase in prices during the recession was contributed by the concentrated industries. In the more competitive industries, prices went up little or went down. The only exception to this tendency was the fuel and power index which rose 11% largely because of the scarcity of pollution-free fuels.

The dismal failure of this attempt to control administrative inflation by the planned creation of stagnation was acknowledged by the New Economic Policy of August 1971 which froze prices and wages after the stagnation plan had already cost the country nearly $50 billion in lost GNP and promised more loss until reflation could restore full employment. But no apology was given to the millions who suffered unnecessary unemployment or to the stockholders whose profits were reduced. Nor was there acknowledgment that the crucial presidential decision to create planned stagnation was in direct conflict with the Employment Act of 1946.

The New Economic Policy

The fifth effort at controlling inflation, the President's *New Economic Policy,* involved a return to price-wage guidance and was more successful. It directly faced both the problem created by the lack of an adequate market control of prices and the necessity of reflation as the stagnation mistake was corrected. The new guidelines introduced in Phase II were a distinct improvement over the Kennedy guideposts in two respects. The wage guideline included a factor for the rise in the cost of living which would accompany the process of reflation. The price guideline focused on the holding of profit *margins* which allowed enterprises to increase their profits by producing more, but not by increasing prices relative to costs except in special cases. In addition, both guidelines were backed by legislative authority to exercise and enforce controls.

In its first sixteen months up to December 1972, the price-wage program was quite successful in preventing *administrative* inflation. The weighted index for the six most concentrated industrial groups in the wholesale price index rose at the annual rate of only 1.8%, while the index for the three mixed groups went up at an annual rate of 2.5% as shown in Table II [Table 17.2]. Both of those increases could have been expected as a part of the normal reflation. The cost-of-living factor meant that the labor cost, per unit of output, increased by around 2%.

Competitive prices went up more than would have been expected on the basis of reflation alone. The partial recovery in this period could have been expected to raise market-dominated prices by perhaps double that of the mixed groups, or

Table 17.2

Wholesale Price Behavior Under Phases I and II (average increase)

Concentrated industries	Percent change August 1971 to December 1972	Annual rate
Rubber and plastic products	0.0	
Machinery and equipment	+2.1	
Non-metallic minerals	+2.5	
Metal and metal products	+2.6	
Transportation equipment	+3.2	
Pulp, paper and allied products	+4.1	
Weighted average	+2.4%	+1.8%
Mixed industries		
Chemicals and allied products	+0.4	
Furniture and household durables	+2.0	
Fuel, power etc.	+6.1	
Weighted average	+3.3%	+2.5%
Competitive industries		
Textile products and apparel	+5.2	
Lumber and wood products	+11.1	
Processed foods and feeds	+12.0	
Farm products	+21.1	
Hides, skins, leathers, etc.	+24.3	
Weighted average	+13.8%	+10.3%
Total wholesale index	+7.0%	5.3%

around 5%. But the weighted index of the five most competitive groups of the B.L.S. index went up at an annual rate of 10.3% to December 1972. A severe drought in Texas and the destructive corn blight in 1970 broke the cattle cycle, so that less meat and fewer hides were available in 1972. Then drought in other parts of the world forced up grain and feed prices and, in turn, produced abnormally high prices for hogs, poultry, eggs, and an added increase in beef prices. The floating of the dollar in August 1971 and its devaluation in May 1972 also contributed, particularly for the flexible market prices. If the special restrictions on supply are excluded, the wholesale price index would have increased during these sixteen months at an annual rate of around 3%, instead of 5.3%, almost all of it an appropriate reflationary response to the partial recovery of the period.

It should also be noted that unlike the guideposts of 1961–65, the effects of Phases I and II were substantially fair to both labor and capital. In the last half of 1972, the division between capital and labor of the income generated by nonfinancial corporations was almost exactly the same as it was in 1969 and in the eight years of the Eisenhower administration: 87.6% to labor and about 12.4% to capital.[8]

The success of Phases I and II in preventing administrative inflation suggests the efficiency of this type of control in a period of recovery. How long the controls could be effective once full employment is achieved still remains a central problem of economic analysis and economic policy.

Compound Inflation and the Problem of Diagnosis

A particular period of inflation may be dominated by a single major source—such as a general excess in demand, as in 1967–68, or by the exercise of market power in the administrative inflation of the 1950's. Diagnosis is a relatively simple problem once the different possible sources of inflation are recognized. But inflation in a particular period may reflect a compound of several different sources. Then diagnosis becomes difficult.

Such is the case with the hyper-inflation from June 1973 to June 1974. In this single year, the wholesale price index rose 14%, in part from the Arab-created rise in fuel prices, in part from the effects of inflation abroad, and in part from administrative inflation at home. But how much should be attributed to each is not easy to determine.

What is easier to determine is the possible sources which did *not* contribute to this inflation.

Clearly there was no general excess in demand. Aggregate demand went up less than prices, and real national income went down. Unemployment increased from 4.8% to 5.2% of the labor force, and the proportion of manufacturing capacity utilized declined from 83.3% to 80.6%. The economy had unused reserves of manpower and plant that could have supplied at least another $50 or $60 billion of demand without establishing the conditions for inflation.

Likewise, there was no element of reflation in the price rise since production declined and unemployment rose.

The rise in farm prices as a result of previous crop failures had come to a practical end with the index of farm prices down more than 7% from June 1973 to June 1974 and the wholesale food and feed index up only 3.7% during the year—together contributing nothing to the 14% rise in the wholesale index.

Finally, it is clear that wages followed, rather than initiated, the price rise. In the twelve months from June 1973 to June 1974, the average hourly earnings for the private nonfarm economy went up 8.0%, but prices went up so much faster than wages that the real income per worker-hour went down 2.8%. Thus wage rates lagged substantially behind the rise in living costs.

The Compound and Three Major Sources

This leaves three sources to account for the 14% price rise: the energy crisis, the domestic effects of foreign inflation, and administrative inflation coming from the side of management.

The direct contribution of the energy crisis is evident in the 57.8% rise in the wholesale index for fuels, related products, and power. This alone accounted directly for nearly a third of the rise in the wholesale index. The rise in fuel and power prices also added to costs of production in nearly every field, and the raw materials for other industries such as chemicals and plastics became more expensive. Perhaps half the year's rise in the wholesale index, seven percentage points, should be attributed to the direct and indirect effects of the energy crisis.

Another part, but probably small in the total, should be attributed to the domestic effects of the rapid inflation in the leading foreign industrial countries. Throughout the year, the U.S. economy was to a considerable degree protected from foreign inflation by the floating exchange rate—but not as completely as traditional theory would lead one to expect. Traditional theory assumes that general demand inflation will lift all prices in about the same degree in the inflating country. In such a case, it could be expected that a floating exchange rate would largely insulate one country from demand inflation in another. The decline in the real value of money in the inflating country would be just offset by the decline in its exchange value. But in modern industrial countries, a general demand inflation operates first and most extensively on market-dominated prices so that they advance ahead of prices dominated by administration. As a result, a floating exchange rate does not give a country complete protection from the effects of foreign inflation. It is in this way that the flexible market prices of many imported raw materials such as lead, zinc, and copper have been raised in the United States, thus adding to domestic costs and contributing to the 14% inflation.

How much of the 14% rise should be attributed to this foreign inflation is difficult to say, but *total* imports in that period amounted to only 8% of GNP, and only a part would be involved in the wholesale index. Even taking account of the indirect as well as the direct effects of these flexible-priced commodities, it is doubtful if they accounted for anything like half of the 14% rise in the wholesale index.

The third claimant, administrative inflation from the side of management, appears to have been a much more important element. First, most of that half of the 14% price rise still to be accounted for came in the more concentrated industries. This is shown in Table III [Table 17.3] which classifies the fourteen B.L.S. group indexes in the same fashion as in Charts III and V and shows the percentage increase from June 1973 to June 1974.

Of the five more competitive groups, only textiles went up as much as the total index; and the five groups taken together increased less than 2%. On the other hand, of the six more concentrated groups, all but transportation equipment went up more than the total index, and the weighted average for the six went up nearly 22%.

This table reinforces the evidence already given that there was no general excess of demand to account for the inflation of the period. The prices most

Table 17.3

Inflation from June 1973 to June 1974

Competitive industry groups	Percent change in price index	Weighted change in price index
Farm products	−7.5%	
Hides, skins, and leather products	+3.6	
Foods and feeds, processed	+3.7	+1.9%
Lumber and wood products	+5.0	
Textile products and apparel	+14.7	
Mixed industry groups		
Furniture and household durables	+9.5%	
Chemicals and allied products	+29.3	
Fuels and related products and power	+57.8	
Concentrated industry groups		
Transportation equipment	+6.8%	
Nonmetallic mineral products	+16.3	
Rubber and plastic products	+20.4	21.9%
Pulp, paper, and allied products	+20.9	
Machinery and equipment	+21.9	
Metals and metal products	+31.3	
All commodity index		+14%

Source: U.S. Bureau of Labor Statistics
Note: A Breakdown of the B.L.S. wholesale price index to reflect the relative role of market-dominated and administration-dominated prices

sensitive to rising demand rose little at the same time that fuel and the administration-dominated prices rose sharply. An outstanding example of the latter is the 31% rise in the index of iron and steel prices. In the year from August 1973 to August 1974, the index for finished steel prices rose a total of 44%.

How much of the 22% price increase in the concentrated industries came from increased fuel and raw material costs, how much from the wage increases which averaged 9.6% per man-hour for all manufacturing, how much from the increase in interest rates, and how much from widened profit margins can only be determined from an industry-by-industry analysis. But corporate profits increased substantially in this period, while real production did not. The reduced profits of the more competitive industries, which could not raise their prices as easily, tended to cover up the greater increase in the more concentrated industries within the total industry figures. The tentative conclusion is justified that a substantial part of the 14% inflation at the wholesale level arose from the excessive widening of profit margins.

A similar compound inflation occurred in the galloping inflation of the two months following June 1974. In that period, the wholesale price index rose 7.5%, or at an annual rate of 45%. This inflation reflected not only the continued rise of fuel prices, but also a renewed rise in the farm and food prices as a result of drought and crop damage in the mid-West. But the price indexes for the other three competitive industry groups went up little or went down, and the bulk of the remaining price increase was in the more concentrated industries whose combined index went up 5.8%, an increase at an annual rate of 35%. Again, the figures point strongly to a further widening of profit margins in those industries in which there is such a degree of concentration that management can exercise substantial market power.

In these two months of galloping inflation, the rate suggests that *the expectation* of further inflation may have played an important role. As traditional theory has explained, the pure speculator can stimulate inflation, pushing up prices through buying a part of the supply. When the speculator unloads, the price is pushed down, and the speculator has no *net* effect on price, once adjustment to the cause of price change has been made. But where an industry is concentrated and management has a substantial degree of market power, there is usually little room for the pure speculator. A speculator outside the auto industry could expect a rise in auto prices and buy, say, 10,000 cars; but it would require more than just a sell order to dispose of them. Thus the independent speculator is not a problem in the concentrated industries.

However, an expectation of inflation can introduce a quite different effect in the concentrated industries—an arbitrary price increase by management. Once there is a *general* expectation of continued inflation, the market controls of cost and demand become even less restrictive in the concentrated industries than they would be in more normal times, and prices can be raised by sizable amounts. Astute management seeks to "beat the gun" on inflation by raising prices more in relation to costs than if there were no general expectation of inflation. Again, only detailed industry studies would show how much this factor contributes to an inflation once it has started. What is important is that this factor can operate when inflation occurs under conditions of stagnation.

Inflation and Public Policy

Once the source or sources of a given inflation have become clear, the appropriate public policy is reasonably clear, except in the case of administrative inflation.

When inflation comes from a *general* demand in excess of what can be met with available resources, traditional theory correctly calls for a tight monetary-fiscal policy to limit demand.

When prices rise for particular market-dominated commodities because of a crop failure or oil crisis, traditional theory again correctly offers the alternative of rationing through price increases or, where the damage through price increases would be great, the alternative of price control and government rationing. Indeed, whether the high price of imported oil calls for rationing through greatly increased prices or calls for domestic price control and government rationing would be a legitimate matter of debate under traditional theory. In either case, the short-run answer to reduced supply is belt tightening, while the longer-run answer is the increase in supply and more efficient use.

Domestic price increases arising from inflation abroad present a more complex problem. Domestic policy would call for a floating exchange rate. Then it might simply treat the increases which bypassed the floating exchange rates in the same fashion as other temporary limitations on supply. Or policy could be aimed at helping other countries to control their own inflation.

The latter course seems indicated by the fact that much of the foreign inflation can be linked to the uncontrolled expansion in eurodollars—dollar deposits held in foreign commercial banks—which have already reached the magnitude of $185 billion. They have arisen in part from imbalances in U.S. payments abroad with the backing of dollars in the U.S. But in substantial part, they have been created abroad and are not in any way an obligation of the U.S. Traditional theory does not concern itself with the effect from the deposit currency of one country when it is created in another. But foreign inflation is likely to continue as long as the stock of eurodollars is allowed to expand without control, and there is an increasing recognition that the effect is inflationary. A eurodollar may have a low velocity of use in a foreign country, but as a liquid store of value, it can take the place of the country's own currency and force a rise in its velocity. This presents a problem, along with that of oil, which requires international cooperation.

Limiting Administrative Inflation

The really immediate issue is that of limiting the abuse of market power in concentrated industries. Because traditional theory does not envisage administrative inflation, it can give little guidance in its control. Indeed, traditional theory could not even provide a basis for setting up the principles to guide management in adjusting its prices to changed conditions. The principle of equating marginal cost and marginal revenue would have no relevance.

The first essential is to provide management with a clear set of guidelines which would define what use of market power is consistent with a national policy to achieve high employment without inflation and what actions constitute an abuse of such power. An effort to "beat the gun" on inflation is obviously such an abuse, and until management is provided with clear guidelines, it cannot be expected to act responsibly.

Labor has shown that it will abide by price-wage guidelines when it believes (1) that the guidelines are fair and (2) that management will also abide by them.

This is partly because labor has a greater interest than management in avoiding inflation and partly because management will tend to act as enforcer of wage guidelines.

In the case of management, there is no possible enforcer in sight except the government. Suppose that a fair set of price and wage guidelines had already been set up. Some more responsible enterprises might abide by them, and most could be expected to enforce them on labor. But most businesses could be expected to continue to abuse their market power, and the result of a simple publication of such guidelines would clearly be unfair to labor.

Yet, consider the advantages to management if all enterprises with significant market power were to abide by a fair set of guidelines. If a given enterprise with market power were offered a contract that would make everyone else adhere to the guidelines providing that it would agree to do so in turn, the signing of such a contract would usually be an excellent piece of business. A small diminution of discretion would promise to remove the headaches of this type of inflation, both with respect to wages and the constant need to readjust to changing prices and the accounting problems this generates. And if it would allow an expansion of real demand, operations under a prosperous economy would yield larger profits.

But only government could enforce such a contract. The problem is to work out a program of enforcement which would interfere minimally with business discretion in the carrying out of its productive activity.

It would probably be sufficient to limit the enforcement to the few hundred largest manufacturing corporations. This is where most of the significant market power resides. It seems likely that, if the abuse of market power were prevented in the more concentrated industries, and for their more important products, administrative inflation could be kept to an acceptable minimum.[9]

It may be said that such government interference with the private administration of prices by the big corporations is an invasion of individual freedom. It should be recognized, however, that the market power of big enterprise is only possible as the result of the power to operate as corporations, and the power to operate as a corporation is a grant of power from the government, not a "natural right" of individuals. This grant of power does not entitle corporations to abuse their market power. And their very size vests them with a public interest.

An alternative approach would be to reduce or eliminate market power through the more stringent enforcement of the antitrust laws and the breakup of big business. The antitrust laws have been outstandingly successful in preventing actual *monopoly,* the industry with only one seller. There are very few industries in which there are not at least several competing producers. But these laws were never designed to prevent *oligopoly*—the current source of market power. A substantial reduction of market power will, in any case, take time.

Public policy might well combine the short-run course of guiding the use of market power with longer-run measures to reduce it, waiting on the success of each to determine the subsequent weight to be given to each.

Figure 17.6. **The Anatomy of the Recent Stagflation,**
September 1973 to September 1974

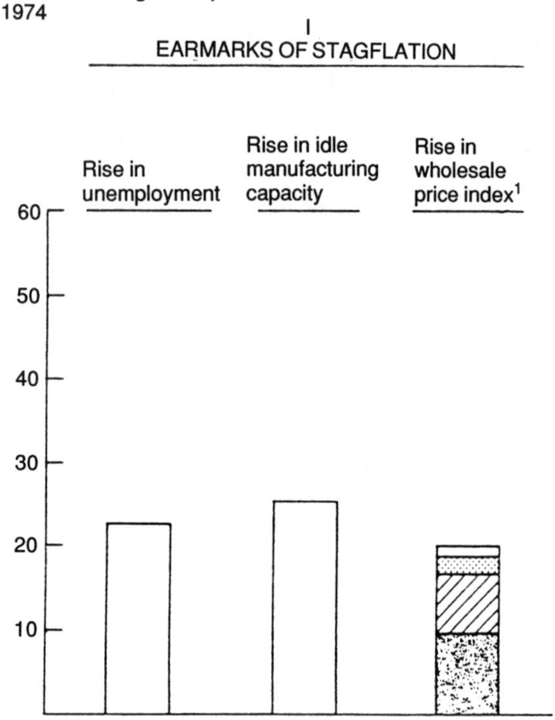

Source: B.L.S. and F.R.B.

[1]In addition to the industry groups included in II, the wholesale price index includes B.L.S. groups ''Miscellaneous'' and ''Furniture and Household Durables'' which cannot be attributed as primarily concentrated or primarily competitive and account for 5% of the increase in the wholesale index.

Conclusions

Simultaneous inflation and stagnation or recession is a relatively new phenomenon which lies outside the framework of traditional theory and traditional policy. It has plagued the American economy for a score of years and clearly cannot be controlled by the traditional measures of fiscal restraint and tight money. In the United States, it has arisen primarily from the abuse of market power by big business, while the compensation of labor has lagged behind the rise in prices. Its essential character can be summarized in the simple Chart VI [Figure 17.6] which shows the anatomy of this inflation from September 1973 to September 1974. In this period of stagflation, the weighted index for the concentration-dominated industries rose 27%, accounting for half the rise in the wholesale index, while average hourly compensation to labor in manufacturing during the

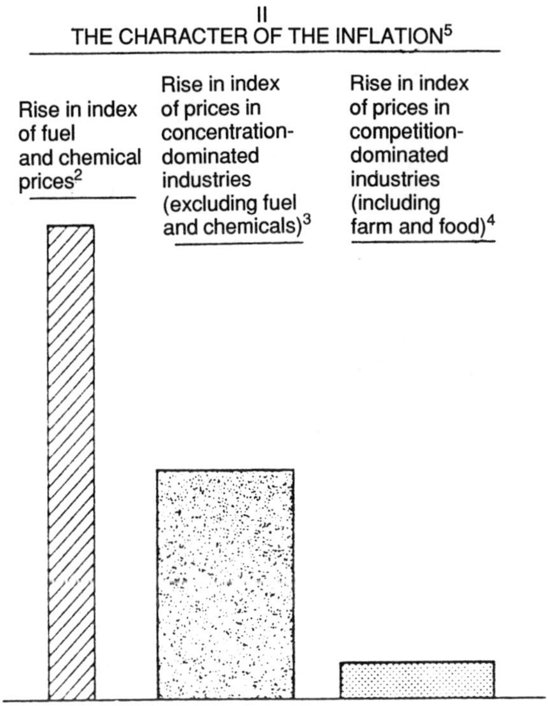

[2]Weighted Average of Wholesale Indexes for Fuel, etc. and Chemicals, etc.
[3]Weighted Average of Wholesale Indexes for Metals, Machinery, Non-metallic Minerals, Rubber, Paper, and Transportation Equipment.
[4]Weighted Average of Wholesale Indexes for Farm, Food, Leather, Lumber, Textiles, and their products.
[5]Width of columns indicate relative weight of groups in the wholesale price index.

same period rose only 10%. The index dominated by competition rose less than 5%.

In the short run, it is likely that this new form of inflation can be substantially controlled by the government through the guidance of pricing of a few hundred of the largest manufacturing corporations. To what extent it can be controlled in the longer run by reducing market power through antitrust action or the break-up of enterprises remains to be seen.

Notes

1. Gardiner C. Means, *The Structure of the American Economy,* National Resources Committee, 1939, pp. 200–201.

2. *The Behavior of Industrial Prices,* National Bureau of Economic Research, 1971, Table 5–5, p. 65. Other data on frequency of price change is presented but in such a

confused fashion that it sheds little light on the frequency of price changes paid by individual buyers. For an analysis of the price data and a critique of this report by the present writer see "The Administered-Price Thesis Reconfirmed." *American Economic Review,* Vol. LXII, No. 3, June 1972, pp. 292–306.

3. See "The Administered Price Thesis Reconfirmed," *Op cit.*

4. *Steel and the Post-War Inflation,* Joint Economic Committee, 86th Congress, 1st Session, Nov. 6, 1959.

5. See John M. Blair, *Economic Concentration,* New York, 1972, pp. 640–642.

6. The total of demand deposits and currency (M_1) was not significantly greater at the end of 1957 than at the end of 1955, $135.9 billion as against $135.2 billion.

7. The corn blight of 1970 contributed some "crop-failure" effect.

8. After paying taxes and allowing for the plant and equipment used up in production (depreciation etc.) the remaining income of nonfinancial corporations in the last half of 1972 amounted to $941 billion. Of this $824 billion went as compensation to employees covering wages, salaries and supplements while $117 billion went as compensation to capital covering interest and profits after taxes whether or not distributed as dividends.

9. The government's power to interfere with the pricing process might be further limited by relating it to the rate of administrative inflation. If there were little administrative inflation as indicated by an appropriate index, the government power might be limited to the issuance of guidelines and the calling on the few corporations subject to its control to report and justify price increases. If the rate of administrative inflation were higher, the government could require pre-reporting of planned price changes which would provide an opportunity to persuade those which appeared to exceed the guidelines. Finally, the power to control prices or force rollbacks might accrue to government only if the rate of administrative inflation were high.

18

Which Was the True Keynesian Theory of Employment?

Modigliani once pointed out that it was possible to find the basis for two quite different theoretical explanations of persistent unemployment in Keynes' *General Theory of Employment, Interest and Money*. The first theory revolved around Keynes' concept of liquidity preference and the effect of interest rates on the willingness or desire of the public to hold money balances. The second theory revolved around money-wage rates and their failure to behave in the classical fashion of equating supply and demand. Either theory *within its own postulates* could explain the failure of Say's Law to operate. One did this at the macro-level of the demand for money balances and the other at the micro-level of specific markets for labor.

The first of these theories, which became widely accepted in the United States, is referred to in Joan Robinson's recent article in *Challenge* (May/June 1976) as "bastard Keynesianism," while the second she treats as the true Keynesian theory. Here I would like to take the reverse view.

My conclusion that Keynes' explanation of unemployment did not depend on the nonclassical behavior of money-wage rates rests in important part on personal experience. By 1934 I had developed a theoretical explanation for persistent unemployment in terms of the nonclassical behavior of administered prices. This theory, with substantial statistical support and a discussion of its policy implications for that period, was published as a U.S. Senate document in 1935. I sent a draft to Keynes and he suggested that I take the statistical material and organize it as an article for the *Economic Journal* which he was then editing. Unfortunately, press of duties prevented my doing this. Then when Keynes' *General Theory* was published in 1936, I was unclear as to whether it was a theory of employment which closely paralleled my own, except that it turned on

Reprinted from *Challenge* (July–August 1976), pp. 61–63.

the nonclassical behavior of money-wage rates instead of administered prices, or was quite a different theory which did not depend on nonclassical wage or price behavior.

In the summer of 1939, on my way to a holiday in Norway, I made it a point to visit Keynes with the specific purpose of asking him to what extent his explanation of persistent unemployment rested on an assumption of wage-rate or price inflexibility. His answer was a categorical: "Not at all." I asked the question in several different ways in order to make sure there was no failure of minds to meet and the answer was always the same. I said, "Suppose that prices and wage-rates met the classical assumption of perfect flexibility so that, if there were excessive unemployment, the price-wage level would fall frictionlessly. Then with the nominal money stock remaining constant, wouldn't the rise in the *real* value of the money stock create added demand which would tend to absorb unemployed workers?" But still the answer was no. Once interest rates had fallen to their limit there would be no further corrective. We were in complete agreement that, in practice, neither prices nor wage-rates were as flexible as classical theory assumed, but he insisted that his theory of unemployment did not depend *at all* on this fact.

On my return, a re-reading of the *General Theory* confirmed the fact that, *if its basic postulates were accepted,* it offered a logical explanation of persistent unemployment even when prices and money-wage rates were classically flexible. It also indicated that this explanation, based on Keynes' interest and money postulates, was *the* General Theory of Employment Keynes was presenting in his book. Two-thirds of the way through the book Keynes summarized his explanation of unemployment in Chapter 18, entitled "The General Theory of Employment Re-stated." In the four-and-a-half pages of this summary there is not a single mention of the inflexibility or the nonclassical behavior of money-wage rates.

A re-reading also indicated why Keynes introduced the inflexibility of money-wage rates into his book. It was not to explain unemployment but to explain the relative *stability* of prices. Keynes clearly recognized that *if money-wage rates and prices were classically flexible,* it was a logical necessity of his theory that once the minimum level of interest rates was reached, continued unemployment would force down money-wage rates with no clear stopping point short of zero. Thus he says, "For if competition between unemployed workers always led to a very great reduction of the money-wage, there would be a violent instability in the price-level" (p. 253). But it was only after he had *completed* this summary of his General Theory of Employment that he faced the empirical fact that the price-level is not violently unstable and sought an explanation.

In a section immediately following his summary, Keynes says: "The above is a summary of the General Theory. But the actual phenomena of the economic system are also colored by certain characteristics of the propensity to consume, the schedule of the marginal efficiency of capital and the rate of interest, about which we can safely generalize from experience, but which are not logically necessary. In particular, it is an outstanding characteristic of the economic system in which we live that, whilst it is subject to severe fluctuations in respect of output and employment, it is not violently unstable'' (p. 249). Keynes then gives four possible conditions *outside the logic of his theory* to explain this relative *stability*. One of these is that ''moderate changes in employment are not associated with very great changes in money-wages. This is a condition of the stability of prices rather than employment'' (p. 251).

Keynes states the problem most clearly in his chapter on ''The Theory of Prices'' when he says: ''In fact we must have *some* factor, the value of which in terms of money is, if not fixed, at least sticky to give us any stability in a monetary system'' (p. 304; emphasis in the original). He introduces the relative inflexibility of money-wage rates as the sticky factor.

In the light of my 1939 interview with Keynes and the re-reading of the *General Theory*, I find it difficult to accept the idea that the employment theory Keynes presented in his book to explain the failure of Say's Law was a theory *based* on the nonclassical behavior of money-wage rates. The evidence seems too strong that his theory of employment was a theory based on the relation between interest rates and money, as the title to his book clearly implies.

Whether Keynes later shifted the basis of his explanation of unemployment away from the logic of his macro-theory of interest and money to the logic of a micro-theory of money-wage inflexibility is open for discussion. Robinson says (*Challenge*, Jan./Feb. 1974, p. 7): ''. . . we had some trouble in getting Maynard to see what the point of his revolution really was but when he came to sum it up after the book was published he got it into focus.'' She cites an article by Keynes in the *Quarterly Journal of Economics*, February 1937, entitled ''The General Theory of Employment.'' In that summarizing article, Keynes discusses ''Certain definite points on which the writer diverges from previous theories'' (Section II) with emphasis on his departure from the classical in respect to interest and money but with no mention of any nonclassical behavior of wage rates or prices. In the section on ''Demand and Supply of output as a whole'' (Section III) Keynes says: ''The theory can be summed up by saying that, given the psychology of the public, the level of output and employment as a whole depends on the amount of investment'' (p. 221). He also says: ''More comprehensively, aggregate output depends on the propensity to hoard, on the policy of the monetary authority as it affects the quantity of money, on the state of confidence concerning the prospective yield of capital-assets, on the propensity to spend and on the social factors which influence the level of the money wage'' (p. 221).

This is the only mention of money-wage rates in his summary and he gives no elaboration with respect to ''social factors.'' If Keynes had had in mind the nonclassical behavior of wage rates, this would have been a major divergence from previous theories of employment, since it would in itself be a sufficient divergence to explain the persistence of unemployment without introducing the concept of liquidity preference or Keynes' particular postulate on the relation of money to aggregate demand. Certainly, in 1939 when Keynes categorically denied that his explanation of unemployment depended on inflexible wage rates, no shift in the basis of his explanation was in evidence. I submit not only that the theory of employment elaborated in the U.S. under the Keynesian banner was not a bastardized version, but that it was the true version developed in his book.

A more interesting question is whether the General Theory of Employment as given in Keynes' book and as elaborated by Keynesians in the U.S. is valid. The issue turns on Keynes' hidden postulate that the only significant way money affects aggregate demand is *indirectly* through interest rates. One can accept Keynes' concept of liquidity preference as an important contribution to theory. One can also accept his liquidity trap so long as it is limited to the idea that at some low level of interest rates (Keynes suggested 2 percent) the public would choose to hold any amount of money *rather than make additional loans*. But it is extremely difficult to accept his postulate that at the "trap" level of interest rates, the public would choose to hold any amount of money *rather than spend more on goods*.

The questionable character of this third postulate can be suggested by an extreme example. Take a closed economy with classically flexible prices and money-wage rates, with a fixed nominal stock of money, and with an initial trap condition combined with excessive unemployment. In this situation, a fall in money-wage rates and prices could be expected which would increase the *real* buying power of the total money stock. Since interest rates are assumed to be already at the trap level, the increase in the real stock of money would have no significant effect on interest rates and thus provide no reduction of interest rates to stimulate investment. On the other hand, the increase in the real buying power of the fixed money stock could, in Ricardo's term, make money *redundant,* i.e., more than the public would choose to hold at the initial level of incomes, prices, and interest rates. If the public started with a real money stock equal to, say, a quarter of a year's real income, a 50 percent drop in the price-wage level with no change in production would mean the public was holding the equal of half a year's real income in the form of cash on hand. A price-wage drop to a quarter of the initial level would mean the public would be holding enough money to buy as much as a full year's real income. The public would be holding the equal of five years' real income if the price-wage level dropped to one-twentieth of its starting level. It is reasonable to believe that long before the public was holding such huge idle balances, it would find that the relative advantage of spending outweighed the advantage of holding more real buying power in the form of money. Then the public would be trying to spend more than its current income, and since the public *in total* could not do this, its production and real income would have to go up, absorbing unemployed workers.

This would mean that real aggregate demand was being affected directly by the increase in the size of the real stock of money even though the liquidity trap precluded any fall of interest rates and there was therefore no indirect interest effect from the increase in the real money stock. Also, there would seem to be no reason to think that a small real increase in the money stock would not operate directly to produce a small increase in real aggregate demand, even when interest rates were so low that the public would choose to hold any amount of money rather than make additional loans. One concludes that the valid postulate is that at the trap level of interest rates, the public would choose *not* to hold any amount of money rather than spend more on goods.

But this change in postulate which makes aggregate demand in part a *direct* function of the real money stock would so modify the Keynes formulation that the modified version could no longer explain persistent involuntary unemployment where prices and money wage rates were classically flexible. Excessive unemployment would then tend to be eliminated through the direct effect of the increase in the real stock of money even when there was no indirect effect from a fall of interest rates. Say's Law would then be vindicated for an economy with classically flexible prices and wage-rates. I therefore conclude not only that the theory of employment presented in Keynes' book and elaborated in America is the true Keynesian theory of employment, but also that it fails to explain persistent unemployment because it rests on the faulty postulate that money does not affect the level of aggregate demand directly.

To explain the obvious failure of Say's Law one should recognize that its validity rests on the classical postulate of price and wage flexibility. Once this is accepted, one can turn to the nonclassical behavior of administered prices or of money-wage rates or both. But this would not be a Keynesian explanation. Its logic would not depend *in any way* on Keynes' valuable concept of liquidity preference.

One could then discuss which plays the major role in explaining persistent unemployment and in explaining simultaneous recession and inflation, the nonclassical behavior of administered prices or the nonclassical behavior of administered wage rates. Perhaps in the U.K. wages play the major role and in the U.S. the major role is played by administered prices. After all the Great Recession in the U.S. from 1929 to 1933 occurred when there was little labor organization in the more concentrated industries. But whether the nonclassical behavior of prices or money-wage rates should be assigned the major role in the unhorsing of Say's Law, the answer is unrelated to the theory of unemployment presented by Keynes in *The General Theory of Employment, Interest and Money.*

19

Corporate Power in the Marketplace

I have been asked to give you my perception at present of the issues raised in our book *The Modern Corporation.* As a macroeconomist concerned with a stable and productive economy, I will focus on the second theme of this issue, the power of corporations. At the same time I will keep in mind the extent to which the separation of ownership and control increases that power. Also I want to make it clear that in speaking of corporate power in the marketplace I am not concerned with monopoly power. Our book does not even list "monopoly" in the index. Rather, I am concerned with the market power that arises naturally from active competition among a few large independent corporations and is reflected in the pricing discretion in the hands of individual competing enterprises.

I

A. The Basic Change in the Structure of the Free Market System

As you know, the central aim of our book was not to give answers to the basic issues we raised but to present a realistic framework to replace the picture of economic life so skillfully painted by Adam Smith in 1776, which still provided the basic framework for the conventional wisdom fifty years ago.

At the time Adam Smith wrote, he was well justified in championing competition among the many small producers of his day as the great macrocoordinator of production and distribution. The individual small producer tended to have no significant market power over the pricing of his product; prices were determined by the invisible hand of market forces; and the free market system not only tended to direct

Reprinted with permission from the *Journal of Law & Economics*, vol. XXVI (June 1983). © 1983 by the University of Chicago. All rights reserved.

resources into optimum uses in the long run but, more important for present purposes, it provided an automatic mechanism tending to maintain full employment through the flexible adjustment of prices. If general demand fell and the total money stock remained constant, a fall in the price level automatically increased the real buying power of the money stock, thereby stimulating real demand and restoring full employment at a lower level of prices.

Then the Industrial and Corporate Revolutions gradually altered the structure of the free market system by transferring much of the task of coordinating productive activity from the marketplace to the administrative actions of the managers of corporations.

This gradual shift from market to administrative coordination had two profound effects. First, it gradually increased the productivity of both labor and capital so that the average level of living rose greatly over the years. Second, it undermined the ability of the free market system to maintain economic stability. It gradually substituted a radically different kind of competition for that relied on by Adam Smith. So long as prices were set by the classical market, they were highly flexible since no one producer could expect to influence a market price ruled by the equating of supply and demand. But the increase in corporate production had the natural and legitimate effect of increasing the proportion of markets in which competition was between a few independent competitors who thereby obtained some degree of pricing discretion. An individual management could estimate its costs and the probable demand for each of its specific products and then set its price in the light of what it thought its few competitors would do if it set one price rather than another. Or it would adopt the price set by a price leader. In either case, the price would usually be set by the seller and would tend to be held constant for a period of time and a series of transactions. Under this different kind of competition, prices were set by the visible hands of competing managements and could perform the function of directing a nation's resources of labor and capital into optimum uses only if close to full employment could be maintained for the economy as a whole. But this is what the free market system cannot do if too large a proportion of prices behave in a nonclassical fashion.

By the time our book was published, the conventional wisdom had registered the great increase in potential productivity due to the corporation, but it still clung to the view that the free market system would operate automatically to eliminate excessive unemployment of labor and capital. Yet at that time (1932) real national income had fallen by nearly a third, 40 percent of the country's industrial plant was idle, and a quarter of its labor force was unemployed. Clearly a new framework was needed within which to work out the economic issues and policies for that day. Laissez faire was no longer a valid policy.

B. Market Power in the New Framework

As I now read what we said at that time, I continue to believe that the most important *economic* conclusion we reached is in the chapter on "Concentration of Economic Power," where we said in our fifth and final conclusion, "Competition has changed in character and the principles applicable to present conditions are radically different from those which apply when the dominant competing units are smaller and more numerous."[1] I fully agree with our final conclusion that the modern corporation has wrought such a change in the free market system that, "[n]ew concepts must be forged and a new picture of economic relationships created."[2]

Our book provided the new framework, showing that by 1930 (1) roughly three quarters of the business wealth of this country was held by corporations; (2) practically half of this corporate wealth was controlled by the 200 largest; (3) a substantial part of this wealth involved a separation between ownership and control; and (4) the free market system had shifted from one dominated by markets in which competition was among the many to a system of such markets combined with markets in which competition was among the few, with significant market power in the hands of managements.

But we did not go much beyond these concepts to answer the basic question how such an economy, with a significant part of its industrial plant and manpower already idle, could be returned to health. What could take the place of the classical automatic corrective of free-falling prices as the mechanism to maintain high employment of resources? This was the economic problem we presented along with the legal and economic implications of the separation of ownership and control, which so greatly increased the power of individual corporations to grow in size.

II

A. New Market Concepts for the Prewar Period

When I turn from my present perception of what we said about market power and consider the new concepts which grew directly out of this new framework, I do not hesitate to say that far and away the most important new economic market concepts were those of "administered price," "administrative competition," and later, "administrative inflation," arising from "perverse pricing." An administered price is a price set for a period of time and a series of transactions. Administrative competition is a nonclassical form of competition in which there are so few independent competitors that each has a significant degree of pricing discretion, so that setting prices becomes an active function of business administration. The other two concepts did not become important until after World War II and will be discussed in Section III.

The difference between classical and administrative competition can easily be seen in the difference between the markets for farm products and for farm implements. Corn and wheat prices are largely determined in public auctions with no one seller setting a price, whereas the price of a new farm tractor is set by the management of the individual tractor maker and kept constant for considerable periods. The difference is also obvious between Adam Smith's retail price arrived at by higgling and bargaining in the market and the modern chain store where there is no higgling and bargaining at the cash register.

What makes these two new concepts important is that they *alone* are sufficient not only to explain why, in the 1930s, the automatic corrective of classical competition could not work, but also to point to an alternative mechanism which could maintain high employment consistent with the free market system.

This problem and a solution were clearly brought out in a paper I gave before a joint session of the American Statistical Association and the Econometric Society in 1934.[3] There I first publicly introduced the concept of an administered price and gave extensive statistical evidence that there were two quite different types of competitive markets, one in which prices changed frequently and were highly flexible and one in which prices changed infrequently and tended to be inflexible. This can be seen in Figure 1 [Figure 19.1].

Briefly, the paper said that in a national economy where all production is sold in classically competitive markets and where there is initial full employment, if for some reason a fall in demand creates unemployment while the money stock remains constant, the conventional corrective will operate. Prices will fall, thereby increasing real aggregate demand, and this will restore high employment at a lower level of prices. The higher real buying power of the money stock will support a high real income. But in an economy where roughly half of production is sold in administratively competitive markets, there is no automatic corrective to maintain production. Only half of prices would fall in an automatically corrective fashion, while half would drop insufficiently to correct the fall in real demand, thereby creating persistent unemployment and a distorted price structure. The resulting distortion in the price structure can be seen in the 1929–32 recession in Figure 2 [Figure 19.2].

In the same paper, I showed that a monetary expansion could be expected to bring about economic recovery by raising classically competitive prices, raising production and employment in administratively competitive markets, and leading to a restoration of full employment with the distortion of prices largely eliminated. The rise in the nominal money stock would take the place of the classical fall in the price level as a whole at the initial price level.

As I look back on this 1934 analysis, I would now modify it only in two important respects. First, I would add Keynes's deficit spending to my monetary expansion as a possible but not a necessary way for government to expand aggregate demand when there is excessive unemployment. Second, I would point out that the 1934 analysis did not envisage the new kind of inflation we have been experiencing over most of the period since 1955, which will be discussed in Section III.

B. The Relevance of Classical Monopoly Theory

When the Great Depression forced economists to rethink macroeconomic theory beyond the range of the business cycle, it is not surprising that the principles of

Figure 19.1. **Relation between Frequency of Price Change and Magnitude of Price Change During Depression, 1929–32.**

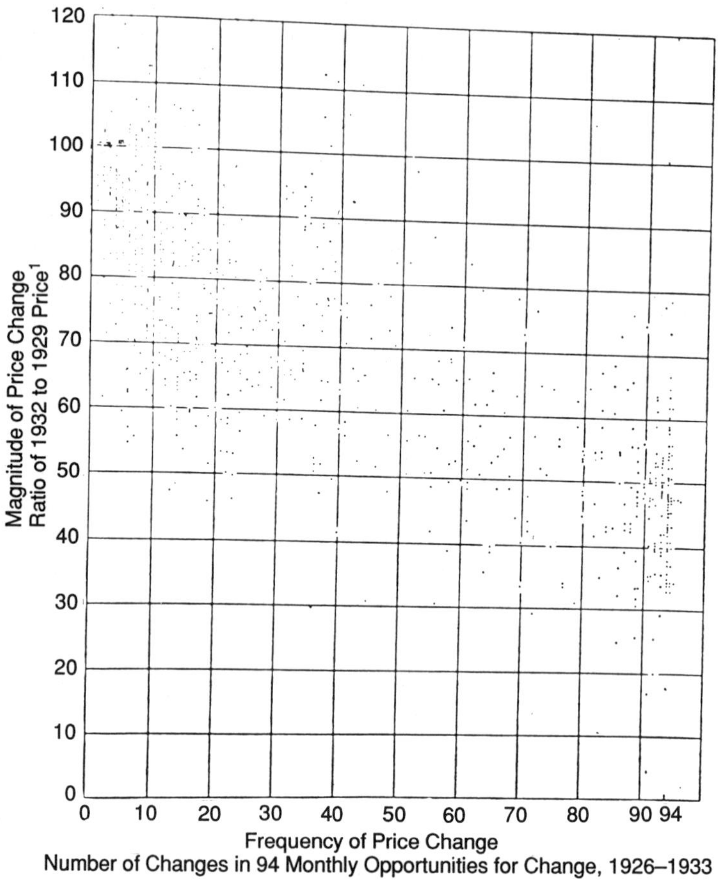

Source: Gardiner C. Means, "Price Inflexibility and Requirements of a Stabilizing Monetary Policy," *Journal of the American Statistical Association* 30 [1935]: 404.
Note: Distribution of 750 price series included in wholesale price index.
[1]Average of monthly prices

classical monopoly theory were applied to competition among the few. This is explicit in Chamberlin's book *The Theory of Monopolistic Competition.*[4] My own experience in running a successful monopoly over a decade led me to reject monopoly theory in writing my 1934 paper. It would have been clarifying if I had given my reason.

My basic reason for rejecting classical monopoly theory turns on the simple

Figure 19.2. **Deflation and Reflation: Wholesale Prices for Five Frequency Groups, 1926 to March, 1942.**

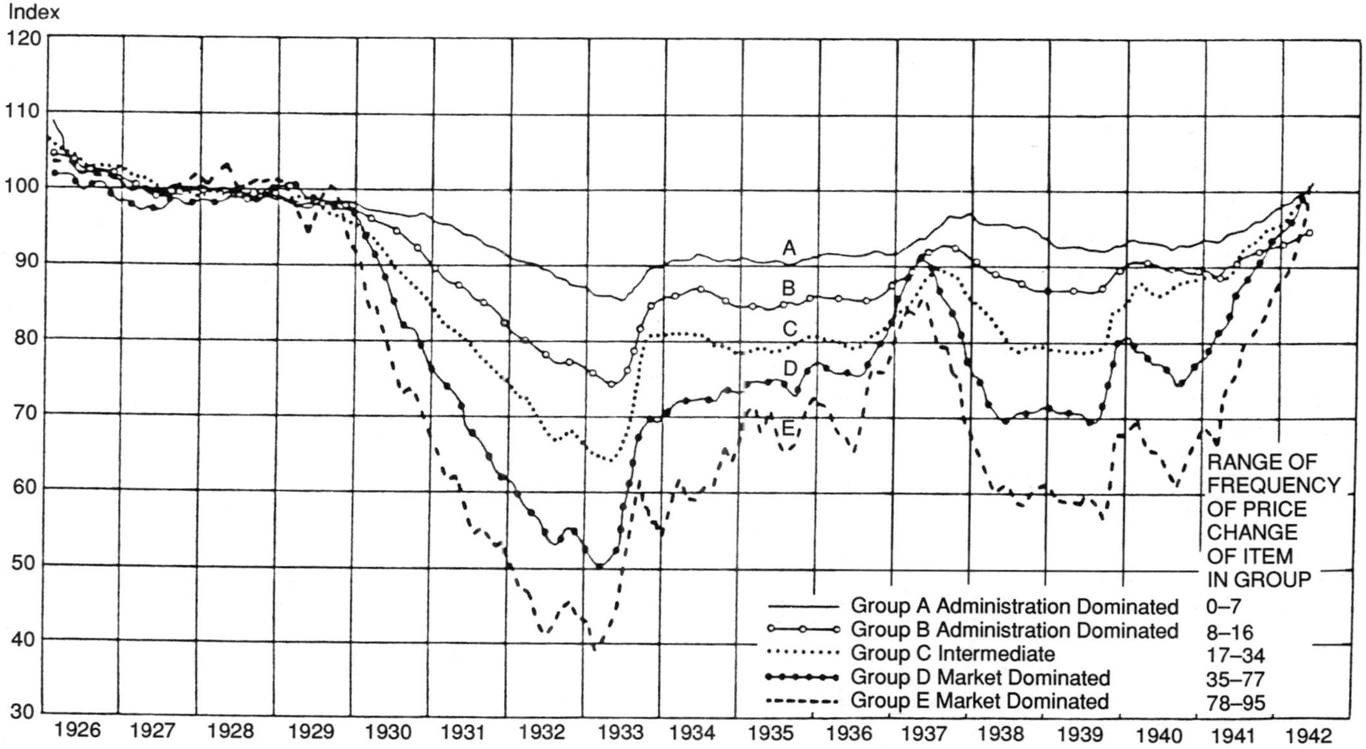

Note: Price indexes are for 731 items included in the wholesale price index grouped according to frequency of monthly price change, 1926–33. Price freeze 1926–29 = 100.

mathematics of monopoly pricing. The textbooks present a correct statement of the mathematics but usually present only two of the three messages the mathematics carry. The first message is that, given figures for costs and revenue at relevant quantities, the most profitable price can easily be calculated. The second message is also clear, namely, that a price well above or below the most profitable price will produce much smaller profits. But the third and crucial message for practical pricing behavior is seldom discussed. It indicates that moderate departures from the most profitable price have little practical effect on profits.

This failure can be seen in the example of monopoly pricing given by Samuelson in his widely used text on economics.[5] He shows in his monopoly example, first, that the most profitable price for his monopolist would be $120 per unit, which would bring in $230 of profits in a given period. He also shows that a $20 departure up or down from this price would lose him $30 of these potential profits and further departures from the most profitable price would bring even more sharp reductions in profits. But he does not point out that a moderate departure from the most profitable price would have only a minor effect on profits. In his example, a price $1 higher or lower than $120 would lose the monopolist less than 8 cents out of $230. A price departure of $2 would reduce profits by a mere 30 cents. Indeed, a $5 departure from the most profitable price or a $10 range would still bring the monopolist more than 99 percent of the full monopoly profit.

Even with perfect knowledge of demand and cost, there would be little inducement for a monopolist to be constantly changing its price because of moderate changes in demand or cost. And in the presence of some uncertainty over costs and demand and with positive costs in announcing price changes, there could easily be substantial periods of constant prices and sizable changes in price when they occurred. If this message, which is inherent in pure monopoly pricing, had been well understood, I believe the infrequency of price change where competition was among a few competitors would have been more quickly accepted.

C. The Actual Recovery from the Great Depression

The role of market power in the recovery from 1932 to 1942 can be seen in Figure 2. The five lines in the chart represent price indexes for wholesale prices grouped according to crude measures of frequency of price change. The difference in behavior is taken to reflect in large degree differences in pricing discretion arising from market power.

In the long period of recovery from the Great Depression, the basic analysis of the 1934 paper receives a remarkable confirmation in spite of the confusions of the period. By 1942, when full employment was finally reached and the price structure was frozen, the substantial unbalance between classically competitive and administratively competitive prices had disappeared and the wholesale price level at full employment in 1942 was almost exactly the same as at full employment in 1929.

During this twelve-year period there was great confusion about recovery policy. By the spring of 1933 the reliance on the classical corrective had been dropped in the 100 days of "new economic policy." By 1934 the Depression panic had been overcome with the introduction of "industrial self government" under the National Recovery Administration. It served an important role and was then declared unconstitutional. The Keynesian explanation of oversaving and my own explanation of price inflexibility began to have some influence, with Keynes emphasizing government spending while I emphasized monetary expansion as a recovery measure. These theories pointed to the constructive use of monetary and fiscal measures by government and thus had some tendency to reinforce each other. But then, after excessive unemployment had been cut in half, unemployment began to rise sharply in 1937 when monetary growth was *unintentionally* brought to a halt, thus producing a new recession which shifted 4.7 percent of the total labor force to the ranks of the unemployed by early 1938, when the mistake was recognized and corrected. But excessive unemployment did not wholly disappear until 1940, when the money stock had been increased by nearly a fifth over the 1938 figure and war spending began. Another source of confusion grew out of the theoretical treatment of competition among the few as a branch of monopoly theory. A third source of policy confusion arose from a basic flaw in Keynes's theory which denied the potency of monetary expansion when interest rates were very low.

This confusion in policy was finally resolved. In place of the classical automatic corrective of a general fall in price level, there has been substituted an increase in aggregate demand generated by monetary and fiscal measures stimulated in part by war demand. This produced the same full-employment price level as before the recession, reversing the distorting decline in flexible prices. The success of this basic shift in policy led to the enactment of the Employment Act of 1946, which made the maintenance of aggregate demand a federal responsibility.

III

A. Structural Change and the New Type of Inflation

When I turn to the role of corporate power in the marketplace during recent years, I find that the creeping increase in the role of administrative competition has created a new dilemma. Concentration has passed a critical point in changing the structure of the free market system and has suddenly brought us a new type of inflation with prices rising sharply in recession.

The conventional wisdom holds that any sustained inflation "always and everywhere comes from too much money chasing too few goods." If this were true it would mean that simultaneous inflation and recession would be impossible. One could not have too much demand for goods in general and too little demand for goods in general at the same time.

Yet in each of the four substantial recessions in the last dozen years, prices rose while demand fell. In the 1969–70 recession the index of industrial prices rose 5 percent while the index of industrial production fell 7 percent. In the 1974–75 recession, industrial prices rose 11 percent while industrial production fell nearly 13 percent. In the 1980 recession, industrial prices rose 6 percent while industrial production fell 8.5 percent. And in the current recession, industrial prices have risen over 5 percent while industrial production dropped over 10 percent.

In the second and third of these recessions the oil cartel contributed somewhat to the price increase. The 1969–70 recession, however, occurred before the cartel was formed, and oil prices have declined in the current recession. Most of the inflation in these four recessions represented not "too much money chasing too few goods" but "too little money chasing goods on well stocked shelves." Obviously, in these recessions, more prices by weight were rising than falling.

At the time we wrote *The Modern Corporation* we did not foresee the possibility that the exercise of pricing discretion could lead to simultaneous recession and inflation. In my 1934 paper on a stabilizing policy, it was enough to show that the inflexibility of industrial prices could explain the failure of the classical automatic corrective. But my statistics showed that while roughly half of the prices in the wholesale price index behaved nonclassically in the 1929–32 recession, 10 percent of the latter actually rose. In a new preface to a 1967 revised edition of *The Modern Corporation,* I pointed out that "in the economy of the modern corporation, a wholly new type of inflation is possible: a rise of administered prices without a general excess in demand."[6] I also added that "just such an inflation occurred between 1953 and 1958" and gave figures showing that the 8 percent rise in the wholesale price index for the preceding five years occurred in administered prices and that the average of flexible market prices as a group did not rise at all. This is shown in Figure 3 [Figure 19.3]. I called this "administrative inflation" to distinguish it from demand inflation. There can be no question of the reality of this new kind of inflation.

Once the reality of simultaneous inflation and recession is accepted, three major questions are posed: What makes it possible? Why did it come suddenly? And how can it be overcome within the framework of the free market system?

B. Sources of Inflation in Recession

Here I will consider only four sources of inflation in recession.[7] I will call them all cases of "perverse pricing" and limit them to cases in which a fall in demand leads a management to raise a price. They include (1) full-cost pricing, (2) the risk of entry, (3) arbitrary wage increases, and (4) the expectation of inflation.

Full-cost pricing takes various forms, most of which can produce perverse

Figure 19.3. **Wholesale Price Changes by Product Groups, 1953 to October 1958** (average increase 8.1 percent)

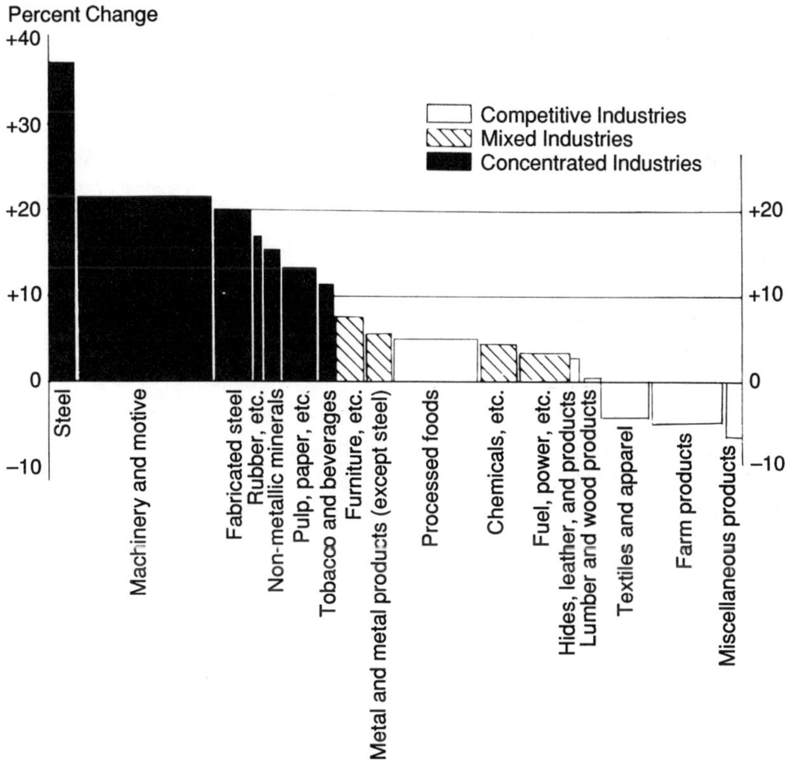

Source: Gardiner C. Means, *Administrative Inflation and Public Policy* [Washington, D.C.: Anderson Kramer Assoc., 1959], chart 4, p. 14.

pricing. In principle, probably the most common is that in which a seller works with three basic concepts—variable cost, total fixed cost, and a total profit target—which are combined to give a target price.

Variable cost covers such input items as raw materials and operating labor, the quantity of which goes up or down with the quantity of output. So long as the prices of these input items remain constant, the variable cost per unit in the target price remains constant even when demand falls.

Fixed cost covers those items of cost—such as supervisory labor, depreciation, interest, and property taxes—that do not vary because of changes in current output and under the target-pricing formula are treated as constant in total but are spread over total output to give a fixed cost per unit to be included in price. This treatment means that under the target-pricing formula when demand falls the fixed cost per unit rises because the total fixed cost has to be spread over a smaller number of units.

The profit target included in price is also treated as if it were a fixed cost of doing business. It aims to provide a targeted return on equity capital invested in producing the product, and applies a total chosen rate of return on equity capital to arrive at a total profit target. This total, like the total of fixed costs, is then spread over the total expected output to give a target profit per unit to be included in price. Also, as in the case of fixed cost, a fall in demand means that, with a fixed stock of capital, the total profit target would have to be spread over a smaller volume of sales and require a larger profit per unit.

Where this target-pricing technique is strictly adhered to, the net effect of spreading the total fixed cost and the targeted return on capital over a smaller volume of sales can explain a rise in price when demand falls. In detail it can take various forms but, with one exception to be discussed later, it can explain why a firm using the method will price perversely. It also plays a part when a single producer modifies the price it sets in the light of an expectation of how its few competitors will react if it sets one price rather than another.

A second source of perverse pricing arises where competition is among a few and the risk of encouraging new entries to the industry is reduced by a fall in demand. If an industry is operating at 90 percent of capacity, there can be considerable risk that each producer's share in the coming market will be reduced by new entrants to the industry if target rates of return are set too high. But when only 70 percent of capacity is in use, this danger is much less and individual firms can risk aiming at a higher target rate of return on their equity capital.

The third possible source of perverse pricing is the arbitrary raising of wage rates. It is well recognized that increases in real productivity justify an increase in real wage rates. But there tends to be confusion over what is a legitimate wage increase in other circumstances, such as a rise in living costs. For example, the Kennedy guideposts were quite unfair to labor. They allowed for increases only in productivity and took no account of the legitimate rise in classically competitive prices in a period of recovery as demand expanded toward full employment. In those days a perfect recovery would bring classically competitive prices up into balance with inflexible prices and produce a rise in the cost of living, which was legitimately passed on in higher wage rates. The net effect of this complex recovery would be a compound of increased real demand and a rise in the average of prices. To distinguish this legitimate price rise from "too much money chasing too few goods," it has often been referred to as "reflation": the Kennedy guideposts should have taken it into account.

In the presence of administrative inflation, the distinction between legitimate wage increases and excessive wage increases becomes much more complex, and here I will suggest only that I have seen little evidence that the wage increases of recent years have been more than a catching up in legitimate wage increases. The matter deserves more careful examination and my perception should not be given too much weight.

The fourth source of perverse pricing when there is "too little money chasing goods on well stocked shelves'' is a widespread expectation of inflation. It bears little relation to the classical ''flight from money.'' Rather, it grows out of the market power of firms that can exercise significant pricing discretion.

In the case of classical markets, an individual firm that expects inflation in the near future can speculate, first adding to demand in the market and then adding to supply in the market by the same quantity when it cashes in, thus canceling out its net effect for a period as a whole.

But in the case of administrative markets, the individual firm can react to an expectation of inflation by using its pricing discretion to raise its price directly with no offsetting inventory effect. Where competition is among a few and those few all expect general inflation, if one raises its price, it would be natural for others to follow. If government forecasts an inflation of say 5 percent, the likelihood increases. And to the extent that firms with significant pricing discretion give way to the expectation of inflation, this expectation becomes self-fulfilling.

There may well be other sources of perverse pricing, but those above are sufficient for present purposes. They raise two major questions: What is their relation to concentration? and, Why did the new type of inflation appear suddenly?

C. Perverse Pricing and the New Measure of Concentration

So long as the price level tended to fall in recession, the measure of concentration used by Berle and Means served well. It focused on nonfinancial corporate assets and showed nearly half of such assets controlled by the 200 largest corporations in 1929. But this included a significant number of corporations whose prices were regulated and were relatively inflexible. When the problem of measuring changing concentration involves *perverse* pricing, the appropriate measure should exclude the government regulated prices. An appropriate measure of concentration under the new conditions would be the index of the assets of the 200 largest manufacturing corporations given by Professor Weiss in his Table I.[8] There he shows the top 200 manufacturing corporations controlling 45.8 percent of all manufacturing corporation assets in 1929, and 59.9 percent in 1980. From 1974 to 1980, the concentration is shown as increasing from 57.6 to 59.9 percent, or significantly faster in percentage points than from 1929 to 1974. Clearly, the concentration has been continuing at a significant rate.

D. Structural Change and the Great Divide

Once one accepts the idea that structural change has been gradually increasing the relative role of perverse pricing, it is easy to see why the appearance of administrative inflation has been sudden. So long as the balance between the two types of competitive market favored classical competition, it meant that in recession more prices would go down than would go up, so that the price level as a whole would go down and the constructive program of monetary and fiscal measures already described could operate effectively. But once a critical point has been passed in this gradual structural change, the role of perverse pricing will have so greatly increased that more prices will go up than will go down and we will have the new type of inflation with the level of prices rising in recession.

This critical turning point is a new conception, and I will christen it the "Great Divide." It seems to have occurred without fanfare somewhere in the 1950s and it is well behind us now. Passing this Great Divide has presented us with the basic problem of eliminating the new type of inflation in a way consistent with the free market system and the optimum use of resources.

E. The Double Dilemma

Once the Great Divide has been passed, we are in unknown territory and are faced with two major dilemmas. First, the monetary and fiscal measures that can be used to control aggregate demand when the economy is on the good side of the Great Divide cannot control the new kind of inflation; and second, the expectation of inflation tends to become self-fulfilling when the economy is on the wrong side of the Divide.

The impotency of monetary and fiscal measures in the new circumstances is beginning to be recognized even by laymen. For example, a tight money policy that limits demand in the hope of controlling inflation can be expected not only to increase idle machines and workers but also raise prices. And an expansion in the money stock to stimulate demand will also stimulate both inflation and the self-fulfilling expectation of inflation.

As I see it, the basic source of this double dilemma is not perverse pricing as such but only the fact that structural change has carried the number of prices set perversely beyond the critical point. The big problem is to bring our economy back to the good side of the Divide so that monetary and fiscal measures can again become effective and perform the function of the classical flexible price corrective.

In theory there are various ways by which this could be done. If enough big companies were pulverized, the amount of perverse pricing could be reduced to the necessary extent, but this would mean a great decline in efficiency. If enough prices were regulated by government, perverse pricing could be limited to the necessary extent, but this would displace the efficiency of the free market system.

A third possibility is to get a sufficient number of big corporations to change their methods of pricing. I think this is the most promising to explore.

F. Toward a Free Market Solution

Ever since I recognized the significance of administration inflation I have spent a great deal of time trying to find a way of eliminating it that would be consistent with the free market system and would not require the breakup of big business.

Then, quite recently, I found a conceptual solution by bringing together a basic concept underlying Adam Smith's optimum use of resources and a special form of target pricing used by several large corporations before the expectation of inflation became general.

Adam Smith drew a sharp distinction between the two concepts "market price" and "natural price." In the short run, equating current supply and current demand would clear the current market, but only by chance would it provide prices that result in optimum use of resources. In the longer run, shifts in market prices would occur which would stimulate an expansion in capacity and production in some directions and reduce them in other directions, so that in addition to equating current supply and demand, market prices would tend to direct resources into optimum uses. Prices that succeeded in performing both functions he called natural, and this strong tendency to optimum use of resources was the crowning feature of his free market system, governed by competition among the many.

The special form of target pricing uses a long-run formula rather than the customary short-run procedure that leads to perverse pricing. This formula starts with figures for variable cost, fixed costs, and a total target profit as in short-run target pricing. But instead of dividing the figures for fixed cost and target profit by the current volume of production, it uses a long-run figure based on the average use of capacity over a period of years. The resulting price tends to approximate Adam Smith's natural price and thus eliminate a major source of perverse pricing when demand falls. If enough firms currently pricing on the basis of short-run techniques shifted to a long-run pricing technique, the economy would be returned to the good side of the Great Divide and monetary measures could again be effective. This long-run target pricing technique deserves to be explored as a possible way to eliminate administrative inflation.

G. Factors Favoring the Needed Shift in Pricing Behavior

At first glance it might be thought that such a shift in the use of market power would be difficult to bring about without regulation. But there are conditions now existing which would facilitate such a shift, once the need for the shift is accepted. These conditions will be discussed under the following heads: (1) The Relative Newness of Administrative Inflation, (2) Corporate Experience with Long-Run Pricing, (3) The Self-Interest of Big Business, (4) Corporate Power and Corporate Responsibility, and (5) Flexible Foreign Exchange Rates.

1. *The Relative Newness of Administrative Inflation*

Because of the slowness of the progressive change in the structure of the free market that has made administrative inflation possible, and because the Great Divide was

Table 19.1.

Results of Long-run Target Pricing, 1953–68 (in percent)

Profit rate	Du Pont	U.S. Steel	General Motors	Alcoa	Standard Oil of New Jersey
Targeted rate	20.0	8.0	20.0	10.0	12.0
Average actual	22.2	8.4	20.2	9.5	12.6
Maximum year	34.1	14.8	30.5	18.7	16.6
Minimum year	13.3	4.9	12.6	4.5	9.4

Source: Table adapted from *Economic Concentration* by John Blair, copyright © 1972 by Harcourt Brace Jovanovich, Inc. Reprinted by permission of the publisher.

passed only thirty years ago, it is unlikely that, in the present structure, the overbalance of prices in recession will be very great. This suggests that if a few hundred big companies now pricing for short-run profits were to shift to long-run pricing, this might be sufficient to eliminate administrative inflation without interfering with the freedom of business action. This does not seem at all an impossible goal.

2. *Corporate Experience with Long-Run Pricing*

A second reason for thinking that the task is not too difficult is that before the expectation of inflation became general a number of big corporations had successful experience with long-run pricing. The pioneer in long-run target pricing appears to be Du Pont. It adopted 80 percent of capacity as its standard rate of operation and a 20 percent return on its stockholders' equity capital as its profit target. Then, for each type of product, it divided its fixed cost and targeted profit for that product by 80 percent of capacity in arriving at its full-cost price. But U.S. Steel has an even longer record of what it calls its "public utility approach" to pricing, using 8 percent return on equity capital as its target. A special tabulation by the Federal Trade Commission (FTC) gives the actual profit experiences of these two industrial leaders and three others that also used long-run pricing techniques in the years 1953–68. The results for the whole fifteen-year period are given in Table I [Table 19.1], which shows the rates of return on stockholder's equity after deducting taxes.

As can be seen from the table, in these five cases the long-run profit targets were fairly closely approximated, while the rate of profits in individual years varied greatly. Because in each case both fixed costs and total profit targets were divided by the standard rate of operation, not by the current rate, total profits varied more than they would have with short-run pricing, while perverse pricing was greatly reduced or eliminated. The profit targets aimed at differ because of the variation in the role of borrowed capital, the competitive position of the corporation, and accounting methods.

3. *The Self-Interest of Big Business*

Where firms have a choice between pricing for short-run profits and pricing for long-run profits, the dictates of self-interest are peculiar. The conditions of the free market do not point to either alternative as clearly more or less profitable. But if the preceding analysis is accepted, it would clearly be in the interest of most firms to have enough other firms price for long-run profits to shift the balance to the favorable side.

4. *Corporate Power and Corporate Responsibility*

A fourth factor is that the increase in the power to choose between short-run and long-run pricing is largely a product of the corporate revolution. In the absence of the power to act as a corporation, it is doubtful that the Great Divide would have been passed. Yet the power to act as a "legal person" comes from government. When Keynes denigrates the long run by saying "In the long-run, we are all dead," he is obviously not speaking of the corporation. It can live as long as the state and should be expected to carry responsibilities which are beyond those required of actual persons. A public attitude toward the use of pricing power could be expected to induce some voluntary shifts from short- to long-run pricing once the importance is understood.

5. *Flexible Exchange Rates*

A fifth factor is the existence of flexible exchange rates between the dollar and the money units of other countries. If the United States and its major trading partners were still on the traditional gold standard, administrative inflation arising abroad would tend to be transmitted to this country.

In the presence of these favorable conditions it seems not impossible to find ways to return to the favorable side of the Great Divide.

H. A Challenging Precedent

I am encouraged to think that the necessary change in business practices can be worked out as I recall the success of business leadership in altering the outlook of business at the close of World War II. At that time there was widespread expectation of a big recession similar to those following other wars. Faced with this problem, a group of progressive business leaders formed the Committee for Economic Development (CED) to consider this threat. Their sampling showed an enormous gap between prospective employment one year after the end of the war and the peacetime labor force, unless a radical change in business attitudes was brought about. To effect such a shift, the CED persuaded the Department of Commerce to make estimates, industry by industry, of the real production that would result if real demand were at the level that would give full employment. These estimates were then published as *Markets after the War* and were very widely distributed.[9] Then CED representatives visited key industrialists to persuade them to be prepared for a much larger demand than they had envisaged. Largely as a result of the shift in business attitudes thus brought about, business was ready to expand its peacetime capacity. The nation avoided a recession.

In the present situation, the needed shift in business attitudes is more complex but could be facilitated by the preparation of current estimates of "markets at full employment" and a similar drive on the part of progressive business leaders to persuade enough enterprises to adopt long-run behavior that will not contribute to the new type of inflation and will not perpetuate the self-fulfilling expectation of inflation.

The estimates of markets at full employment would be stated in real terms and to be most effective would need to be supplemented by a set of guidelines to distinguish between price and wage behavior that would generate inflation and that would not.

This is my present perception of the problems raised in our 1932 book. I must reiterate our conclusions that: "Competition has changed in character and the principles applicable to present conditions are radically different from those which apply when the dominant competing units are smaller and more numerous"; and that "New concepts must be forged and a new picture of economic relationships created."

These words ring as urgently today as they did fifty years ago.

Notes

1. Adolf A. Berle & Gardiner C. Means, *The Modern Corporation and Private Property*, 45 (1932).
2. *Id.* at 351.
3. Gardiner C. Means, "Price Inflexibility and the Requirements of a Stabilizing Monetary Policy," 30 *J. Am. Stat. Ass'n* 401 (1935).
4. Edward Chamberlin, *The Theory of Monopolistic Competition* (1933).
5. Paul Anthony Samuelson, *Economics: An Introductory Analysis* (10th ed. 1976).
6. Berle & Means, *The Modern Corporation* (2d ed. 1967), at xxxii.
7. I would point out that even conventional theory recognizes that if all production were carried on under conditions of classical competition, a rise in price would occasionally occur for specific products when demand falls so low that out-of-pocket costs per unit rise as the volume of output falls. This is usually disregarded in the general statement that under conditions of classical competition a fall in demand produces a fall in price. It will also be disregarded in the following analysis.
8. Leonard W. Weiss, "The Extent and Effects of Aggregate Concentration," in this issue [*Journal of Law & Economics*, vol. 26, June 1983].
9. U.S. Department of Commerce, *Markets after the War* (1944).

Part II
Caroline F. Ware

20

Academic Resistance to Administered Prices

by Caroline F. Ware

More than fifty years ago, *The Modern Corporation and Private Property* by Adolf A. Berle, Jr., and Gardiner C. Means[1] called attention to the role of the modern corporation as the dominant institution in one-half of the modern American economy. The book was immediately acclaimed and continues to be quoted.[2] When a new edition came out in 1967, the *New York Times* book reviewer referred to it as a classic: "a book which nobody has read recently but everybody knows what it says."[3] In 1982, the Hoover Institution at Stanford organized a conference in celebration of the fiftieth anniversary of "one of the most influential books of this Century."

Yet in spite of its acclaim and durability, this study's findings and conclusions have been largely ignored and at times actively resisted by the economics profession, spokesmen for business, and makers of public policy. The book pointed out that the modern corporation has so altered the nature of competition as to require a reexamination of the processes and mechanisms of economic adjustment assumed by traditional economic theory and a rethinking of macro-theory itself.[5] Yet the principal economic textbooks have continued to be couched in terms of a highly competitive market economy. The conventional wisdom has continued to assume that "the law of supply and demand" guided by the "unseen hand" of market forces brings adjustment through the mechanism of prices with the support of monetary and fiscal measures.

Although the names of the giant corporations are household words, their advertising fills the nation's eyes and ears, and their activities become headline news in relation to such dramatic events as major failures, bail-outs by government, dramatic mergers, or disastrous impacts on the environment, the manner and effects of the day-by-day exercise of corporate power in the market and their implications for the functioning of the economy as a whole have not begun to receive the systematic study and analysis that their importance requires. Almost the only follow-up of the points brought out in *The Modern Corporation* has come from the authors themselves. Berle, the lawyer, addressed himself to the investment aspect of the corporation. He helped to develop and provided the legislation that established the Securities and Exchange Commission and supported, unsuccessfully, an effort to provide for federal incorporation for companies in interstate commerce. Means, the economist, addressed himself to the implications for the economy of the exercise of corporate power over prices.

The present article examines the failure of the economics profession to consider the implications of corporate power over price for the economy as a whole and its resistance to such study, analysis, and modification of economic theory.

The first indications of academic resistance to the idea that corporate power has implications for the functioning of the economy came from the Harvard Economics Department. As his doctoral dissertation, Means submitted three factual articles that had been published in the economic journals[6] and incorporated into *The Modern Corporation,* together with an essay pointing to some of the implications for economic theory of the facts disclosed. The Department rejected the theoretical analysis but accepted the factual material alone as fulfillment of the thesis requirement. Inadvertently, the summary of the entire thesis, including the theoretical implications, was published in the summaries of Harvard theses for the year 1933.[7] The summary opens with the statement:

> This thesis presents statistical evidence of a change in the fundamental character of economic organization which has been brought about through the growth of corporate activity, and attempts to indicate certain of the important changes in the assumptions of economic analysis which the development requires.

Among such changes in assumptions, the summary lists "the modern corporation . . . has altered the character of the market by making *price* not an outgrowth of trading but of administration."[8]

Means then undertook a detailed study of the effect of corporate power and administration upon price setting and its consequences for the economy, a subject that he pursued for fifty years. The setting for his first study was the depression of the early 1930s when he was an economic adviser to the secretary of agriculture. His assignment was to examine relations between agriculture and the rest of the economy. Using the raw price data supplied to the Bureau of Labor Statistics by reporters for compiling the BLS Wholesale Price Indexes, he observed two distinct patterns of price behavior: the flexible behavior of prices for agriculture and some other products which fell drastically under depression conditions, and the relatively inflexible behavior of prices of many industrial products which did not fall correspondingly. Examination of employment in these two sectors revealed quite different patterns of behavior: employment was maintained where farmers and other small producers tried to make a living by continuing production at the lower prices. Where prices of industrial products were held above the levels that would have maintained sales and resulted in full employment, workers were laid off and unemployment grew.[9]

Within the Department of Agriculture, the implications of the study were known and accepted and the concept that agriculture, operating in terms of classical market prices, was up against industry, much of which operated with administered prices, became a fundamental premise for agricultural policy. In respect to industrial policy, the role of administered prices was generally recognized by the principal government economists who constituted the industrial committee of the National Resources Planning Board during the mid-1930s and it was basic to the study undertaken by that agency on *The Structure of the American Economy*.[10] This study, the first comprehensive effort to delineate the structural anatomy of the prevailing American economy, included an analysis that divided the BLS Wholesale Price Index into five indexes based upon the frequency of price change for each price.[11] This device permitted the observation of differential price behavior over a period of time among prices with differing degrees of flexibility. The use of these indexes dramatically showed how the price relationships that existed in 1929 at the beginning of the depression became distorted as the flexible price index fell greatly while each of the other four indexes fell proportionately less. In the period of recovery, the separate indexes moved back toward their pre-depression relationships, only to diverge again in the recession of 1937. The indexes came back together by early 1942 and served as a guide for the timing of wartime price controls. They made it possible to identify the point at which price relationships appeared to be consistent with full employment and to reflect a potentially stable relationship, thus facilitating the maintenance of price controls.[12]

It is noteworthy, however, that these price relationships and tools of analysis were not effectively used for *further* exploration of pricing practices by corporations. The separate indexes of prices with varying degrees of flexibility which showed such differential behavior in depression and recovery were not continued by the BLS in their regular reporting in spite of their obvious usefulness for public policy. The concept of inflexible prices did not fit the deep-seated classical conviction that all prices tend to equate marginal cost and marginal revenue.[13]

The concept of administered prices, moreover, was subject to not only normal levels of criticism but attacks that sought to demolish the whole idea. Criticism at that time came mainly from two sources, business economists and those participating in the TNEC (Temporary National Economic Committee) study. None of the critics challenged the basic observation that part of the economy adjusted to depression primarily through declines in price while part adjusted primarily through reduction in production with limited price change. Some business economists, however, regarded the concept of administered prices as an attack on business and repudiated the concept on that ground.[14] Some economists engaged in the TNEC study questioned parts of the BLS statistics.[15] They used other data, which were in turn criticized,[16] to explain that they had "exploded" the administered price thesis and had "controverted" Means.[17]

Interest in administered prices and their relevance to public policy was centered in Washington among government economists, not in academic circles. The initial thesis had, indeed, been presented to an academic audience, at the meetings of the American Statistical Association in 1934.[18] It did not, however, get into the mainstream of academic thinking at that time.

What did reach the universities during these years was an alternative explanation for the failure of the automatic classical mechanism to bring recovery from depression, namely Keynes's *General Theory*[19] published a year after Means's pamphlet on *Industrial Prices*.[20] Keynes's thesis, presented as a full-length treatise, soon became a matter of serious study in the universities; it was reviewed in the professional journals[21] and discussed at the professional meetings.

In terms of immediate policy, there was no conflict between Keynes and Means. Keynes's prescription for the use of fiscal policy to raise the level of aggregate demand and employment was consistent with Means's emphasis on maintaining the level of aggregate demand through the use of monetary measures. The difference lay in the theoretical analysis, and even that difference was obscured by the fact that Keynes used examples of inflexible wage rates and prices in his presentation although these were not relevant or necessary to his theory.[22]

Keynes's explanation of persistent involuntary unemployment, which focused on the relation between savings and investment and the effect of interest rates, did not require the abandonment of the basic major premise with respect to price behavior and thus call for a rethinking of the main body of economic price theory. The economic textbooks, of which Samuelson's *Economics* can be taken as representative, present an amalgamation of classical and Keynesian theory in which students find no basic conflicts to be reconciled.[23] Successive generations of economics students were thus trained either by the more traditional and theoretical economists who remained in the classrooms when the great trek to Washington in the 1930s drew the pragmatically minded into the operations of government, or by the growing number of followers of Keynes, whose influence spread widely in academic circles and reached into government. While there was discussion of competition among a limited number of concerns in particular markets,[24] there was little recognition of the extent to which the existence of corporate power over prices had changed the structure of the free market system as a whole. There was little concern as to how administered prices were actually set—what considerations corporate executives actually used in determining prices within the range of discretion that they could exercise and what mechanisms they employed. Such inquiries as were made were often stonewalled by corporations as business secrets to which only the company insiders were privy. Economists did not develop tools of analysis to penetrate this area.

World War II brought an end to preoccupation with the causes of depression and produced a series of administrative agencies—War Production Board, Office of Price Administration, Board of Economic Warfare, War Labor Board, etc.—designed to direct various aspects of the economy under conditions of total war and government price controls. At the close of the war, in the face of an unknown future and many predictions of a postwar depression, and with the memory of the Great Depression still fresh, the Congress enacted the Employment Act of 1946 committing the government to the maintenance of "maximum employment, production and purchasing power"[25] as a matter of public policy. It is noteworthy that this important Act takes no position with respect to the theoretical question of the causes of depression or unemployment. Its principal architects were followers of no particular theoretical line and it left entirely open the question of the economic premises upon which measures to carry out the Act would be based. The only assumption that underlies the Employment Act of 1946 is that the traditional automatic mechanisms of classical economics cannot be relied upon to maintain full employment and government intervention toward this end is needed and can be effective.

The principal mechanism of intervention, which came to be accepted as standard operating procedure, was the use of monetary and fiscal policy to create a level of aggregate demand that would be sufficient to sustain full employment but would not be so great as to produce an inflationary situation with too much money chasing too few goods.

Price Discretion and the New Inflation

For a decade after the war, the economy appeared to be relatively stable and questions relating to price behavior and the exercise of corporate power were not subjects of major discussion. Then, in the late 1950s, a new phenomenon appeared—what seemed to be a general inflationary rise in prices while unemployment was increasing and much industrial capacity stood idle for lack of orders. This was a situation—simultaneous inflation and excessive unemployment—that was theoretically impossible in a free market system of flexible prices. But there it was.

Faced with this unexplained reality, the Senate Sub-committee on Antitrust and Monopoly, chaired by Senator Estes Kefauver, announced hearings that again focused attention on the effects of price administration. These hearings, on "Administered Prices," were organized by the subcommittee's staff economist, John M. Blair, and continued from July 1957 to Kefauver's death in 1963,[26] and were extended by his successor, Senator Philip Hart. They brought out an immense amount of evidence on practices in many different industries. Means, along with four other economists, was asked to testify at the opening session[27] and on several other occasions.[28] In these presentations he offered clear evidence that the price rise of these years was not general but was largely confined to industries where competition was among a few large corporations that could set their prices within a significant zone of discretion. He noted that flexible prices in market-dominated industries had not risen, or had even dropped during the middle 1950s, indicating no *general* excess in demand, yet the wholesale price index rose 8 percent from 1953 to 1958. Monetary and fiscal measures designed to control inflation by restricting demand could therefore not be expected to be effective. The evidence was sufficiently strong to lead one of the two chief economists of the Federal Reserve Board to conclude in 1959 that a new factor was present which could not be controlled by the Fed's traditional methods.[29]

In the 1960s the Kennedy administration made an attempt to deal directly with arbitrary price increases. In May 1962 it talked U.S. Steel into rolling back a price increase that the company had announced. Following this action, it sought to counteract further administrative inflation by setting up a series of guideposts to indicate the limits of appropriate price and wage changes. Although without enforcement authority, these guideposts were offered in the hope that the powerful corporations and labor unions would see that the maintenance of a stable economy served their self-interest. At first, the system worked reasonably well. Labor unions kept their wage demands within the prescribed limits and management's violations of price ceilings were small. After a year and a half, however, a defect in the guideposts' design resulted in action by labor to overcome the disadvantage in which workers found they had been placed by the failure of the guideposts to take account of reflationary increases in flexible market prices which raised workers' cost of living. Workers, finding that their real wages were dropping, pressed for catch-up wage increases.

Thereafter the guidepost approach was generally discredited and labor was blamed.

An article published in the *Journal of Political Economy* for April 1963 by DePodwin and Selden opened with the statement:

> The notion that administered prices play a major role in determining the course of economic activity has served for nearly three decades as a rallying point for those who believe that the economy is improperly dominated by business. Although the evidence failed to support his original theory, Means has recently revived the administered price theory and put it to another use. Whereas concentrated industries were formerly accused of aggravating the unemployment problem because they allegedly maintained prices in the face of falling demand, Means now blames them for the inflationary trends in the United States during the 1950's. Prices that were supposed to have displayed downward inflexibility are now discovered to be characterized by upward flexibility, independently of demand and cost changes.[30]

The article cites the attacks of the 1930s,[31] accepts them at face value, and conspicuously fails to cite John Blair's criticism of these 1930s attacks.[32] The article concludes: "We suggest that it is time to put the administrative inflation hypothesis to rest."[33] The article failed to recognize that both types of price behavior reflected the same exercise of price discretion in the market by the visible hands of corporate executives. When Means submitted to the *Journal of Political Economy* a comment taking exception to what he considered misinterpretations of the positions of his original critics and also to some of the data and conclusions presented by the authors, the *Journal* refused to publish the comment on the ground that it had been printed in the record of the Senate hearings.[34] Means had offered it there as a supplementary note after an earlier witness had inserted the DePodwin-Selden article into the record with the aim of refuting the testimony Means had given.[35]

The most vigorous and persistent attacks came from Professor George Stigler of the University of Chicago.[36] In the 1960s Stigler and his associates undertook to study the prices actually paid for items listed in the BLS Wholesale Price Index, presuming that the practice of discounts and other price concessions might result in quite different prices from those reported to the BLS.[37] Their results showed various patterns among concentrated industries, including some price increases in the face of falling demand of the inflationary sort noted by Means. In the text Stigler concluded that this new evidence "destroys the administered price thesis."[38] But when Means analyzed the Stigler data, he came to the directly opposite conclusion and set forth his interpretation of Stigler's material in the *American Economic Review* under the title "The Administered Price Thesis Reconfirmed."[39] Stigler replied with an article in the same journal, "Industrial Prices as Administered by Dr. Means,"[40] but when Means submitted a rejoinder alleging no less than seventeen errors of fact or in the interpretation of his position, the *Review* refused publication. Since the *Review* is the official journal of the American Economic Association, Means appealed to the executive committee of the association,[41] but the latter left the matter in the hands of the editor who indicated that he felt no obligation to keep the controversy alive.[42]

During this whole period, the main body of economists disregarded the presence of administered prices. Most economists were preoccupied with model building, econometrics, and related theory based on traditional assumptions about price behavior. The large body of material contained in the Kefauver hearings remained practically unnoticed in the macroeconomic literature. When a pamphlet containing Means's testimony under the title *Administrative Inflation and Public Policy*[43] was sent to all members of the American Economic Association, it failed to generate interest in academic circles.

It remained for Blair himself, after he left the subcommittee and returned to academic life, to exploit the mine of price information contained in the hearings and to point out some of the theoretical implications.[44] His book on *Economic*

Concentration, however, drawn from this material, received no reviews in the major economic journals when it appeared.

Blair's studies called special attention to the ever-increasing tendency of prices set by corporations to *rise* in response to falling demand. He called the practice "perverse pricing" since it ran directly counter to expected price behavior. This was the same phenomenon that Means had found to be responsible for price increases in the inflation of the 1950s. Such perverse pricing had actually existed for a long time—it characterized 10 percent of the "inflexible" prices noted in Means's 1934 study—but it was not until the 1950s that it had become sufficiently widespread to produce a rise in the wholesale price index in recession.

Meantime, the main body of economic writing and teaching continued to ignore the theoretical implications of inflexible and perverse administrative price behavior and the reality of inflation in the presence of recession for which none of the received theories offered an explanation.

When the phenomenon of simultaneous recession and inflation again appeared in the 1970s, the Nixon administration disregarded the experience of the 1950s and sought to control a nondemand inflation with the same measures, applicable to a traditional demand inflation, which had proved futile two decades before. The Fed ignored its earlier experience and applied the same techniques for limiting demand to a situation where demand was already insufficient to sustain full employment. Once more the concept of administrative inflation and the evidence to support it were put forth by Means in congressional hearings[45] and in 1975 legislation was proposed in both houses which accepted the administrative hypothesis and tried to check administrative inflation by dealing directly with its source in price administration and the exercise of market power.[46] The proposed legislation would have required major corporations to announce intended price increases in advance on the assumption that public disclosure and the force of public opinion would make it necessary for the wielders of market power to justify their actions. The proposed legislation, however, received little support.

Thus, for more than half a century the economic fraternity has turned its back on the implications for macro-theory of the fact that the large corporation is the principal economic institution of modern life, and has criticized the evidence and rejected this fact for the essential mechanism of price. It has built elaborate macro-models on unreal assumptions of price behavior where competition is among the few, rather than redesigning models to incorporate more realistic premises on price behavior.

The history set forth in this record leads the cultural and economic historian to ask the question "why?"

We might look for an explanation in the nature and circumstances of the economic profession itself: we might find it in the dominant influence and interest of powerful corporations; it could lie in the value systems and institutions of modern American society with its traditional business orientation; it could be explained perhaps by one or another theory of how basic changes in thought take place.

The most obvious answer would appear to lie in the self-defense of the economics profession. No established profession holding a given body of thought willingly tolerates challenges to its basic premises. To admit that prices that equate supply and demand do not provide the essential mechanism of macroeconomic adjustment is to pull the foundations out from under traditional economic theory and to undermine the expertise built on this foundation. It is not reasonable to expect the high priests of the temple to recast their basic doctrine or tools of analysis. The indifference of the BLS to the demonstrably useful indexes for prices grouped by degree of flexibility has been noted. The suggestion in the 1950s and again in the 1970s that an index of prices in highly concentrated industries be developed with which to distinguish administrative inflation from that resulting from excess demand met with no response. Likewise, there has been no effort to distinguish these sensitive prices whose rise could be expected to signalize ''reflation'' in a period of recovery. The growing practice of ''perverse'' pricing has been almost completely ignored.

The mechanisms for perpetuating patterns of economic thought are well entrenched. A flourishing industry, complete with popular and profitable textbooks, sustains a more or less standard series of basic and advanced economics courses in universities from one end of the country to the other. The major economic journals that publish articles by means of which young scholars achieve their professional reputations are edited by persons committed to prevailing views. Persons applying to the National Science Foundation for study grants in Economics have been given forms that inquire into the mathematical processes to be used, thus implying that the study will be an econometric one.

The second alternative explanation, the influence of corporate power, is also plausible. It is in the interest of corporations to perpetuate the assumption that they are subject to the conditions of the traditional competitive market and to discourage attention to their exercise of market power.

If they can be assumed to behave like small businesses without influence over the market they will enjoy greater freedom of action.

They have strong and subtle means of exercising influence in respect to economic ideas as well as economic behavior. For example, General Motors is reported to have indirectly secured the determination of the original publisher, Commerce Clearinghouse, not to reissue *The Modern Corporation and Private Property*. But this did not prevent the latter from selling the plates to another publisher with a wider system of distribution.[47]

It seems unlikely, however, that even a concerted effort within the corporate community would have had as general an effect on economic thinking and writing as that which has been discussed here. It is more likely that the general attitudes and institutions that characterized America during these years have been responsible for the indifference and opposition to the ideas here discussed. Basic economic concepts that have been incorporated into the traditional wisdom include a deeply ingrained resistance to government intervention in the operations of the economy except in customary ways that facilitate business and are not recognized as "intervention," such as protection of contracts, regulation of weights and measures, and the act of incorporation itself. The appeal of a laissez faire attitude is increased by the sense that the complexity of the economy is so great and the knowledge of the factors affecting its operation is so limited that any intervention is expected to make matters worse rather than better. What is noteworthy is the failure to recognize that the decision-making process by corporate executives is a major form of intervention into the traditional processes of the free market.[48]

When it comes to the fourth possible explanation, the basic process of change in ideas, it may well be that the disparity between experienced reality and inherited assumptions has now produced the need for a revolutionary change in point of view. As Thomas Kuhn points out in *The Structure of Scientific Revolution*[49] resistance to disorganizing change in prevailing concepts serves the double purpose of enabling a society to function with the necessary degree of consensus and of canalizing scientific advance into central channels instead of being dissipated. A quantum shift in thought takes place when changes in reality reach a point where they must be faced and a new framework built. It may be that in the economic confusion of today we are at such a point.

It seems time to focus research, economic analysis, and public policy on the reality of corporate power in the market place which *The Modern Corporation and Private Property* so vividly delineated more than fifty years ago and which is of even greater impact today.[50]

Notes

1. Adolf A. Berle, Jr., and Gardiner C. Means, *The Modern Corporation and Private Property* (New York: Commerce Clearing House, 1932; and New York: Macmillan, 1932).

2. See "The Very Modern Corporation," *New York Times* Editorial, February 19, 1988.

3. Robert Lekachman, "The Corporation Gap," *New York Times Book Review*, September 15, 1968.

4. Letter from Thomas G. Moore, Hoover Institution, to Gardiner C. Means, September 23, 1982.

5. Berle and Means, op. cit., pp. 45 and 308.

6. "Diffusion of Stock Ownership in the United States," *Quarterly Journal of Economics* 44 (August 1930): 561–600; "Growth in the Relative Importance of the Large Corporation in American Life," *American Economic Review* 21 (March 1931): 10–42; "Separation of Ownership and Control in American Industry," *Quarterly Journal of Economics* 46 (November 1931): 68–100.

7. Gardiner C. Means, "The Corporate Revolution," in *Summaries of Ph.D. Theses—*

1933 (Cambridge, Mass.: Harvard University, 1934); reprinted in Gardiner C. Means, *The Corporate Revolution* (New York: Crowell-Collier, 1962), pp. 15–19.

8. Ibid., p. 18.

9. Gardiner C. Means, "Industrial Prices and Their Relative Inflexibility," Senate Document No. 13, 74th Cong., 1st sess., Washington, D.C., January 1935.

10. National Resources Committee, Industrial Section, *The Structure of the American Economy*, Washington, D.C., June 1939.

11. Ibid., pp. 146–47.

12. See NRC, *The Structure of the American Economy*, p. 147; Gardiner C. Means, John Blair, et al., *The Roots of Inflation* (New York: Burt Franklin, 1975), p. 9.

13. In 1958, at the request of Senator Paul Douglas, the BLS made a special study of its Wholesale Prices in the 1947–56 period grouped by frequency of change, and at John Blair's request, the series was extended to 1966 (M.E. Riley, *Frequency of Change in Wholesale Prices: A Study of Price Inflexibility*, U.S. Department of Labor, Bureau of Labor Statistics, Report Number 142, Washington, D.C., 1958; John M. Blair, *Economic Concentration* [New York: Harcourt, Brace, Jovanovich, 1972]: 438–48).

14. See, for example, W.L. Crum, "On the Alleged Concentration of Economic Power," *American Economic Review* (March 1934): 69–83, with "A Reply by Gardiner C. Means," pp. 84–87, and a "Rejoinder," pp. 87–88.

15. Willard L. Thorp and Walter F. Crowder, *The Structure of Industry*, TNEC Monograph no. 27 (Washington, D.C.: GPO, 1941); Alfred C. Neal, *Industrial Concentration and Price Inflexibility* (Washington, D.C.: American Council on Public Affairs, 1941).

16. John M. Blair, "Means, Thorp and Neal on Price Inflexibility," *Review of Economics and Statistics* (November 1958).

17. Neal, *Industrial Concentration*, pp. 2, 124.

18. Gardiner C. Means, "Price Inflexibility and the Requirements of a Stabilizing Monetary Policy," *Journal of the American Statistical Association* 30 (June 1935): 401–13.

19. John M. Keynes, *The General Theory of Employment, Interest and Money* (London: Harcourt, Brace, 1936).

20. "Industrial Prices and Their Relative Inflexibility."

21. See reviews of *The General Theory of Employment, Interest and Money* by Frank Taussig, Wassily W. Leontief, D.H. Robertson, and Jacob Viner in *Quarterly Journal of Economics* 51 (November 1936); and reply by J.M. Keynes, "The General Theory of Employment," *Quarterly Journal of Economics* 51 (February 1937): 209–13.

22. In 1939 Means visited Keynes at his home for the express purpose of clearing up this point and received from Keynes a categorical affirmation that his theory was not based on any assumption other than the classical assumption of perfectly flexible prices and wage rates. The present writer attended these discussions. See also John M. Blair, *Economic Concentration* (New York: Burt Franklin, 1972), p. 437.

23. Paul A. Samuelson, *Economics*, 8th ed. (New York: McGraw-Hill, 1970).

24. As in the works of Edward Chamberlin and Joan Robinson.

25. Employment Act of 1946, Sec. 5 of Public Law 304 (79th Congress).

26. Hearings on Administered Prices, Subcommittee on Antitrust and Monopoly, Committee on the Judiciary, U.S. Senate, 85th Cong., 1st sess., 1957, through 88th Cong., 2nd sess., 1963.

27. *Ibid.*, July 12, 1957, pp. 74–125.

28. Ibid., January 24, 1959, pp. 4746–79; March 10, 1959, pp. 4827–923; May 12, 1959, pp. 5778–83; May 21, 1963, pp. 17972–77. See also *Hearings on Economic Concentration*, Senate Antitrust and Monopoly Subcommittee, July 1, 1964, pp. 8–36, 88th Cong., 2nd sess.; and "Pricing Power and the Public Interest," in *Administered Prices: A*

Compendium on Public Policy, Senate and Antitrust Monopoly Subcommittee, Committee Print, March 1963, 88th Cong., 1st sess., pp. 213–39.

29. Woodlief Thomas, Letter to the *Washington Post,* March 12, 1959.

30. Horace J. DePodwin and Richard T. Selden, "Business Pricing Policies and Inflation," *Journal of Political Economy* 71, 2 (April 1963): 116–27.

31. See note 14.

32. See note 14. Blair concluded: "In the opinion of this observer, there is more to Means and less to Thorp and Neal than has generally been assumed. . . . A little more attention to these shortcomings [of the statistical studies by Thorp and Neal] and a little less emphasis on the weakness of the BLS prices, would help to put the whole controversy in balance."

33. DePodwin and Selden, "Business Pricing Policies," p. 126.

34. *Hearings on Economic Concentration,* Part I, p. 88, and pp. 489–97.

35. *Hearings on Administered Prices,* Part 29, May 21, 1963, pp. 17972–77, and pp. 18197–208.

36. George J. Stigler, "Administered Prices and Oligopolistic Inflation," *Journal of Business* 25 (January 1962): 1–13; George J. Stigler and James K. Kindahl, *The Behavior of Industrial Prices* (New York: National Bureau of Economic Research, 1970).

37. Stigler and Kindahl, *The Behavior of Industrial Prices.*

38. Ibid., p. 9.

39. Gardiner C. Means, "The Administered Price Thesis Reconfirmed," *American Economic Review* 62 (June 1972): 292–306.

40. George J. Stigler and James K. Kindahl, "Industrial Prices, as Administered by Dr. Means," *American Economic Review* 63, 4 (September 1973): 717.

41. G.C. Means correspondence with R.A. Gordon and George H. Borts, 1975.

42. Means wrote: "Say Stigler apologized in the public print." I do not know where the apology by Stigler was printed.

43. Gardiner C. Means, *Administrative Inflation and Public Policy* (Washington, D.C.: Anderson Kramer Associates, 1959).

44. See Blair, *Economic Concentration.*

45. See statements by G.C. Means at: *Hearings on Renewal of the Stabilization Act,* March 27, 1973; "Control of the Current Administrative Inflation," statement before the Joint Economic Committee, November 18, 1974; *Hearings on a Bill to Amend the Council on Wage and Price Stability Act,* Senate Committee on Banking, Housing and Urban Affairs, March 7, 1975; *Hearings on Renewal of Price Stability Act,* House Banking and Currency Committee, June 15, 1975.

46. 94th Cong., 1st sess., S 409, HR 4594 and 4214.

47. See note 1 above.

48. Council on Wage and Price Stability, Conference on Concentration, Administered Prices and Inflation, April 15, 1975, Transcript.

49. Thomas S. Kuhn, *The Structure of Scientific Revolutions,* International Encyclopedia of Unified Science, Vol. 2, no. 2, 2d ed., enlarged (Chicago: University of Chicago Press, 1970).

50. See "The Very Modern Corporation," *New York Times,* February 19, 1988.

Chronological Bibliography of the Writings of Gardiner C. Means

Books and Monographs

The Modern Corporation and Private Property (with Adolf A. Berle). 1932. New York: Commerce Clearing House; reissued, New York: The Macmillan Company, 1933; Revised Edition, New York: Harcourt, Brace & World, Inc., 1967. Japanese translation, Tokyo, Bungado Shoten, 1958; Portuguese translation, Rio de Janeiro, Editora Ipanema, 1957; Italian translation, Turin, Giulio Einaudi, 1966.

The Holding Company (with James Bonbright). 1932. New York: McGraw-Hill Book Company, Inc.

Industrial Prices and Their Relative Inflexibility. 1935. Senate Document No. 13. 74th Cong., 1st sess. Washington, D.C.

The Modern Economy in Action (with Caroline F. Ware). 1936. New York: Harcourt, Brace and Company.

Patterns of Resource Use. 1938. Washington, D.C.: GPO.

The Structure of the American Economy. Part I: *Basic Characteristics*. 1939. Washington, D.C.: GPO.

Jobs and Markets: How to Prevent Inflation and Depression in the Transition (with others). 1946. New York: McGraw-Hill.

Administrative Inflation and Public Policy. 1959. Washington, D.C.: Anderson Kramer Associates.

The Corporate Revolution in America. 1962. New York: The Crowell-Collier Press.

Pricing Power and the Public Interest. 1962. New York: Harper & Brothers.

Articles and Other Published Papers and Comments

"Corporations and the Public Investor" (with A.A. Berle). 1930. *American Economic Review* 20 (March): 54–71.

"The Diffusion of Stock Ownership in the United States." 1930. *Quarterly Journal Of Economics* 44 (August): 561–600.

"Growth in the Relative Importance of the Large Corporation in American Economic Life." 1931. *American Economic Review* 21 (March): 10–42.

"Stock Dividends, Large Scale Business and Corporation Savings—A Criticism." 1931. *Quarterly Journal of Economics* 45 (May): 536–40.

"Separation of Ownership and Control in American Industry." 1931. *Quarterly Journal of Economics* 46 (November): 68–100.

"Bank Debts." 1933. In *The Internal Debts of the United States*, ed. by Evans Clark, pp. 326–84. New York: The Macmillan Company.

"The Corporation Revolution." 1933. In *Summaries of PhD Theses*. Cambridge, Mass.: Harvard University Press. Reprinted in *The Corporate Revolution in America*. 1962. New York: The Crowell-Collier Press.

"Debts of Industrial Corporations." 1933. In *The Internal Debts of the United States*, ed. by Evans Clark, pp. 171–203. New York: The Macmillan Company.

"Debts of Industrial Corporations." 1933. *Survey Graphic* 22 (June): 305.

"A Reply." 1934. *American Economic Review* 24 (March): 84–87.

"The Consumer and the New Deal." 1934. *Annals of the American Academy of Political and Social Science* 173 (May): 7–17.

"Corporation" (with A.A. Berle). 1935. In *Encyclopaedia of the Social Sciences*, ed. by Edwin R.A. Seligman and Alvin Johnson, vol. 4, pp. 414–23. New York: The Macmillan Company.

"The Distribution of Control and Responsibility in a Modern Economy." 1935. *Political Science Quarterly* 50 (March): 59–69.

"Price Inflexibility and the Requirements of a Stabilizing Monetary Policy." 1935. *Journal of the American Statistical Association* 30 (June): 401–413.

"Notes on Inflexible Prices." 1936. *American Economic Review—Supplement* 26 (March): 23–35.

Review of *Big Business: Its Growth and Its Place*. 1937. *Journal of the American Statistical Association* 32 (December): 777–81.

"Business Combinations and Agriculture." 1938. *Journal of Farm Economics* 20 (February): 53–57.

"The Causes: Price Relations and Economic Instability" (with Louis H. Bean and J.P. Gavin). 1938. In *Soils and Men: Yearbook of Agriculture 1938*, pp. 171–97. Washington, D.C.: GPO.

"Financial Control of Large-Scale Enterprise." 1939. *American Economic Review—Supplement* 29 (March): 110–15.

"Big Business, Administered Prices, and the Problem of Full Employment." 1939–40. *Journal of Marketing* 4 (April): 370–81.

"Basic Structural Characteristics and the Problem of Full Employment." 1940. In *Structure of the American Economy*. Part II: *Toward Full Use of Resources*, pp. 3–9. National Resources Planning Board. Washington, D.C.: GPO.

"The Controversy over the Problem of Full Employment." 1940. In *Structure of the American Economy*. Part II: *Toward Full Use of Resources*, pp. 9–17. National Resources Planning Board. Washington, D.C.: GPO.

"Economic Institutions." 1942. *American Journal of Sociology* 47 (May): 941–57.

"The American Economy in the Interwar Period: Discussion." 1946. *American Economic Review* 36 (May): 32–35.

"Comment." 1953. *American Economic Review* 43 (March): 146–48.

"Statement." 1957. U.S. Congress. Senate. Committee on the Judiciary. *Administered Prices—Part I: Opening Phase—Economists' Views. Hearings before the Subcommittee on Antitrust and Monopoly*, pp. 74–125. 85th Cong., 1st sess.

"Collective Capitalism and Economic Theory." 1957. *Science* 126 (August 16): 287–93. Reprinted in *The Corporation Take-over*, ed. by A. Hacker, pp. 65–90. New York: Harper & Row.

"Administrative Inflation." 1957. *Current Business Studies* 28 (October): 29–46.
"This Recession Is Different." 1958. *The Nation* 186 (May 17): 442–48.
"Looking Around: Is Economic Theory Outmoded?" 1958. *Harvard Business Review* 36 (May-June): 27–40. Japanese translation in *Americana*, U.S. Information Service, Tokyo, January 1959, pp. 59–70.
"Requiem for the Modern Age." Review of *Landmarks of Tomorrow*. 1959. *Saturday Review* 42 (January 17): 55.
"Statement of Gardiner C. Means, Economist." 1959. U.S. Congress. Senate. Committee on the Judiciary. *Administered Prices—Part 9: Administered Price Inflation: Alternative Public Policies. Hearings before the Subcommittee on Antitrust and Monopoly*, pp. 4746–79. 86th Cong., 1st sess.
"Statement of Dr. Gardiner C. Means, Washington, D.C." 1959. U. S. Congress. Senate. Committee on the Judiciary. *Administered Prices—Part 10: Administered Price Inflation: Alternative Public (Continued). Hearings before the Subcommittee on Antitrust and Monopoly*, pp. 4897–923. 86th Cong., 1st sess.
Statement submitted to the Joint Economic Committee, *Hearings on the Economic Report of the President*, February 16, 1959, pp. 755–64.
Statement before the House Committee on Government Operation, *Hearings on Amendment of Employment Act of 1946*, March 25, 1959, pp. 44–59.
"Discussion." 1959. *American Economic Review* 49 (May): 451–54.
"The New-Style 'Administrative' Inflation." 1959. *The New Republic* 140 (May 4): 9–13.
Statement submitted to the Senate Antitrust and Monopoly Subcommittee, Hearings on Administered Prices, May 12, 1959, pp. 5778–83.
Statement before the Senate Banking and Currency Committee, *Hearings on the Employment Act Amendments*, February 24, 1960, pp. 41–64.
"Collective Enterprise and Economic Theory." In *Die Konzentration in der Wirtschaft*, ed. by Helmut Arndt, pp. 1523–43. Berlin: 1960, rev. ed. 1971.
"Inflation and Full Employment." Statement before the Joint Economic Committee. *Hearings on the Economic Report of the President*, February 2, 1962, pp. 363–74.
"Thoughts on Concentration." 1962. *Proceedings of the American Statistical Association: The Business and Economic Statistics Section* (September): 118–26.
"Pricing Power and the Public Interest." In *Administered Prices: A Compendium on Public Policy*, Senate Antitrust and Monopoly Subcommittee, Committee Print, March 1963, pp. 213–39.
"Letter from Dr. Gardiner C. Means to Senator Estes Kefauver, May 31, 1963." 1963. U.S. Congress. Senate. Committee on the Judiciary. *Administered Prices—Part 29: Public Policy on Administered Prices. Hearings before the Subcommittee on Antitrust and Monopoly*, pp. 18192–96. 88th Cong., 1st sess.
"Statement of Dr. Gardiner C. Means, Vienna, Va." 1963. U.S. Congress. Senate. Committee on the Judiciary. *Administered Prices—Part 29: Public Policy on Administered Prices. Hearings before the Subcommittee on Antitrust and Monopoly*, pp. 17972–77. 88th Cong., 1st sess.
Review of *The Business Conscience* by Luther H. Hodges, Englewood Cliffs, N.J., 1963. In *The New York Times Book Review*, September 1, 1963.
"Collective Capitalism and Economic Theory." 1964. In *The Corporation Take-Over*, ed. by A. Hacker, pp. 65–90. New York: Harper & Row.
"Business Pricing Policies and Inflation: A Comment." 1964. U.S. Congress. Senate. Committee on the Judiciary. *Economic Concentration—Part 1: Overall and Conglomerate Aspects. Hearings before the Subcommittee on Antitrust and Monopoly on S. Res. 262*, pp. 8–36, 281–324, and 489–97. 88th Cong., 2nd sess.
"Dr. Gardiner C. Means, Economist, Vienna, Va." 1964. U.S. Congress. Senate. Com-

mittee on the Judiciary. *Economic Concentration—Part 1: Overall and Conglomerate Aspects. Hearings before the Subcommittee on Antitrust and Monopoly on S. Res. 262*, pp. 8–36, 281–324, and 489–97. 88th Cong., 2nd sess.

"Job Opportunities and Poverty." 1965. In *Poverty as a Public Issue*, ed. by Ben Seligman, pp. 321–35. New York: Free Press.

"Monetary Institutions to Serve the Modern Economy." 1967. In *Institutional Adjustment*, ed. by Carey C. Thompson, pp. 149–77. Austin: University of Texas Press.

"The Problems and Prospects of Collective Capitalism." 1969. *Journal of Economic Issues* 3 (March): 18–31.

"Government Policy toward the Large Corporation." In *Big Business in Australia*, Australian Institute of Political Science, Proceedings of the 36th Summer School, Sydney, Australia, 1970, pp. 108–20. Japanese translation, *The Oriental Economist*, Tokyo, March 14, 1970, no. 3524, pp. 98–105, and in *The Economic Club Lecture Series*, Tokyo, April 1970, pp. 2–34.

"The National Bureau Study of Industrial Prices." 1970. U.S. Congress. Joint Economic Committee. *The 1970 Midyear Review of the State of the Economy—Part 2. Hearings before the Joint Economic Committee*, pp. 299–302. 91st Cong., 2nd sess.

"Statement of Gardiner C. Means, Consultant." 1970. U.S. Congress. Joint Economic Committee. *The 1970 Midyear Review of the State of the Economy—Part 2. Hearings before the Joint Economic Committee*, pp. 226–30. 91st Cong., 2nd sess.

"Prepared Statement of Gardiner C. Means: Inflation and Unemployment." 1970. U.S. Congress. Joint Economic Committee. *The 1970 Midyear Review of the State of the Economy—Part 2. Hearings before the Joint Economic Committee*, pp. 230–44. 91st Cong., 2nd sess.

"Conglomerates and Concentration." 1970. *University of Miami Law Review* 25 (Fall): 1–40.

"The Administered-Price Thesis Reconfirmed." 1972. *American Economic Review* 62 (June): 292–306.

"Beware of Phase III." 1973. U.S. Congress. House of Representatives. Committee on Banking and Currency. *Economic Stabilization—1973. Hearings before the Committee on Banking and Currency on H.R. 2099 and H.R. 6168*, pp. 162–170. 93rd Cong., 1st sess.

"Statement of Dr. Gardiner C. Means, Economic Consultant." 1973. U.S. Congress. House of Representatives. Committee on Banking and Currency. *Economic Stabilization—1973. Hearings before the Committee on Banking and Currency on H.R. 2099 and H.R. 6168*, pp. 157–61. 93rd Cong., 1st sess.

"Statement by Gardiner C. Means at Conference on Concentration, Administered Prices and Inflation" and "Prepared Statement of Gardiner C. Means." 1974. U.S. Congress. *Market Power, The Federal Trade Commission, and Inflation. Hearings before the Joint Economic Committee*. 93rd Cong., 2nd sess.

"Statement of Dr. Gardiner C. Means, Economic Consultant." 1975. U. S. Congress. Senate. Committee on Banking, Housing and Urban Affairs. *Council on Wage and Price Stability Act Amendments of 1975. Hearings before the Committee on Banking, Housing and Urban Affairs on S. 409*, pp. 215–24. 94th Cong., 1st sess.

"Will We Repeat 1929?" 1975. U.S. Congress. Senate. Committee on Banking, Housing and Urban Affairs. *Council on Wage and Price Stability Act Amendments of 1975. Hearings before the Committee on Banking, Housing and Urban Affairs on S. 409*, pp. 224–31. 94th Cong., 1st sess.

"Additional Statement of Gardiner C. Means." 1975. U.S. Congress. Senate. Committee on Banking, Housing and Urban Affairs. *Council on Wage and Price Stability Act Amendments of 1975. Hearings before the Committee on Banking, Housing and*

Urban Affairs on S. 409, pp. 283–84. 94th Cong., 1st sess.
"How to Control Inflation in the United States: An Alternative to 'Planned Stagnation'." 1975. *Wage-Price Law & Economic Review* 1: 47–74.
"Prepared Statement of Gardiner C. Means, Economic Consultant." 1975. U.S. Congress. House. *Incomes Policy Legislation—1975. Hearings before the Committee on Banking, Currency and Housing on H. R. 4594, HR. 6577, H.R. 4214, and H.R. 5142.* 94th Cong., 1st sess.
"Remarks upon Receipt of the Veblen-Commons Award." 1975. *Journal of Economic Issues* 9 (June): 149–57.
"Simultaneous Inflation and Unemployment: A Challenge to Theory and Policy." 1975. In *The Roots of Inflation*, ed. by Gardiner C. Means, et al, pp. 1–31. New York: Burt Franklin & Co., Inc.
"Which was the True Keynesian Theory of Employment?" 1976. *Challenge* 19, no. 3 (July–August): 61–63.
"Administered Prices." 1982. In *Encyclopedia of Economics*, ed. by Douglas Greenwald, pp. 10–15. New York: McGraw-Hill Book Company.
"Consumer Participation at the Federal Level" (with Caroline F. Ware and Thomas C. Blaisdell, Jr.). 1982. In *Consumer Activists: They Made a Difference*, ed. by Erma Angevine, pp. 171–97. Mount Vernon, NY: Consumers Union Foundation, Inc.
"Corporate Power in the Marketplace." 1983. *The Journal of Law and Economics* 26: 467–85.
"Hessen's 'Reappraisal'." 1983. *The Journal of Law and Economics* 26 (June): 297–300.

Unpublished Manuscripts and Papers

"The Corporate Revolution." 1933. G.C. Means Papers.
"Currency Issue." 1934. President's Personal File.
"Monetary Policy and the New Function of the Banking System." 1934. G.C. Means Papers.
"NRA and AAA and the Reorganization of Industrial Policy Making." (August) 1934. Washington, D.C.
"NRA and AAA and the Reorganization of Industrial Policy Making." (October) 1934. Charles E. Merriam Papers.
"The Price Problem." 1934. G.C. Means Papers.
"The Relations between Government and Economic Activity." 1934. G.C. Means Papers.
"The Major Causes of the Depression." 1935. G.C. Means Papers.
"Outline of Approach to Economic Planning." 1935. G.C. Means Papers.
"Princeton Talk." 1935. G.C. Means Papers.
"Report Covering the Development of Techniques for Making Industrial Capacity Studies." 1935. G.C. Means Papers.
"Proposals for bringing the technical phases of national planning to a national focus." 1936. Charles E. Merriam Papers.
"Technology and Capital Obsolescence." 1936. William F. Ogburn Papers.
"Utilizing National Resources: Production-Consumption Patterns as a Means to More Effective Resource Use." 1937. Charles E. Merriam Papers.
"Incentives to Capital Creation." 1938. Jerome Frank Papers.
"Chapter X: Conclusion." 1939. National Archives.
"Characteristics of the September Price Rise." 1939. Charles E. Merriam Papers.

"Possibilities and Limitations of Antitrust Policy." 1939. G.C. Means Papers.
"Public Administration and the Character of a Positive Economic Program." 1939. G.C. Means Papers.
"Public Administration and Current Policy Conflicts." 1939. G.C. Means Papers.
"Public Administration and the Tools of Economic Policy." 1939. G.C. Means Papers.
"The Economics of Administered Prices: Introductory Explorations for an Atomistic Economy." 1940. G.C. Means Papers.
"An Insensitive-price Mechanism of International Trade Adjustment and its Policy Implications." 1943. G.C. Means Papers.
"A Monetary Theory of Employment." 1947. G.C. Means Papers.
"Further Consideration of Price Flexibility and Full Employment." 1948. G.C. Means Papers.
"Administered Prices and Individual Firm Theory." 1953. G.C. Means Papers.
"Price Administration by a Monopolist." 1953. G.C. Means Papers.
"A General Formulation of Macro-Economic Equilibrium." 1957. G.C. Means Papers.
Letter to Jerry Cohen. 1964. J.M. Blair Papers.
"Industrial Prices, as Administered by Dr. Means—A Reply." 1975. G.C. Means Papers.
"The New Non-Monetary Source of Inflation and Its Elimination." 1988. Vienna, Virginia.

Gardiner C. Means Papers (description of the papers at FDR Library)

Series I: National Recovery Administration, 1933–1935.
Correspondence, memoranda, reports, charts, notes, reprints of articles, and printed material arranged alphabetically by subject. The subjects include NRA codes, Consumers' Advisory Board, banking and monetary policy, corporate revolution, corporate concentration, and prices.

Series II: National Resources Planning, 1935–1940.
Correspondence, memoranda, reports, charts, notes, reprints of articles, and printed material arranged alphabetically by subject. The subjects include capital requirements of the iron and steel industry, minutes of the Industrial Committee, prices, production-consumption study, and patterns of resource use.

Series III: Bureau of the Budget, 1940–1941.
Correspondence, memoranda, reports, charts, and printed material arranged alphabetically by subject. The subjects include defense, inflation, and prices.

Series IV: Committee for Economic Development, 1943–1958.
Correspondence, memoranda, reports, charts, graphs, notes, handwritten and typed drafts of books and articles, and printed material arranged alphabetically by subject. The subjects include CED material, collective enterprise and pricing power, macroeconomics, inflation, monetary theory of employment, prices, and the United Nations Economic Commission for Asia and the Far East.

Series V: Personal Business Files, 1955–1975.
Correspondence, reports, sales records, bills, receipts, notes, charts, graphs, legal documents, drafts and reprints of articles, clippings and printed material arranged alphabetically by subject. This series reflects Means's work as a consultant for the Central Railroad of New Jersey, Fund for the Republic, Puerto Rico, Schenley, and Sun Oil, operation of the Lawn Green Grass Development Company and Bucks Harbor Skiff Company, interest in the economic development of Maine, physics, the quantum theory, and his patents for light machinery design.

List of Manuscript Collections That Contain Material by Gardiner C. Means

Blair, John M. National Archives.
Bonbright, James C. Papers, Columbia University.
Central Records of the National Resources Planning Board. National Archives.
Frank, Jerome. Papers, Yale University.
Kaplan, A.D.H. Papers, University of Wyoming.
Merriam, Charles E. University of Chicago.
Ogburn, William F. Papers, University of Chicago.
Records of the National Recovery Administration. National Archives.
Roosevelt, Franklin D. Papers, Franklin D. Roosevelt Library.

Other Collections with Related Material

Bean, Louis H. Papers, Franklin D. Roosevelt Library.
Berle, A.A. Papers, Franklin D. Roosevelt Library.
Colm, Gerhard. Papers, Franklin D. Roosevelt Library.
Columbia University Oral History Collection. Columbia University.
Coy, Wayne. Papers, Franklin D. Roosevelt Library.
Henderson, Leon. Papers, Franklin D. Roosevelt Library.
Mitchell, Wesley C. Papers, Columbia University.
President's Official File. Franklin D. Roosevelt Library.
Ware, Caroline. Papers, Franklin D. Roosevelt Library.
Women in Federal Government Project. Radcliffe College.

Index

About the Editors

Frederic S. Lee is a senior lecturer at Leicester Polytechnic, Leicester, England. He has written articles on Post Keynesian price theory, Gardiner C. Means, and the marginalist controversy, which have appeared in *The Journal of Post Keynesian Economics, Journal of Economic Issues,* and *Review of Social Economy,* among others. He is also preparing two books, one on Oxford economists and Oxford economics, and the second on the foundations of Post Keynesian price theory.

Warren J. Samuels is currently professor of economics at Michigan State University. He earned his M.S. and Ph.D. degrees at the University of Wisconsin. Professor Samuels has written extensively on the history of economic thought, Post Keynesian economics, and institutional economics.